FRANCE

From the Source

*Authentic recipes from the
people who know them best*

Written by Carolyn Boyd
Photographed by River Thompson

CONTENTS

INTRODUCTION

No other nation's cuisine has given as much to the world as France. It's a country where food is the very glue that binds society together, where restaurants were invented and where the term 'cuisine' was first coined. Served the world over, French food conjures up images of sophisticated bistros in Paris and sun-drenched terraces in Provence, with such iconic dishes as beef bourguignon and lemon tarts bringing people the taste of France wherever they are.

Trace these dishes back to their source and you'll find a treasure trove of stories, told by passionate cooks, chefs and bakers. They'll tell you about the produce grown in their land, the legends that accompany the recipes, and the generations of families who have perfected these recipes over centuries.

We've gathered together 63 recipes that tell those stories, with the help of the people who know them best. The dishes, from simple starters to sophisticated desserts, are drawn from France's wonderfully varied geography, climate and terrain, which results in a bounty of produce from the wild, western tip of Brittany to the golden shores of Provence.

The French term that describes the total of these conditions is *terroir* and, as any chef will tell you, it is as important for raising cattle and growing vegetables as it is for making wine. Each region's *terroir* dictates its regional culinary identity, which is why, for example, you find dairy-rich dishes in Normandy, wine-infused stews in Burgundy and vibrant vegetables at the heart of Provençal cuisine. Even Michelin-starred chefs, whose reputations may be national or even global, are bound to the *terroir* of their region and use produce that is grown nearby, sometimes just a few steps from the kitchen door, just as it was in homes centuries ago. Although kitchens have modernised and a variety of food has become readily available, many of the best chefs will still use ingredients and techniques that were born in simpler times, because flavours and combinations have been perfected over centuries and still make the mouth water.

Of course, French food is renowned for its sophistication, its elegance and its multiple accolades, including the revered Michelin stars, but what all chefs and cooks will tell you is that good food is what brings people together here, whether it's a family around the dinner table, a group of friends at a restaurant or the chance for neighbours to chat over the *boulangerie* counter and the market stall. Restaurants play a big part in the daily tempo of life here, with families working together to serve their customers, while cooks at guesthouses make their *tables d'hôtes* (hosts' tables) a chance for guests from around the world to share some of French cuisine's most rustic dishes.

These dishes may well lead you on a journey to discover the foods in the places they originate, as well as try them at home. So whether the recipes inspire you to make a simple cake to share with friends over coffee, or an ambitious dish for a dinner party, there is something here to fit every occasion and all are provided by chefs and cooks who are passionate about their food, their ingredients and their region.

Bon appétit!

Northern France

16e 8e

Seine

Right Bank

1er 6

3e 11e

7e

Faubourg St-Germain 19

Le Marais

18 17

5

4e

PARIS

Left Bank

6e

Latin Quarter

15e

5e

11 12e

Montparnasse

14e 13e

UNITED KINGDOM

NETHERLANDS

Wales

England

NORTH SEA

Calais

BELGIUM

Nord-Pas-de-Calais

English Channel

Dieppe

Amiens

LUXEMBOUR

Guernsey

Cherbourg

Haute-Normandie

Picardie

Jersey

4

LE HAVRE

Rouen

Reims

Metz

1

ROSCOFF

Caen

Basse-Normandie

8

14

See Enlargement

COMMERCY

NANC

Brest

15 VIRE

PARIS

Champagne-Ardenne

16

2

DOUARNENEZ

3

Île-de-France

10

12

Bretagne

9

13

Troyes

Lorrair

7 QUIMPER

Rennes

ALENÇON

FRANCE

Le Mans

Dijon

Franche-Comté

Pays de la Loire

Nantes

Centre

Bourgogne

Bay of Biscay

La Rochelle

Poitou-Charentes

Limoges

Rhône-Alpes

Lyon

Limousin

Clermont-Ferrand

Auvergne

NORTHERN FRANCE

The fishing ports, apple orchards and dairy farms of Brittany and Normandy offer up some heart-warming classics, while Lorraine's much-loved baked goods date from centuries ago. In Paris, the classic bistro cuisine includes some of France's most iconic dishes.

CRÉMEUX DE CHOU-FLEUR, SAINT-JACQUES CARAMÉLISÉES, PIGLENS DE ROSCOFF

Cream of cauliflower soup, with caramelised scallops & pickled Roscoff onions

The stereotypical image of a Frenchman – with a striped jersey, a bicycle and a string of onions– is thanks to the Onion Johnnies of Roscoff who came to England in the early 20th century to sell their delicately flavoured pink onions. Here, they're combined with cauliflower to produce a deliciously warming soup.

Chef //
Loïc le Bail
Location //
Hôtel Brittany, Roscoff

There can be few areas of France more spoiled for choice of ingredients than the northern tip of the Finistère *département* (county) in Brittany: not only is its port town of Roscoff known for the sweet, pink onions made famous by the 'Onion Johnnies', but the area is rich in other produce. In the fields that lie around the pretty harbour town, artichokes, cauliflower and asparagus grow in plentiful supply.

'I call it a big garden,' says Loïc Le Bail, who returned to his native Finistère after several years training with top chefs in Paris. 'There's a strong history of growing vegetables and there is so much here. As well as the fish and the seafood, there are lots of different seaweeds that we use in the kitchen. It wasn't till I came here that I got to know these products. In Paris, there's nothing like that.' Central to his recipe is the cauliflower, 'I use a summer cauliflower, it's smaller and has a subtler flavour,' says Loïc. 'The flavour is stronger in the winter.'

Also in his recipe is the product for which locals hold most pride: the Roscoff onion. It's celebrated throughout the town with a festival every August, there's a *confrérie* (a brotherhood, or guild) devoted to promoting them, and even a small museum dedicated to the Onion Johnnies' history. So what makes them so special? 'When you look at a Roscoff onion,' Loïc says, 'it's handsome, it's nice and round. You feel like biting into it, like you would an apple. You can eat it raw, too, as it's quite sweet.' Despite his passion for the ingredient, Loïc explains it doesn't have to be the central ingredient to his dishes, 'I don't think of it as a vegetable, it's a condiment,' he says. Pickled, the onions provide the pièce de résistance to his dish: the sweet, sharp taste cuts through the smooth and welcoming flavours of the soup and, together, it's the perfect recipe to encapsulate this beautiful corner of Brittany.

CRÉMEUX DE CHOU-FLEUR, SAINT-JACQUES CARAMÉLISÉES, PIGLENS DE ROSCOFF

Cream of cauliflower soup, with caramelised scallops & pickled Roscoff onions

Serves 6

Preparation and cooking time: 45min (not including soaking time for onions)

For the pickled onions
3 small Roscoff onions
500ml (17½fl oz) white vinegar

For the soup
1 medium-sized cauliflower
salted water, for boiling cauliflower
40g (1½oz) butter, plus 2 tbsp for frying scallops
1 large onion, finely chopped
tip of a garlic clove (approx 2mm/¾in)
250ml (8¾fl oz) milk
250ml (8¾fl oz) single cream
300ml (10½fl oz) thick cream
salt, to taste
pinch of cayenne pepper
12 scallops
croutons, to serve
chervil (or half flat-leaf parsley /half tarragon), to serve

Tip
For a midweek meal, the soup can be served without the scallops. Loïc prefers to add a pinch of cayenne pepper, rather than black pepper, as it gives a warmer flavour.

For the pickled onions

1 Peel the Roscoff onions and slice them thinly. Put them in a bowl of white vinegar for two hours, then drain and blot them on absorbent kitchen paper. The vinegar should be pink, having taken the colour from the onions. Set the pickled onions aside to garnish the soup.

For the soup

1 Cut the cauliflower into large florets. Bring a pan of water to the boil, add a sprinkle of salt and the cauliflower florets, and cook for ten minutes. Drain and set aside.

2 Melt the 40g of butter in a casserole dish, add the chopped onion, the garlic and the cauliflower florets.

3 Mix together the milk and single cream, then pour into the casserole dish to just cover the cauliflower. Simmer for 15 minutes then blitz the mixture with a hand blender/liquidiser.

4 Add the thick cream, heat through and add salt and a pinch of cayenne pepper.

5 In a separate pan, fry the scallops in 2 tbsp of butter for one minute on each side.

6 Serve the soup in a dish, placing the scallops, pickled onion slices, croutons and springs of chervil on top.

'Why onion "Johnnies"? Well, because back then, all the men were called Jean-this, or Jean-that, so the English just started calling them all "Johnny".'

Loïc Le Bail

RILLETTES DE SARDINES
Sardine pâté

The fishing port of Douarnenez, on the far northern tip of Brittany, was made famous in the 19th century by its booming industry producing tins of sardines, enabling the world to enjoy the fresh taste of the sea. Local chef Gaël Ruscart uses this simple ingredient in a delicious pâté.

As one of France's biggest ports for sardine fishing, the Finistère town of Douarnenez is inhabited by those who know how best to eat the small oily fish. The son of a fisher, chef Gaël Ruscart remembers his parents' advice: 'Just fillet them, and eat them fresh and raw on bread and butter,' he says. 'That's how they used to eat them.' These days, however, chefs and home cooks are a little more ambitious with the town's freshest catch and prefer to eat their sardines grilled on a barbecue or in a salad. 'They just need a drizzle of olive oil, a squeeze of lemon. There's no need to mess around with them too much.'

Yet, not all of us are lucky enough to enjoy the daily catch that lands on the Finistère coast, but a revolutionary canning technique made the town its fortune in preserving that fresh taste for a wider market. After the first *conserverie* (canning factory) opened in 1853, dozens more followed, and by the end of the 19th century Douarnenez's 32 factories were supplying the world with canned sardines. These eye-catching tins, with colourful labels and designs, became the emblem of the town. Among the most famous producers is La Maison Chancerelle, which remained in the same family for six generations and still produces canned fish under the label Connétable.

In the local shops, you'll find dozens of varieties of sardines in different marinades and sauces – such as tomato sauce, olive oil and lemon – stacked in their neat, glossy tins. For this recipe, sardines canned simply in oil or brine are used, which, together with fresh herbs, tangy fromage frais and sharp mustard, makes an ideal topping for toasted bread or crackers. 'It's a little more sophisticated than how the fishermen ate them, and perfect with a drink of cider,' says Gaël.

Chef //
Gaël Ruscart
Location //
L'Insolite, Douarnenez

RILLETTES DE SARDINES
Sardine pâté

Serves 4

Preparation and cooking time: 20min

1 x 100g (3½oz) can of sardines in olive
  oil, or water
250g (8¾oz) butter
20g (¾oz) parsley, chopped
80g (3oz) Dijon mustard
660g (1½lb) fromage frais
150g (5¼oz) shallots, finely chopped
salt, to taste
pepper, to taste
toasted rye bread or pain de campagne
  (country bread), to serve

1 Drain the sardines, then pull out the largest bones.

2 Melt the butter and combine it with the sardines and parsley, mashing together with a fork.

3 Add the mustard, fromage frais and shallots and continue mashing until it has a smooth consistency. Add salt and pepper, then refrigerate for an hour.

4 Remove the rillettes from the fridge and serve cold on rye bread or toasted *pain de campagne*.

CAMEMBERT AU FOUR, FLAMBÉE AU CALVADOS

Baked Camembert, flambéed with Calvados

World-renowned Camembert cheese is one of Normandy's most prized products and once combined with the region's other delicacies – apples and Calvados – and baked in the oven, it makes a dish that is ideal for sharing. Chef Charles-Henry de Valbray serves it at his ancestral home-turned-hotel, the Château de Saint Paterne.

Chef //
Charles-Henry de Valbray
Location //
Château de Saint-Paterne,
Alençon

Whether it's baked in the box as some cooks suggest, or with a few embellishments, as per chef Charles-Henry de Valbray's recipe, baked Camembert is the perfect dish for when good company is complemented by good food. 'It's so easy,' laughs Charles-Henry de Valbray as he unwraps the characteristic balsa-wood box.

The world-famous cheese lies at the heart of this unctuous dish, and although its preparation is minimal, Charles-Henry's other ingredients – apple and Calvados – lend it a touch of class. It's fitting then, that this sophisticated version of a simple recipe should come from the owner of an elegant 15th-century château that has been in his family for generations and is now a stylish hotel. The château was once the venue for the French King Henry IV's *liaisons romantiques*, but it was the monarchy's subsequent demise that lies at the heart of Camembert's backstory. 'During the French revolution there was a priest who escaped from Coulommiers in the Brie area [east of Paris],' explains Charles-Henry. 'He hid with a family at a farm called Le Manoir of Beaumoncel and, as thanks to the family, the priest gave them the recipe for Brie.' But this was just the start: Marie Harel, who worked at the farm, used local Normandy ingredients to improve on the recipe for Brie, and Camembert cheese was born.

'The milk here is so good, so rich, so creamy,' says Charles-Henry. The charismatic chef sources his cheese from one of the local farms near the tiny village of Camembert itself, but he admits not all Camemberts are equal: 'They never patented the recipe, which is why it has become so industrialised.' Of course a farm-produced cheese will reap the best results, but, as this recipe has the Camembert served alongside caramelised apples and flambéed with a heady dose of Calvados, the brand of cheese is immaterial. The most important thing is to eat, drink and be merry.

CAMEMBERT AU FOUR, FLAMBÉE AU CALVADOS
Baked Camembert, flambéed with Calvados

Serves 2

Preparation and cooking time: 40min

1 cooking apple
1 tbsp salted butter
120ml (4¼oz) Calvados
1x 250g (8¾oz) box of Camembert cheese
  (preferably made with unpasteurised milk)
black pepper, to taste
salad, to serve
French bread, to serve

1 Preheat the oven to 180°C–190°C (350°F–375°F).

2 Peel and core the apple, and cut into eight pieces.

3 In a pan, fry the apple in butter until soft on the outside but firm in the middle.

4 Flambée the apple with 1 tbsp of the Calvados until the alcohol burns out, then set aside.

5 Cut the Camembert in two through the middle horizontally, and then each half into eight pieces to make a total of 16.

6 Place eight pieces of the cheese in one ovenproof dish and eight pieces in another dish, place the apple quarters in-between each wedge of cheese, so you have alternate pieces of apple and cheese. Grind black pepper over the top.

7 Bake the Camembert and apple in the oven for 15 minutes.

8 Heat the rest of the Calvados in a small saucepan. With a long kitchen match, set the Calvados alight and when the flame turns white, remove from the heat and pour the Calvados over the Camembert and apples in the dishes.

9 Serve with a small salad and French bread.

RAMEQUINES AVEC TROIS FROMAGES NORMANDS

Ramekins with three Normandy cheeses

Near Le Havre, not far from the sights that inspired many of the Impressionist artists of the 19th century, chef Régine's Boidin draws on the cuisine created by Claude Monet's cook. One of her favourite recipes is this comforting soufflé that incorporates three of Normandy's unique cheeses.

Chef //
Régine Boidin
Location //
Le Mirlibut, Étainhus

Claude Monet's paintings are known the world over, but few people know that the founding father of the Impressionist art movement was a true gastronome. In the garden of his country retreat at Giverny, in the south of Normandy, the plants he grew were as much about his palate as his palette, and Monet would host dozens of guests for lavish lunches.

Not far from Le Havre – the port that inspired Monet's painting *Soleil Levant*, which heralded the start of the Impressionist movement – chef Régine Boidin recreates some of the recipes that were served to Monet's guests more than a century ago. This deliciously warming soufflé uses three of Normandy's quartet of cheeses – Pont l'Évêque, Livarot and Camembert all melted together, leaving out the fourth Norman cheese (it's too salty for this dish), the heart-shaped Neufchâtel.

'Claude Monet loved his food,' Régine says. 'When he was in Paris for the big exhibitions, he would eat in the best restaurants, but in the countryside there were only *auberges* (inns). He had a very good cook and he invited guests to his house for lunch and to buy his paintings, and the cuisine became well known.' Guests would dine in his blue and yellow kitchen at Giverny. 'When I bought the house, I decorated the dining room and – by complete accident – ended up choosing the same colours as the kitchen in Giverny,' says Régine, who has modernised the recipes, as eating habits have changed. 'It was a simple cuisine that used local products, such as eggs, butter, cheese and bread. I've made it a bit lighter. People back then didn't eat meat every day: they used lots of butter, and cream and eggs to fill themselves up.' While her soothing dish is intended as a starter, Régine harks back to the past to transform it into a main course. 'Some people put a piece of stale bread in the bottom of the ramekin to save throwing it [the bread] away. If you eat that with a salad, you have a complete meal.'

RAMEQUINES AVEC TROIS FROMAGES NORMANDS

Ramekins with three Normandy cheeses

Serves 6

Preparation and cooking time: 1hr

300g (10½oz) cream cheese
2 eggs
2 tbsp plain flour
pinch of nutmeg
salt, to taste
pepper, to taste
50g (1¾oz) Camembert
50g (1¾oz) Livarot
50g (1¾oz) Pont L'Évêque
40g (1½oz) butter
crusty bread, to serve

1 Preheat the oven to 200°C (390°F).

2 In a mixing bowl, stir in the soft white cheese with the eggs.

3 Add the flour, nutmeg, salt and pepper. Mix well.

4 Cut the three Normandy cheeses into small pieces and add them to the egg-cheese mixture in the bowl.

5 Butter six ramekins and half fill them with the creamy mixture.

6 Put a tiny bit of butter on top of each ramekin and put them in the oven on a baking tray for 20 minutes.

7 Remove the ramekins from the oven and serve warm with crusty bread.

Tip

If you stir the mixture continuously in one direction, without lifting the whisk out of the mixture, you shouldn't get any lumps.

'A true Pont l'Évêque cheese has five raffia bands around it – like a colonel in the army. If it has four, it's not the real thing!'

Régine Boidin

BAGUETTE
French bread

The traditional baguette is as familiar a French icon as the Eiffel Tower, a beret and a bicycle. While its recipe may be simple, the technique involved in achieving the ideal taste and texture can take years to perfect, but the effort is worth it, says Parisian baker Mickaël Reydellet.

Chef //
Mickaël Reydellet
Location //
Boulangerie La Parisienne, Paris

If you had to sum up the whole of French cuisine in one item, the humble baguette would surely be it. With its golden crust hiding a tender white dough inside, all it needs is a hunk of cheese or some cool, salted butter and it's a meal in itself. The slender loaf's exact origins are hazy, but some date it to 1920 when a law was passed forbidding bakeries from operating between 10pm and 4am. This created the need for a quick-to-bake bread that could be made in time for customers' breakfasts.

Today, the quality of the loaf will vary between bakeries, but the version that has been voted the best in Paris is that of Mickaël Reydellet. With seven outlets of his La Parisienne bakery, the first of which he opened aged just 22, he has spent the last ten years perfecting his formula and now sells 10,000 traditional baguettes every day. 'It's something with a life of its own; you have to respect the temperature, the yeast, the flour – our flour has 21 types of wheat in it. The ideal is that it has a dark golden crust, so that it has all the aromas,' he says, squeezing the loaf so that it gently cracks or, as he says, 'sings'.

Mickaël's efforts were rewarded in 2016 when he won the *Concours de la Meilleure Baguette de Paris* (Best Baguette in Paris) competition, an accolade that brings with it the chance to supply the French President's residence – the Élysée Palace – with bread for a year. With such passion and success, you might imagine Mickaël had been born into the profession, but in fact he stumbled on it almost by accident. 'I studied science until I was 20, and that had nothing to do with baking. But a friend invited me to work in a bakery in the holidays in Normandy, where I'm from, and as soon as I entered that bakery, that was it.'

BAGUETTE
French bread

Serves 6–8

*Preparation and cooking time: 1 hr
(not including 5½hr waiting time)*

*1 kg (2¼lb) flour, plus extra for
 sprinkling
18g (⅔oz) salt
720ml (1¼pt) water
10g (⅓oz) yeast*

1 Place all the ingredients in a food mixer with a dough hook, and knead for ten minutes until it's a smooth and well-combined paste.

2 Leave to stand for five hours.

3 Divide the dough into three 350g (12⅓oz) pieces and shape into a long baguette shape.

4 Let stand for 30 minutes.

5 Preheat the oven to 250°C (480°F).

6 Sprinkle with flour and make five diagonal scores with a knife down the length of each baguette.

7 Bake the baguettes in the oven for 20 minutes. Best served within three hours of baking.

'The waiting time is important, and the way of cooking it. There are lots of little details in making it that, at the end, can completely change the result.'

Mickaël Reydellet

SOUPE À L'OIGNON GRATINÉE
French onion soup

French onion
soup has been on
the menu at the
classic Parisian
restaurant Café
de la Paix since it
opened in 1862,
and it's down
to chef Laurent
André to perfect
the recipe of this
quintessential
brasserie dish
to ensure it is as
popular as ever.

'My dream is to find the recipe from 1862!' says the enthusiastic chef Laurent André, when asked of the origins of the Café de la Paix's most famous dish – gratinée à l'oignon. 'We know the soup was on the menu when the restaurant opened, but we don't have the original recipe. For every soupe à l'oignon there are 50 ways of doing it. For some places it's just the stock and onions,' he shrugs, 'but then there's how to cook the onions, the quality of the beef [stock], whether to add sugar. It's the little things that make all the difference.'

With up to 100 orders for the soup being fulfilled every day at this large, busy brasserie in Paris, which sits next to the magnificent Palais Garnier, Laurent has the restaurant's reputation to uphold, and for him this means using good produce. 'There are about 50 varieties of onions, some good, some bad, and you can't make simple dishes with bad products.' For Laurent, his preferred onions are those from the Cévennes, a rural area of south-central France, which have a soft, sweeter taste. Laurent sources them from the capital's enormous Rungis food market, which supplies almost all restaurants in the city. 'It's a treasure trove for me. To go to Rungis is like being a child in a toyshop!'

When it comes to the white wine in the recipe, Laurent also has his preferences: 'It's not good to use the big-name wines, but you can't use the cheap ones either. I use Côtes du Rhône or Val de Loire wines because they're quite dry. You don't want too much sugar in it.' For the cheese, the taste is also very important, but so too is the texture. 'I'm still looking for the right combination, because some cheeses are difficult to eat and go all stringy when you take the spoon to your mouth,' he says, as he mimes getting it all down his front. 'And that just won't do.'

Chef //
Laurent André
Location //
Café de la Paix, Paris

SOUPE À L'OIGNON GRATINÉE
French onion soup

Serves 4

Preparation and cooking time: 45min

30g (1oz) butter
6 onions, sliced finely in rings
juice of ½ a lemon
1 tsp sugar
8g (⅓oz) salt, plus extra to taste
2 cloves of garlic, finely chopped
100ml (3½fl oz) dry white wine
1L (1¾pt) beef stock
1L (1¾pt) chicken stock
freshly ground black pepper, to taste
8 slices of small baguette, sliced into 2cm
   (¾in) cubes
60g (2oz) grated Gruyère cheese, to serve

1 Preheat the oven to 200°C (390°F).

2 In a large casserole pot, melt 20g (¾oz) of the butter on a medium heat. Add the onions, lemon juice, sugar and 8g of salt, and stir to combine.

3 Cover and leave to cook, stirring frequently, for 12 minutes or until the onions are turning a light golden colour.

4 Turn the heat up and stir for a further three minutes or until the onions are golden.

5 Add the finely chopped garlic, and stir for another 10 seconds.

6 Add the white wine and bring to the boil. Stir, making sure to scrape the bottom of the casserole to loosen the onions that have stuck, and leave to simmer for 8 minutes, or until the liquid has reduced by two thirds.

7 Add the beef and chicken stock and bring to the boil again. Add salt and pepper and reduce the heat, cover and leave to simmer for 10 minutes.

8 Paint the two sides of the bread with the remaining melted butter, and put on a baking tray. Bake in the oven, turning frequently until the bread has turned into lightly golden and crispy croutons (approx three minutes).

9 To serve, distribute half the croutons between four oven-safe bowls and sprinkle with a third of the cheese. Pour over the soup and then add the rest of the croutons to the top, and sprinkle on the rest of the cheese.

GALETTES BRETON

Breton pancakes

At one of the oldest crêperies in the town of Quimper, Myriam Frances uses an age-old recipe for the savoury pancake known as a galette. Popular all over Brittany and beyond, they are made with buckwheat flour, which was first popularised by Queen Anne of Brittany in the 15th century.

Chef //
Myriam Frances
Location //
Au Vieux Quimper, Quimper

For all the mod cons that have been introduced to kitchens since the crêperie Au Vieux Quimper opened over 60 years ago, owner Myriam Frances prefers to use the most ancient of tools to mix her batter – her hand. Tapping the side of the bowl as she beats the greyish flour, eggs and water together, she explains how this adds in the air. While the recipe may be simple, the perfect galette cannot be rushed. 'If you leave it overnight, the colour is better, the texture is less elastic. It's better to wait.'

Known as *blé de sarrasin* or *blé noir* (black wheat), buckwheat is related to the rhubarb family, and the conditions in Brittany are perfect for growing it. Naturally gluten-free, it lacks the elasticity required for bread dough, but for galettes it is perfect – beautifully golden and crispy. As Myriam pours the mixture on to the *billig* (the Breton name for the pancake griddle), she guides the batter into a circle using a wooden T-shaped tool, the *rozell*, that's almost the same age as her.

The crêperie is one of the two oldest in Quimper, in the south of Finistère (a department in the west of Brittany), and its rustic interior features Breton pottery on shelves built against the stone walls. On each table, a small jar of buckwheat kernels shows diners the raw ingredient – tiny green triangles that jangle when you shake the jar. The recipe for Myriam's galettes has been handed down from the crêperie's previous owners: 'Some customers are around 70 years old, and remember coming since they were ten,' she says. Nowadays, Au Vieux Quimper offers dozens of fillings, such as ham and cheese, mushroom and cream, but back then, there was just one flavour – Brittany's most famous product: butter. 'It's the simplest,' says Myriam, 'but it's the best.'

GALETTES BRETON
Breton pancakes

Serves 5 (two galettes each)

**Preparation and cooking time: 30min
(not including overnight refrigeration)**

500g (1lb) buckwheat flour
1 tsp sea-salt flakes
2 eggs
*1L (1¾pt) water [or half milk and half
   water, if you prefer]*
melted butter, for frying
*galette filling of your choice
   (eg ham and cheese, mushroom and cream)*

1 Add the flour, salt, eggs and half of the water in a bowl.

2 Mix it with your hand, in a wave motion, tapping the side of the bowl as you do so with your mixing hand. This brings in the air to the mixture. After four or five minutes, there should be bubbles rising and popping on the surface. Refrigerate the mixture overnight.

3 The next day, the mixture will be very thick. Add the remaining litre of water and mix until well blended.

4 Apply a thin layer of butter to the base of a large frying pan, either by smearing a knob of butter into the base, or by painting the base with melted butter (softened in the microwave) and a pastry brush.

5 Pour a ladleful amount of the galette mixture into the frying pan and turn the pan so it coats the bottom. Fry until golden on the bottom.

6 Place a filling of your choice in the middle of the galette and then fold the four sides in to make a square, pushing down with the spatula to seal it together. Cook a little longer until the filling has been heated through, and serve.

POULET DE VALLEE DE L'AUGE

Auge Valley chicken

In the heart of Normandy's apple orchards, where cider farms and Calvados distilleries abound, Anne Bourbeau brings together the region's prized produce of butter, cream, apples and chicken to create a hearty and indulgent dish.

Just south of the chic Norman coast, the rustic heart of the region offers up a delicious bounty. The local cheeses, cream and butter are rich in temptation, while the apples that grow in abundance are at the heart of many of the dishes served in the Pays d'Auges. In spring, the orchards are a sea of white blossom, and in summer the trees come into fruit that hangs low in autumn, ripe for picking when the trees turn a riot of colour.

Throughout the area, farm shops sell direct to visitors all manner of apple variations: heady ciders, cloudy ciders, even ice ciders, the moreish *apéritif pommeau*, and the woozy apple brandy that gives its name to the department – Calvados. Being just a couple of hours from the capital, it's an area that has captured the heart of many a Parisian, with the rolling hills and woodlands being exceptionally popular as a weekend bolthole.

Anne Bourbeau was one of those who fell for the area, eventually moving here permanently and restoring a 17th-century farm into a B&B, though she has recently retired. 'When I lived in Paris, I ate in restaurants every day, but when I came here, I began cooking.' Her recipe uses a whole chicken rather than just the legs of the traditional version and the juicy, sticky chicken is further enhanced by the caramelised apples. The recipe is a simple yet decadent treat, even without the Calvados that many cooks use to flambé it at the end. Instead, Anne is keen to suggest another Normandy custom that aids further indulgence: the wicked *trou Normand* is a shot of Calvados served between courses. 'The idea is that you eat so much in the first course, that you need a digestif in-between,' explains Anne. 'And then you have room for dessert.'

Chef //
Anne Bourbeau
Location //
Les Petits Matins Bleus,
Sainte Marguerite de Viette

POULET DE VALLEE DE L'AUGE

Auge Valley chicken

Serves 4

Preparation and cooking time:
1hr 20min

selection of garden herbs
  (such as bay, thyme, tarragon)
1 x 1.8kg (4lb) free-range chicken
salt, to taste
pepper, to taste
1 tbsp olive oil
1 tbsp butter, plus 1 tbsp for caramelising
  apples
250ml–500ml (8¾fl oz–17½floz) dry
  cider (less for smaller chickens)
4 firm-fleshed apples
  (such as Golden Delicious)
fleur de sel
1 tbsp demerara/golden cane sugar
pinch of cinnamon
pinch of ginger
2 sprigs of tarragon
2 tbsp crème fraiche

1 Preheat the oven to 180°C (350°F).

2 Put the herbs inside the chicken's carcass and add salt and pepper. Put the chicken in the roasting dish and massage it with the olive oil and butter. Roast in the oven until golden (approx 30–45 minutes).

3 Pour the cider over the chicken and put back in the oven for another 30 minutes. Cook until the juices run clear.

4 Core the apples and cut them into quarters.

5 Put 1 tbsp of butter on the apples, add *fleur de sel* and pepper to taste, then fry them until golden. Then add 1 tbsp sugar, a pinch of cinnamon and a pinch of ginger to the pan and caramelise the apples.

6 Remove the chicken from the oven and reserve the pan of roasting juices. Place the chicken in a shallow dish with the apples, and sprinkle with 2 tbsp of the tarragon leaves.

7 Add 2 tbsp of crème fraiche to the warm juices in the roasting pan. Mix together and pour into a gravy boat. Pour some of the sauce over the chicken and serve.

LE SAINT PIERRE AVEC GIROLLES ET ABRICOTS

John Dory with chanterelle mushrooms & apricots

The dense Andaine Forest that surrounds the Normandy spa town of Bagnoles-de-l'Orne provides the perfect conditions for mushrooms to grow naturally, and it's these fabulous fungi that have been at the heart of chef Franck Quinton's cuisine for more than 25 years.

At the Manoir du Lys hotel in the heart of the Andaine Forest, it's no longer wild boar or deer that most people come searching for, but a more mysterious ingredient: mushrooms. In autumn, at the peak of their production, the former hunting lodge is packed with food-lovers in search of all manner of fungi, under the guidance of a professional mycologist. Armed with baskets of their bounty, the foragers will return to put their mushrooms to good use in Franck Quinton's cookery classes.

While autumn is undoubtedly the most popular time to go foraging in the forest, the summer will yield a different variety. It is then – when the sunshine glances through the tall Scots pines and beech trees, shedding dappled light on the forest floor – that the chanterelles are in season. These exotic golden fungi, like a trumpet with a pretty frilly edge, have the aroma of apricots, making them the perfect pairing with the summer fruit, along with fresh John Dory fillets sourced from small fishing crews on the Normandy coast.

'My cuisine is quite simple,' says Franck. 'Just two flavours, three flavours. I don't have lots of things on the plate. It's the quality of ingredients that counts.' But in every dish, there's a place for the ingredient that has inspired him since childhood, when his parents opened the hotel and his father started cooking with the mushrooms, which were available all year round. 'In summer, you have the chanterelles, in autumn lots and lots of varieties and then more in winter and then others in spring,' says Franck. But if you're one of those hunters who think that the best mushroom varieties are more easily found than the forest's wild game, then you'd be wrong. 'The mushrooms are – and this is what fascinates me – ephemeral," says Franck. 'One day you see them, and the next day they're gone.'

Chef //
Franck Quinton
Location //
Manoir du Lys, Bagnoles-de-l'Orne

LE SAINT PIERRE AVEC GIROLLES ET ABRICOTS

John Dory with chanterelle mushrooms & apricots

Serves 4

Preparation and cooking time: 40min

100g (3½oz) dried apricots
1 tbsp cider vinegar
4 fresh apricots
*1 sprig of rosemary, cut into 8 x 2cm (¾in)
  portions, with leaves leftover*
200g (7oz) girolles/chanterelles mushrooms
1 tbsp olive oil
4 x 150g (5¼oz) John Dory fillets
1 tbsp butter

Tip

Don't get the mushrooms too wet, as they are like a sponge and soak up water, which will affect the recipe. A quick rinse will suffice, or a wipe with kitchen paper. Peel the stalks if they are particularly muddy.

---

1 Preheat the oven to 180°C (350°F).

2 Purée the dried apricots in a blender with the cider vinegar.

3 Cut the fresh apricots in half, remove the stone and fill with the dried apricot paste to form a round shape over the top. Put one of the little rosemary sprig pieces in the centre of each apricot half. Refrigerate in an ovenproof dish.

4 Peel the stalks of the mushrooms and rinse quickly under water.

5 In a frying pan, heat the olive oil and fry the fish for three minutes on each side. Set aside.

6 Fry the mushrooms in the butter and a scattering of rosemary leaves.

7 Bake the apricots in the oven for seven or eight minutes.

8 To serve, place each fish fillet on a plate, with the mushrooms and apricots alongside.

'Apricots and rosemary are often paired together in cooking, so, as the chanterelles have an aroma of apricots, they go well together.'

Franck Quinton

QUICHE LORRAINE

Quiche lorraine

At Maison Gwizdak, a charming bakery in the heart of the elegant city of Nancy, Fabrice Gwizdak is dedicated to making the region's signature dish, quiche lorraine, in a way that is true to its origins, using the area's best ingredients.

'The quiche lorraine is known the world over, but no one knows where Lorraine is!' declares Fabrice Gwizdak, one of the region's most successful bakers. 'My son went on holiday to Thailand, and he even found it there!' Southeast Asia is indeed a world away from Lorraine, but no matter how ubiquitous this delicious cream, bacon and egg tart is, its origins are firmly rooted in eastern France.

'There's a big culture of breeding cows here, so there's a lot of milk production. The bacon comes from our Germanic culture; in the Vosges mountains [which covers parts of both Alsace and Lorraine], there's lots of pork,' says Fabrice.

Areas of Lorraine and its neighbouring region Alsace have been part of Germany at various times in their history, and the word 'quiche' comes from the German word '*Kuchen*', for cake. But, as Fabrice explains, the quiche evolved from one of Alsace's best-known dishes. 'In Alsace there's the *tarte flambée*, which is how Quiche Lorraine started in the 18th century. This has bread dough, lardons, *fromage blanc* [soft cheese] and egg yolks. Theirs is flat, like a galette, but ours evolved to be a tart, and we changed the texture by making a mixture with eggs and cream. And so the quiche lorraine was born,' explains Fabrice. 'People put in leeks, ham and other ingredients, but that's mad. I want to make a quiche lorraine that is true to its origins, that is one of France's favourite dishes.'

Fabrice's approach is clearly successful; his bakery in the handsome city of Nancy has won numerous accolades, including being a finalist in the French TV show *La Meilleure Boulangerie de France* (Best Bakery in France), and Fabrice is proud to represent the best of Lorraine's cuisine. 'When people come to a place, they want to try the local cuisine, but here in Nancy there isn't a restaurant that serves quiche lorraine! So we artisans are working hard to change that.'

Chef //
Fabrice Gwizdak
Location //
Maison Gwizdak, Nancy

QUICHE LORRAINE
Quiche lorraine

Serves 4-6

Preparation and cooking time: 1hr 30min (not including 1–2hr for pastry refrigeration)

For the pastry
125g (4½oz) plain flour, plus extra for rolling pastry
65g (2¼oz) corn starch
5g (¼oz) salt
115g (4oz) softened butter, plus extra to serve
1 egg
40ml (1½oz) water

For the filling
water, to soak lardons/bacon
200g (7oz) lardons/chopped bacon
4 eggs
250g (8¾oz) full fat milk
250g (8¾oz) cream (single or double)
salt, to taste
pepper, to taste

1. To make the pastry, mix the flour, baking powder and salt in a bowl. Mix in the butter until it resembles breadcrumbs.

2. In another bowl, whisk the egg with the 40ml of water, then gently combine with the breadcrumb-like mixture to form the pastry. Gently knead the pastry, form a ball and leave in the fridge for at least an hour (two is better, overnight also works).

3. Roll out the pastry on a lightly floured surface and place in a mould measuring 26cm (10in) in diameter. Set this pastry case aside.

4. To make the filling, bring a pot of water to the boil, and then reduce the heat. Place the lardons into the water for a few minutes to reduce their salt content. Drain them and set aside.

5. Whisk the four eggs in a bowl and then add the milk, the cream and the salt and pepper. Leave to rest for 15 to 20 minutes.

6. Preheat the oven to 180°C (350°F).

7. Sprinkle the drained lardons into the pastry case, and then pour the egg mixture over the top.

8. Bake in the oven for 30 to 40 minutes. When the quiche comes out of the oven, spread a knob of butter across the top (it should melt gently), and serve.

GRATIN DAUPHINOIS
Dauphinois potato gratin

Le Train Bleu at Paris' Gare de Lyon is one of France's most recognisable restaurants, having opened in an era when luxury train travel was all the rage. On its menu is this soothing cream and potato dish, a French classic for which today's travellers still have an appetite.

Lunch at a railway station usually consists of a quick sandwich while dashing for the train, but linger a while at Paris' Gare de Lyon and an elegant dining experience awaits. Le Train Bleu is not your typical railway station diner: an awe-inspiring belle époque brasserie, it is one of France's best-known restaurants and harks back to an era when luxury train travel was the height of sophistication. With its sumptuous decor featuring brass fixtures and fittings, chandeliers, gilt mouldings and carvings, its intricately painted frescoes will inspire any traveller. Each scene depicts a destination served by trains leaving from the Gare de Lyon, including – as the station's name suggests – Lyon and the 'Dauphiné' area of the Alps, from which the much-loved recipe gratin dauphinois originates. This rich and warming dish of potatoes, cream and cheese is one of the restaurant's most iconic dishes and chef Jean-Pierre Hocquet adds his own touch by adding a layer of the blue-veined Auvergne cheese *Fourme d'Ambert* on top, before serving it with lamb.

'Gratin Dauphinois and leg of lamb is a classic combination in traditional French cuisine. I've worked here 13 years and it's always been the number one dish of the restaurant. We serve it from a trolley, with the lamb being sliced in front of the guests, and they really like that,' says Jean-Pierre, who notes how high-speed train travel has changed dramatically since the restaurant opened in 1901: 'The TGV *[Trains Grand Vitesse]* changed everything, there used to be the overnight Wagon-Lits, where you would board at eight in the evening, and arrive at the Côte d'Azur for breakfast.'

Although the train services leaving from Gare de Lyon have changed, the classic French dining experience on offer at Le Train Bleu endures. 'Because the restaurant is so old, a lot of people come whose parents brought them here, and their parents brought them, and so on. People still look for that traditional cuisine.'

Chef //
Jean-Pierre Hocquet
Location //
Le Train Bleu, Paris

GRATIN DAUPHINOIS
Dauphinois potato gratin

Serves 6

Preparation and cooking time:
1hr 30 min

2kg (4½lb) firm-fleshed potatoes
butter, for greasing dish
3 cloves garlic
600ml (1pt) single cream
400ml (14fl oz) full-cream milk
20g (¾oz) salt
pinch ground nutmeg
20ml (¾fl oz) thick cream
1 egg yolk
50g (1¾oz) grated cheese
   (such as Gruyère or Emmental)
100g (3½oz) Fourme d'Ambert cheese
   (or another blue cheese, if unavailable)

1 Preheat the oven to 150°C (300°F).

2 Peel and slice the potatoes into thin slivers, ideally using a mandolin.

3 Rub the surface of a 15cm x 20cm (6in x 8in) oven-safe porcelain dish with butter and arrange the potato slices in layers.

4 Peel the garlic cloves, discard the green sprouts, and chop the garlic finely.

5 In a bowl, mix the single cream, milk and garlic. Add the salt and nutmeg, and pour the mixture over the potatoes. The milk mixture should just about cover the potatoes.

6 Bake in the oven for an hour, then remove from the oven and leave to cool.

7 In a bowl, mix the thick cream, the egg yolk and the 50g of grated cheese, then pour over the top of the potatoes.

8 Add thin slices of Fourme d'Ambert cheese across the top of the potatoes.

9 Put the dish back in the oven, at 180°C (350°F) for 10 minutes.

Tip
Serve with roast shoulder of lamb: a 2kg
(4½lb) joint will serve six people. Cover
with foil and cook for four hours in a
preheated oven at 170°C (340°F).

KOUIGN-AMANN
Butter cake

This famous butter pastry can be found across Brittany, but its origins lie in the remotest corner of Finistère, where it was created by accident around 1860. In the village of Locronan, baker Alain le Guillou continues the tradition, noting the secret to success is in the technique.

L ike many classic recipes, the kouign-amann (pronounced 'queen amon') is the result of an accident; or at least an experiment, according to baker Alain le Guillou. 'The story goes that baker Yves René Scordia wanted to pack up his shop at the end of the day, but the only ingredients he had to hand were the bread dough, butter and sugar.' He put it all together as a layered pastry and the 'butter cake', or Kouign-Amann in the Breton language, was born.

While you'll find kouign-amann in most bakeries across Brittany, its birthplace is the town of Douarnenez, where Scordia's original bakery still stands (though it is now a gift shop). The pride of most bakers in the region, this golden pastry combines the best of sweet and savoury, with the sweetened dough punctuated by the salted butter.

There is much debate over how many times the pastry should be rolled, with some bakers claiming it requires up to five or six rounds of folding and rolling. It's a time-consuming business, too, so home bakers need to be dedicated to the timings, and experiment with further rolls if it becomes too dense. Different bakers have their own techniques and, as the fifth generation of his family to run the picture-perfect Boulangerie Le Guillou in Locronan, Alain's formula clearly works a treat – he sells up to 250 of the pastries a day. The difficulty, he says, is 'it sticks, so keep flouring the surface.' And when it comes to the key ingredient, 'make sure the butter is the same softness as the pastry, not too soft, not too hard.'

Under the granite arches of the bakery's back rooms, racks of the kouign-amann are ready to be wrapped and sold to the hundreds of customers who pass through every day. And with Locronan being one of France's most beautiful villages, there can be scarcely any prettier place to enjoy one.

Chef //
Alain le Guillou
Location //
Boulangerie Le Guillou,
Locronan

KOUIGN-AMANN
Butter cake

Serves 4

Preparation and cooking time:
2hr 30min

300g (10½oz) plain flour, plus extra for
* rolling dough*
3g (¼oz) yeast
pinch of salt
200ml (7fl oz) water
250g (8¾oz) salted butter
* (with salt crystals inside)*
220g (7¾oz) granulated sugar, plus
* extra for sprinkling*

1 Make the bread mixture by combining the flour, yeast and pinch of salt. Gradually add the water and blend with a palette knife until a dough forms.

2 Knead the dough for about 10 minutes, or five minutes in a mixer with a dough hook. Leave to rise for 30 minutes.

3 On a floured surface, with a floured rolling pin, roll out your dough to a rectangle measuring 25cm by 20cm (10in by 8in).

4 Flatten the butter in its own packaging, or on greaseproof paper, with the heel of your hand and when it is 1–2cm (½in) smaller than the dough, place the butter on top of the dough.

5 Pour the sugar into the centre of the butter and with your fingers spread it around until it covers the butter.

6 Fold in the four sides, starting with the longer sides, so that it forms a parcel. Then, with your rolling pin, roll out the buttered, sugared dough so it is 25cm by 20cm (10in by 8in) again. Repeat this step – fold into a parcel, roll out to a rectangle – three times.

7 After the third rolling, cut the rectangle into two squares. Fold each side of the squares in, and then the corners, so that each square becomes a hexagon.

8 Place the hexagons into two round cake tins, each 20cm (8in) in diameter, and leave to rest for 30 minutes.

9 Preheat the oven to 180°C (370°F).

10 Sprinkle each cake mixture with sugar and gently score the top with a knife.

11 Bake in the oven for 30 minutes. Because of the sugar, it can burn very easily, so place the cake tins on the bottom of the oven to prevent this happening.

12 Remove from the tins, cool on a cooling rack and serve.

LA TEURGOULE
Rice pudding three ways

This aromatic rice pudding was once a staple food for sailors setting off from the Normandy coast. These days, the much-loved dish is found in restaurants and hotels throughout the region, served for breakfast or, as in the case of chef Freddy Pommier, reinvented as an elegant three-part dessert.

If patience is a virtue, then the reward must surely be this delectable rice pudding from Normandy. Its preparation is simple but, with six hours in the oven, it takes time. Those who do go to the effort of making it will be rewarded with a generous supply of a rich, creamy and heart-warming dessert. Its unusual name comes from the old French for 'twist mouth', which is how your face is supposed to look if you burn your tongue when eating it hot. It was traditionally intended to be kept for a long time: the sticky, golden crust preserving the rich treat beneath. It was this crust that gave it an in-built 'lid', making it perfect for Normandy's sailors.

'It was a food taken on the ships,' explains young chef Freddy Pommier, whose modern interpretation of the dish graces the menu at the charming Hôtel du Tribunal in Mortagne-au-Perche. The town is in the heart of the Perche Regional Nature Park, a couple of hours from the Normandy coast, where sailors would set off with a plentiful supply of teurgoule. 'It keeps well at room temperature,' says Freddy. 'It's rich in calories and so it allowed them to feed themselves well at sea.'

These days, the rice pudding is often combined with cinnamon and is popular for breakfast or as dessert served at home, but Freddy's version uses the teurgoule to make two other stages of the dessert that he serves in a jar – a light mousse that sits on top of the base layer and a cool refreshing ice cream served on the side. On top, he uses a cinnamon crumble to give it some crunch. 'It's always on the menu,' he says. 'Other desserts come and go, but this is a classic.' And for the leftovers? Why not try the Norman custom of having it for breakfast?

Chef //
Freddy Pommier
Location //
Hôtel du Tribunal,
Mortagne-au-Perche

LA TEURGOULE
Rice pudding three ways

Serves 8

Preparation and cooking time:
7hr 15min

For the teurgoule base (makes
1¼kg/2¾lb teurgoule)
1½L (2½pt) unpasteurised full fat milk
(or pasteurised, if unpasteurised is
unavailable)
140g (5oz) short-grained white rice
160g (5½oz) caster sugar
½ vanilla pod
1 bay leaf
½ tsp ground cinnamon (optional)

For the teurgoule mousse
250g (8¾oz) cooled teurgoule
500ml (17½fl oz) whipped cream
50g (1¾oz) sugar
½ tsp ground cinnamon

For the teurgoule ice cream
500g (17½oz) teurgoule
400g (14oz) whipped cream
3 egg yolks
40g (1½oz) caster sugar
½ tsp ground cinnamon

For the cinnamon crumble
110g (3¾oz) plain flour
2 tbsp granulated sugar
110g (3¾oz) caster sugar
100g (3½oz) chilled butter, cut into cubes

1 Preheat the oven to 110°C (230°F).

2 To make the teurgoule base, mix all the ingredients in a terracotta baking dish and bake in the oven for six hours. Set aside to cool.

3 Increase the oven temperature to 180°C (350°F) in preparation for the cinnamon crumble in step 6.

4 To make the teurgoule mousse, mix 250g of the cooled teurgoule with the other mousse ingredients. Pass through a conical sieve to eliminate any grains of rice. Place in a piping bag and refrigerate until ready to serve.

5 To make the teurgoule ice cream, mix all the ice cream ingredients and place in an ice-cream maker until ready to serve.

6 To make the cinnamon crumble, put all the crumble ingredients in a bowl and rub the mixture between your fingers to create a breadcrumb-like consistency. Spread the crumble on a baking sheet/oven tray and bake for 10 minutes at 180°C (350°F).

7 To assemble per serving, place warmed teurgoule base in the bottom of a jar or ramekin, pipe the mousse on the top, sprinkle with the cinnamon crumble and serve with a scoop of the ice cream on the side.

TARTELETTE POMME RHUBARBE
Apple & rhubarb tartlet

Among the farms and fields of eastern Normandy, chef Jordan Fouchet makes the most of the best local produce for his delicate apple and rhubarb tartlet served at the chic Manoir de Surville. And when the ingredients aren't available, seasonality still provides a perfect solution.

Chef //
Jordan Fouchet
Location //
Manoir de Surville, Surville

In the land around the pristine village of Surville, south of Rouen in eastern Normandy, the wheat fields roll with the seasons. In spring, the crop is just burgeoning green sprouts, but by late summer the fields have become a sea of gold, rippling in the breeze. The harvested wheat is then ground to become flour and goes on to be used in a wonderful array of bread, cakes and tarts across France.

In the heart of the village, the seasons also come into play for a simple fruit tart created by chef Jordan Fouchet, which is served at the Manoir de Surville, a favourite escape for Parisians. At the stylish B&B, set in a beautifully restored farmhouse, Jordan picks the best produce to create his dessert. 'It's better to work with local products. They're fresh, seasonal and that's important,' he says. This being Normandy, the obvious fruit to include are its famous apples, which he couples with rhubarb, sourced from a farmer just 15 minutes from the Manoir. But in the height of summer, when the rhubarb harvest is slowed to allow the plant to gain energy stores for the winter, there is less available. So what to do when you can't find your chosen ingredient? Jordan's answer is simple: adapt the recipe.

'The compote can be any fruit. In summer, you can use strawberries, cherries, peaches. As long as the compote is reduced down [and not too watery], it will work well in the tart.' You can then simply caramelise slices of another fruit to put on the top. For added freshness, his cuisine draws on garden herbs, particularly *verveine* (lemon verbena), a herb that the French adore, thanks to its citrus aroma. As he places the tiny green leaf on the top of the perfectly poised apple globes, Jordan declares, 'Voila! It's ready to taste!'

TARTELETTE POMME RHUBARBE
Apple & rhubarb tartlet

Serves 4

Preparation and cooking time: 1hr 15min

For the pastry

250g (8¾oz) plain flour, plus extra for rolling
   pastry
100g (3½oz) icing sugar
30g (1oz) ground hazelnuts
   (or ground almonds)
pinch of salt
100g (3½oz) butter
1 egg yolk

For the compote

2 sticks of rhubarb
seeds from 1 vanilla pod
20g (¾oz) butter
100g (3½oz) caster sugar
water, optional
2 Jonagold apples (or firm-fleshed apples)

verbena leaves, to serve
vanilla ice cream, to serve

For the pastry

1 In a bowl (or food processor), mix the flour, icing sugar, ground hazelnuts and salt. Then add the 100g of butter.

2 Add the egg yolk and combine.

3 Form the mixture into a ball, wrap in clingfilm and put in the fridge for 30 minutes.

For the compote

1 Wash the rhubarb and cut it into small cubes.

2 In a saucepan, add the rhubarb, vanilla seeds, the 20g of butter and half of the sugar and cook for 30 minutes. Add a small amount of water if it starts to boil dry. Put in a bowl and bring to room temperature before setting aside in the fridge until ready to serve.

3 Peel and core the apples, and then use a melon baller to create small globes.

4 Pour the remainder of the sugar into a frying pan and add the apple globes. Fry for six to eight minutes until the apples are caramelised.

Tip
The apple globes are quite tricky to create (it takes practice!), half-circles do just as well or cut them into cubes. You can also make one large tart, rather than four small ones.

To assemble

1   Preheat the oven to 170°C (340°F).

2   Take the pastry from the fridge. Roll out with a floured rolling pin on a lightly floured surface and cut the pastry into circles to fit 14cm (5½in) small round tins or rings to form the tartlets. Bake in the oven for 10 to 15 minutes then leave to cool.

3   To assemble a tartlet, spread 1 tbsp of rhubarb compote on the bottom of a cooled pastry circle, and then place the apple globes on top. Top with a small verbena leaf and serve with a scoop of vanilla ice cream.

MACARON À LA FRAISE ET YUZU
Strawberry yuzu macaron

Macarons have become a modern icon of French patisserie, presented in all manner of flavours and colours. Combine these decadent almond meringues with Normandy's rich cream and the citrus twist of the Japanese yuzu fruit, and the dessert becomes the perfect emblem of Normandy-Japanese husband-wife team Julien and Masako Guérard.

Chef //
Julien and Masako Guérard
Location //
Restaurant Pommeraie Vire,
Roullours Vire

French patisserie is nothing without a good helping of cream, so what better region for a Japanese patisserie chef to be perfecting her techniques than in Normandy, where the milk, cream and butter is the richest in France? It was here that Masako met her French chef husband Julien, and the couple settled in the place he grew up –Roullours Vire, where the Guérards now create a wonderful array of patisserie for their restaurant.

'It's a region with a lot of rain,' explains Julien, 'and this makes the grass good quality. The Normande breed of cow also makes milk that is fattier than other breeds, so it's richer, thicker, tastier. There are even farmers who can tell the season from the colour of the butter – in summer, when the cows are eating the grass, it's yellow. In winter, when they're eating hay, it's whiter and less flavourful. So, whatever the cows eat, it affects the quality of the milk, cream and butter.'

While Normandy's dairy produce has been its speciality for centuries, the Japanese citrus fruit, the yuzu, is something of a new arrival. 'It's very fashionable, but what is interesting is that it's grown in Normandy, near Falaise,' says Julien. 'A local saffron producer imported six mature yuzu trees from Japan five years ago. It was a risk as to whether the trees would stand the journey, and they didn't grow much fruit for the first couple of years. Now though, they harvest quite a few each October. It's a very special flavour.'

For Masako's macaron dessert, the two ingredients work perfectly together: the sharpness of the yuzu cutting through the rich buttery crème patissière that is later mixed with cream. The final flourish comes with the strawberries, perched delicately around the edge. Taste the sweetness of the sugar and the cream, then the zing of yuzu before the macaron cracks and melts in your mouth.

MACARON À LA FRAISE ET YUZU
Strawberry yuzu macaron

Serves 6

Preparation and cooking time: 2hr

For the yuzu cream
sugar
2 eggs
10g (⅓oz) cornflour
100ml (3½fl oz) yuzu juice
  (or lime juice, if unavailable)
75g (2½oz) butter

For the macarons
150g (5¼oz) caster sugar
38ml (1⅓fl oz) water
96g (3½oz) egg whites
150g (5¼oz) ground almonds
100g (3½oz) icing sugar

To assemble
150g (5¼oz) whipped cream
18 good-sized strawberries, cut into
  quarters

To serve
strawberry coulis
broken pistachio nuts
white chocolate tuile

For the yuzu cream

1 Whisk the sugar, eggs and cornflour together in a bowl.

2 Heat the yuzu juice in a saucepan (but do not boil) and add it to the mixture. Pour the whole mixture back into the saucepan and continue to heat, whisking vigorously so that it becomes as thick as a crème patissière.

3 Once cooled to room temperature, add the butter and mix together.

4 Set aside in the fridge until ready to use.

For the macarons

1 Preheat the oven to 130°C (265°F).

2 Cook the sugar and water together at 116°C (240°F).

3 In a clean bowl, whisk half of the egg white mixture until it stands in peaks. Fold the sugar water in gently.

4 Mix ground almonds, icing sugar and the remaining egg whites. Then fold the egg white and sugar mixture in gently with a flexible spatula, over and over until blended (it should look shiny). If you mix too hard the macarons will be too flat.

5 Spoon the mixture into a piping bag and, on a silicone sheet, pipe out in circles of around 4cm (1½in) diameter.

6 Bake in the oven for 20 to 25 minutes until crispy on the outside, but not cooked throughout. Leave to cool on a cooling rack.

To assemble and serve

1 Remove the yuzu cream from the fridge, and blend with the whipped cream before spooning the mixture into a piping bag.

2 Pipe a small blob of yuzu cream on the plate and fix a macaron shell upside down on it. Pipe the yuzu cream in a spiral onto the macaron and then place the quartered strawberries around the edge. Place the second macaron on top. Repeat with the remaining yuzu cream and macarons.

3 Serve the macarons with a strawberry coulis, broken pistachio nuts and a white chocolate tuile.

MADELEINES
Madeleine cakes

These moreish cockle-shaped cakes, with a hint of lemon, are known throughout France. Yet few will know that their origins lie in the tiny town of Commercy in the heart of the Lorraine countryside, where baker Stéphane Zins makes thousands every day using his popular artisanal recipe.

Chef //
Stéphane Zins
Location //
La Boîte à Madeleines,
Commercy

It's easy to see why the great French scribe Marcel Proust wrote so eloquently about madeleines in his great tome *Remembrance of Things Past*, describing them 'as though they had been moulded in the fluted scallop of a pilgrim's shell'. For these light buttery cakes, with their characteristic bump and gentle lemon flavour, have such an allure that they are almost impossible to resist. Little wonder that baker Stéphane Zins sells up to 20,000 of them a day at his bakery La Boîte à Madeleines, in Commercy – the little town in Lorraine where they originated.

The legend goes that, in 1755, the Polish King Stanislas, who was also Duke of Lorraine, held an important dinner at the château in Commercy. 'The baker fell ill, so the king asked the young servant to make a little dessert,' says Stéphane. 'The king really liked it and asked her what the cake was called and she said she didn't know; it was something her grandmother made. He asked her name, which was Madeleine, and said: "From this day, we'll call them Madeleines de Commercy."'

The little cakes became popular in the region, and once Napoleon's Paris-to-Strasbourg railway line was opened in the mid-1800s, the rest of France discovered them. 'The madeleine sellers were allowed to stand on the platform at Commercy's station, so when the locomotives stopped to refill with water and so on, people would buy them, take them home and this really helped madeleines become known across France,' says Stéphane.

La Boîte à Madeleines is one of two remaining madeleine bakeries in Commercy. Stéphane and his brother Thierry only started making madeleines in 2002 (though the family business dates from 1951) and are proud to use artisanal methods. 'There used to be 15 producers of madeleines in Commercy, but now there are just two: us and another more industrialised operation. We don't use preservatives or chemicals. If we started doing that, we'd end up being just like the factory-produced ones.'

MADELEINES
Madeleine cakes

Makes 20 madeleines

Preparation and cooking time: 40min
(not including 6hr waiting time)

3 eggs
80g (2¾oz) caster sugar
30g (1oz) honey
200g (7oz) flour
5g (¼oz) baking powder
120g (4¼oz) butter, melted
4ml (¼fl oz) lemon juice
½ tsp Guérande salt (or any sea salt)

1 In a bowl, whisk the eggs, sugar and honey for three minutes.

2 Add the flour and baking powder, and mix for four minutes.

3 Add the melted butter while it is still hot, the lemon juice and salt. Mix for one minute.

4 Leave to rest for six hours at room temperature.

5 Preheat the oven to 220°C (430°F).

6 Pour the mixture into madeleine moulds and bake in the oven for 11 minutes. Serve warm or cold.

'The deeper the mould, the higher the bump. People have trouble getting a good-sized bump, but it's often because the mould is too flat and therefore there's not enough batter in the centre, so it doesn't rise very high.'

Stéphane Zins

ÎLE FLOTTANTE
'Floating island'

The much-loved île flottante – a fluffy meringue island on a sea of custard – has been a favourite dessert across France since time immemorial. At Paris' historic French bistro La Fontaine de Mars, chef Pierre Saugrain's version is given some added pizazz with the addition of caramel and praline.

When it comes to classic desserts, the enticing île flottante is one of France's favourites. Served everywhere, from school canteens to high-end restaurants, it consists of an 'island' of light-as-a-feather egg white, floating on a 'sea' of crème anglaise, the French version of custard. At Paris' La Fontaine de Mars bistro, chef Pierre Saugrain knows first-hand how popular it is, as he serves between 35 and 40 of them every day.

While the basic recipe is fairly simple, Pierre gives this sweet confection some added wow factor with by incorporating caramel and praline, but this also means the moment of truth – when you float the '*île*' on the crème anglaise – can be a bit fiddly. 'If you wet your hand in cold water, then the meringue won't stick to your fingers. Don't use a knife or anything, as that will just stick,' Pierre advises.

Also known as *oeufs à la neige* ('eggs made into snow'), the dish is considered a Parisian bistro classic, along with snails (p104), boeuf bourguignon (p124) and *sole meunière*, which all appear on the Fontaine de Mars' menu. 'Seven of our dishes, including île flottante, have been on the menu since the day we opened in 1992,' says the bistro's owner Christiane Boudon, who is proud of the restaurant's history.

Named after the neighbouring water fountain, the bistro was first a bar frequented by Napoleon's troops, whose horses were stabled nearby, before becoming a restaurant in 1908. These days, it's considered such a classic Parisian bistro that it was the venue chosen to host US President Barack Obama when he visited France in 2009. As the restaurant is just a short walk from the Eiffel Tower, it's no surprise that its île flottante has many international fans, but it is Christiane who might be the dessert's greatest devotee. 'I've probably eaten about 5000 of them! If ever I feel a bit down, I'll eat an île flottante.'

Chef //
Pierre Saugrain
Location //
La Fontaine de Mars, Paris

ÎLE FLOTTANTE
'Floating island'

Serves 12

Preparation and cooking time
1hr 30min

For the crème anglaise
10 egg yolks
200g (7oz) granulated sugar
1 vanilla pod
1L (1¾pt) milk

For the caramel
1kg (2¼lb) sugar
330ml (11½fl oz) water

For the meringue îles
pinch of salt/sugar
1 kg (2¼lb) egg whites
160g (5½oz) chopped pralines

1 Preheat the oven to 150°C (300°F).

2 To make the crème anglaise (custard), whisk the egg yolks in a bowl with 200g sugar and the seeds from the vanilla pod. Set aside.

3 Place the vanilla pod and the milk in a pan, and bring to the boil.

4 Remove the vanilla pod, reduce the heat and whisk in the egg yolks, until the mixture is thick enough to coat the back of a spoon. Set aside to cool.

5 Make the caramel by placing the sugar in a frying pan over the heat. When it has turned a golden colour, cover with the water and stir until it becomes a syrup.

6 Put 1–2 tbsp of caramel in the bottom of 12 ramekin dishes, and keep the rest of the caramel aside for later.

7 To make the meringue '*îles*', add a pinch of salt or sugar to the egg whites and whisk until they are stiff.

8 Carefully fold the remainder of the caramel into the egg whites and whisk gently.

9 Fill each ramekin with some egg white mixture and level off, then sprinkle with 1 tsp of chopped pralines. Then add another 3–4 tbsp of egg white mixture to create a 'mountain' shape, and sprinkle with the rest of the pralines.

10 Place the ramekins in a baking tray filled with water, to create a bain-marie, and cook for 15 minutes in the oven.

11 Fill 12 bowls with the cooled crème anglaise.

12 To serve, remove the cooked meringue from the ramekin by wetting your fingers in cold water and then turn the meringue within the ramekin with your fingers gently clockwise to loosen it. Then gently tip out the meringue on to your hand. Still holding the meringue, use your other hand to drizzle the warm caramel from the base of the ramekin across the crème anglaise. Then place the meringue on top, so that it floats upright on top of the dish.

BABA À L'ARMAGNAC
Brioche-style cake with brandy

The Michelin-starred Jules Verne restaurant perches on the second level of the Eiffel Tower and offers a stunning view of Paris. Pastry chef Thomas Croizé is charged with making the restaurant's signature dessert, baba à l'Armagnac, a new take on a 300-year-old recipe.

As one of the world's most famous monuments, the Eiffel Tower has been wowing visitors to Paris since it opened as part of the Universal Exhibition in 1889. Every year, some 7 million visitors ascend its lofty heights to admire the City of Lights from above, but for gastronomes, the way to truly enjoy it is from a table at the Jules Verne restaurant. Part of culinary legend Alain Ducasse's restaurant empire, its menu is created by the multi-Michelin starred chef, and prepared by a busy team in a tiny kitchen. Thomas Croizé is *chef de patisserie* and it is up to him to make the baba à l'Armagnac, Ducasse's signature dessert – a take on the classic rum baba, which has been part of French cuisine since the 18th century.

The origins of this dense brioche bun, soaked in syrup and then served with alcohol, can be traced to Stanislas I, King of Poland, who – when exiled in Lorraine – had fond memories of raisin brioches served with Hungarian Tokaji wine. His chef Nicolas Stohrer was charged with creating something similar, which the king, being a fan of the *Arabian Nights* stories, named after Ali Baba. When Stanislas' daughter Marie married King Louis XV, Stohrer relocated to Paris and opened his own bakery.

Now, nearly 300 years later, the dessert is served at the Jules Verne with a sprinkling of Armagnac, a brandy from Southwest France. While diners enjoy gazing through the girders of the mighty monument as a rare treat, Thomas is delighted by the view every day and knows how best to enjoy it: 'In the spring or summer you should arrive at 7pm or 8pm, when it's still daylight, but as the meal goes on, the sun sets and you see a beautiful sky – all pink and orange. Then after the sunset, you see Paris by night. It's just magic.'

Chef //
Thomas Croizé
Location //
Le Jules Verne, Paris

BABA À L'ARMAGNAC
Brioche-style cake with brandy

Serves 4
Preparation and cooking time: 3hr

For the baba dough
415g (14½oz) flour
pinch of salt
140g (5oz) butter
17g (½oz) honey
500g (1lb) eggs
34g (1¼oz) yeast

For the apricot glaze (alternatively use apricot jam)
500g (17½oz) apricot purée
125g + 25g (4½oz + 1oz) granulated
  sugar
81g (3oz) glucose syrup
8g (⅓oz) pectin

For the soaking syrup
1L (1¾pt) water
465g (1lb) granulated sugar
1 empty vanilla pod
zest of 1 orange
zest of 1 lemon

For the vanilla cream
80g (3oz) icing sugar
seeds from 2 vanilla pods
1L (1¾pt) cream

1 To make the baba dough, place the flour, salt, butter and honey in a food mixer with a dough hook and leave to mix for 20 minutes.

2 Add half the eggs and the yeast, and increase the speed (to second level), adding the other half of the eggs little by little, until the mixture comes completely away from the sides of the bowl. The ideal temperature for the dough is 24°C (75°F).

3 Place the dough in a piping bag and leave to rest at room temperature for 15 minutes, then in the fridge for a further 15 minutes. The dough will be stretchy but will have some resistance in it.

4 Preheat the oven to 180°C (350°F).

5 Pipe 32g (1oz) of dough into each mould (individual baking moulds work best, you can place each mould on an electronic scale as you do it, for accuracy). Tap the base of each mould on a teacloth on the counter to settle it and knock out any bubbles.

6 Bake in the oven for 20–25 minutes, then unmould the cakes while they're still warm.

7 To make the apricot glaze, bring the apricot purée, 125g of the sugar and the glucose to the boil. Add the pectin and the remaining 25g sugar. Boil for one minute then keep cool.

8 To make the soaking syrup, boil the water with the sugar, then add the vanilla pod and the citrus zests and leave to soak. Reduce heat to lukewarm then dip the baba cakes in it. Hold them down until they soak up enough syrup to sink into the mixture.

9 To make the vanilla cream, mix the icing sugar with the vanilla seeds in a bowl, then sieve into the cream. Whip the cream until it stands in soft peaks.

10 Before serving, spread the apricot glaze around the outside of the cake, and cut the cake vertically into two. To eat, spoon the cream into the centre of the two cake halves.

CRÈME BRÛLÉE
Crème brûlée

*On Paris'
fashionable
Boulevard Saint
German, Les Deux
Magots is one of
France's most
famous cafes and
is renowned for
its literary and
artistic clientele.
Its menu offers
classic bistro
cuisine, including
the much-loved
dessert crème
brûlée made by
chef Magesh
Arumugam.*

W ho can resist making that unmistakable sound – 'tap, tap, crunch' – as a spoon is used to break through the sugary crust of a crème brûlée? What follows is the taste of the smooth vanilla cream, contrasted perfectly by the angular crust, in a dessert that is adored the world over.

The history of the crème brûlée is much debated, with both England and Spain staking claims on its origins, but France's version dates from 1691 when it was mentioned in a cookery book by François Massialot, chef to Philippe I, brother of Louis XIV. It came back into vogue in the 1980s, and since then it has appeared on menus throughout France – and indeed the world – including one of the country's most famous restaurants, Les Deux Magots.

Named after two Chinese figurines that perch above the tightly packed tables of the restaurant's main room, Les Deux Magots started its life as a shop, before becoming a cafe in 1812. It soon became known as a hang-out for artists and writers, including Pablo Picasso, Ernest Hemingway and the philosophers Simone de Beauvoir and Jean-Paul Sartre. 'It's great to work somewhere that has such an interesting history,' says Magesh Arumugam who has been working at the cafe since 2005. As *Chef de Cuisine*, he knows the secrets of creating the restaurant's popular crème brûlée, which is made with vanilla pods that he soaks in the mixture overnight before baking it the next day.

'The vanilla is key to the classic version of the crème brûlée, but you can add whatever you like to it, chocolate, even green tea,' he says. Yet the true skill comes in achieving that delicate shell with the flaming torch – sprinkle the sugar too thinly and it won't hold together; layer it too thickly and you risk heating the vanilla cream beneath and burning the sugar, making it bitter. But, however it is done, it must result in the all-important 'tap, tap, crunch'.

Chef //
Mageswaran 'Magesh'
Arumugam
Location //
Les Deux Magots, Paris

CRÈME BRÛLÉE
Crème brûlée

Serves 6

Preparation and cooking time: 1hr 30min (not including overnight refrigeration and waiting time)

10 egg yolks
180g (6⅓oz) sugar
2 vanilla pods
150ml (5¼fl oz) milk
1L (1¾pt) single cream
6 tbsp demerara sugar

1 In a bowl, beat together the egg yolks and sugar.

2 Cut the vanilla pods, and scrape out the seeds, reserving the pods. Add the seeds only to the mixture at this stage.

3 Pour in the milk, whisking the mixture as you do so.

4 Pour in the cream, whisking the mixture as you do so.

5 Add the empty vanilla pods and leave overnight in the fridge.

6 Preheat the oven to 95°C (200°F).

7 Drain the mixture through a sieve, and discard the vanilla pods.

8 Pour the mixture into six ramekins and bake in the oven for an hour.

9 Leave to cool, and place in the fridge for at least two hours.

10 When ready to serve, sprinkle 1 tbsp of demerara sugar over each ramekin, and tip the dish so it spreads evenly across the top.

11 With a culinary blowtorch, evenly caramelise the sugar across the top (or put under a very hot grill for a couple of minutes and watch until the sugar is caramelised). Serve immediately.

Tip
It's not obligatory to refrigerate this dish overnight, but it will be better if the mixture has had time to absorb the flavour from the vanilla seeds and pods.

BELGIUM

English Channel

Amiens

Picardie

Rouen

Reims

Caen

Haute-
Normandie

Basse-Normandie

PARIS

Île-de-France

Champagne-
Ardenne

Troyes

Rennes
Bretagne

Le Mans

Orleans

Auxerre

26

33

22

MONTIVAULT

27

AVALLON

37

Dijon

Pays de la Loire

ANGERS

AMBOISE

31

32

36

28

Tours

34

21

NANTES

CHÉDIGNY

Bourges

29

BEAUNE

25

35

20

Poitier

Centre

Nevers

Bourgogne

23

La Rochelle

Poitou-Charentes

24

30

MÂCON

FRANCE

Vichy

Lyon

Limoges
Limousin

Clermont-Ferrand

Rhône-Alpes

Auvergne

Central France

Midi-Pyrénées

Languedoc-
Roussillon

Nimes

CENTRAL FRANCE

Discover the heart of France, where some of the country's most rewarding gastronomic experiences are found among the vineyards of Burgundy, where wine is the most essential ingredient. Meanwhile, the River Loire offers a bounty of dishes, from creamy desserts to easy-to-bake cakes.

LES CUISSES DE GRENOUILLE À LA CRÈME D'AIL ET PERSIL

Frogs' legs with garlic cream & parsley

It's thanks to frogs' legs that the English-speaking world nicknamed the French 'frogs' and although it was originally considered peasant food, it now graces the tables of elegant restaurants throughout the country. At Le Clos aux Roses in the Loire Valley, chef Armelle Krause is proud to serve the typical French dish.

For chef Armelle Krause, there is a very good reason for serving the quintessential French dish of frogs' legs in her restaurant: 'I love them!' she smiles. 'It's such a classic dish and people love it.'

It was in the 12th century in Southeast France, in the lakes of Dombes near Lyon, that people started the tradition of eating frogs' legs. The story goes that the Catholic Church forbade the eating of meat on certain days of the year. Canny monks got around the problem by having frogs classified as fish; the food caught on among local peasants and a national dish was born.

The dish is served throughout France, and different chefs will have their own recipes for the amphibious creatures that were once dubbed 'nymph's thighs' when served at the London Ritz by the renowned French chef Auguste Escoffier in 1908. Whichever way they are served by the world's top chefs, the traditional recipe is with garlic and parsley, which is how Armelle serves them at her restaurant in the heart of the Loire Valley.

Armelle first discovered the dish while training in Paris under the three-Michelin-starred Guy Martin. 'I cooked them at Le Grand Véfour and they were really popular,' she says. 'My cuisine is traditional and so I've kept much of the original recipe. They don't have that much flavour themselves, hence the garlic and parsley.' While the dish dates from centuries ago, today's foreign visitors are somewhat amused. 'In some countries, there are animals that people just don't eat, like frogs and snails, so diners are shocked to see them on the menu. They're intrigued and want to try them as a bit of a joke, but then they like them. Then there are the people over 60 years old, who have childhood memories of eating them,' she says. But whether it's history or curiosity that drives people to try them, the description of the taste will generally be the same: a cross between chicken and fish.

Chef //
Armelle Krause
Location //
Le Clos aux Roses, Chédigny

LES CUISSES DE GRENOUILLE À LA CRÈME D'AIL ET PERSIL

Frogs' legs with garlic cream & parsley

Serves 4

Preparation and cooking time: 45min

4 cloves garlic
200ml (6¾fl oz) single cream
pinch of salt
salted water, for boiling potatoes
500g (1lb) floury potatoes
100ml (3½fl oz) milk
25g (¾oz) butter, for potato purée
24 pairs of frogs' legs
plain flour, seasoned with salt & pepper,
  for dipping
1 tbsp olive oil, for frying
1 tbsp butter, for frying
bunch of flat-leaf parsley
cooking oil (sunflower or rapeseed),
  for frying parsley

1 Peel the garlic and take out the small green sprout (it makes it bitter), put into a saucepan with cream and bring to the boil.

2 When it comes to the boil, add a pinch of salt, then remove from the heat and mix with a hand blender/liquidiser.

3 Strain through a pointed sieve into a saucepan, then keep warm over a low heat.

4 Boil the potatoes in salted water for approx 15–20 minutes. Drain and add the milk and 25g of butter. Mash until smooth and set aside.

5 Dip the frogs' legs in seasoned flour on a plate, until well covered.

6 Fry the frogs' legs in 1 tbsp olive oil and 1 tbsp butter in a frying pan until golden, then drain on a plate lined with absorbent kitchen paper.

7 For the parsley chips, dip the parsley leaves in cooking oil (sunflower, rapeseed) and fry gently in a frying pan until they are crispy but not coloured.

8 Serve the frogs' legs with the warm garlic cream and mashed potato purée, and parsley chips to garnish.

Tip

These portions are for frogs' legs served as a main course – divide the ingredients by three to serve as a starter (as pictured).

SALADE DE TOMATES AVEC SOUPE FROIDE DE TOMATES
Tomato salad & chilled tomato soup

There are 650 varieties of tomatoes growing in the walled garden of Château de la Bourdaisière, the passion project of an aristocrat nicknamed 'the gardening prince' that inspires visitors to plant, grow and cook their own. Here, chef Yacinthe de Geyer serves simple dishes at the Bar à Tomates.

Chef //
Yacinthe de Geyer
Location //
Château de la Bourdaisière,
Montlouis-sur-Loire

There can be no better taste than that of a tomato you've grown yourself; it's the taste of sunshine, with a sweetness not often achieved by the shop-bought varieties. Imagine, then, the bounty of flavours that come with growing some 650 varieties, in all manner of shapes, sizes and colours. Their names read like characters in a Roald Dahl book – Magellan Burgess Purple, Caspian Pink, Ponderosa Golden, to name just a few – and each bring something different to the open kitchen of the Bar à Tomates in the Château de la Bourdaisière's garden.

Here, chef Yacinthe de Geyer cooks simple dishes that let the fruit's flavours shine through, using them for the salad and then the leftovers for a gazpacho-style soup. Ask him to name his favourites and it's like asking him to name a favourite child, but when pushed he admits to a few. 'I like the Coeur de Boeuf, it has very thin skin and very few seeds and it just melts in the mouth,' he says. 'Then there are some that are like tiny yellow pears [*poires jaunes*] and they are so tasty. The tiny ones are the tastiest.' For the tomato salad, there are others that win the day. 'Varieties like Green Zebra, with a stripy skin; Rose de Berne that is more acidic, and the Paul Robeson, named after the African-American jazz man who fought for human rights. That's the great thing about creating new varieties, you can give them new names.'

It was this diversity that inspired the château's owner, Louis Albert de Broglie – the so-called Prince Jardinier – to start his project in 1992. 'When he learned there were more than 10,000 varieties of tomato in the world, that was a big inspiration,' says Yacinthe. 'The whole thing about this place is to educate people. We want to inspire them to live a healthier life, and that starts with food.'

SALADE DE TOMATES AVEC SOUPE FROIDE DE TOMATES

Tomato salad & chilled tomato soup

Serves 4

Preparation and cooking time: 30min

For the salad

12 garden tomatoes (three different
  varieties x four tomatoes), sliced
32 fresh basil leaves
dash of olive oil
sea salt flakes, to taste
black pepper, to taste

For the cold tomato soup

1.4kg (3lb) tomatoes
4 or 5 cloves of garlic
150g (5¼oz) white onion, finely chopped
100ml (3½fl oz) extra virgin olive oil
20ml (¾fl oz) sherry vinegar
6 good pinches of black pepper
4 good pinches of salt
250ml (8¾fl oz) water

drizzle of olive oil, to serve
16 croutons (1.5cm x 1.5cm/½in x ½in),
  to serve (see p102)
4 basil leaves, to serve

1 For the salad, slice the tomatoes and arrange on the plate, decorate with torn basil leaves. Drizzle with olive oil, and season with salt and pepper, to taste.

2 To make the cold tomato soup, put all ingredients, apart from the water, in a blender and blitz until smooth.

3 Add the water and blend again.

4 Push the liquid through a conical sieve to eliminate the seeds and other bits.

5 For each person, serve the soup in a bowl with a drizzle of olive oil, croutons and a basil leaf. Serve the salad on the side.

MOUSSE DE CHÈVRE FRAIS
Goat's cheese mousse

The wide open plains that surround the River Loire are the perfect environment for breeding goats, making their cheese a local speciality, which chef Christophe Hay pairs with the wild flowers that grow in the fertile plains at his Michelin-starred restaurant in the small village of Montlivault.

N ot far from the mighty Château de Chambord, where kings and queens resided for centuries, Christophe Hay's Michelin-starred kitchen uses ingredients that are somewhat more rustic than their royal surroundings would suggest. The humble goat thrives on the plains here and, as a result, the cheese is a local speciality. 'There is so much goat's cheese here: we have the prairies, we have the climate, and life is – in general – perfect for rearing goats,' says Christophe.

He admits the cheese can be an acquired taste, and everyone has a preference how to eat it. 'Some people like the strength and just have it with butter, which softens it slightly. Others, they like to balance it with something sweet, with honey or fruit. When a cheese is strong like that, it's good to balance it with something softer.' To get that balance right, Christophe chooses a cheese from a producer that specialises in a more delicate product. 'He makes it differently to others because he presses on the cheese more than usual, which eliminates more whey, and this makes it softer,' he explains. 'It's the whey that makes a cheese acidic.'

For his recipe, which is served as a starter, Christophe combines it with ingredients that also thrive in the countryside here in the royal heart of France. 'My cuisine is really attached to the terroir here, the wild flowers and herbs of this area. In the Val de Loire, we're still in the riverbed. The water has gone now; it flowed here 150 years ago, but the earth is still wild and rich in nutrients. By using the flowers, we link the river to our cuisine.' The flowers he uses include wood sorrel, salad burnet, wild geranium and chickweed. So, with a trickle of honey, some croutons for crunch, and a sprinkling of these pretty flowers, the dish is a rich, enticing start to any meal.

Chef //
Christophe Hay
Location //
La Maison d'à Côté,
Montlivault

MOUSSE DE CHÈVRE FRAIS
Goat's cheese mousse

Serves 5

*Preparation and cooking time: 45min
(not including 3hr refrigeration time)*

*3 leaves of gelatine
water, for soaking
360ml (12½fl oz) milk
190ml (6¾fl oz) single cream
300g (10½oz) fresh goat's cheese
bowl of iced water
salt, to taste
pepper, to taste
40ml (1½fl oz) good quality sherry
   vinegar
1 slice of bread, for croutons
butter, for frying
shavings of hard goat's cheese, to garnish
clear honey, to garnish
wild herbs (eg thyme, dill), to garnish
wild flowers, to garnish (see Tip)*

1 Soak the gelatine leaves in cold water for approx five minutes until dissolved.

2 Bring the milk and cream to the boil in a saucepan, then immediately pour over the goat's cheese in a food processor.

3 Add in the drained gelatine leaves straight-away and mix on full speed to get a smooth mixture.

4 Transfer to a mixing bowl over iced water (the opposite to a bain-marie) and whip in the salt, pepper and sherry vinegar. Transfer the mixture to a piping bag or siphon, and put into the fridge for a minimum of three hours.

5 To make the croutons, cut the bread into very small cubes. Fry in a pan with butter until golden then drain on a plate lined with absorbent kitchen paper.

6 Remove the piping bag/siphon from the fridge and pipe a neat dome of goat's cheese mousse in the centre of a plate. Garnish with slices of hard cheese, drizzle over a small amount of honey and decorate with croutons, wild herbs and edible flowers.

Tip

You can buy edible flower seed mixes to plant in the garden. They might not be the same flowers as found in the Loire, but any edible flowers will add a pretty dimension to the dish.

'When you're buying your cheese at the market, make sure it has a good shape and doesn't move. If it's leaking whey, then it won't be a good product. Too much whey makes it acidic.'

Christophe Hay

ESCARGOTS À LA BOURGUIGNONNE
Snails with butter & parsley

The quintessential French dish may have had humble beginnings, but thanks to gourmet chefs both past and present, snails in garlic butter have never been more popular, as Michelin-starred chef Luc Filoé proves at Le Montrachet in the wine-making village of Puligny-Montrachet.

Chef //
Luc Filoé
Location //
Le Montrachet, Puligny-Montrachet

History tells us that it was the Romans who first introduced snails to the Gaulish diet, but it is the French who are now famous the world over for eating the humble gastropod. The modern dish was born in Burgundy in 1796 when Père Vallée, the landlord of an auberge in Yonne, began serving them with the obligatory lashings of garlic butter to overnight guests en route from Paris to Lyon. A little later, in 1814, they became fashionable thanks to Marie-Antonin Carême, the chef of Louis XVIII's minister of foreign affairs, who served them to Tsar Alexander I. From this moment on, the snail was a firm favourite among the French.

'Before this, they were more of a peasant dish,' explains Luc Filoé, a Michelin-starred chef working at a restaurant surrounded by the prestigious Côte d'Or vineyards in Burgundy. Nowadays, snails are served by chefs of all levels in many different recipes. 'Not many gastronomic restaurants serve them as we do,' explains Luc. 'They do them in new ways, but we serve them in the traditional way, in their shells.' There's a ritual to eating them this way, with a set of small tongs and a special fork required to tease them out of their spiral carapace. After this comes the juicy, buttery sauce, with the kick of the garlic and parsley to follow.

'Snails themselves don't have that much taste. So the herbs and garlic give them some flavour,' says Luc. But a true Burgundy snail can be hard to come by. 'You can't cultivate them, they have to grow in the wild, and because they're now a protected species, you can only collect them in July and August.' So now the French look to Eastern Europe for their supplies. 'I don't think they eat them there,' laughs Luc. 'They just send them to the French!'

ESCARGOTS À LA BOURGUIGNONNE
Snails with butter & parsley

Serves 8

Preparation and cooking time:
30–40min

80–100 large snails (10–12 per person)
300g (10½oz) parsley
20g (¾oz) tarragon
500g (1lb) butter (at room temperature)
7g (¼oz) salt
4g (⅛oz) pepper
½ tsp mixed spice
30g (1oz) garlic, chopped finely
30g (1oz) spring onions, chopped
2 tbsp white wine
crusty baguette, to serve

1 Preheat the oven to 180°C (350°F).

2 Remove the snails from their shells.

3 Chop the parsley and tarragon finely then combine with all other ingredients (except the snails) in a bowl to make a thick paste.

4 Place a small spoonful of this mixture into the shell of each snail, return each snail to its shell, then add another spoonful of the butter mixture on the top.

5 Bake in the oven for 10–15 minutes in a baking dish. Serve immediately with a crusty baguette to mop up the excess butter.

Tip
If you don't have a snail serving dish (as only a dedicated escargot fan would), use any excess butter mixture to 'glue' the snails to the plate.

GOUGÈRES AU FROMAGE
Cheese pastries

These delicious little pastry puffs are cooked with Comté cheese and are served before meals with an aperitif at restaurants throughout Burgundy and Franche-Comté. At Ma Table en Ville, a friendly modern restaurant in Mâcon, chef Gilles Bérard serves these addictive savoury treats to whet the appetite.

Chef //
Gilles Bérard
Location //
Ma Table en Ville, Mâcon

The list of French delicacies that are made with choux pastry is long, but among the indulgent cream and caramel buns, which are the pride of many a patissier, is the simple yet delicious gougère. This small choux bun might look like a profiterole, but its contents are entirely savoury, which – according to chef Gilles Bérard – is a rarity for this kind of pastry: 'They're the only savoury choux pastry I know,' he says. 'A choux is usually sweet, like eclairs, *choux à la crème, les religieuses, les Saint-Honorés.*' Unlike these pastries that may come at the end of a meal, gougères arrive at the start and are ubiquitous in Burgundy and neighbouring Franche-Comté, being served as an aperitif before the main meal, with the obligatory glass of white Burgundy wine. They're a favourite, whether served at a rustic auberge or at a gourmet establishment, such as Ma Table en Ville, which Gilles runs with his wife Laurence, and two friends.

The key to the true gougère is the cheese, which comes from across the regional border – Comté is a hard cheese made in huge wheels up to 70cm (27½in) in diameter. It grates particularly well, making it perfect for stirring into the choux pastry. 'Some people use Emmental,' says Gilles, 'but Emmental doesn't have much taste, whereas Comté has more flavour. The longer it ages, the drier the cheese gets and the more aromas it has. A Comté *fruité* is the youngest and is matured for up to 18 months. It's not too powerful.' With a buttery pastry and the slightly salty cheese, *gougères* are nothing if not moreish, making them the perfect start to any meal. 'That moment when you take your seat at the table is a nice one,' describes Gilles. 'We would naturally have an aperitif and take some time out. And it's always nice to have some nibbles to go along with it.'

GOUGÈRES AU FROMAGE

Cheese pastries

Serves 40–50 gougères

Preparation and cooking time: 45min

250ml (8¾fl oz) water
125g (4½oz) butter
salt, to taste
pepper, to taste
250g (8¾oz) plain flour
8 eggs
150g (5¼oz) Comté fruité cheese, grated

1 Preheat the oven to 190°C–200°C (375°F–390°F).

2 In a saucepan, bring the water with the butter to the boil, add salt and pepper to taste.

3 Once the butter has melted in the boiling water, add the flour quickly and stir into a pastry. Lower the heat and keep stirring rapidly for about five minutes until the mixture thickens and leaves the sides of the pan.

4 Put the mixture into a food mixer (or use an electric whisk) and add the eight eggs gradually. Mix until the batter is well combined.

5 Add the grated cheese and mix well.

6 Spoon the whole mixture into a piping bag and then, on a lined baking sheet/tray, pipe (or spoon, if not using a piping bag) out a quantity the size of a quail's egg every 4cm to 5cm (1½in–2in).

7 Bake in the oven for 10–12 minutes, then serve warm.

CAKE À L'AMI DE CHAMBERTIN
Savoury cheese loaf

Contrary to English-speakers' expectations, the French 'cake' is a savoury loaf, sliced and served as the perfect accompaniment to an aperitif, a pre-dinner drink with friends. For chef Roland Chanliaud, it's the ideal food to serve at his laid-back 'gastro-bar' in the heart of Beaune.

When chef Roland Chanliaud left behind his Michelin-starred kitchen at Le Jardin des Remparts in 2013 to start a wine bar, he did so with one thing in mind: 'I wanted it to be more sociable, to be able to chat with my clients,' he says. 'With a gourmet restaurant, the kitchen is separate from the dining room and the terrace.' His wine bar, or 'gastro-bar' as he calls it, is set in La Maison du Colombier, a 16th-century turreted building in the heart of Beaune, itself the centre of the Burgundy wine industry. Be careful not to order the local drink Kir (aligoté white wine and crème de cassis). 'We don't serve it here. We have so many good white wines now, there's no need to hide the bad wines with crème de cassis.'

In Beaune, wine boutiques, cellars and high-end restaurants abound, selling some of the world's most expensive food and wines. In contrast to these more formal places, La Maison du Colombier has a more modern, casual approach, where eating and drinking is a laid-back affair; something to share with friends. Among the plates of charcuterie, cheese and *tartines* (grilled open sandwiches), there are also 'cakes', savoury loaves that are sliced and served with pre-dinner drinks.

Roland's recipe for his savoury loaf draws on one of Burgundy's local cheeses, called l'Ami de Chambertin. Created in 1950 by a cheesemaker who worked near the Gevrey-Chambertin vineyards, it became a firm favourite with winemakers, hence the name, 'Friend of Chambertin wines'. Similar to the local soft cheese Époisses, its rind is washed with Marc de Bourgogne (a pomace brandy that is a by-product of winemaking), which gives it an orange colour and a wrinkled texture. 'It tastes good, not too strong,' says Roland. And when mixed into a savoury cake, its buttery flavour is perfect alongside the hint of mustard.

Chef //
Roland Chanliaud
Location //
La Maison du Colombier, Beaune

CAKE À L'AMI DE CHAMBERTIN
Savoury cheese loaf

Serves 10–12

Preparation and cooking time:
1hr 30min

125g (4½oz) butter
70g (2½oz) Dijon mustard
125g (4½oz) cheese
  (preferably Ami du Chambertin,
  or Époisses if unavailable)
5 eggs
25g (¾oz) parsley
1 clove of garlic, finely chopped
125g (4½oz) flour, plus extra to coat loaf tin
25g (¾oz) baking powder
butter, for greasing loaf tin

1 Preheat the oven to 160°C (320°F).

2 In a food processor, blend the butter, mustard and cheese.

3 Little by little, add the eggs to the mixture in the food processor, then the parsley and finely chopped garlic.

4 Add the sieved flour and baking powder.

5 Grease and flour a loaf tin or mould.

6 Pour the mixture into the mould and bake for one hour.

7 Remove the loaf from the oven and turn it out onto a cooling rack. Wait two to three hours before slicing and serving.

'You can adapt it [this recipe] and use ham, or ham and olives, smoked salmon or goat's cheese.'

Roland Chanliaud

POISSON AU BEURRE BLANC
White fish with white wine butter sauce

The Loire region's famous dish of river fish with an indulgent white wine and butter sauce may have uncomplicated ingredients, but the trick is in the technique. It's a dish that has evolved to grace the tables of the region's elegant châteaux, such as the beautiful Château des Briottières.

Chef //
Hedwige de Valbray
Location //
Château des Briottières,
Champigné

Ask any local from the Loire – from Orleans to Nantes – to name a classic dish from the region and it is the beurre blanc with river fish they will undoubtedly recommend. Made with butter and white wine, it is similar to hollandaise or Béarnaise sauce but without the egg yolks. Despite its simple ingredients, its technique is one to master over time. After 30 years serving it to guests at the magical Château des Briottières, Hedwige de Valbray has perfected the art: 'The hard part is stopping the butter from melting. That's why people add in the cream, it emulsifies it,' she says. 'You have to serve it immediately. It's quite rare to see [on menus] – you don't often find it in Paris restaurants, because it's so fragile.'

The traditional fish to serve it with was pike, found in abundance in the River Loire, but Hedwige is not a fan. 'It has lots of bones and rather a muddy flavour.' Little wonder, then, that those living along France's longest river found a way to make it more enticing. 'That's why they invented a sauce, to soften it,' she says. While pike is not often the order of the day now, the sauce remains a classic and is used to enhance white fish, scallops, pork and chicken.

Hedwige serve the mouthwatering beurre blanc over zander, or pike-perch, as she has always done here. Her kitchen is just metres from the elegant dining room, so the dish can be whisked quickly to the table. These more delicate river fish are more fitting for the setting – one of the most elegant châteaux in the Western Loire. 'The pike was eaten by fishermen, it was a poor person's food,' says Hedwige, 'but in the châteaux, they would eat zander with beurre blanc. It's a very old recipe.'

POISSON AU BEURRE BLANC
White fish with white wine butter sauce

Serves 4

Preparation and cooking time: 40min

boiled potatoes, to serve
garden vegetables, to serve
4 shallots, chopped finely
250ml (8¾fl oz) white wine
    (ideally Muscadet)
200g (8¾oz) white fish per person
    (ideally zander, or cod if unavailable)
250g (8¾oz) unsalted butter, cut into cubes
3 tbsp single cream (optional)
squeeze of lemon juice (optional)
salt, to taste
pepper, to taste

1 Bring a saucepan of water to boil and add the potatoes. Simmer until cooked (roughly 15 minutes), then set aside.

2 Add your choice of garden vegetables to a steamer. Steam for 5–10 minutes until cooked, then set aside.

3 Put the shallots and wine in a casserole dish with a large base. Simmer until the wine has all evaporated (approx five minutes).

4 In a steamer, steam the fish over a medium heat until it is cooked through. Keep warm and covered until ready to serve.

5 Over a very low heat, vigorously stir (or whisk) in the butter a little at a time so it softens and thickens, but don't let it melt. If it starts to melt, add the single cream and a squeeze of lemon juice.

6 Add salt and pepper, then pass the sauce through a sieve to eliminate the shallots.

7 Pour over the fish and serve immediately.

8 Serve with the boiled potatoes and garden vegetables.

OEUFS EN MEURETTE

Poached eggs in red wine sauce

This warming dish of poached eggs in a red wine sauce is a classic Burgundy dish born of Sunday leftovers, but Stéphane and Nathalie Oudot's version, served at their charming table d'hôte, is a dish worth making for its own sake.

'Every home in Burgundy has a recipe for oeufs en meurette,' says Stéphane Oudot as he stirs a pot in the kitchen at the heart of his cosy and welcoming B&B. 'Beef bourguignon (p124) is famous all over the world, but oeufs en meurette is like a local secret. We do ours with mushrooms and bread and onions,' he confides. 'It's very popular with the British, American and Australian guests. Sometimes, people don't know what it is, so they don't try it; but as we have a set menu here they have a nice surprise.'

The rich red wine sauce might be seen as an indulgence when served with simple poached eggs, but when you discover its origins it makes perfect sense. 'When people spent three days cooking beef bourguignon, with lots of meat, it was important to have a lot of sauce,' says Stéphane. 'On Saturday night, or Sunday, people would eat all the beef and there would be lots of sauce left but no money. So people used eggs to use up the sauce.'

As with beef bourguignon, the choice of wine is essential: 'You can't do oeufs en meurette without Pinot Noir,' he insists. 'Some chefs use other wines, but the characteristic of it is that it is brown when cooked and not acidic. If you use Syrah [Shiraz], that's the worst one: you will have an acidic, purple sauce, and that's just rubbish!' The other key element is fresh eggs: the fresher they are, the less likely the whites will have turned watery and will not adhere to the yolks. 'Some chefs poach the eggs in the sauce itself but we do it separately, as we then have the contrast of the white and the sauce.'

With finishing touches, such as crispy bacon, tasty mushrooms fried in butter and a sprinkling of chives, the meal makes the perfect starter or, with the addition of a slice of bread or croutons, a satisfying dish – even for a Sunday.

Chef //
Stéphane & Nathalie Oudot
Location //
La Cimentelle,
Vassy-les-Avallon

OEUFS EN MEURETTE

Poached eggs in red wine sauce

Serves 4

Preparation and cooking time: 1hr 30min

1½L (2½pt) veal or beef stock
12–18 small onions
1 tbsp sugar
salt, to taste
pepper, to taste
water, for simmering onions
400g (14oz) beef & bones
   (leftover cuts to flavour stock only)
olive oil, for frying
150g (5¼oz) carrots, chopped finely
150g (5¼oz) celery, chopped finely
700ml (1¼pt) Pinot Noir red wine
bowl of salted iced water, to hold cooked eggs
water, for boiling eggs
1 tsp white wine vinegar
8 very fresh eggs
250g (8¾oz) mushrooms
squeeze of lemon juice
lardons/chopped bacon
20g (¾oz) chilled butter, cubed
8 pieces toasted bread
chopped chives, to serve

1 Pour the stock into a saucepan and bring to the boil. Cook until the quantity is reduced by half then set aside.

2 Peel the onions and place in a shallow saucepan with a tablespoon of sugar, salt and pepper. Barely cover with water and leave to simmer for an hour.

3 In a large saucepan, sear the beef pieces and bones in the olive oil. Don't move the meat around too much, let it stick to the pan and turn it just enough to brown on each side.

4 Once the meat is coloured on each side, add the chopped carrots and celery to the pan and fry until they're cooked through. Remove the meat and veg from the pan and set aside.

5 Add the wine to the pan and deglaze the base, loosening all the browned bits. Leave to simmer for 30 minutes, melting all the cooking residues.

6 Drain the wine in a conical sieve, return the wine to the pan and continue simmering until the wine has reduced by a quarter.

7 Mix together the reduced stock from step 1 and the reduced wine. Take off the heat and set aside.

8 Prepare a bowl of salted, iced water and place near the hob/hot plate. Bring a large pan of water to the boil and add a teaspoon of white vinegar.

9 Reduce the heat on the boiling water to a low simmer. Crack each egg into a ramekin dish and then tip gently into the boiling water one by one. Leave to poach for three minutes. Scoop each egg out gently and place into the iced water.

10 Wipe or peel the mushrooms and cut each one into four pieces. Fry in a pan for 10 minutes with a squeeze of lemon juice. Set aside.

11 Ten minutes before serving, fry the lardons until they're crispy. Then reheat the sauce from step 7 and add 20g (¾oz) of chilled butter cut into cubes, mix with a whisk, then place the poached eggs in the sauce until they're warmed through.

12 For each serving, place two pieces of toasted bread on a plate (or shallow bowl), ladle an egg on top of each slice, then add the onions (from step 2), mushrooms and lardons/bacon around it. Cover with the red wine sauce and sprinkle with chopped chives.

BOEUF BOURGUIGNON
Burgundy beef

Legendary American cook Julia Child described boeuf bourguignon as: 'Certainly one of the most delicious beef dishes concocted.' The recipe uses two of Burgundy's most prized ingredients, beef and red wine, but techniques to create the hearty stew vary throughout the region, as chef Cécile Riotte explains.

Chef //
Cécile Riotte
Location //
Le Vaudésir, Avallon

As one of France's most iconic dishes, it's little wonder this hearty stew is so well loved considering its central ingredients are two of Burgundy's most delicious products – hunks of beef stewed for hours in a rich red wine. While there is no debate about which wine is used – it should always be Pinot Noir – the cuts of beef can be open to discussion. But coming from a family of cattle farmers, chef Cécile Riotte knows which are best: 'I use the *gite* (shin or topside), as it stews well; but you can use chuck cuts too,' she advises. 'It's better to use the tastiest cuts, but then you would never use fillet, it just wouldn't stand being stewed for three hours – it would be rock hard.'

Cécile's restaurant, Le Vaudésir, in the town of Avallon in the north of Burgundy, is decorated with such memorabilia as agricultural medals and pictures that celebrate the region's strong culture of raising Charolais cows, the cream-coloured breed that graze throughout the Burgundy countryside. 'They're a large animal, so the cuts you get are very big,' she says. Naturally, the key stage to any Beef Bourguignon recipe is the long stewing time, and Cécile also gives the meat a head start by marinating it in wine overnight. And she has a trick for thickening the sauce that avoids the flour used in many recipes. 'I blend the onions and carrots in a food processor to create a thickener for the gravy,' she explains. 'Don't roll the meat in flour, you need more oil to fry it; then it gets too thick and you need more water. No, never flour.' Cécile also dispenses with mushrooms, often found in other recipes. But between the marinade, the rich aromatic gravy and the caramelised onions to top it off, there is plenty of warming flavour.

BOEUF BOURGUIGNON
Burgundy beef

Serves 6

Preparation and cooking time: 4hr
(not including overnight marinating)

1L (1¾pt) Pinot Noir red wine
1⅔kg (3½lb) beef
  (preferably chuck or topside)
150g (5¼oz) carrots
  (preferably small, fine ones)
2 large onions
100ml (3½fl oz) olive or sunflower oil
1 bouquet garni
salt, to taste
freshly ground black pepper, to taste
150g (5¼oz) small onions
1 tbsp butter
4 tsp sugar
water, to cover small onions
4 squares of dark chocolate
  (at least 44% cocoa)
150g (5¼oz) lardons or chopped bacon
water, for blanching lardons
mashed potatoes, to serve
steamed carrots, to serve

1 To prepare the marinade, pour the wine into a saucepan and bring to the boil (approx 10 minutes) to reduce the amount of alcohol in it.

2 Cut the meat into pieces of around 4cm (1½in) square, slice the carrots and the two large onions. Put the meat, 150g of carrots and onions into the wine and leave in the fridge overnight.

3 Remove the marinade from the fridge and drain the meat and vegetables in a sieve. Reserve the wine marinade.

4 In a large oven-safe casserole pot, fry the meat in the oil and brown on each side, then add the drained onions and carrots and fry for a further five minutes.

5 Add the wine marinade to the pot and the bouquet garni, bring to the boil and skim off any foam that rises on the surface.

6 Add salt and pepper. Put the lid on the pot and leave to simmer on low heat for three hours. If the liquid reduces too much, top up with a little water.

7 Peel and trim the ends of the small onions. In another saucepan, melt the butter and add the onions and sugar, cover with water. Leave to simmer until all the water has evaporated, leaving you with caramelised onions.

8 Once the meat is cooked, drain the casserole in a sieve. Keep the wine mixture aside in one container and the meat in another. Place the drained fried onions and carrots in a food processor, and blend until a smooth purée. This will serve to thicken the final dish.

9 Put the wine back into the pot and reduce further, adding salt and pepper, and the chocolate until it melts.

10 Blanch the lardons in boiling water, then add to the casserole pot. Add enough carrot and onion mixture to the casserole to make it a thick gravy consistency.

11 Arrange the meat on a plate and pour over the sauce. Arrange the caramelised onions on top and serve with mashed potatoes and steamed carrots.

POULET FROID À LA MOUTARDE DE DIJON

Cold chicken with Dijon mustard

In the heart of the world-famous vineyards of the Côte d'Or, chef Lionel Freitas uses Dijon's famous mustard in a fresh and enticing chicken dish designed to match Burgundy's elegant white wines at the Olivier Leflaive winery restaurant in Puligny-Montrachet.

Mention the regional capital of Burgundy and one product springs to mind: Dijon mustard. The condiment is an essential for the region's cooks and the world beyond – its strong and pungent flavour playing a starring role in many sauces, marinades and dressings. Its history dates back to the 14th century, but its popularity rose in the 18th century, when Beaune-born artist Jean Naigeon replaced the vinegar in the mustard's recipe with verjuice, the sour juice of unripe white grapes. These days, the verjuice is replaced by white wine vinegar, in what is a simple recipe consisting only of the mustard grains, salt and the vinegar. Chef Lionel Freitas often uses the condiment in his dishes, due to this simplicity.

'Mustards from elsewhere can often have a lot of spices in them; ginger, olive oil, things that don't so much mask the flavour, but give a different taste,' he says. 'With Dijon mustard, it's just the grains on their own, it's a raw and original product, without any taste of the spices.' Despite this, it pays to be cautious when using it because it can overpower other ingredients. 'Often it can mask the flavour; it can be too strong for cod, for example. You have to be careful.'

Lionel's sense of flavour comes to the fore in the restaurant where he works, which belongs to the Olivier Leflaive winery in the village of Puligny-Montrachet. It produces some of Burgundy's most acclaimed white wines. 'I work with the sommelier to get a good balance,' he says. Served chilled, the wines are the perfect match for this summery chicken dish, which, along with the mustard emulsion, draws on the fresh flavours of lemon, apple and celeriac to create a refreshing alternative to the rich red wine sauces found elsewhere in Burgundy.

Chef //
Lionel Freitas
Location //
Olivier Leflaive,
Puligny-Montrachet

POULET FROID À LA MOUTARDE DE DIJON

Cold chicken with Dijon mustard

Serves 4

Preparation and cooking time:
2hr 30min (not including overnight
marinating)

For the chicken marinade
100g (3½oz) preserved lemons
150ml (5¼fl oz) white balsamic vinegar
300ml (10½fl oz) olive oil
2 chicken breasts weighing 200g (7oz) each

For the mustard emulsion
250g (8¾oz) single cream
150g (5¼oz) Dijon mustard
200g (7oz) egg whites

For the celeriac remoulade
1 Granny Smith apple (or Braeburn, if
*   unavailable), chopped*
250g (8¾oz) celeriac, grated
20g (¾oz) mayonnaise
10g (⅓oz) Dijon mustard
salt, to taste
freshly cracked pepper, to taste

1 For the chicken marinade, blend the preserved lemons in a food processor until smooth. Add the vinegar and olive oil.

2 Cut the chicken breasts in half and put in a freezer bag. Pour over the marinade, making sure the chicken pieces are well covered. Leave in the fridge overnight.

3 Remove the chicken from the fridge and scrape off the excess marinade. Place the chicken pieces in a preheated steamer and steam until cooked through (approx 10 minutes). Leave to cool.

4 To make the mustard emulsion, mix the cream, the mustard and the egg whites in a bowl. Spoon the mixture into a whipping siphon, with two cartridges of gas. Alternatively, whisk with a hand whisk until the egg whites become thick and frothy.

5 To make the celeriac remoulade, chop the apple into tiny cubes and mix with the celeriac in a bowl.

6 In a separate bowl, combine the mayonnaise and mustard, then fold it into the celeriac and apple mixture, along with salt and black pepper.

7 To arrange an individual portion, cut each chicken breast half into three pieces, and add a spoonful of celeriac remoulade on the side of the chicken, a smear of mustard emulsion, with salt and pepper, to taste.

Tip
To give the dish some extra crunch, you can
make a savoury mustard crumble by combining
wholegrain mustard (25g/¾oz), plain flour
(30g/1oz), sugar (6g/¼oz) and softened butter
(60g/2oz), and bake in a moderate oven until
golden. Spoon over the chicken, to serve.

COQ AU VIN
Chicken in red wine

The traditional coq au vin stew is one of world's best-loved French recipes and, for purists, the chicken at its heart should be the Poule de Bresse, which is bred just a few miles away from the charming chambres d'hôtes run by the passionate cook Marie-Eugénie Dupuy.

'You want a good cock!' declares Marie-Eugénie Dupuy. 'It's a big animal, not a ridiculous little chicken,' she laughs as she sits in the bucolic garden of her enchanting B&B in the heart of Bresse. This area of eastern France, which straddles three different departments, is fiercely proud of its poultry farming heritage. Each winter, just before Christmas, the world descends for an amazing poultry fayre called the Glorieuses de Bresse. Farmers primp and preen their prized produce for everyone – from Michelin-starred chefs to weekend visitors from Belgium and Switzerland – to buy their birds for their Christmas or New Year celebrations. 'The chickens are coiffed like stars,' says Marie-Eugénie. 'There are gold medals, and well-known chefs and specialists all come down for it.'

The Poule de Bresse is the only breed of chicken to be given *appellation d'origine protégée* (AOP), the prestigious status given to only the most carefully produced regional foods. This chicken with blue feet, pure white feathers and bright red comb (which is said to represent the colours of France) is fed on only corn and milk, and it is allowed to roam freely before being fattened up in cages at the end.

When it comes to making coq au vin, one of Burgundy's most famous stews, the male of the species plays the starring role. 'It's a recipe that dates from the Middle Ages. In Burgundy, we've always had chicken and wine. You'll find it in all Burgundy cookery books,' says Marie-Eugénie. Her own recipe, however, brings together tips she has gathered in her years cooking for her large family and friends, and makes the most of the local specialities. 'The original recipe says to use Chambertin wine, but Côte de Nuits will be just as good, and I add some chocolate – it works really well. And then, it's "*bon appétit!*"'

Chef //
Marie-Eugénie Dupuy
Location //
La Ferme de Marie-Eugénie,
Bruailles

COQ AU VIN
Chicken in red wine

Serves 8

Preparation and cooking time: 1hr 30min (not including 12hr marinating)

2 bottles of Chambertin (or Côte de
    Nuits) red wine
2 onions, chopped in large pieces
1 carrot, chopped in large pieces
5 peppercorns
3 sprigs of thyme
1 bay leaf
sprig of parsley
a large cock/chicken, cut into pieces
200g (7oz) mushrooms
1 tbsp butter
squeeze of lemon juice
200g (7oz) lean bacon, cut into large pieces
80g (2¾oz) plain flour
2 squares of dark chocolate
25–30 pearl onions, peeled
1 tbsp crème fraiche (optional)
steamed potatoes (or bread), to serve

1 In a mixing bowl, add the red wine, onion, carrots, peppercorns, thyme, bay leaf and parsley. Then add the chicken pieces. Leave in the fridge for at least 12 hours.

2 Remove the marinade from the fridge, scoop out the chicken pieces and set aside, reserving the marinade mixture.

3 Cut the mushrooms and fry them in butter in a pan with a squeeze of lemon. Set aside.

4 In a large casserole pot, fry the bacon pieces and cook through. Add the chicken pieces and colour on all sides. Sprinkle on the flour and stir until all the chicken pieces and bacon are covered.

5 Pour the marinade into the casserole pot, add the chocolate squares and bring to the boil. Reduce the heat and leave to simmer, covered, for an hour or until you can easily pierce the thickest piece of meat with a sharp knife.

6 Add the whole onions and the mushrooms, and leave to simmer further until the onions are cooked and the sauce has reduced a little further.

7 Just before serving, add a spoonful of the same wine, or add a spoonful of crème fraiche if desired. Serve with steamed potatoes or bread to soak up the sauce.

'With a cock, if it's been running around, it has big thighs and is muscly, so you need three hours. With a chicken, it only takes three-quarters [of an hour] or an hour, but it's better to cook it too much than not enough.'

Marie-Eugénie Dupuy

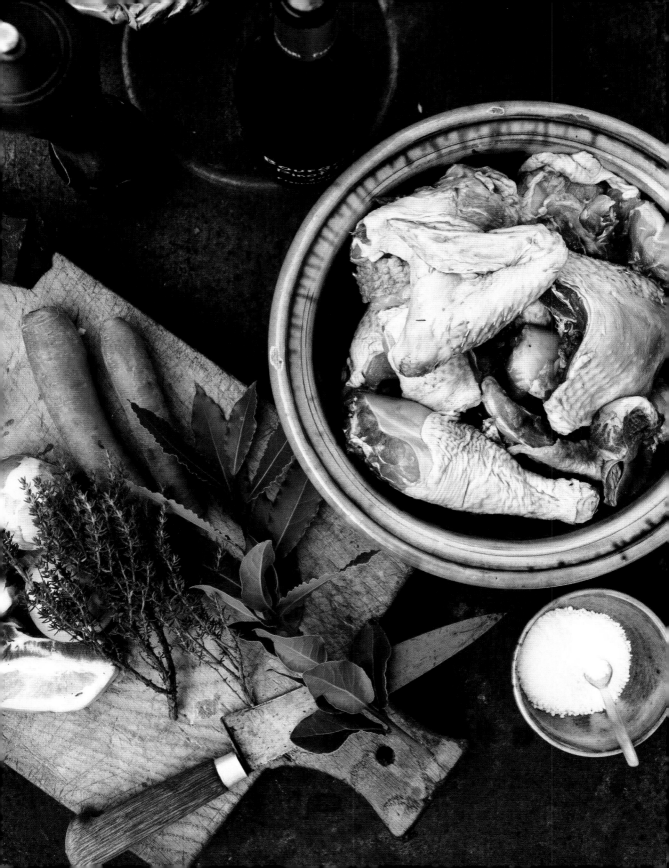

NOUGAT
DE TOURS
Sweet tart with dried fruit filling

*For more than
a century, the
family-run Maison
Bigot in the heart
of Amboise has
been baking the
nougat de tours, an
indulgent tart with
a macaron topping
and dried fruit (an
ingredient made
popular during
the Renaissance)
hidden inside,
with rum-infused
raisins.*

In the shadow of the Château Royal d'Amboise, where Leonardo da Vinci is said to be buried, the Maison Bigot patisserie and *salon de thé* (tearoom) has been delighting visitors to the Loire Valley for three generations. Among the confections on display under the shiny glass counters is the nougat de tours, a cake that is said to date from the Renaissance. This period of the 15th and 16th century, when Kings Charles VIII and François I ruled, resulted in craftworkers and artists coming from Italy to build and elaborate the glorious châteaux found throughout the region. They also brought a new kind of delicacy, dried fruit, which became the central ingredient in the nougat de tours, hidden between a delicate sweet pastry and a macaron-like topping.

'We use real *fruits confits* [dried fruit],' says Christiane Mason, whose grandfather first opened the Amboise bakery in 1913. 'Some people say they don't like them, but poor quality dried fruit can just be dyed beetroot with no taste.' Christiane's head baker, Flavien, uses a blend of fruits, most importantly big, juicy cherries, while the raisins get a dose of rum before use. Rather than nougat de tours, Christiane has nicknamed her version nougat de touraine after the traditional name of the local area. 'I'm a rebel!' she laughs.

For Christiane, the nougat has been one of myriad cakes created in the bakery since she was a child and she holds strong memories of watching her grandfather bake bread. The premises have expanded over the years and the ovens are now upstairs, while the old bakery is now the *salon du thé*. Christiane points to where the old oven used to be and reminisces about her childhood. 'My grandfather used to give me choux buns when my grandmother wasn't around, as she didn't want me eating them. As soon as she arrived, I'd have to gobble them all up, and sometimes I'd even have to swallow them whole!'

Chef //
Flavien Ferrand &
Christiane Mason
Location //
Maison Bigot, Amboise

NOUGAT DE TOURS
Sweet tart with dried fruit filling

Serves 10–12
Preparation and cooking time: 2hr
(not including overnight refrigeration)

For the sweet pastry
250g (8¾oz) flour
95g (3⅓oz) icing sugar
30g (1oz) ground almonds
pinch of salt
165g (6oz) unsalted butter, cubed, plus
   extra for greasing pie mould
1 egg
170g (6oz) apricot jam

For the dried fruit filling
60g (2oz) raisins
50–60ml (1¾–2fl oz) rum to cover the
   raisins
75g (2¾oz) dried cherries
130g (4½oz) other dried fruit, cubed

For the macaron topping
200g (7oz) ground almonds
200g (7oz) icing sugar, plus extra to
   decorate
1 x 8g (⅓oz) sachet of vanilla sugar
1 tbsp flour
4 egg whites

custard, to serve (optional)
ice cream, to serve (optional)

Tip
Vanilla sugar is a popular ingredient in France, but if you can't buy it, it's easy to make: simply put empty vanilla pods in an airtight jar with sugar and leave for a few days for the sugar to be infused with the vanilla.

---

1 To make the sweet pastry, place all dry ingredients in a food processor and combine. Add the butter and the eggs. Blend until you have a soft ball. Place in the fridge overnight.

2 For the dried fruit filling, cover the raisins in the rum, and leave overnight at room temperature.

3 Remove the pastry from the fridge and roll it on a lightly floured surface then press into a pie baking mould, lightly greased with butter. Paint the apricot jam across the bottom of the base. Place in the fridge for 30 minutes.

4 Preheat the oven to 190°C (375°F).

5 Drain the raisins from the rum (if it hasn't all been soaked up) and mix with the other dried fruit.

6 For the macaron topping, in a bowl blend the ground almonds, icing sugar, vanilla sugar and flour. In a separate, clean bowl, whisk the egg whites until they stand in peaks, then fold the egg whites gently into the dry ingredients.

7 Remove the pastry case from the fridge and sprinkle the dried fruit mixture (from step 5) evenly across the apricot jam base (press it down gently so it sticks into the jam), then cover with the macaron topping and smooth evenly, being careful not to lift any of the dried fruit into the topping.

8 Sieve a little extra icing sugar across the top, and bake in the oven for 30 minutes.

9 Serve alone, or with custard or ice cream.

TARTE TATIN
Upside-down apple tart

It's said that this world famous apple tart, which is cooked upside-down, was created by accident in the Sologne area of central France in the 1880s; but today, protecting its quality has become the passion of the 'Brotherhood of the Tarte Tatin'.

I n the sunny garden of 'Grand Master' Jean-Paul Cousin-Martin, a meeting of the *confrérie* of the tarte tatin is in full swing. The eight members present have all declared their allegiance to the 'true' recipe of the tarte tatin. It's just one of France's hundreds of *confréries* (brotherhoods) and its role is to uphold the reputation of the dish and promote it.

The *confrérie* tour around festivals and events wearing traditional blue robes and hats, and offer the public the chance to taste what they consider to be the real tarte tatin. Such devotion to purity is ironic, given the original tart is said to have been made by accident: the most popular story goes that Stephanie Tatin, one of two sisters running the Hôtel Tatin in the town of Lamotte-Beuvron, was overworked one day and forgot to make the base of the tart, so instead she baked it with the pastry over the top, turning it the right way up to serve. 'Like many recipes, it was done by mistake,' says Jean-Paul. 'But that error has given us one of the best loved desserts in France.'

The Hôtel Tatin still serves the dish, but keeps its recipe a closely guarded secret. Meanwhile, the *confrérie* is proud to share its own method, in which the caramelisation of the apples comes from slowly evaporating the juice. After half an hour in the oven the apples are transferred across to the hob, where a watchful eye is crucial to its success. 'The last five or 10 minutes of the evaporation are the most important in the whole process,' says Jean-Paul. 'You wait until the very last bubbles disappear through evaporation and then take it off the heat. Too late, and it will burn.' And the effect? 'If you have made the caramel separately in advance, the apples will be white inside. If you do it this way, they will be caramelised and golden all the way through.'

Chef //
Jean-Paul Cousin-Martin
Location //
Les Lichonneux de Tarte
Tatin, Lamotte-Beuvron

TARTE TATIN
Upside-down apple tart

Serves 8–10

Preparation and cooking time: 2hr

80g (3oz) butter, melted
120g (4¼oz) caster sugar
1⅔kg (3½lb) apples (Royal Gala, Jonagold,
  Golden Delicious), average size
scattering of flour, for rolling pastry
500g (1lb) shortcrust pastry
vanilla ice cream, to serve

1 Preheat the oven to 200°C (400°F).

2 Pour the melted butter into a 24cm (9½in) diameter baking pan (which can also be used on a gas hob/hot plate), then scatter the sugar on top, to cover evenly.

3 Peel and quarter the apples. In a circle, place a layer of quarters around the edge of the baking tin, with the outside of the apples face-down. Add a second layer of apple quarters within this first circle, but have the outside of the apples facing up. Use smaller apple pieces to fill the remaining central space.

4 Place the baking tin in the hot oven for 30 minutes.

5 Keeping the oven switched on, remove the baking tin and then cook on the hob/hot plate on a medium heat for a further 25–30 minutes, until the water and apple juice has evaporated. You will know this once you can no longer hear liquid bubbling: the apples should be caramelised. Remove from the heat and set aside.

6 With a lightly floured rolling pin, roll out the shortcrust pastry on a floured surface to a thickness of around 5mm to 8mm (¼in to ⅓in).

7 Place the pastry across the top of the baking tin and trim any excess with a knife. Pierce the pastry lid several times with a fork.

8 Bake in the oven for 25 minutes, then remove and let cool in the tin.

9 Once the tart is cool, warm the base of the tin gently over a low heat for a few minutes. The heat should loosen the tart a little, so then place a plate over the top of the tin and in one swift movement turn the tin upside down (being careful not to burn yourself on any caramel that leaks out).

10 Leave the tart to cool and then cut into slices. Warm in the oven for 10 minutes at 160°C–180°C (320°F–360°F) before serving with vanilla ice cream.

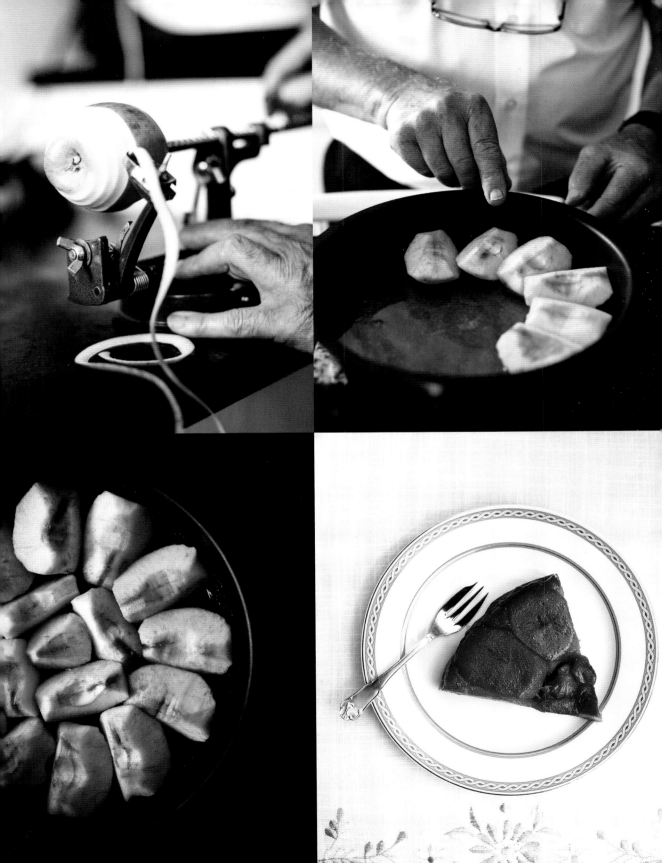

CRÉMETS D'ANJOU

Anjou cream cheese dessert

This versatile dessert may have been created by accident in the 19th century, but it remains a classic in bistros and restaurants in Angers and the Anjou area of the Western Loire region. Chef David Gasnier gives his version a tipsy twist at this restaurant in the Loire countryside.

Like many classic French recipes, the legend behind the crémets d'Anjou tells of a quick-thinking cook making the best of a difficult situation. The story goes that Marie Renéaume, a young cook working in a large house in 1890, hadn't prepared a dessert for the evening meal. Having only eggs, cream, fromage blanc and her own ingenuity at her disposal, Marie created the light and creamy dessert that delighted her employers. A decade later, having married and opened a small grocery shop in Angers with her husband, she started to create the crémets d'Anjou on a larger scale. From then on, the dessert became a favourite in most cafés and restaurants, while the early 20th-century critic known as Curnonsky (dubbed the 'Prince of Gastronomes') declared the crémet d'Anjou his favourite dessert, saying that it was like eating a cloud.

It is still a much loved dessert, according to chef David Gasnier, who has had it on the menu of the many Angers restaurants he's worked in. While the basic version has changed little over the years, its versatility gives cooks the chance to add their own touch of flair. For David, this means including another classic ingredient from Angers, the orange liqueur Cointreau. 'The real crémets d'Anjou is the same mixture, but without the Cointreau. I add it in because it's another taste of the region. But if you leave it out, you can complement it with whatever you like: fresh fruit, citrus fruit, a fruit coulis.'

David serves it in a glass dish, but traditionally the mould used to make the dessert was a small, white, heart-shaped porcelain dish with small holes to allow the excess water to drain out. Yet, however you make it and whatever you serve it with, the same is true. 'It's easy to do, and makes for a really fresh and light dessert at the end of the meal,' says David.

Chef //
David Gasnier
Location //
Anjou Golf & Country Club

CRÉMETS D'ANJOU
Anjou cream cheese dessert

Serves 5

**Preparation and cooking time: 45min
(not including 3hr refrigeration)**

300ml (10½fl oz) single cream
1 tsp icing sugar
200g (7oz) fromage blanc (see Tip)
1 tbsp clear honey
50ml (1¾fl oz) Cointreau
6 egg whites
pinch of salt
1 lime, zested
fresh fruit, to serve

1 Whip the cream with 1 tsp of icing sugar until soft peaks form, then put in the fridge for 30 minutes..

2 Mix the fromage blanc in a bowl with the honey and Cointreau. Set aside.

3 In a clean bowl, whip the egg whites with a pinch of salt and the zest of the lime until they stand in peaks.

4 Remove the cream from the fridge and fold it together with the fromage blanc mixture, then fold in the egg whites gently.

5 Pour the mixture into a mould or glass dish and refrigerate for at least three hours.

6 Serve with your choice of fresh fruit.

Tip
Fromage blanc is a much loved ingredient for French cooks, but not so easily found outside France. Try substituting it with crème fraiche, thick Greek yoghurt, quark or cream cheese. Italian cheeses ricotta and mascarpone could also be used.

SOUFFLÉ COINTREAU
Cointreau-flavoured soufflé

The classic soufflé has a reputation for being a rather difficult dessert to master, but at the Moulin Cavier, a restaurant based in a former windmill near Angers, chef Franck Houdebine reveals that the secret is in the simplicity of its ingredients.

It would be hard to imagine a more fitting signature dish at a restaurant set in an 18th-century windmill than a soufflé: a concoction where the most important ingredient is air. While many home cooks may blanch at the idea of creating the perfect soufflé, chef Franck Houdebine is always confident of success: 'People are scared that it will go flat, or about taking it out of the oven too soon,' he says, before revealing the secret to his light-as-a-feather dessert. 'Classic soufflé recipes often have starch in them, such as flour, to hold it together, and the hot, sweet soufflé often has a *crème patissière* (thick, creamy custard) base to it. But here, there's only egg whites, egg yolks and sugar, which makes it much lighter and that gives it some air.'

Once it's out of the oven, the dessert is served swiftly to diners, who pierce the golden crown with their spoons as if to burst a bubble. In so doing, the opening lets out a woozy, orangey aroma from the liqueur Cointreau – the ingredient that gives this soufflé a local flavour. The liqueur was created in 1849 and is distilled to this day in Angers at a state-of-the art distillery, which also tells its colourful history. The windmill, meanwhile, pre-dates the town's love of its orange liqueur, having been built in 1730 in an era when the flat, wide landscape north of the River Loire had hundreds of windmills operating across it. The mill's surviving machinery stands as testament to its history, and diners can admire the millstones, cogs and wheels above the bar as they sip their aperitifs, Cointreau-based of course. The restaurant's soufflé has also developed something of its own history. 'We've been serving Cointreau soufflé here since the restaurant opened, more than 20 years ago,' says Franck, 'People come here especially to eat it.'

Chef //
Franck Houdebine
Location //
Domaine du Moulin Cavier,
Avrillé

SOUFFLÉ COINTREAU

Cointreau-flavoured soufflé

Serves 2

Preparation and cooking time: 35min

4 tbsp granulated sugar, plus extra for
*   sprinkling*
3 egg yolks
4 tbsp Cointreau
30g (1oz) butter, melted
4 egg whites
icing sugar, to serve

1 Preheat the oven to 200°C (400°F).

2 Whisk together 2 tbsp of the sugar and the egg yolks in a bowl, then add the Cointreau and whisk together. Set aside.

3 Melt the butter and, using a pastry brush, grease the insides of two large ramekin dishes.

4 Dust the ramekins with a further sprinkling of sugar, so it sticks to the butter.

5 In a clean bowl, whisk the egg whites and, just before they start to form peaks, whisk in the remaining 2 tbsp of sugar. Continue whisking until the mixture stands in peaks.

6 Fold the egg whites to the yolk and sugar mixture from step 2. Pour into the ramekins.

7 Bake in the oven for 17–20 minutes until the top is golden and has risen nicely (don't open the oven door to check prior to this or else your soufflé may deflate). Sieve icing sugar over the top to serve.

GÂTEAU NANTAIS
Nantes cake

This simple cake brings together ingredients from the other side of the Atlantic, and it is thanks to the prowess of Nantes' bakers past and present that it has become the much-loved treat it is today. At the popular La Petite Boulangerie, Franck Dépériers wants the whole world to discover its delightful flavour.

Chef //
Franck Dépériers
Location //
La Petite Boulangerie, Nantes

Ask baker Franck Dépériers about the gâteau nantais and his eyes light up. 'It's magic,' he says. 'It's simple to make, it has very few ingredients. Everyone all over the world loves the gâteau nantais!' His claim isn't without proof: Franck has taught bakers in Japan, the US and across Europe the secrets to making good French bread, and every time he made the gâteau nantais it went down well. 'It was a bit like a calling card,' he says of the light and tasty cake topped with a heady, alcoholic glaze.

The cake has something of a global background itself, with its key ingredients – rum and sugar - being gathered from across the Atlantic. 'It's part of the dark history of the town,' explains Franck. 'Nantes was a port of slavery, and as the ships transported the slaves, they also brought back spices and rum from the Antilles.' But it was a local patisserie that created the gâteau nantais.

'It's a large, industrialised company now, but when Lefèvre-Utile (LU) started out, it was just a family of bakers in the centre of town making biscuits, such as the *petit-beurre* [a Nantes buttery biscuit],' explains Franck. 'They took those ingredients and made the gâteau nantais. So the cake is really linked to the town's industries.'

As a native of Normandy, rather than Nantes, Franck had never heard of the cake when he first opened his boulangerie in a suburb of Nantes – it was his customers who told him about it. He tracked down a recipe and adapted it slightly, and it is now a firm favourite with his clientele. He sells 100 of the gâteaux every week, and there are queues out of the door on a daily basis. 'I wanted to make a cake that told a story of the country, that was very simple. The gâteau nantais was considered very expensive, but we've popularised it. I wanted everyone to have a bit of luxury.'

GÂTEAU NANTAIS
Nantes cake

Serves 8–10

Preparation and cooking time: 1hr

For the gâteau

190g (6¾oz) butter
225g (8oz) caster sugar
150g (5¼oz) ground almonds
60g (2oz) plain flour
7g (¼oz) baking powder
225g (8oz)/4 medium eggs, whisked
45ml (1½fl oz) rum
butter, for greasing
sprinkle of flour, for cake tin

For the icing

200g (7oz) icing sugar
40ml (1½fl oz) dark rum
20ml (¾fl oz) sugar syrup

1 Preheat the oven to 190°C (375°F).

2 Mix the butter and sugar together in a bowl. Add the ground almonds, the 60g of flour and the baking powder and combine.

3 Add the whisked eggs bit by bit, and mix together, then mix in the 45ml of rum.

4 Butter and flour a round cake mould measuring 28cm (11in) diameter.

5 Pour the gâteau mixture into the mould then bake for 30 minutes or until a skewer pressed into the gateau comes out clean. Turn the gâteau out of the tin and leave to cool on a wire rack.

6 Combine the icing sugar in a bowl with the dark rum and sugar syrup, and then pour over the cooled cake and spread evenly with a spatula. Slice the gâteau into pieces and serve.

LES POIRES
AU VIN ROUGE
Pears in red wine

*Based on the
traditional recipe
of pears stewed
in Beaujolais
red wine, chef
Stéphanie Moreau
creates a dessert
that brings
together three
of Burgundy's
favourite fruits: the
pear, the grape and
the blackcurrant.*

From hearty stews to savoury cakes, wine seems to find its way into most recipes that originate in Burgundy, and that doesn't stop at the dessert trolley. The traditional recipe, *poires à la bonne femme*, was designed to use up the pears that had not properly ripened and consisted of the fruit being boiled in sugar to disguise its grainy texture before wine was added for colour rather than flavour. During this process, the skin would go wrinkly, supposedly like an 'old wife', or *'bonne femme'*, which is how it got its name.

In this aromatic dessert, created by chef Stéphanie Moreau, the pears get a further boost in flavour by being marinated in wine for two days, along with citrus fruit, and cinnamon, which lend it a festive feel. As chef at the bucolic Moulin des Ruats, hidden in woods in the wildly beautiful Parc Naturel Régional du Morvan near Avallon, Stéphanie's favoured method sees the wine infuse the pears gently, rather than boil them in it. 'It improves the taste of the wine,' she explains.

Working at the cosy former watermill, Stéphanie has developed the dish into a sophisticated dessert that leaves its rustic roots firmly in the past. She serves it with a chocolate sorbet or ice cream, a red wine jelly and a tuile wafer that is made with one of Burgundy's other key ingredients: blackcurrants. 'The tuile gives the dish an extra crunch, which works with the softness of the pears,' says Stéphanie. This extra touch is a nod to the blackcurrants that were traditionally grown alongside the grapes by the wives of Burgundy winegrowers. While the main harvest was, of course, the wine, the blackcurrants were used to create the local liqueur named crème de cassis, which – like the wine – also finds its way into many a dessert.

Chef //
Stephanie Moreau
Location //
Moulin des Ruats, Avallon

LES POIRES AU VIN ROUGE
Pears in red wine

Serves 10

Preparation and cooking time: 1hr 30min
(not including 48hr to marinate pears)

For the pears & red wine jelly

10 pears
1L (1¾pt) Pinot Noir red wine
1L (1¾pt) water
zest & juice of 1 orange
zest & juice of 1 lemon
1 cinnamon stick
6g (¼oz) agar-agar powder

For the tuile

410g (14½oz) blackcurrant purée
35g (1¼oz) flour
220g (7¾oz) icing sugar
20g (¾oz) butter

chocolate sorbet, to serve
mint leaves, to garnish

Tip

When cutting the pears, if you want to make it very neat, use three different sized smooth-sided pastry cutters to cut out the largest three pieces. Roll up the excess from the largest piece into a rose-like shape to decorate the plate.

'You can use blackcurrant sorbet instead of chocolate to carry through the blackcurrant theme.'

Stéphanie Moreau

1 Peel the pears (leaving the stalk in place) and place in an airtight container with the red wine, the water, orange juice and its zest, lemon juice and its zest, and cinnamon stick, and leave in the fridge for 48 hours.

2 Prepare the tuile by combining the blackcurrant purée, flour, icing sugar and butter in a food processor.

3 Place teaspoons of the tuile onto a sheet of greaseproof paper and spread the mixture out in circles of approx 5cm (2in) in diameter with your finger. Place in the fridge overnight.

4 Take the pears from the fridge and remove them from the red wine, reserving the liquid. Cut the pears in quarters horizontally and core each piece with an apple corer (this indentation will be filled with chocolate sorbet later).

5 To make the jelly, put 200ml (7fl oz) of the reserved wine mixture in a pan with the agar-agar and bring to the boil until it starts to thicken.

6 Line a large baking sheet with clingfilm/plastic wrap and pour the warm jelly mixture onto it. Spread out to a thickness of about 3mm–5mm (up to ¼in). Place in the fridge for about 30 minutes.

7 Remove the tray of tuiles (from step 3) from the fridge and bake in a preheated oven for 10 minutes at 150°C (300°F). They should appear slightly transparent. While still warm, cut each tuile in a neat circle with a pastry cutter. Leave to cool.

8 When ready to serve, fill the centre of each piece of pear with the chocolate sorbet, and arrange the pears on the plate with slices of the jelly and the tuile, and small mint leaves to garnish.

DESSERT DE MIEL
Honey dessert

The flavour of this sweet and delicate dessert owes everything to the character of the honey at its heart. Chef Guillaume Royer takes his straight from the hives in the grounds of the 12th-century abbey that's home to his restaurant in the middle of Burgundy.

There's a special kind of tranquillity that pervades the atmosphere at the Abbaye de la Bussière. It is easy to see why it appealed as a venue for a hotel and restaurant once the abbey fell out of use. But for all the calmness in the elegant grounds, salons and bedrooms, it's a hub of activity in the Michelin-starred restaurant where chef Guillaume Royer and his team work their magic.

Born in a neighbouring village, Guillaume is passionate about the delicious regional produce, and one of his most prized ingredients is the honey from the beehives in the abbey's grounds; so much so, it inspires his signature dessert. 'The former chef had the beehives installed and used to use the honey for breakfast,' he recounts. 'One day, the beekeeper came to collect the honey and there was tons of it. It got me thinking, how can I use it in a dessert?'

The result is a sweet and indulgent honey cream – served with ice cream, a tiny madeleine and a *langue de chat* biscuit. But it's Guillaume's extra touches that make it even more special: lemon and orange zest, a sprinkle of delicate edible flowers and a small glass of *hydromel*, or honey wine, on the side.

The dessert connects the hotel to its long history, because for several centuries in the Middle Ages the abbey's Cistercian monks cultivated honey themselves. 'Everyone made honey back then,' says Guillaume. 'It was a way to sweeten things, as they didn't have sugar.' While the honey is rooted in the abbey's past, it also captures the ephemeral, due to the varied nature of the garden's flowers imbuing the honey's character. 'We do two harvests a year and the taste in every harvest of every year is different,' says Guillaume. 'This year, there's been a lot of rain and fewer flowers, so it's a very gentle taste; more subtle, more feminine.'

Chef //
Guillaume Royer
Location //
Abbaye de la Bussière,
La Bussière-sur-Ouche

DESSERT DE MIEL
Honey dessert

Serves 6

Preparation and cooking time: 1hr
(not including 6hr refrigeration time)

For the crème patissière
2 egg yolks
30g (1oz) caster sugar
15g (½oz) plain flour
1 tsp cornflour
140ml (5fl oz) milk

For the honey cream
90g (3¼oz) cream
100g (3½oz) eggs (two medium), whisked
85g (3oz) honey
45g (1½oz) butter
½ leaf of gelatine
90g (3¼oz) crème patissière
edible flower petals, to garnish
½ tsp orange zest, to garnish
½ tsp lemon zest, to garnish
madeleine and/or langue de chat biscuits,
  to serve

1 To make the crème patissière, whisk the egg yolks and sugar until pale and slightly thickened. Add in the flour and cornflour and whisk.

2 Heat the milk in a saucepan until it just comes to boiling point, and then whisk the milk into the egg mixture. Put the whole lot back into the pan, stirring all the time until thick and boiling. Take the pan off the heat, cover with clingfilm/plastic wrap and leave to cool.

3 To make the honey cream, start by warming the cream and whisked eggs in a pan but don't let them boil.

4 Add the honey, butter and gelatine and 90g of the crème patissière made in step 1. Whisk until thoroughly blended. Spoon into in a piping bag and leave in the fridge for six hours.

5 Take the piping bag from the fridge and pipe the mixture out on to a dish, approx 2cm (¾in) in length. Decorate with edible flower petals, and orange and lemon zest. Serve with madeleines and/or *langue de chat* biscuits.

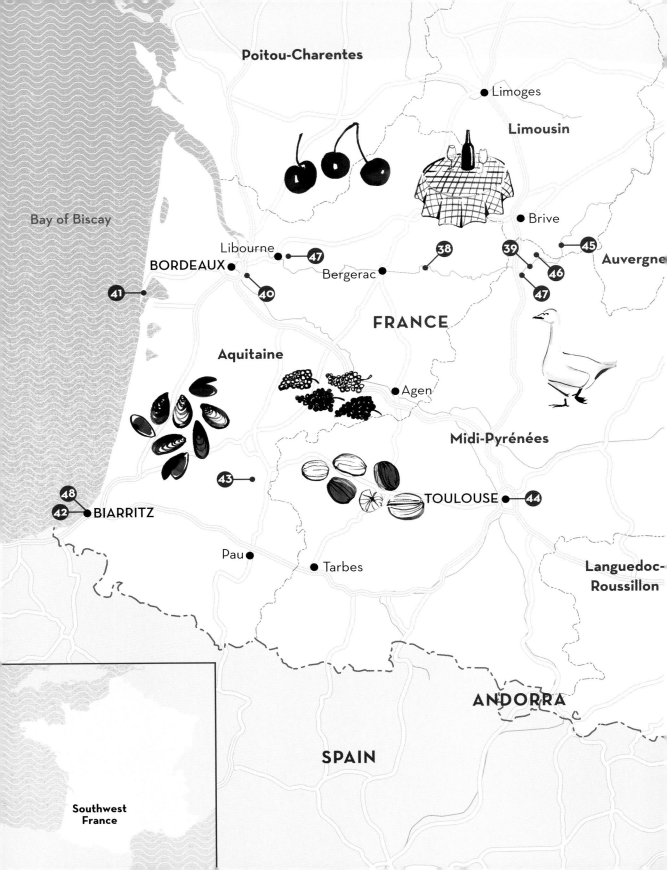

Poitou-Charentes

Limoges

Limousin

Bay of Biscay

Brive

Libourne

47

38

39

45

BORDEAUX

Bergerac

46

Auvergne

41

40

47

FRANCE

Aquitaine

Agen

Midi-Pyrénées

43

TOULOUSE

44

48

42

BIARRITZ

Pau

Languedoc-
Roussillon

Tarbes

ANDORRA

SPAIN

Southwest
France

SOUTHWEST FRANCE

From the walnut groves of the Dordogne valley to the spicy menus of France's Basque country, the southwest offers an enormous variety of produce, including the region's famed poultry, used in classic stews and delicious roasts.

CROUSTILLANT DE CONFITS DE CANARD DU PÉRIGORD

*Filo parcels of duck
& vegetable terrine*

For centuries, in the heart of the ancient province of Périgord, now known as the Dordogne, the locals have been using duck in myriad ways. The classic dish Confit de Canard – duck thighs preserved in duck fat – is at the heart of these filo parcels.

Ask a local in the Périgord region what they'd like to eat and chef Vincent Arnould will tell you that they have only one answer: 'Duck, duck, duck. It's incredible!' he laughs. Having arrived from Provence for what he thought would be a two- or three-year stint, Vincent fell in love with the land of honey-stone villages, where the gentle River Dordogne winds its way through the idyllic landscape. That was nearly 20 years ago and he has been head chef at the charming inn, Le Vieux Logis, ever since. Here, he soon discovered that duck was surprisingly versatile, thanks to the locals' propensity for preserving all they can of it, a habit born of an era when food was scarce.

'The Périgord was one of the first places to use conserving, they looked for the best ways to preserve the whole duck,' says Vincent. 'First they'd use the liver, as foie gras, then the breast, there's no problem cooking that. Then they thought, "What are we going to do with the rest?" With the thighs, they'd do confit, and the advantage of tinning it is that it lasts a long time. With the carcass they'd make soup, with the skin they'd make scratchings. For some old Périgordians, they'd even eat the duck's feet. Then, it's only the beak they'd throw away.'

Vincent's recipe for a terrine wrapped in filo pastry is inspired by this 'waste not, want not' attitude, and is perfect for using up the leftover vegetables from the classic French stew, *pot-au-feu*. Add to this the rich flavour of the foie gras and the tender meat of the confit de canard, and you have a dish that brings together the many flavours offered by the humble duck. For an elegant and modern touch befitting the hotel's charming bistro, it is wrapped up in a perfect filo parcel and served with the classic French accompaniment, *sauce gribiche*.

Chef //
Vincent Arnould
Location //
Le Vieux Logis, Trémolat

CROUSTILLANT DE CONFITS DE CANARD DU PÉRIGORD
Filo parcels of duck & vegetable terrine

Serves 8

Preparation and cooking time: 2hr
(not including overnight refrigeration)

100g (3½oz) foie gras, cut into tiny cubes
500g (17½oz) confit de canard
(duck preserved in fat, in a tin/jar)
100g (3½oz) duck gizzards, preserved in fat
100g (3½oz) carrot
100g (3½oz) celery
100g (3½oz) onions
a few chanterelle mushrooms
2 tbsp parsley, finely chopped
salt, to taste
pepper, to taste

For the sauce gribiche
2 hard-boiled eggs
40g (1½oz) capers
40g (1½oz) cornichons
40g (1½oz) onion
1 tsp flat parsley
1 tsp tarragon
200g (7oz) mayonnaise

8 layers of filo pastry
green salad, to serve

1 Put the cubes of foie gras in the freezer, so they become hard.

2 Remove the duck pieces from the tin/jar of confit de canard, but leave the fat inside and reserve. Take off the duck skin (it's easier if it is slightly warm), and break up the meat with your fingers and then cut it finely.

3 Do the same with the gizzards, cut them into very small pieces.

4 Cut the vegetables into very small cubes.

5 Put a small amount of fat from the jar/tin of confit de canard into a frying pan and heat it gently. Add the vegetables (except the mushrooms) and cook gently.

6 In a separate pan, also toss the mushrooms in some of the duck fat and season them. Cook until they soften slightly, they should release some water; pour this into the other pan of vegetables then add the duck and gizzards.

7 The mixture should be lukewarm, which is important for the ingredients to stick together. Add the 2 tbsp chopped parsley, salt and pepper to taste, then take the foie gras out of the freezer and mix with all the ingredients together until well combined.

8 Tip the mixture into a long, flat tray or mould, like a flat terrine, and put in the fridge overnight.

9 For the *sauce gribiche*, chop the eggs, capers, cornichons, onion, parsley and tarragon, and combine with the mayonnaise. Refrigerate for a few hours.

10 Turn the terrine out and cut it into eight long rectangles. Wrap each one in one layer of filo pastry, and seal the end.

11 Add some duck fat to a frying pan, and fry each filo rectangle on all sides until the pastry goes golden. Serve with the *sauce gribiche*, and a small green side salad.

CARRE D'AGNEAU DU QUERCY ROTI ET SES PETITS FARCIS

Roasted Quercy lamb with stuffed vegetables

In the Quercy regional park, a particular breed of lamb grazes on the dry and rocky landscape and is carefully farmed. The result is excellent quality meat that needs little effort to become the highlight of any dish. Michelin-starred chef Stéphane Andrieux always has it on his menus.

Chef //
Stéphane Andrieux
Location //
Château de la Treyne, Lacave

Even as long ago as 1770, the old province of Quercy in the Lot was known for its good quality lamb. The 'Caussenarde du Lot' breed are known as 'sheep in sunglasses' on account of the black patches on their eyes and ears, and they thrive on the arid, rocky plateaux of the Quercy regional park. It's a landscape that comprises walnut groves, oak trees, sinuous rivers and golden cliffs, as well as many idyllic villages and the ancient pilgrimage sight Rocamadour.

The sheep are known for their wool, milk and, of course, their tender meat. To qualify for the prestigious 'red label' that guarantees good quality, farmers must meet certain criteria in production, including keeping the sheep in excellent conditions, allowing the lambs to be fed by the mothers' milk for 70 days, and feeding them with hay and cereals for up to 150 days. The result is a tender, succulent meat that is a highlight on the menus offered by Michelin-starred chef Stéphane Andrieux at the fairytale Château de la Treyne in Lacave. 'It's always on the menu, to represent the terroir here,' he says. 'The taste of the lamb is good on its own. There's no need to do anything complicated. Just season it, make a good gravy and cook it the right way.'

For a summery dish, Stéphane took inspiration from Provence and marries the lamb with stuffed vegetables known as *petits farcis*, with the courgettes (zucchinis) and mint being an ideal accompaniment. 'I wanted to leave the lamb as untouched as possible, so I looked for something light to go with it for the summer.' Indeed, summer is the best time to enjoy it: the restaurant's walled terrace sits on a clifftop overlooking the River Dordogne. Here, guests can look out over the forests and golden cliffs and tuck into the deliciously delicate lamb and vegetables while the river glides gently by.

CARRE D'AGNEAU DU QUERCY ROTI ET SES PETITS FARCIS

Roasted Quercy lamb with stuffed vegetables

Serves 4

Preparation and cooking time: 2hr
(not including overnight soaking of bread)

For the stuffed tomatoes & potatoes
500ml (17½oz) milk
100g (3½oz) bread
4 eggs
1 clove garlic, chopped
200g (7oz) sausage-meat or minced lamb
60g (2oz) tomato passata
10g (⅓oz) pesto
10g (⅓oz) tomato purée with basil
20g (¾oz) grated parmesan
4 small potatoes
water, to boil potatoes
4 tomatoes (approx 3½cm/1⅓in diameter)

For the gravy
1 carrot, chopped
1 onion, chopped
1 stick of celery, chopped
1 tbsp olive oil
40g (1½oz) flour
20g (¾oz) tomato concentrate
water, to cover vegetables

1 To make the tomato and potato stuffing, first soak the bread in the milk and leave in the refrigerator overnight. Then drain the bread and set aside.

2 Preheat the oven to 180°C (350°F).

3 To make the gravy, fry the chopped carrot, onions and celery in an ovenproof pan with 1 tbsp olive oil until soft. Sprinkle over the flour and place in the oven, uncovered, for five minutes.

4 Remove the vegetables from the oven, add the tomato concentrate and cover with water.

5 Simmer for 30 minutes on the hob/hotplate, uncovered, then pass through a sieve and set aside. If the gravy is too watery, simmer it further to reduce and intensify the flavour.

6 To make the stuffing for the tomatoes and potatoes, whisk one egg in a bowl, and add the chopped garlic. Separately whisk the other three eggs and soak the bread (from step 1) in them for 20 minutes.

7 Place the egg-soaked bread in a food processor along with the sausage meat, tomato passata, pesto, tomato purée and parmesan, and blend until smooth. Spoon into a piping bag.

For the stuffed courgette (zucchini) flowers
4 courgettes (zucchini) chopped into tiny
  dice (brunoise)
4 shallots, finely chopped
1 tbsp olive oil
100g (3½oz) cream
100g (3½ oz) bread
2 garlic cloves, chopped
3 eggs
1 tsp peppermint leaf
1 tsp parsley
1 tsp basil
½ tsp tarragon
1 tsp chives
salt, to taste
pepper, to taste
4 courgette (zucchini) flowers

2 racks of Quercy lamb
40g (1½oz) butter
40g (1½oz) olive oil

8 Peel the potatoes, cut the top and bottom off to make flat ends, and carve out a small well in the middle of each. Place in cold, salted water, and bring to the boil. Once tender, leave to cool and fill with the stuffing, and set aside.

9 Cut the top off each of the tomatoes – keep it aside – and scoop out the flesh inside, also fill with the stuffing, then replace the top.

10 To make the stuffed courgette flowers, chop the courgettes and shallots into tiny dice. Fry them in a pan with 1 tbsp olive oil, until the water has evaporated. Add the cream and reduce further. Leave to cool.

11 Soak the bread in a bowl with the three whisked eggs and two cloves of chopped garlic for 20 minutes, then add to a food processor, along with the peppermint leaf, parsley, basil, tarragon, chives, salt and pepper. Blend until smooth. Spoon into a piping bag and pipe into the centre of each of the four courgette flowers until they are full.

12 Wrap the courgette flowers, tomatoes and potatoes individually in clingfilm/plastic wrap to seal, and then place on the top level of a steamer. Steam over boiling water for 10 minutes (or you can bake the potatoes in the oven for 20 minutes).

13 To cook the racks of lamb in a hot oven (230°C/450°F), first add the olive oil to a pan, heat it, then add butter. When the butter is melted and foamy, add the lamb and roast for 10–15 minutes, basting frequently.

14 Serve the racks of lamb on a plate together with the stuffed potatoes, stuffed tomatoes and stuffed courgette flowers, and pour the gravy over the meat.

ROUGET À LA BORDELAISE

Red mullet with Bordeaux sauce

Bordelaise sauce has long been a favourite accompaniment for red meat, poultry and fish, and the simplicity of its ingredients means it is perfect for enhancing a dish whichever way you choose. Just outside Bordeaux, Le Saint-James restaurant's Michelin-starred chef Nicolas Magie blends tradition with innovation.

It should come as no surprise that the central ingredient in Bordeaux's eponymous sauce consists of red wine. Combined with just a few other ingredients – shallots, onions and beef bone marrow – the sauce isn't complicated, but this doesn't mean that chef Nicolas Magie eschews it in favour of more sophisticated dishes. Traditionally served with the local Bavardaise beef, the sauce grew out of another method of using up the scraps from the winemaking industry. 'In the early days, during the wine harvest, they'd find all the stalks which had been filtered out of the wine. These had a whole year in the barrels soaking up the flavour of the wine, so they'd burn these stalks and grill their meat over it for flavour,' explains Nicolas, whose Michelin-starred restaurant Le Saint-James looks out over a small vineyard towards the city of Bordeaux.

Beef has long been associated with the sauce, hence the use of bone marrow in it, but the chef prefers to use it with a fish that is sourced from the Atlantic coast. 'The sauce goes really well with red mullet. It's a fish with lots of taste and character.' Along with the fish, the chef also cherry-picks a few other flavours from the region to create a dish that marries the traditional ingredients from the land, and the sophisticated flavours of the sea. 'The oyster leaves and the samphire taste of the ocean,' says Nicolas. Meanwhile, the marrow and chitterlings will appeal to the most carnivorous diners. 'They're not obligatory,' laughs Nicolas, 'but they're traditional. This is a recipe you can reinvent, but tradition is the base of our cuisine.' So, with the bounty of the Atlantic Ocean, locally sourced beef and the great swathes of vineyards that surround Bordeaux, Nicolas can work magic – as his surname suggests – and turn something simple into something utterly delicious.

Chef //
Nicolas Magie
Location //
Le Saint-James, Bouliac

ROUGET À LA BORDELAISE
Red mullet with Bordeaux sauce

Serves 4

Preparation and cooking time:
2hr 30min

4 red mullet fish
  (200g–300g/7oz–10½oz each)
salt, to taste
piment d'Espelette
  (or paprika/cayenne pepper), to taste
300g (10½oz) shallots
4 tbsp olive oil
knob of butter, plus 1 tbsp for puréeing
  shallots
500ml (17½fl oz) red Bordeaux wine
4 pieces of beef bone marrow
80g (3oz) chitterlings
pepper, to taste
10g (⅓oz) roasted buckwheat grains,
  to serve
60g (2oz) samphire
12 oyster leaves

1 Descale the red mullets, taking care not to damage the flesh, then cut the fish horizontally up to the tail, leaving it intact, then open it like a 'wallet'. Pull out the bones, using tweezers if necessary. Season with salt and *piment d'Espelette* to taste and put the fish fillets back together.

2 Wrap each fish in baking parchment (not greaseproof paper) that has been lightly oiled, and seal at the top with a stapler. The fish should be able to stand lengthways on its base, rather than lie flat.

3 Peel the shallots and chop very finely. Fry them in 1 tbsp of olive oil and a knob of butter without letting them colour, for about three or four minutes. Then deglaze the pan with the red wine. Leave to simmer uncovered for a further 30 minutes. Once cooked, drain the shallots in a sieve, reserving both the wine and the shallots separately.

4 Preheat the oven to 160°C (320°F).

5 Purée the shallots in a food processor with 1 tbsp of butter, salt and *piment d'Espelette* to taste, cover to keep warm.

6 In a saucepan, cook the bone marrow in the wine reserved from the shallots for four or five minutes. Keep warm.

7 Break the chitterlings into pieces of 1cm–2cm (⅓in–¾in) then fry them over a high heat (without any oil/butter – they contain enough fat of their own) until they are crispy. Remove from the pan, season them with salt and pepper, to taste, and keep warm.

8 In the oven, place the fish upright on a baking tray (if you can't get them to stand up, then place them flat directly on the oven shelf) and cook for about 12 minutes.

9 Remove the fish from the oven and discard the baking parchment. Paint the fish with 2–3 tbsp olive oil to make them shine. Sprinkle with a little *fleur de sel* and *piment d'Espelette*, to taste.

10 To serve, place a spoonful of the shallot purée on the plate and sprinkle with the grains of buckwheat. Steam the samphire for two minutes then place on the plate with the chitterlings and oyster leaves. Then add the bone marrow on the plate, then finally the red mullet. Sprinkle the plate with the red wine used to cook the shallots and bone marrow.

MOULES MARINIÈRE
Moules marinière

Mussels have been consumed on the Atlantic coast since the 13th century, and the classic dish moules marinières is eaten throughout France. The dish holds a special place in chef Bruno Grand-Clément's heart as he serves them at the historic Hôtel de la Plage on the Cap Ferret peninsula.

From the moment you remove the lid of the characteristic black enamel pot and reveal the steaming mussels, laced with white wine and parsley, the briny aroma of moules marinière will instantly transport you to the seaside. You may well be there already, for moules marinière is served in almost every beachside bistro in France. You could also be miles from the sea, such is the ubiquity of this favourite seafood dish.

At the Hôtel de la Plage, a 19th-century canteen for forestry workers, which is tucked between oyster-farmers' huts on the Cap Ferret peninsula, it's a favourite dish for both locals and tourists. Here, the clatter of empty mussel shells being dropped into the pot's deep lid is as familiar a sound as the clinking of glasses.

For his version of moules marinière, which uses olive oil as well as butter, chef Bruno Grand-Clément is proud to use the local catch, *moules de bouchot*. These small black-shelled molluscs are cultivated all along the Atlantic and Normandy coasts and their story dates from 1235 when an Irish sailor Patrick Walton was shipwrecked in the Bay of Aiguillon, just north of La Rochelle. He settled and began catching sea birds with nets. Before long, he noticed that mussels were growing on the stakes holding his nets in the water. He added more stakes, along with racks, and named his invention *bout et choat* (a wooden fence) and the cultivation of mussels was born.

'You can cook them anyway you like, there's no limitations. Add spices, different herbs, such as coriander or basil, chorizo, cream, bacon,' says Bruno. The classic is, of course, moules marinière: 'It's a simple recipe, just shallots, garlic, thyme, butter, white wine and parsley at the end. My mother is Breton, so I grew up with lots of seafood, fish, shellfish. I ate moules marinière all the time as a child. Everyone has their own story to tell about them.'

Chef //
Bruno Grand-Clément
Location //
Hôtel de la Plage, Cap Ferret

MOULES MARINIÈRE
Moules marinière

Serves 4

Preparation and cooking time: 1hr

*2kg (4½lb) mussels
   (moules de bouchot, preferably)
40g (1½oz) shallots
40g (1½oz) parsley, plus extra to garnish
80g (3oz) butter
1 tbsp olive oil
1 sprig of thyme
½ head of garlic, peeled
800ml (1½pt) dry white wine
freshly ground black pepper, to taste*

1 Scrub the mussels, pull off the 'beards' and wash in several baths of cold water.

2 Discard the mussels that are already open or damaged. Drain the remaining mussels.

3 Peel and finely chop the shallots. Wash and blot the parsley, then chop finely.

4 In a large casserole pot, melt half the butter with 1 tbsp olive oil, and fry the shallots until soft. Add the mussels along with half of the chopped parsley, the thyme and whole garlic cloves.

5 Deglaze the base of the pan with the white wine, add freshly ground black pepper. Bring to the boil on a high heat, and cover for six to eight minutes. Stir the mussels gently.

6 As soon as some of the mussels start to open, take off the heat.

7 Drain the mussels over a bowl and sieve to eliminate any bits of sand and shell, reserving the juice. Discard any mussels that haven't opened. Add the filtered juice back to the pan and simmer over a high heat until the liquid has reduced by a third.

8 Take off the heat, and add the rest of the butter, cut into pieces.

9 Pour the sauce over the mussels, and sprinkle over the rest of the parsley.

AXOA AUX PIMENTS D'ESPELETTES

Veal stew with Espelette pepper

The town of Biarritz has a proud Basque heritage with a cuisine that draws on influences from Spain and South America. At the vibrant Tantina de Burgos restaurant, chef-owner David Arruabarrena uses the fragrant local chilli pepper piment d'Espelette in a traditional veal stew known as axoa.

On arrival in France's Basque country, it isn't long before you're seeing red: red berets, red flags, red-timber-framed buildings and strings of the local red peppers, the *piments d'Espelettes*. These deep red chilli peppers, which are strung together in *ristras,* adorn buildings, decorate the interiors of restaurants and feature heavily across market stalls – their ubiquity illustrates just how important they are to Basque cuisine.

Originating in South America, the peppers were first introduced to this region of France in the 16th century as medicine, but quickly began replacing black pepper in local dishes. 'It's a condiment that is very fragrant, but at the same time it gives just a bit of a kick at the end,' says chef David Arruabarrena, who owns La Tantina de Burgos, a charming Basque restaurant in the suburbs of Biarritz, and uses the pepper in a traditional stew called *axoa* (pronounced 'Atch-oh-a'). 'It's a typical dish, every Basque family makes the *axoa.* [In the past] when they couldn't preserve the meat, they'd make a dish like this with sauce, which keeps more easily,' he says.

The recipe is a simple one, with few ingredients, and there's no doubt that the *piment* play the starring role. 'They gives the dish its red colour, but you always add it at the end, 10 minutes before serving. If you put it in from the start, it loses all its flavour and you're just left with the spicy kick,' explains David. For the *axoa,* the simplicity of the other ingredients allows the *piments* to shine with deliciously smoky-sweet flavour. The aromatic stew is served with steamed potatoes on typical Basque crockery – white with blue and red stripes – at the Tantina, which is the perfect venue (think red-checked tablecloths, stone walls and bright artwork) to enjoy the lively spirit of the Basque country.

Chef //
David Arruabarrena
Location //
La Tantina de Burgos,
Biarritz

AXOA AUX PIMENTS D'ESPELETTES
Veal stew with Espelette pepper

Serves 4

Preparation and cooking time: 2hr

2 onions
1 red pepper
1 green pepper
olive oil, for frying
1kg (2¼lb) minced veal (see Tip)
250ml (8¾fl oz) dry white wine
salt, to taste
pepper, to taste
1–2 pinches of piment d'Espelette
*   (or paprika) to taste*
boiled potatoes (ideally Agata variety),
*   to serve*

Tip
You can replace the minced veal with minced beef or pork. Rather than use minced meat, you can also chop the meat very finely with a knife, but this would require a longer cooking time.

1 Peel the onions and chop them finely.

2 Chop the peppers into large pieces (approx 2cm/¾in) and fry in the saucepan with the onions in olive oil until soft.

3 In a large saucepan, fry the mince in olive oil until it is cooked through.

4 Add the wine and season with salt and pepper.

5 Leave to simmer on low heat, uncovered, for 1½ hours.

6 Ten minutes before serving, add the *piment d'Espelette*. This gives the colour.

7 Serve with boiled potatoes.

'*Piment d'Espelette isn't limited to the local cuisine; it is fast becoming the condiment of choice among chefs throughout France. All the top chefs, such as Alain Ducasse, are using a lot of piment d'Espelette. It's easy to work with.*'

David Arruabarrena

LA POITRINE DE VOLAILLE DES LANDES, CUISINE AU LARD

Chicken breast stuffed with bacon & foie gras

Michel Guérard is one of the founding fathers of France's nouvelle cuisine movement and has held three Michelin stars since 1977. While his reputation is truly global, he is fiercely proud of using local ingredients – here, his mouthwatering recipe brings together chicken, bacon and foie gras.

A tiny village among the cornfields of the Landes, an area just north of the Pyrenees, may seem an unexpected setting for one of France's most famous restaurants, but three-Michelin-starred chef Michel Guérard had a good reason for settling there in the mid-1970s. 'It was love that led me here, simple as that,' he says on the subject of meeting his wife Christine, whose family business was in the small spa resort of Eugénie-les-Bains.

Having left Paris behind, Michel discovered that the local produce provided ample inspiration for his cuisine. 'In the Landes there's a lot of poultry, there are ducks for foie gras, the chicken and the guinea fowl and other game birds are extraordinary,' he says. 'I wrote the recipe more than 20 years ago and people love it, it's one of those we call the "classics". The foie gras inside the chicken breast is a way of incorporating some softness and moisture into it. We're lucky in France, each recipe is born of each region, the tradition, the customs, the hunting and gathering, all these things. The products are like notes of music for a composer, or the words for a novelist,' says the chef, who has been championing the use of local produce for decades. 'There's a kind of globalisation for cooking, so you can eat the same thing from Los Angeles to Copenhagen... I prefer to keep our traditions, our unique characteristics and I fight for that.'

Among those traditions is the notion of using every part of the chicken – so as not to waste it – and the same applies today. Far from being a cost-saving measure, now it's all a matter of flavour. For the gravy, almost everything is tossed in: the giblets, the extra bones, even the feet ('We don't eat the beak!') and the result is a rich, flavoursome gravy that provides the perfect accompaniment to the utterly delectable chicken.

Chef //
Michel Guérard
Location //
Les Prés d'Eugénie,
Eugénie-les-Bains

LA POITRINE DE VOLAILLE DES LANDES, CUISINE AU LARD

Chicken breast stuffed with bacon & foie gras

Serves 4

Preparation and cooking time:
1hr 30min (not including 2 x overnight refrigeration)

80g (3oz) Boursin cheese (or cream
    cheese), with pepper
16g (½oz) fromage blanc (see the
    Tip on p146)
12g (½oz) parsley, chopped
5g (¼oz) tarragon, chopped
pinch of salt
pinch of pepper
4 slices of very thinly sliced smoked
    streaky bacon
4 chicken breasts
    (with bones and skin, ideally cut from
    whole chickens yourself)
80g (3oz) foie gras
    (cut into sticks of ½cm)
1 clove of garlic, crushed
1 shallot, finely chopped
1 bay leaf
1 sprig of rosemary
1 tbsp olive oil

1 Mix the Boursin cheese with the fromage blanc, parsley and tarragon, salt and pepper, and refrigerate overnight.

2 Slip a slice of smoked streaky bacon underneath the skin of each of the chicken breasts.

3 Open each chicken breast like a 'wallet' by cutting them in halves (but not all the way through). Take out the vein/tendon and spread the Boursin cheese mix thinly onto each side.

4 Arrange the foie gras sticks on one of the breast halves and fold the other breast half back on top. Pull the chicken skin around it so the meat is completely covered and pin it together with four toothpicks/cocktail sticks.

5 In a bowl, mix together the garlic, shallot, bay leaf, rosemary and olive oil and brush it over the chicken breast. Wrap the chicken breasts in clingfilm/plastic wrap and keep in the fridge overnight.

6 Preheat the oven to 180°C (350°F).

7 To make the gravy, put the giblets on a baking sheet/tray and bake in the oven for

For the gravy

the giblets & remaining parts
  of the chicken (see Tip)
1 onion, cubed
1 carrot, cubed
2 shallots, cubed
3 cloves of garlic, whole
fresh herbs
  (such as rosemary, thyme, bay)
1L (1¾pt) water
1 tbsp butter

roast potatoes, to serve
caramelised onions, to serve

20 minutes (no need to use oil, there's enough fat in them already). Add the giblets to a casserole pot, with onion, carrot, shallots, garlic and herbs and cover with 1L of water. Cook on a low heat for at least an hour.

8 Remove the chicken breasts from the fridge and put in a casserole pot or heavy-based saucepan on a low heat (ideally heat to 48°C/120°F if you have a meat thermometer), then let it rest (the temperature will go up to 59°C/140°F).

9 When ready to serve, slice the chicken breast and arrange it on the plate. Drain the gravy in a sieve, and add 1 tbsp of butter, stirring until it melts, and pour over the chicken.

10 Serve with roast potatoes and caramelised onions.

> ### *Tip*
> *The advantage of having cut the chicken breasts from a whole chicken is that you can take extra skin from the leg to allow you to wrap the whole breast. You can use the legs for another dish, and use the giblets and bones for the gravy.*

CASSOULET

Cassoulet

This rustic dish of beans, pork, poultry and sausages is one of the true French classics. Allegedly created in the town of Castelnaudary, the cities of Carcassonne and Toulouse also lay claim to the dish. In central Toulouse, chef Alain Lacoste tries to remain as loyal to its origins as he can.

There are few dishes that evoke such passion as cassoulet; speak to anyone who lives near the short section of the Canal du Midi that runs between Toulouse and Carcassonne, and they'll tell you this stew, crammed with pork, poultry, sausage and beans, has been part of everyday life here for centuries. 'It's a dish of seven days. On the Monday, they would add some water and a few root vegetables to make a soup. They would eat that and leave the coating in the pot,' explains chef Alain Lacoste, owner of Le Colombier restaurant in Toulouse. The routine would continue each day with different ingredients, the pot would build up seven layers of flavour. 'Then on the Sunday they'd put in something a bit richer – meat or whatever they could afford – go off to Mass, then come back and eat everything. Only then would they wash the pot.'

Traditionally, cassoulet was cooked in the embers of the fire in a glazed earthenware pot called a *cassole*, from which it takes its name. While this aspect is undisputed, its history is hotly contested between the towns of Carcassonne, Toulouse and Castelnaudary. The latter cites a tale from the Hundred Years War in which the town was under siege by the English; the inhabitants pooled their meagre resources to feed their ailing troops. So fortifying was their concoction of duck, beans and sausages, the soldiers went on to defeat the enemy. While most cooks will agree on using haricot beans and Toulouse sausages, other ingredients – such as the poultry – are subject to fierce debate. 'In the beginning it was goose, but I think we're the only place in France that uses it,' claims Alain. His tried-and-tested recipe attracts a steady stream of international customers but, he admits, very few locals. 'The French people who come are from [for example] Lille, Strasbourg or Brest, but not many *Toulousains*. Everyone here has a grandmother who makes it for them!'

Chef //
Alain Lacoste
Location //
Le Colombier, Toulouse

CASSOULET

Cassoulet

Serves 10

Preparation and cooking time: 5hr
(not including overnight soaking of beans)

1¼kg (2¾lb) dried white haricot beans
water, for soaking beans
800g (1¾lb) pork rind
1 medium ham hock
2 pork knuckles
800g (1¾lb) saucisses de couenne
    (local sausage made with pork rind,
    alternatively use pork sausage)
2 large onions
2 carrots
3L (5¼pt) water, for ham hock stock
2 bouquet garni
1 duck (or goose) carcass
water for duck/goose stock
2 celery sticks
100g (3½oz) garlic
100g (3½oz) smoked bacon
3–4 tbsp goose fat
2 pinches of quatre-épices
    (French spice mix, comprising nutmeg,
    pepper, cloves and ginger/cinnamon)
2 pinches of nutmeg
2 pinches of salt
2 pinches of freshly ground black pepper
cold water, for cooking beans
10 Toulouse sausages
1 tsp vegetable oil
2–3 tbsp water, to deglaze sausage pan
12 confit goose wings or 5 thighs
    (use duck or guinea fowl if goose is
    unavailable)

1 Cover the haricot beans in water and soak them overnight.

2 Place the pork rind, the ham hock (off the bone), the pork knuckles (off the bone), the *saucisses de couenne*, half a peeled onion and half a peeled carrot in a large casserole pot, cover with 3L of water and simmer on a low heat, uncovered, for two hours.

3 At the same time, in another casserole pot, place the goose/duck carcass, the remaining half of the peeled onion, the remaining half of the peeled carrot and the bouquet garni, cover with water and simmer on a low heat, uncovered, for two hours.

4 After one hour, take out the *saucisses de couenne* and the pork rind, and put into cold water. Drain and keep cool.

5 When the two-hour cooking time is up, take out the pork knuckles, place in cold water to cool, then drain and keep cool. Take out the ham hock and pass the liquid through a sieve, and set this pork stock aside.

6 Drain the goose/duck carcass and save the stock. Combine this with the pork stock.

7 Finely chop the other onion, the other carrot, celery sticks, garlic and smoked bacon. Fry them in a casserole pot in goose fat until they start to soften.

8 Pour over most of the combined stocks until covered (keeping approx 500ml/17½fl oz stock back for later), add the spices and cook, uncovered, for 15 minutes.

> *'The top needs to be golden and quite thick, with a rich sauce underneath. Some people put on breadcrumbs, but with all the meats, the top should be golden anyway. There's no need to add anything else.'*
>
> **Alain Lacoste**

9 Drain the beans and place them in a large pot. Cover with cold water and bring to the boil for three minutes. Drain again, and put them in the pot with the vegetables and stock. Leave to simmer uncovered for 1½ –2 hours, until the beans become very soft.

10 Once the beans are cooked, leave to rest for 15–30 minutes, add more stock if it has been completely absorbed.

11 Preheat the oven to 180°C (350°F).

12 Cut the pork rind (from step 4) into strips, cut the *saucisses de couenne* into rounds, lay the pork knuckles (from step 5) flat and chop them up.

13 Line the base of a *cassole* pot with the strips of pork rind, then fill the pot up to half depth with the beans. Lay on the sausage rounds, sliced pork knuckle and then cover with the rest of the beans.

14 Pour over the stock to the top and bake in the oven for 45 minutes. Add further stock during cooking if needed.

15 Brown the Toulouse sausages in a frying pan with 1 tsp vegetable oil for 10 minutes. Remove and set aside the sausages and deglaze the pan with water. Reserve this liquid.

16 Remove the *cassole* from the oven, arrange the sausages and confit goose on the top and sink them gently under the beans. Pour over the deglazed water from cooking the sausages and more stock if needed. Place back in the oven for 10–15 minutes to lightly brown the surface.

17 Remove from the oven and serve.

CLAFOUTIS
Cherry flan

This dessert is famous throughout France, but its origins lie in the central region of Limousin, where wild cherries once grew in the dense forests. At Château de la Grèze, which looks out over the River Dordogne, chef Anne France sticks close to tradition with her clafoutis.

It's thanks to the fruits of the dense forests in Limousin that the dessert known as clafoutis was born. Coming from *clafi* (the dialect word for 'full'), the dessert was a simple way to use a particular variety of cherry – the *franche noire* – that grew wild in the woods. The small black cherries with a tiny stone are difficult to find these days, which means cook Anne France, who runs a *chambre d'hôtes* at the Château de la Grèze, has to compromise on what she uses to fill the dessert's light batter. She sticks to tradition where she can: 'You must keep the stones in: it's traditional, and I like to respect that,' she says.

In the past, the recipe was just one of many ways the cherries would be used by the people of Limousin. 'You don't need a large quantity of cherries. If they had just a few, they would make clafoutis. If they had a lot, they would make lots of things: jam, cherry brandy, clafoutis. The cherries don't last very long.' The rarity of the cherries meant different fruits were also used in the dessert. 'When you use another fruit and keep the recipe just the same it becomes a *flognarde*,' explains Anne. 'It's a really 'Limousin' word.'

Surrounded by forest, the château is located close to the village of Beaulieu-sur-Dordogne, famed for its annual strawberry festival each May, its 8m strawberry tart, and myriad uses for the fruit. For Anne, the obvious choice is to use them in her *flognarde*, but whichever fruit is hidden beneath the golden batter, the taste is always a treat – the sharpness of the fruit in contrast to the sweet, smooth taste of the cake. 'It's really a dessert but, in the summer, I make a clafoutis or a *flognarde* every day, with cherries, strawberries or apple, and serve it at breakfast. The guests just love the surprise!'

Chef //
Anne France
Location //
Château de la Grèze,
Brivezac

CLAFOUTIS
Cherry flan

Serves 8

Preparation and cooking time: 1hr 15min

3 eggs
250ml (8¾fl oz) milk
100g (3½oz) caster sugar
sachet of vanilla sugar, or 1 tsp vanilla extract
100g (3½oz) flour
40g (1½oz) butter, plus extra for greasing
sprinkle of icing sugar
500g (17½oz) cherries, with stone in

1 Preheat the oven to 180°C (350°F).

2 In a bowl, beat the eggs, then add the sugar and vanilla, and beat well.

3 Add the flour and beat well.

4 Melt the butter in a microwave and then beat it into the mixture.

5 Grease a baking dish (at least 4½cm/1¾in deep) with butter, and sprinkle icing sugar over the dish: shake it until it is evenly coated. Tip out the excess sugar.

6 Add the cherries to the baking dish and then pour over the mixture.

7 Bake for 45 minutes then slice and serve warm.

> ## *Tip*
> *Some cooks soak the cherries in cherry brandy to give*
> *it an extra kick, but if Anne is going to use alcohol, she*
> *uses rum – 'Rum works very well in all desserts.'*

GÂTEAU DE NOIX
Walnut cake

Walnut groves have peppered the plains of the winding River Dordogne for a millennium, and near the enchanting town of Martel, Marie-Claude Castagné uses her family's own walnuts and their golden walnut oil to produce a light and tasty cake to serve at her delightful restaurant.

Chef //
Marie-Claude Castagné
Location //
Moulin à Huile de Noix,
Martel

In the cosy cellar of the Moulin à Huile de Noix, a huge millstone trundles around its base, crushing thousands of walnuts as it goes. The resulting oil trickles out, ready to be bottled by the Castagné family, who have been growing walnuts here for six generations. 'When we got married, we bought a house near the groves and we planted, planted, planted. When you grow walnuts, no generation should ever stop planting,' says chef Marie-Claude Castagné.

The humble *noix* (walnut) has been part of the landscape here alongside the River Dordogne since the 10th century, when peasants would pay their debts with bushels of nuts. The trees last, on average, 30 to 40 years and so the planting must never stop. It takes Marie-Claude's whole family to keep production going: her husband, two sons and even her octogenarian father-in-law all play a vital role. For Marie-Claude, however, it is the *ferme-auberge*, a charming restaurant above the mill, which keeps her busy. The mill's history would suggest a rustic affair, but with dainty glassware and white porcelain dishes set on oak tables, Marie-Claude achieves a more sophisticated ambience.

'I don't want to give the idea we're stuck in the past,' she says. 'My kitchen isn't old, with straw, wood and fire, those days are over. We are making a quality product, and we're working hard to achieve certain standards.' As well as walnut wine, and dishes of foie gras and the local Quercy lamb (see p170), the menu offers a deliciously moreish walnut cake. 'People think a nut cake is going to be heavy, but by using half flour, half cornflour, and separating the eggs, it makes it light and that's why it's good. I never cook with butter, never,' she says, and why would she? Her kitchen is just a few metres from the groves and the golden walnut oil is the pride of the Castagné family, and will be for generations to come.

GÂTEAU DE NOIX
Walnut cake

Serves 8

Preparation and cooking time:
1hr 20min

200g (7oz) walnuts, plus a handful of
   walnut halves to garnish
4 eggs
250g (8¾oz) sugar
100ml (3½fl oz) white wine
1 pinch of salt
100ml (3½fl oz) walnut oil, plus extra for
   greasing
125g (4½oz) plain flour, plus extra for
   dusting
125g (4½oz) cornflour
2 tsp baking powder

For the icing
250g (8¾oz) dark chocolate/cooking
   chocolate (at least 47% cocoa)
100ml (3½fl oz) milk

1 Preheat the oven to 180°C (350°F).

2 Blend the walnuts in a food processor until
they become a fine crumb texture.

3 In another bowl, separate the eggs and whisk
the whites until they stand in peaks.

4 In a separate bowl, whisk the egg yolks
with the sugar. Add the white wine, the salt,
walnuts, walnut oil and the flour, cornflour
and baking powder.

5 Fold in the egg whites.

6 Grease a cake tin (approx 20cm/8in in
diameter) with walnut oil, then dust with
flour and pour in the cake mixture.

7 Bake for 30 minutes.

8 When the cake is cooled, cut in half
horizontally with a large knife.

9 To make the icing, in a bain-marie, melt the
chocolate, take off the heat and whisk in the
milk until it thickens slightly.

10 Spread the icing on top of both halves of the
cake with a palette knife or spatula. Put the cake
back together and decorate with walnut halves.

CANELÉS
Fluted rum & vanilla cakes

The true history of the Bordeaux region's iconic cakes may have been lost in time, but local pastry chef Sébastien Antoine knows the efforts required to make the perfect canelé, with its dark caramelised crust, and its soft, vanilla and rum-laden centre.

The pretty fluted cake known as the canelé is synonymous with Bordeaux and its region, but until 1985 they were almost lost in time. It's thanks to a small number of bakers from the Gironde area, who developed a unique recipe and relaunched the canelés (this 'true' Bordeaux version is spelt with one 'n'), that they were not lost to posterity. Pastry chef Sébastien Antoine's father was one of those bakers who put it 'back on the map' and, as such, Sébastien has had the insider knowledge on making these small cakes with an almost burnt, bittersweet crust and a soft, custardy interior.

Achieving the perfectly fluted crust is crucial to the canelé and Sébastien recommends copper moulds. 'You can get plastic, but the best are copper because it transmits the heat which allows for the caramelisation,' he says. 'You must never wash them, just wipe them clean. It's important they build up a layer of grease, which is necessary for turning them out cleanly and caramelising them evenly.'

While the canelés' recipe has been rescued from the past, the exact details of its origins has been muddled over time. The most popular story tells of when Bordeaux was a busy port: 'The nuns of the Couvent des Annonciades would gather what they could from the merchants, such as the flour, the rum, and then sell the cakes to raise money for the poor,' explains Sébastien. An alternative tale links the canelé to the tradition of using egg whites for clarifying wine in the winemaking process, which left great quantities of egg yolks needing a purpose. Certainly, at La Terrasse Rouge in Saint-Émilion, one of many restaurants for which Sébastien creates his wonderful cakes, it's the latter story that fits best. Surrounded by some of the world's most famous vineyards and cellars, the restaurant's tables offer an exquisite view, making it the perfect place to sip a coffee and bite into the alluring dark crust of a canelé.

Chef //
Sébastien Antoine
Location //
La Terrasse Rouge,
Saint-Émilion

CANELÉS
Fluted rum & vanilla cakes

Makes 30-35 cakes

Preparation and cooking time: 1 hr
(not including overnight refrigeration)

1L (1¾pt) milk
100g (3½oz) butter
seeds from 2 vanilla pods
500g (17½oz) granulated sugar
250g (8¾oz) flour
1 pinch salt
120g (4¼oz) egg yolks
1 whole egg
½ tsp vanilla extract
120ml (4¼fl oz) dark rum
grapeseed oil (or rapeseed oil) for coating
   approx 30 canelé moulds

'Try not to mix the batter too much, as this will release the elasticity in the gluten in the flour and make it blow up like a mushroom. Better to use flour with not much gluten content – which tends to be the cheapest kind. The best flour has most gluten in it.

Sébastien Antoine

1 Boil the milk, butter and vanilla seeds in a saucepan.

2 In a bowl, mix the sugar, flour and salt.

3 In a separate bowl, whisk the egg yolks and whole egg. Add the vanilla extract.

4 Add half the milk mixture (from step 1) to the flour mixture (from step 2) and whisk. Add the egg mixture (from step 3) and whisk.

5 Add the remainder of the milk mixture and whisk.

6 Leave overnight in the fridge.

7 Remove the bowl from the fridge and preheat the oven to 240°C (460°F).

8 Add the rum to the mixture and whisk.

9 Use a pastry brush to coat all the canelé moulds in oil (not butter, as it will burn, see also Tip) and pour or pipe in the canelé mixture.

10 Bake for eight minutes, then reduce the oven temperature to 180°C (350°F) and bake for a further 30 to 35 minutes. Remove from their moulds while still warm, and serve.

Tip
To build up the special layer of grease on the mould, grease them with the grapeseed/rapeseed oil (the traditional method was with beeswax) and then bake the empty moulds for 15 minutes, then grease them again, and bake them again. The third time, fill them with the canelé mixture, as with the recipe.

LE BERET BASQUE
Chocolate mousse cake

In the stylish resort of Biarritz, chocolate has long been the indulgence of the seaside town's well-heeled visitors, but the beret basque has a more poignant history, having been inspired by soldiers going to WWI. The mousse-filled cake is still made to this day by baker Flavie Coutin.

As you plunge your fork into the enticing chocolate dome known as the beret basque, it's hard to think of anything except the taste of the smooth chocolate mousse and sweet biscuit crust. Yet, look beyond the glossy surface and the cake also holds the key to several tales from this corner of southwest France, most of which originate from the historic Miremont tea room in Biarritz.

Founded in 1872 before being bought by Joseph Miremont in 1880, the Miremont is today owned by Jean-Marcel Toledo, who loves to tell the story of one of the bakery's most popular cakes: 'When the Basque men had to go and fight in WWI, they handed over their berets to their wives, fiancées and girlfriends, before taking their helmets and guns and boarding the train to go to war. The idea was that the women would look after the berets until the men returned. Monsieur Miremont had the idea to create a cake to console the women left behind – a cake that would help morale – made completely from chocolate.'

Jean-Marcel's team, including Flavie Coutin, make hundreds of the cakes each week, proving its popularity has endured. The patisserie itself has an even longer history: when it first opened, Biarritz was becoming a fashionable resort for Europe's elite. Miremont's cake and pastry selection were famously a favourite of royalty, including the young Spanish King Alphonso XIII and King Edward VII of England. The poet Edmond Rostand wrote: 'At teatime at Miremont, there are fewer pastries than queens and fewer rum babas than grand dukes.' But to trace the full history of chocolate in the Basque country you need to go back to the early 16th-century when Jews were driven out of Spain and Portugal. Many settled in the town of Bayonne, just across the border. Among them were the renowned Jewish chocolate-makers and the rest, as they say, is history.

Chef //
Flavie Coutin
Location //
Miremont, Biarritz

LE BERET BASQUE

Chocolate mousse cake

Serves 8

*Preparation and cooking time: 2hr
(not including overnight refrigeration)*

For the biscuit

2 egg yolks
2 eggs
75g (2¾oz) sugar
63g (2¼oz) egg whites
28g (1oz) cane sugar
23g (¾oz) flour
23g (¾oz) cocoa powder

For the dipping mixture

150ml (5¼fl oz) water
100g (3½oz) dark chocolate (70% cocoa)

For the mousse

*170g (6oz) dark chocolate
   (at least 66% cocoa)*
17g (⅔oz) dark chocolate (100% cocoa)
85g (3oz) butter
*45g (1½oz) sugar syrup
   (sirop à 30° Baumés – see Tip)*
140g (5oz) egg whites
40g (1½oz) granulated sugar

1 Preheat the oven to 180°C (350°F).

2 To make the biscuit, whisk the egg yolks, whole eggs and 75g sugar in a bowl.

3 In a separate bowl, whisk the egg whites and cane sugar together.

4 In a third bowl, sift the flour and cocoa, and mix together.

5 Fold the egg white mixture into the other egg mixture (from step 2), and then fold in the flour and cocoa. Spread the mixture onto a baking sheet and bake for 10 minutes.

6 To make the dipping mixture, bring the water to the boil in a kettle, then pour over the chocolate in a bowl to melt it. Whisk until it's all combined.

7 When the biscuit has cooled, use a cookie cutter to cut out the circles for the eight 'beret' moulds (each half-sphere silicone mould approx 10cm/4in). For each mould, you'll need three different-sized circles of biscuit: one very large circle (to form the outer case) and two smaller ones (one for inside and another to seal the bottom of the beret). Dip the eight larger biscuit circles in the water-and-chocolate mixture, then place inside the moulds and push into shape. Leave the 16 smaller biscuit circles aside.

For the icing
80ml (2¾fl oz) water
240g (8½ oz) sugar
80g (3oz) cocoa
160g (5½oz) liquid cream
12g (½oz) gelatine leaves

chocolate vermicelli, to garnish

8 To make the mousse, place the dark chocolate and butter and sugar syrup in a bain-marie until the chocolate and butter has melted, ideally to 50°C (120°F).

9 Whisk the egg whites and sugar until it stands in peaks, fold into the chocolate mixture. Use a piping bag, or spoon the mousse into the moulds until it is half full. Tap the moulds on the counter to eliminate the largest bubbles.

10 Dip eight of the smaller biscuit circles in the water and chocolate mixture, place inside each mould, then fill up with mousse and level off. Tap again to eliminate bubbles.

11 For the final eight small biscuit circles, dip them in the water and chocolate mixture and place on the bottom of each mould to seal, then leave to set in the freezer (the fridge isn't cold enough) overnight.

12 Make the icing by bringing the water and sugar to the boil in a saucepan, then pour it over the cocoa powder in a bowl. Stir into a chocolate mixture and set aside.

13 Bring the cream to the boil in a saucepan and pour over the gelatine in a bowl. Then add the chocolate mixture and whisk until well-combined. Cool to 20°C–25°C (70°F –77°F).

14 Remove the berets from the freezer, push out of the moulds and then immediately pour over the icing. Decorate with chocolate vermicelli around the base.

Tip
A 30°C Baumé syrup is frequently used in patisserie cooking (and cocktails). To make the sugar syrup, boil 100ml (3½fl oz) water with 125g (4½oz) granulated sugar until it dissolves, then leave to cool.

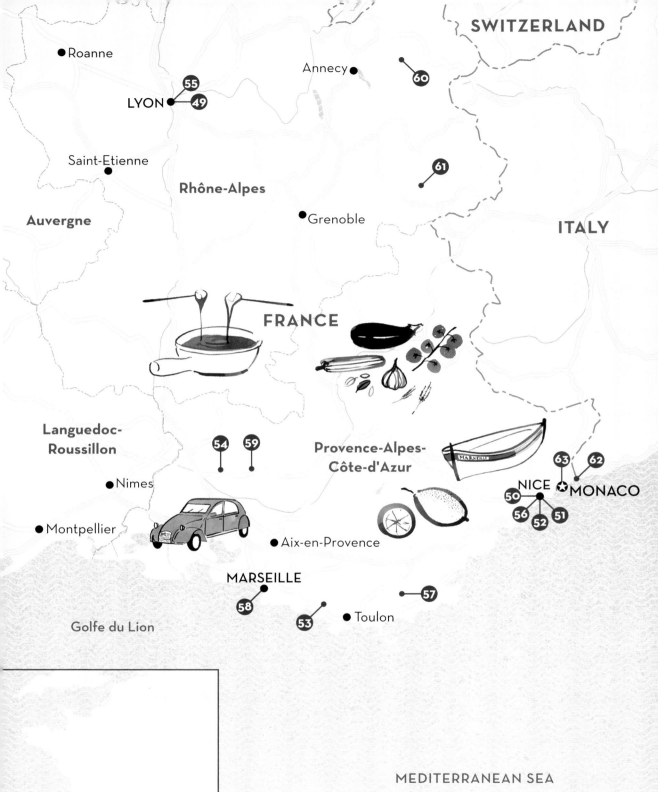

SWITZERLAND

● Roanne

Annecy ●

55
LYON ●
49

60

Saint-Etienne ●

Rhône-Alpes

61

Auvergne

● Grenoble

ITALY

FRANCE

Languedoc-
Roussillon

54 **59**

Provence-Alpes-
Côte-d'Azur

MARSEILLE

63 **62**

NICE ☆ MONACO

50
56 **51**
52

● Nîmes

● Montpellier

● Aix-en-Provence

MARSEILLE

57

58

53

● Toulon

Golfe du Lion

MEDITERRANEAN SEA

Southeast
France

SOUTHEAST FRANCE

The sun-drenched vegetables of Provence combine to create some of the Mediterranean's most vibrant dishes, while the hearty cuisine of the mountains soothe the soul. In France's gastronomic capital Lyon, the menus tell stories of days gone by.

SALADE LYONNAISE
Lyon salad

Many of Lyon's homely restaurants, known as bouchons, were established by local women known as the mères lyonnaises (mothers of Lyon). At the Café du Peintre, Florence Périer continues the tradition. Here she serves the city's eponymous dish, salade lyonnaise.

Just inside the door at the Café du Pientre, dozens of large bibs hang on a hat stand; each bears the name, embroidered into the crisp white cotton, of one of the many loyal clients who visit the restaurant several times a week. 'The *bouchons* (small rustic bistros) in the city centre have a lot of tourists because of their location, but we serve a lot of local lyonnaise, and that's why we have the bibs,' explains Florence Périer, who first helped her parents in their own restaurant, then worked for 30 years across the city before opening Le Café de Peintre in 2009.

Lyon is France's gastronomic capital, and Florence's restaurant is one of the *bouchons* established by the *mères lyonnaises* (mothers of Lyon). 'Originally the *mères* were women who worked in the big houses of the bourgeoisie, they did housekeeping, cooking. After the French Revolution, they lost their jobs, so they needed to find another means of income and what they did best was cook. At the same time, the silk industry was just starting in Lyon and so there was a need to cater for the people coming to buy, sell and transport the silk.'

The *bouchons* had menus that offered, and still do, dishes made with offal because it was cheap. The iconic salade lyonnaise was born of the same circumstances: 'It's a recipe that was created out of necessity, the idea of creating something out of nothing,' says Florence. 'You have to choose a good lettuce according to the season. In winter, the lettuce is very crunchy: frisée salad, or chicory, these aren't good in the summer. It's really a dish that comes with the winter.' Along with the crunchy lettuce comes lardons, a fresh egg (poached), croutons and a good dressing. 'When it comes to making a good salad, and this goes for everything in cooking, you can't make something good with bad produce.'

Chef //
Florence Périer
Location //
Le Café du Peintre, Lyon

SALADE LYONNAISE
Lyon salad

Serves 4

Preparation and cooking time: 30min

For the dressing
1 tbsp strong mustard
1 tbsp wholegrain mustard
2 tbsp olive oil
2 tbsp sunflower oil
1 tbsp sherry vinegar
1 clove of garlic

For the salad
4 eggs
1L water, for poaching eggs
200ml (7fl oz) white vinegar
225g (8oz) slab of bacon
water, for de-salting bacon
1 tbsp sherry vinegar
4 slices of bread, for croutons
oil, for frying
300g (10½oz) salad leaves
   (dandelion in spring, mesclun in
   summer, curly endive in winter)
fresh herbs (such as chervil, chives), to serve

1 In a jug or bowl, whisk together the mustards, olive oil, sunflower oil and sherry vinegar for the dressing. Chop the garlic very finely and whisk in as well.

2 To poach the eggs, bring a saucepan of water to the boil, add the white vinegar and reduce the heat so the water is simmering. Break the eggs into a ramekin or small bowl.

3 Stir the water with a spoon to create a vortex, and tip the eggs from the ramekin into the centre of the vortex. After three minutes, take the eggs out of the water using a slotted spoon and place gently on some absorbent kitchen paper.

4 Cut the bacon into 2cm (¾in) pieces, and place them in cold water to remove the salt. Drain the bacon on absorbent paper then brown them in a frying pan. Deglaze the pan with 1 tbsp sherry vinegar and keep the bacon warm.

5 To make the croutons, cut the bread into squares and fry with a little oil until golden.

6 Place the lettuce leaves on each plate and put the egg in the centre. Add the bacon and sprinkle with the vinegar used to deglaze the pan. Scatter over the croutons, along with some fresh herbs, and serve.

'When visitors come to Lyon they have two aims: eat in a Paul Bocuse restaurant and eat in a Bouchon de Lyon.'

Florence Périer

SALADE NIÇOISE
Salade niçoise

Away from the Côte d'Azur, the salade niçoise can include myriad ingredients but at A Buteghinn'a, a friendly restaurant in the heart of Nice's old town, Sophie Agrofoglio is proud to serve the true and traditional version, which is rather different to those served elsewhere.

D are, if you will, to suggest what might be included in a salade niçoise and you risk the wrath of Sophie Agrofoglio and her two colleagues. Potatoes, green beans, lettuce are all met with a loud '*Non!*' and the grave shaking of heads. As popular as Salade Niçoise is around the world, over time its ingredients have fallen victim to culinary Chinese whispers and those salads served elsewhere often bear no resemblance to the true version.

'The salad provokes passion, and we fight for the respect of the real salade niçoise,' says Sophie. 'The original version – in the 16th and 17th centuries – was just tomatoes and anchovies, then as the port of Nice began receiving produce from elsewhere, the salad developed and began to contain other ingredients: artichokes, green pepper, radish and spring onions, but never red pepper or white onions. The only beans it contains are broad beans, and that's only in the spring. People often put tuna and anchovies in it, but it should be either one or the other – never both. And there are never any leaves in a Salade Niçoise, I've eaten it all my life and there's never been any salad leaves.'

Sophie's version is a rainbow of colours: the flavours of the tomatoes, artichokes and peppers coming together to create a salad that packs a punch – from the piquancy of the garlic that is used to season the plate, to the crunch of the vegetables and the peppery kick of the olive oil. It's one of many typical Niçois dishes on the menu of her bijoux restaurant, which has a bright homely kitchen and a triangular terrace that is sandwiched between the narrow streets of Nice's old town. Sophie, her partner Marcelle and her friend Evelyne have run the restaurant – its name means 'little boutique' in Genoese patois – since 1992. 'I serve food that I like to eat. We do everything ourselves, so I know what goes into everything and we eat well.'

Chef //
Sophie Agrofoglio
Location //
A Buteghinn'a, Nice

SALADE NIÇOISE
Salade niçoise

Serves 4

Preparation and cooking time: 30min

1 clove garlic
4 tomatoes
8 radishes, finely sliced
1 long green pepper, finely sliced
8 small artichokes, finely sliced
4–5 spring onions, finely sliced
50g (1¾oz) tin of anchovy fillets, sliced in
    half lengthways
4 hard-boiled eggs, sliced
40 small whole olives
    (caillettes variety, if possible)
a handful of basil
drizzle of extra virgin olive oil, to garnish

1 Rub the plate with garlic.

2 Cut each tomato in half, then into squares. Layer onto the plate.

3 Add a layer of radish, then pepper, then artichokes and spring onions.

4 Add the anchovies, the egg and then the olives. Chop the basil finely, and sprinkle over.

5 Drizzle the olive oil over the salad and serve.

'You only need extra virgin olive oil. You never add vinegar, it's too acidic with the tomatoes.'

Sophie Agrofoglio

SOCCA
Chickpea pancake

Despite having its origins in Italy, this chickpea pancake is one of Nice's iconic foods, and at Chez Pipo, one of the city's most popular restaurants, local families have been enjoying it for generations. Owner Steeve Bernardo explains its enduring appeal.

When you bite into a hot, crispy, golden slice of socca, it's hard to believe that something this simple could be so enticingly good. Yet this chickpea pancake with just four ingredients – chickpea flour, water, salt and olive oil – will almost certainly have you coming back for more.

The recipe first originated in the south of Italy in the 8th and 9th centuries and, over time, variations of it crept slowly north to find a welcoming home in Nice. 'It first arrived in the Mediterranean when Saracens invaded the south of Italy,' explains Steeve Bernardo, who owns Nice's popular socca restaurant Chez Pipo. 'By the 18th century it had made its way to Liguria in the form of the Italian version, *farinata*. Then it arrived in France at the end of the 19th century, being brought over by the Italian workers who came to build Napoleon's naval dockyards on the Côte d'Azur. It has become so rooted in Niçois cuisine that it is actually better known here now than it is in Italy.'

In the early 20th century, socca was sold as a takeaway food, wrapped in paper and sold by street vendors on Nice's waterfront, but at Chez Pipo (established in 1923 and named after its original owner, whose family ran it until 1986), Steeve and his team go to great lengths to make sure their socca is perfect, baking the batter in large copper pans in a wood-fired oven at the heart of the restaurant. 'What the Niçois look for is that it is crispy on the top but soft in the middle, and not too greasy,' explains Steeve, who bought the restaurant in 2009, 15 years after working there as a student. 'My career wasn't in restaurants, but [to buy it] was a *coup de cœur*. It's a special place in Nice; there's the history, the atmosphere and the clientele and socca is something that carries on through the generations.'

Chef //
Steeve Bernardo
Location //
Chez Pipo, Nice

SOCCA
Chickpea pancake

Serves 8

Preparation and cooking time: 25min

500ml (17½fl oz) cold water
250g (8¾oz) chickpea flour
6 tbsp olive oil
1 tsp fine salt

<u>*Tip*</u>

The wood-fired oven at Chez Pipo reaches temperatures of 500°C (930°F), which is obviously hard to recreate in a domestic oven. A pizza oven is an ideal alternative, but otherwise make sure the oven is thoroughly preheated to the highest temperature before putting the socca inside.

1 Preheat the oven to its maximum temperature for 10 minutes.

2 Put the water in a deep mixing bowl and whisk in the chickpea flour. Add 2 tbsp of the olive oil and the salt. Mix thoroughly to make sure there are no lumps, but if necessary pass through a sieve. The batter should have the consistency of full-fat milk. Add more water if it's still too thick. Set aside.

3 In two 15cm (6in) diameter circular baking tins, pour in the remaining 4 tbsp of the olive oil and place the oiled tins in the oven for five minutes.

4 Remove the tins from the oven, pour in the batter and spread it evenly. Put the tins straight back in the oven on the top shelf.

5 After two minutes, change the oven setting to grill (or move the tins to a separate, preheated grill) and leave to cook for five to seven minutes until it is golden on top, even a little burned in places. During cooking, you can pierce the bubbles that form with a sharp knife.

6 Remove from the grill, slice into sections and serve.

'The good thing about socca is that you eat it very hot – almost burning your fingers. If you leave it to cool down, it continues to cook in the middle and so little by little it gets harder, so it really is best to eat straight out of the oven, with a little bit of pepper.'

Steeve Bernardo

PISSALADIÈRE
Caramelised onion tart

This tempting onion tart is a speciality of Nice and is served as a starter in restaurants, such as Lou Balico, where chef Jo Issautier continues the family tradition of serving Niçois classics that are true to his mother's recipes.

It seems a shame to shed tears for the sake of a classic Niçois dish, but when it comes to pissaladière, it's the onions that will set you off. Thankfully, the finished onion tart provides many good reasons to smile; from the crunch of its biscuity base, to the oozy, slow-cooked onion topping, and then the salty kick of the olives and anchovies on top. Its name derives from the anchovies or, more specifically, the paste made from these salty Mediterranean fish. 'The paste was called *pissala*, which is how the tart gets its name, and it used to be added to the onions as they cooked,' explains chef Jo Issautier, who owns Lou Balico, one of the best-loved traditional restaurants in Nice, an establishment found just behind the city's Musée d'Art Moderne et d'Art Contemporain.

Pissala (also spelled *pissalat* or *pei salat*) was made by macerating the fish (originally it was made with sardines) in salt and spices over two weeks to create a pungent grey concoction. Needless to say, it doesn't find many fans among today's diners. 'Now we just add anchovies on the top, to make it more appealing,' says Jo.

The recipe is one of the many local specialities on offer at Lou Balico: its name means 'basil' in the old Niçois language. Established in 1979 by Jo's mother, Adrienne, who died aged 91 in 2009, the restaurant is now run by Jo and his family. 'My mother started the restaurant, and I'm helped by my wife Brigitte and daughter Sara, who will carry it on. I promised my mother I'd respect all her recipes, because she expected me to adapt them,' he says, saluting the sky every time he mentions her. While the restaurant's founder is still revered, it is the youngest family member who now brings cheer to the restaurant's customers: Sara's nine-year-old son Leo is already becoming familiar with the recipes that the family hold dear and, until he's allowed to chop the onions, his face is all smiles.

Chef //
Jo Issautier
Location //
Lou Balico, Nice

PISSALADIÈRE
Caramelised onion tart

Serves 6

Preparation and cooking time:
2hr 15min

For the topping
1kg (2lb) onions, sliced finely
2 cloves of garlic, peeled & crushed
1 tsp Herbes de Provence
salt, to taste
pepper, to taste
50g (1¾oz) anchovy fillets
black olives, to garnish
sundried cherry tomatoes, to garnish
green salad, to serve (optional)

For the pastry base
250g (8¾oz) flour, plus extra for rolling
  dough
25ml (¾fl oz) olive oil
10g (⅓oz) fresh baker's yeast (or 3g dried
  yeast), dissolved in a small amount of
  water
1 egg
½ tbsp fine salt
250ml (8½fl oz) water

1 Fry the onions, garlic, Herbes de Provence, salt and pepper in a saucepan on a low heat without letting them colour. Then cover and cook gently for about an hour, until the onions are meltingly soft. If there is liquid left, then cook uncovered for a few minutes until it evaporates.

2 Preheat the oven to 180°C–200°C (350°F–390°F).

3 To make the base, place the flour in a bowl and form a well in the middle. Add the rest of the pastry base ingredients into the middle and mix, pouring the water in last, gradually, until it creates a dough.

4 Knead the dough on a lightly floured surface and then form a ball, and leave to rest at room temperature for an hour.

5 Roll out the dough with a lightly floured rolling pin to a depth of about 7mm–8mm (¼in–⅓in), and place in a large, lightly oiled (or lined with greaseproof paper) baking sheet/tray.

6 Spread the cooked onion mixture (from step 1) on top of the pastry base, and arrange the anchovy fillets across the top. Garnish with the olives and sundried tomatoes.

7 Bake in the oven for 30–40 minutes.

8 Cut into small slices and serve alone or with a green salad.

APERITIF PROVENÇALE
Provençal dips & vegetables

The selection of dips and dishes, including tapenade and anchoïade, that come together to make the Aperitif Provençale can be as few or numerous as you like, but the most important element is that the dishes are shared, says chef René Bérard.

It is hard to imagine a more idyllic place to learn the art of cooking Provençal cuisine than the Bastide des Saveurs, the cookery school linked to the Hostellerie Bérard hotel and restaurant in the Var *département* (county). Here at this 19th-century farmhouse, surrounded by a beautifully kept vegetable garden and orchard, octogenarian chef René Bérard shares his wisdom of the sunshine-infused dishes he grew up with. 'I was born [in a house] at the foot of the clock tower. I've never gone far,' he says. With views over a breathtaking landscape that is dotted with cypress and poplar trees, including his home village of La Cadière-d'Azur perched on a hilltop, it's easy to see why he wouldn't stray.

In the kitchen where René teaches budding Provençal cooks, dried herbs hang from the ceiling, rustic pots balance on shelves, and the colours chosen for the tiles and walls represent the terracotta soil and the yellow sun. 'The symbols of Provence are hospitality and sharing; we like to welcome people here and share. That's the *art de vivre* in Provence. Sharing is my passion,' says René. And when it comes to sharing, there could be no better occasion than the traditional aperitif: a table spread with numerous dips, crudités and vegetable dishes, eaten while sipping the obligatory glass of Provençal rosé wine, as the sun goes down. 'Everyone helps themselves; you could say it's a bit like communion.'

For numerous guests, there are myriad dishes included in the 'aperitif', but two of the most loved dips are *anchoïade*, made with anchovies; and tapenade, made with olives and capers. '*Tapen* is the old Provençal word for capers,' explains René. And when it comes to chopping the vegetables, though it may be a simple task, there is also an art to it lest you hamper your guests' conversation: 'Cut the vegetables so they're bite-size, otherwise your guests will have a huge mouthful!'

Chef //
René Bérard
Location //
Bastide des Saveurs,
Hostellerie Bérard, La
Cadière-d'Azur

APERITIF PROVENÇALE
Provençal dips & vegetables

Serves 8–10

Preparation and cooking time:
1hr 30min

For the garlic purée
1 clove garlic
water, to cover
1 tbsp olive oil
pinch of salt

For the tapenade
600g (1⅓lb) stoned black olives
6–8 anchovy fillets in oil, cubed
50g (1¾oz) capers, finely chopped
drizzle of olive oil
pinch of cayenne pepper
1 tbsp garlic puree
1 sliced baguette, to serve

For the anchoïade
250g (8¾oz) anchovy fillets in oil
150g (5¼oz) garlic purée
500ml (17½fl oz) olive oil
15g (½oz) basil, finely chopped
1 tsp thyme flowers, ground in a mortar
  & pestle
2 tbsp mustard
3 tbsp red wine vinegar

For the crudités
3 carrots, cut into bite-size pieces
1 cauliflower, cut into bite-size pieces
5 sticks celery, cut into bite-size pieces
1 fennel bulb, cut into bite-size pieces

1 To make the garlic purée, peel the cloves of one head of garlic. Cut each clove of garlic in half and remove the green sprout in each. Cover with cold water and bring to the boil in a saucepan for one minute. Change the water, then repeat this process three times. Drain very well, then place in a blender with 1 tbsp of olive oil and a pinch of salt, and mix until smooth (unused mixture can be kept in the fridge for other recipes for up to 12 days).

2 To make the tapenade, chop the olives very finely. Add the anchovy fillets, cut into tiny cubes, then the chopped capers and continue to chop all ingredients until all very fine.

3 Add enough olive oil, 1 tsp at a time, until you have a paste consistency.

4 Add a pinch of cayenne pepper and 1 tbsp (or more if desired) of garlic purée and mix. Set the tapenade aside.

5 To make the *anchoïade*, put the anchovies and 150g of garlic purée in a food processor and blend, then drizzle in the olive oil through the processor's lid as it mixes.

6 Add the basil and 1 tsp of the thyme flowers.

7 Add the mustard, then the vinegar and blend until a purée consistency.

8 Serve the *anchoïade* with the crudités, and the tapenade with the sliced baguette, along with additional dips, such as ratatouille (p250) and caviar d'aubergine (p264).

Tip
To remove the smell of garlic from your fingers, rub the leaves of the celery and it will eliminate the odour.

Tip
If you make more anchoïade than you think you'll need, don't add the herbs into the whole mixture. Just add them at the end to the quantity you need, and the rest of the dip will keep in the fridge for up to 10 days.

SOUPE AU PISTOU
Pesto soup

In the idyllic surrounds of an 18th-century farmhouse, chef Thierry Crovara uses the fresh basil grown in his bountiful herb garden in a soup that has long been a favourite dish among the people of Provence, but which also bears a striking resemblance to a famous Italian dish.

'We are in the garden of France, here in the Luberon,' says the jovial chef Thierry Crovara, as he surveys his large herb garden, which is just a few steps from the kitchen of his homely hotel-restaurant. 'We have the sun here and we have the water. It's green everywhere because the water table is just five metres underneath the ground.'

Perhaps better known for its acres of lavender and vineyards, the Luberon area of Provence is home to farms and growers providing a bounty of vegetables to kitchens near and far. Many of the vegetables find their way into the Provençal dish, soupe au pistou – a soup that encompasses a host of different flavours. 'It's traditional recipe from the Mediterranean with basil, garlic and olive oil. We eat it hot, but also cold. It's a country recipe, so if they didn't have beans, for example, they'd just put in something else. You can put in whatever you like,' says Thierry, who cooks a variety of Provençal and French dishes for the hotel's daily *table d'hôte*, served in the dappled shade of the wisteria-clad terrace. 'The people of Provence will tell you, "It's our recipe", but in Italy it's called minestrone, it's almost exactly the same thing – only they use pasta and we use potatoes,' he explains. The clue to the Italian connection also comes in its name: pistou and pesto are largely the same thing and the French and Italians will gladly debate the ingredients of their pistous and pestos, with the latter containing pine nuts and cheese. Some will insist that the basil leaves are small and young, others that they are torn from their stalks to ensure a smooth consistency. Yet whatever is decided by the individual cook, the highlight of soupe au pistou, or indeed minestrone, is the dollop of pesto stirred in at the end, giving the dish the refreshing aroma of basil and the heady taste of garlic.

Chef //
Thierry Crovara
Location //
Le Mas des Grès, Lagnes

SOUPE AU PISTOU
Pesto soup

Serves 4

*Preparation and cooking time: 1hr
(not including soaking of beans)*

500g (1lb) uncooked white haricot beans
100g (3½oz) onion
200g (7oz) carrots
100g (3½oz) celeriac
150g (5⅓oz) courgettes (zucchini)
150g (5⅓oz) French beans
3 tsp olive oil
2L (70 fl oz) chicken stock
salt, to taste
freshly ground pepper, to taste
150g (5⅓oz) potatoes
100g (3½oz) basil
1 head garlic, peeled and chopped finely

1 Put the dried beans in a bowl covered with water and soak overnight.

2 Peel and cut the onion, carrots and celeriac into cubes. Wash and cut the courgette into cubes. Cut the French beans into 2½cm (1in) sections.

3 In a saucepan, heat 1 tsp of the olive oil and sauté the onions, carrots and celeriac until they soften slightly, but don't let them colour.

4 Add two litres of stock.

5 Drain the white beans and add them to the soup, simmer for 30 minutes, season.

6 Peel and cut the potatoes into cubes. Then add the potatoes, French beans and courgettes and cook for 20 minutes.

7 Just before taking off the heat, season again.

8 Mix the basil with the remaining 2 tsp of olive oil, then add to the soup. Add the chopped garlic, without reheating the soup. Serve in warmed bowls.

Tip
To turn this dish into a main meal, add fillets of red mullet (30g/1oz a piece), simply season them and fry them in a bit of olive oil on the skin side, then turn them until cooked through. Place them on top of the soup just before serving.

QUENELLES DE BROCHET À LA LYONNAISE, SAUCE NANTUA

Pike dumplings & crayfish sauce

Lyon's iconic quenelles are the French version of dumplings and have their origins in the fishing lakes of La Dombes, northwest of Lyon. Most often made with pike and served with a crayfish sauce that originates in the village of Nantua, they are a staple dish at bouchons.

The lakes of La Dombes are an impressive sight: more than 1000 fishing ponds are squeezed onto a 50 mile (80km) plateau just northwest of Lyon. It's here that the two key ingredients for quenelles are cultivated: the pike forms the basis for a dumpling that is either poached or baked, the crayfish lend their flavour to the rich Nantua sauce. 'It's always been a dish that is crucial to lyonnaise cuisine,' explains chef Joseph Viola. 'Each kitchen has its own way, but I prefer to steam them, because it gives a smooth texture. We serve it with the Nantua sauce, which has lots of vegetables, garlic, it's flambéed in cognac and has white wine and cream.'

As president of the Association of Bouchons de Lyon, Joseph works hard to protect the traditions of the restaurants that serve this iconic dish. 'In the *bouchons*, we cook all the specialities of the region: offal, river and lake fish, a lot of pork-based dishes, beef, lamb, poultry. They grew out of the old *relais de poste* (coach houses), where the owners would work in the kitchen, in the dining room, but also tend to the horses. They'd use bunches of twisted hay – called *bouchons* – to wipe down the horses. That's how the *bouchons* were born,' says Joseph, who took over Daniel et Denise, one of the city's best-known *bouchons*, in 2004, before opening a further two restaurants with the same name. The original, in Rue de Créqui in the Croix-Rousse district, is characteristic of the style seen in all *bouchons*. 'They're all a bit different, but you see the same materials: copper, wood, iron in a cosy atmosphere. There are sausages and hams hanging from the ceiling, tables are close together, with red-and-white-checked tablecloths, the traditional pot lyonnais wine bottles. It's a warming cuisine and when you're in a *bouchon*, it's like being at home. When you're in a *bouchon*, you feel like time has stood still.'

Chef //
Joseph Viola
Location //
Daniel et Denise, Lyon

QUENELLES DE BROCHET À LA LYONNAISE, SAUCE NANTUA

Pike dumplings & crayfish sauce

Serves 8

Preparation and cooking time: 3hr (not including overnight refrigeration)

For the quenelle pastry
250ml (8¾fl oz) milk
1 grating of nutmeg
70g (2½oz) butter
160g (5½oz) flour

For the quenelles
500g (17½oz) skinless pike fillets (or any
    firm white fish), cut into cubes of 2cm
    (¾in) and then frozen
2 egg whites
5 whole eggs
10g (⅓oz) salt
pinch of ground white pepper
1 grating of nutmeg
125g (4½oz) butter, melted
salted water, to cook quenelles

1 To make the quenelle pastry, boil the milk with the nutmeg and the butter in a saucepan. Add the flour in one go, stir vigorously with a spatula and cook over a low heat for six to seven minutes (like a choux pastry). Pour this pastry mixture into a bowl and put in the fridge overnight.

2 To make the quenelles, place the frozen cubes of pike into a food processor and blend until they are like a sawdust consistency.

3 Add the pastry mixture from step 1 to the processor until well combined. Then add the egg whites, then the eggs one by one.

4 Add the salt, pepper, nutmeg and then the melted butter until well combined.

5 Transfer this quenelle mixture into a bowl, cover with clingfilm/plastic wrap, and leave in the fridge for six hours.

6 Bring a casserole pot of salted water to the boil. With a dessert spoon, mould the quenelles into oval shapes and place into the water for 20 minutes. Then turn them and cook for a further 20 minutes. Remove the cooked quenelles from the casserole pot and place them into iced water, then put in the fridge overnight.

For the sauce Nantua

100ml (3½fl oz) olive oil

40 live crayfish

100g (3½oz) carrot, cut into small
  cubes

60g (2oz) onion, chopped finely

60g (2oz) shallot, chopped finely

2 tbsp tomato purée

50ml (1¾fl oz) brandy

150ml (5¼fl oz) dry white wine

1L (1¾pt) liquid crème fraiche

1 sprig of thyme

1 bay leaf

10g (⅓oz) salt

pinch of ground white pepper

7 To make the sauce Nantua, put the olive oil in a cast iron pot and, over a high heat, cook the crayfish until they turn red. Add the carrot, onion and shallots and cook until tender.

8 Mix in the tomato purée and then flambée with the brandy. Deglaze the pan with the white wine and reduce the liquid. Then add the crème fraiche, thyme and bay leaf. Bring to the boil for two minutes. Lift out the crayfish, remove the shells and put the heads back in the sauce. Cook for a further 20 minutes.

9 At the end of the cooking time, pass the sauce through a conical sieve, pressing the crayfish heads with a spoon to squeeze out all the juice.

10 Remove the quenelles from the fridge and steam them for 20 minutes; they should double in volume.

11 To serve, place a quenelle in the centre of a shallow bowl, add the crayfish tails and cover with the sauce Nantua. Add salt and pepper, to taste.

Tip

Freezing the fish makes for a smoother texture, because the food processor splinters it much more finely.

RATATOUILLE
Ratatouille

The Acchiardo family have run their convivial family restaurant for nearly a century, and among the many Niçois specialities that grace the menu is the classic dish ratatouille. This vibrant stew with its five different vegetables may be simple, but there is a secret to making the perfect version.

In the narrow streets of Old Nice, where the towering buildings cast a shadowy refuge from the hot Provençal sun, a warm welcome awaits at Restaurant Acchiardo. With its closely packed red-clothed tables and a well-stocked bar, the restaurant has been offering classic Niçois dishes since 1927. 'My great grandmother came from the Piémontaise [in Italy] on the other side of the mountains at the age of 16. She started working for an English family in Nice, as a servant, and little by little she learned to cook,' explains Raphaël, the fourth generation to run the restaurant. 'Then in 1927 she opened a restaurant with her daughter-in-law, and it became the place to be for Italian immigrants in Nice.'

The restaurant is now run by Raphaël, his parents Joseph and Evelyne, his brother Jean-François and sister Virginie, who has always loved the friendly atmosphere: 'People come in, sit down next to each other and, to start with, they don't talk to each other, but by the end of the meal they're chatting away and exchanging phone numbers,' she says.

The first records mentioning ratatouille date from the 1930s, and it has pride of place on most traditional restaurant menus in Nice. Its name is related to the French word *touiller*, which means to 'stir up' but the question of when to stir together the five different vegetables is crucial to the final flavour. 'You have to cook each vegetable separately, which allows you to have the taste of each element. At home, if you cook it all together, all the vegetables mix up and come out as one taste,' says Raphaël. The result is a fresh, juicy concoction that is greater than the sum of its parts; each vegetable having been drenched in Mediterranean sunshine before being stirred together in one great big pot at the end. In some ways, it's a fine metaphor for the clients at Restaurant Acchiardo: they arrive as individuals and leave as one big happy family.

Chef //
Virginie Acchiardo &
Gianluca Toselli
Location //
Restaurant Acchiardo, Nice

RATATOUILLE
Ratatouille

Serves 10–12
Preparation and cooking time:
2hr 30min

5 tomatoes
5 white onions
3 yellow peppers
3 red peppers
5 courgettes/zucchinis
5 aubergines/eggplants
2 tbsp olive oil
1 head of garlic
salt, to taste
200g (7oz) crushed tinned tomatoes
pepper, to taste
10 basil leaves

1 Cut the fresh tomatoes into cubes and set this fruit aside until step 5.

2 Chop all the vegetables into cubes and keep them separate from one another.

3 In separate pans, or one ingredient at a time, fry the vegetables in 1 tbsp olive oil with one whole clove of garlic in each pan, season with salt and keep tossing until they are cooked but not too soft. For the aubergines/eggplants, fry on a high heat so it doesn't become a sponge for the oil.

4 When each vegetable is cooked, discard the garlic clove and place the vegetables in a colander to drain off the oil.

5 In a large pot, put in 1 tbsp olive oil, the remaining garlic, crushed tomatoes, fresh tomatoes, salt and pepper, to taste. Fold together with the cooked vegatables and heat through. Lift out and discard the garlic cloves, then heat for a further 10 minutes. Sprinkle on the basil and serve the dish as an accompaniment to meat or fish.

'My great-grandmother walked here over the mountains from Italy in bare feet, so as not to damage her shoes, then when she arrived in Nice to meet her new boss, she put them back on.'

Raphaël Acchiardo

Tip
Not everyone has enough pans to cook all the vegetables at the same time, so two pans will do. The vegetable that takes longest to cook is the aubergine/ eggplant, and the shortest is the courgette/zucchini, so use one pan for the onions followed by the peppers, and the other for the aubergines/eggplants followed by the courgettes/zucchini.

SAUTÉ DE SANGLIER À LA CHÂTAIGNE

Wild boar stew with chestnuts

Autumn is the perfect time to venture inland from St-Tropez to Collobrières in the Massif des Maures, where chef Michel Mattei takes pride in cooking the village's famous chestnuts in a delicious stew that has echoes of the area's centuries-old cuisine.

Just an hour from the chic harbour town of St-Tropez, the dense forests of the Massif des Maures tell a different story of Provence. Here among the ancient chestnut trees, where wild boar and deer roam, the village of Collobrières seems not to have changed for years, decades, even centuries. The chestnut trees were first planted here in the 10th century by an order of monks, who resided here at the Chartreuse de la Verne, subsisting on chestnuts and game for some 600 years (before the French Revolution ousted them).

While life around this rustic oasis has moved on, the diet hasn't much changed in all that time and the wild boar still seem to rule the roost. 'They eat everything, even the best chestnuts – they know how to find them and they leave the bad ones,' says Michel Mattei, chef-owner of Clos du Père Louis restaurant, which is just outside the village. The boar do offer up a robust meat, however, that Michel uses in a delicious yet simple stew. 'You have to stew it for two hours. It can be a tough meat – after all, they run around all day long,' says Michel.

The stew brings together the *sanglier* (boar), with the aromatic spices of cloves and juniper berries, all covered in a light Riesling. The final touch – unsurprisingly – comes from the local chestnuts, which are incorporated towards the end. It's just one of the ways these glossy brown jewels are used. At the annual Fête de la Châtaigne, the chestnuts are showcased in all their guises: liqueurs, beer, cakes, bread, pancakes, biscuits and ice cream are all made with the local harvest, while the pride of the town are the sweet *marrons glacés*, conserved in syrup for up to 10 years. It's all served to the thousands of visitors who descend on the village for the festival each October, packing onto the long refectory tables to enjoy an altogether rustic side of Provence.

Chef //
Michel Mattei
Location //
Le Clos du Père Louis,
Collobrières

SAUTÉ DE SANGLIER À LA CHÂTAIGNE

Wild boar stew with chestnuts

Serves 8

Preparation and cooking time:
  3hr 30min (not including 1hr
  refrigeration time)

For the puréed chestnuts & polenta
500ml (17½fl oz) water
45g (1½oz) fine polenta grains
45g (1½oz) medium polenta grains
50g (1¾oz) butter
200g (7oz) chestnut purée

For the wild boar stew
4 shallots, finely chopped
4 onions, finely chopped
4 or 5 cloves of garlic, finely chopped
2 pinches of salt
freshly ground pepper, to taste
1 pinch of ground cloves
3 pinches of ground juniper berries
2 bay leaves
1 sprig of thyme
1 tbsp sunflower oil
2kg (4½lb) wild boar, diced (see Tip)
750ml (1⅓pt) Riesling wine
250g (8¾oz) blanched chestnuts

1 To make the puréed chestnuts and polenta, bring the water to the boil in a saucepan, then whisk in the polenta grains until the mixture starts to thicken. Cover the pan and leave to simmer on low heat for 45 minutes.

2 Add the butter to the polenta and mix through.

3 Remove approximately a quarter of the cooked polenta mixture from the saucepan and blend it with the chestnut purée until very smooth.

4 In a loaf tin, spoon in the remaining three-quarters of the cooked polenta and smooth it down to form a base layer. Spoon over the puréed chestnut and polenta mixture and smooth it down. Cover with clingfilm/plastic wrap and leave in the fridge to cool for at least an hour.

5 For the wild boar stew, in a heavy-based saucepan or casserole pot, fry the shallots, onion, garlic, salt, pepper, cloves, juniper berries, bay leaves and thyme in the sunflower oil until tender.

6 Add the pieces of wild boar and increase the heat, stirring until the meat changes colour.

7 Pour over the wine and leave, uncovered, to simmer for 10 minutes.

8 Reduce the heat, cover and leave to simmer for two hours.

9 Ten minutes before serving, add the blanched chestnuts to the pan.

10 Remove the puréed chestnuts and polenta from the fridge and turn it out of the loaf tin. Cut into 1½cm (⅔in) slices and microwave individually for 1½–2 minutes to serve alongside the stew.

Tip
You can use pork, or venison, or even beef in place of the wild boar.

BOUILLABAISSE
Provençal fish stew

In the vibrant city of Marseille, a vast array of fish, vegetables, spices and pastis all play a part in bouillabaisse, a rich soup served alongside a platter of Mediterranean fish. At Le Miramar, chef Michel Leydet upholds the restaurant's long tradition of serving the local speciality.

On the quayside of Le Vieux Port, the fish market is in full swing. Under an azure sky, the freshly landed catch is set out for sale: fearsome monkfish, prickly anemones and still-crawling crustaceans, to name a few. In the harbour behind the stalls, yachts and motorboats all jostle for space in a scene that could be nowhere but Marseille.

Just a few steps away, in the kitchen of the Miramar restaurant, a similar array of fish is being prepared for the signature dish, bouillabaisse. 'This one's a conger,' says chef Michel Leydet, holding up an eel caught less than 12 hours before. 'It gives a great taste to the soup.' Along with the conger eel and a number of other more common Mediterranean fish, there are dozens of small fish in a rainbow of colours. 'Those are rockfish, we use them to make the stock and they give the flavour. In the old days, the fishermen couldn't sell them because they're too small, so their wives would use them at home to make a soup, and that's how bouillabaisse was born.'

Made with several vegetables, and the treasured spice saffron, the thick, piquant soup (served alongside the fish) is a meal in itself. 'The sailors were poor, so they needed a bit more substance. All those fish were too expensive, so they would just eat the soup with the potatoes and bread,' says Michel, as he places each fish into the huge bubbling pot. 'It's called bouillabaisse, because you bring it to the boil (*bouiller*) and then you turn it down (*baisser*).'

The restaurant is proud to have been making the city's famous fish stew for some 30 years, serving between 50 and 100 bouillabaisses a day. For the final touch comes another local speciality – pastis. Stirred in at the end, the anise-flavoured spirit brings added piquancy to the soup.

Chef //
Michel Leydet
Location //
Le Miramar, Marseille

BOUILLABAISSE
Provençal fish stew

Serves 10+ (see overleaf for quantities)

Preparation & cooking time: 2½hr

2 onions, thinly sliced
4 cloves garlic, crushed
250ml (8¾fl oz) olive oil
1 tbsp tomato purée
3 large tomatoes, cut into pieces
2kg (4½lb) rockfish (see Quote)
1 conger eel
1 head of fennel
250ml (8¾ fl oz) sunflower oil
1 tsp fennel seeds
1 tsp paprika
1 tsp chilli powder
4 pinches of saffron
water, for fish stock
salt, to taste
pepper, to taste
8 potatoes, peeled & sliced 2cm (¾in)
   thick
4 gurnards
4 weevers
2 John Dory fish
1 monkfish
2 capon fish (or red scorpion fish)
200ml (7fl oz) pastis

1 Brown the onions and garlic in a large saucepan with 3 tbsp of the olive oil.

2 Add 1 tbsp of tomato purée and the tomato pieces. Add the rockfish, the head and tail of the conger eel (reserve the body), the fennel, sunflower oil, fennel seeds, paprika, chilli powder and two pinches of the saffron, and fill up the pan with water (up to 4cm/1½in over the fish). Add salt and pepper and cook, covered, for 20 minutes..

3 Blend the fish soup, pass it through a sieve and cook, uncovered, for an extra 10 minutes.

4 Add the sliced potatoes to the fish soup.

5 Cut up the fish into large pieces, place it into the soup starting with the largest first (the body of the conger eel) down to the smallest.

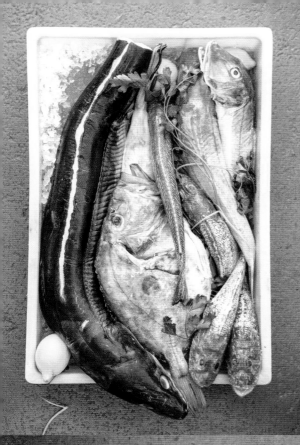

For the rouille (spicy Provençal sauce)

3 egg yolks

½ tsp salt

4 cloves garlic, crushed, plus extra for rubbing bread

1–2 tbsp olive oil, plus 2 tbsp to soak bread

1 baguette, to serve

'If you're making it at home, you don't need so much fish, just the monkfish and maybe a few others. If you don't have one, replace it with another. The important thing is that it's a fish with firm flesh [which won't fall apart].'

Michel Leydet

6 Check the seasoning; add more salt or pepper as desired. Add a pinch of the saffron, bring to the boil for five minutes then lower the heat and cook, uncovered, for 30 minutes.

7 Preheat the oven to 220°C (430°F).

8 To make the *rouille*, place three egg yolks in a food processor. Add the salt, crushed garlic and mix again, then, through the lid, drizzle with olive oil until it becomes thick and then add a final pinch of the saffron.

9 Slice the baguette into croutons (1cm/⅓in thick), rub with garlic and soak in 2 tbsp of olive oil. Put them in the hot oven until golden (approx five minutes). Then spread with the *rouille*.

10 Lift out the fish from the soup and place in a serving dish. Pass the soup through a sieve and, just before serving, whisk the pastis into the soup. Serve the soup, topped with the croutons, in small tureens, with the fish served separately.

TARTINE DE CAVIAR D'AUBERGINE

Aubergine & hazelnut dip on grilled aubergine

Across Provence, caviar d'aubergines is most often served as a dip with crudités, but Christophe Renaud uses fresh herbs and flowers from his kitchen garden to create a delectable version of the dish to serve at his restaurant in the heart of the Luberon.

Just a few steps from the kitchen at La Coquillade, the *potager* (small kitchen garden) is surrounded by the property's famous vineyards, and features a number of raised flower and vegetable beds that are known as *carrés* (squares). Each one offers a medley of produce that chef Christophe Renaud uses in his menu, in which each dish is described by using the vegetable as the key ingredient, accompanied by meat or fish.

'We create combinations that put value on the vegetables so as not to hide them. With meat, you turn it in a pan, or cut it into slices, or stew it for a long time and then it's done,' he shrugs. 'I love working with vegetables, they have so many different possibilities.' The aubergine (eggplant) is the perfect example; for his side dish or starter, tartine de caviar d'aubergine, Christophe uses the vegetable three different ways. 'Aubergines can be white, yellow, big, small, long or round, and this recipe works with all of them. I choose the aubergine de Florence because it has white flesh and very few seeds.'

Central to the dish is the caviar d'aubergines, a purée made by cutting the vegetable in half and baking it until the centre becomes sumptuously soft. Popular across Provence, it's usually served as a dip with raw vegetables, but Christophe mixes the aubergine purée with grilled hazelnuts, chives and olives to create an extravagant mixture that is placed on grilled slices of the large, round aubergine de Florence. In addition to this, he slices the garden's 5cm (2in)-long aubergines with a mandolin to create the delicate, transparent aubergine crisps, and then he sprinkles the whole dish with edible flowers. In many ways, the dish is the perfect tribute to the garden – tasty, pretty and, best of all, as fresh as the day it was picked.

Chef //
Christophe Renaud
Location //
Le Coquillade

TARTINE DE CAVIAR D'AUBERGINE

Aubergine & hazelnut dip on grilled aubergine

Serves 5

Preparation and cooking time:
1hr 30min (not including overnight refrigeration)

1kg (2¼lb) aubergines/eggplants
    (ideally aubergine de Florence)
olive oil, for painting aubergines
salt, to taste
3 pinches of piment d'Espelette
    (or paprika)
1 small bunch chives, finely chopped
100g (3½oz) sundried tomatoes, finely
    chopped
100g (3½oz) grilled hazelnuts, roughly
    chopped, plus extra to garnish
100g (3½oz) black olives (ideally
    Taggiasca variety), crushed, plus extra
    to garnish
100ml (3½fl oz) hazelnut oil
1 sprig of agastache flowers (nasturtiums
    can also be used), finely chopped, plus
    extra to garnish
fresh herbs (such as parsley and dill), to
    garnish

'The olive brings some saltiness and the grilled hazelnuts bring another taste and some texture. The flowers add a bit of pepper.'

Christophe Renaud

1 Preheat the oven to 180°C (360°F).

2 Wash the aubergines and, with one aubergine, cut five slices of about 1cm (⅓in) and set aside until step 7.

3 Cut the other aubergines in half lengthwise, then make an incision around 5mm–1cm (¼in–⅓in) from the edge without cutting all the way through. Score the interior in diagonal lines, and then again in the other direction to make a chequerboard pattern.

4 Use a pastry brush to season with olive oil, sprinkle with salt and a pinch of *piment d'Espelette* and bake in the oven for about 30 minutes.

5 Once they're cooked, scrape out the inside of the aubergines with a spoon into a bowl and leave this mixture overnight in the fridge.

6 Remove the bowl of aubergines from the fridge and add the chives, sundried tomatoes, hazelnuts and crushed olives, and stir with a fork. Add the hazelnut oil, salt, a pinch of *piment d'Espelette* and agastache flowers to make the Caviar d'Aubergines.

7 Rub the slices of aubergine from step 2 with olive oil, salt and a pinch of *piment d'Espelette*, and then grill them until golden. Then place them in the oven on a rack over a baking tray and bake for 10 minutes in a medium oven to drain the oil. They should be fairly thin and crispy. Leave them to cool.

8 To serve, place the aubergine slices on plates, and top with the Caviar d'Aubergines. Sprinkle with toasted hazelnuts, a few chopped olives, sprigs of agastache and other fresh herbs.

TARTIFLETTE
Reblochon, bacon & potato gratin

This warming dish of potatoes, cheese, cream and bacon, enjoyed all over the Alps, is a favourite among locals and visitors. Made with reblochon cheese, which originates in the Aravis mountain range, tartiflette is served by chef Gisèle Angelloz-Pessey at her cosy Alpine restaurant in Le Grand-Bornand.

After a few chilly hours on the ski slopes, or a breathtaking hike up a mountain, there's nothing quite like the unctuous tartiflette to restore the energy levels. This creamy, oven-baked dish, layered with potato, onion and bacon, is food for the soul. Its key ingredient is the pungent, semi-soft reblochon cheese, mixed into the sauce and layered on top to provide a bubbling, orange crown.

Although tartiflette itself is a fairly recent invention, the reblochon cheese – for which tartiflette was invented in the 1980s – dates from centuries ago, as chef Gisèle Angelloz-Pessey explains: 'Tartiflette is based on another dish called *péla*, which was cooked in a frying pan. The reblochon was invented here in the Aravis mountains in the 13th century when the *seigneur* [the lord or landed gentry] would come to collect the milk from the locals. The farmers wouldn't take all the milk from the cow, and when the *seigneur* had gone away, they'd finish milking it and have some milk of their own. Then they'd make it into cheese almost straight away, to preserve it. In old French, *blocher* means to milk, so *reblocher* means do it again. That's how it was born.'

High above the resort of Le Grand-Bornand in the cosy wooden rooms of Gisèle's restaurant, which she runs with her two sons and husband, it's easy to see how tartiflette is the perfect remedy for rosy-cheeked skiers in winter, and a hearty meal for hikers for the rest of the year. Once inside, the wood-burning stoves, antique skis and rustic furniture give you the sense that things haven't changed for years. Indeed, the chalet itself dates from 1796, becoming a restaurant in 2009 after being the family's weekend getaway for decades before. Through the windows, diners can admire the stunning Aravis mountain range, the perfect view to accompany a dish that was born in the very same place.

Chef //
Gisèle Angelloz-Pessey
Location //
Auberge du Croix, Le Grand-Bornand

TARTIFLETTE

Reblochon, bacon & potato gratin

Serves 4

**Preparation and cooking time:
1hr 15min**

1kg (2¼lb) Charlotte/Amandine
    potatoes
2 onions
olive oil, for frying
200g (7oz) lardons/chopped bacon
450g (1lb)/1 wheel reblochon cheese
250ml (8¾fl oz) liquid cream, plus
    extra if needed

1 Preheat the oven to 180°C (350°F).

2 Peel and steam the whole potatoes until tender.

3 Chop the onions and fry them in a pan of olive oil with the lardons until well browned, or even slightly burned. Add more olive oil if it sticks to the pan.

4 Cut off the cheese's rind, and then cut half of it into slices (approx 3–5mm or up to ¼in thick) to cover the final dish, and then cut the remaining half into 2cm (¾in) cubes.

5 Pour the cream into the pan with the onions and lardons. Add the cubed cheese to the pan and stir until the cheese melts.

6 Slice the potatoes and arrange them in a separate dish, then pour the warm cheese and lardon mixture over the potatoes.

7 Arrange the slices of cheese on top of the dish and then bake for 30–40 minutes in the oven. Add more cream if the dish starts to dry up. Serve straight from the oven.

FONDUE DE BEAUFORT
Beaufort cheese fondue

This pot of melted cheese, into which everyone at the table dips a chunk of bread, makes fondue the ultimate communal meal. It's a staple dish throughout the Alps, with its origins in Switzerland, and the mountain restaurant Chez Pépé Nicolas makes sure its fondue is a truly Savoyard experience.

Chef //
Martial Vuillemin
Location //
Chez Pépé Nicolas, Saint-Martin-de-Belleville

Surrounded on all sides by snowy mountains, Chez Pépé Nicolas is a little oasis of bonhomie. Perched between the resorts of Val Thorens, Les Menuires and Saint-Martin-de-Belleville, the lively restaurant was once a remote cabin, where owner Thierry Suchet's grandfather, Nicolas Jay, would bring his animals to graze on the higher pastures during the summer months. In the mid-1980s, Nicolas' grandsons Thierry, Bruno and Eric opened a little bar and eatery on the premises, which steadily grew in reputation. When a ski lift was installed nearby in 2014, and a ski run added in 2015, the chalet restaurant grew to be one of the most popular in Les Trois Vallées (The Three Valleys).

At the heart of the menu is the most famous Alpine dish of them all – fondue – for which chef Martial Vuillemin insists on using the local cheese, Beaufort, created by a cooperative at the bottom of the valley. 'Other chalets use Comté or Gruyère, or a mixture. For Beaufort, they use special wooden hoops to make it, the outside edge is a concave. The taste of the cheese changes according to the season; for fondue the winter cheese is better than the summer Beaufort. In the winter, the cows are eating hay, which makes the cheese fruitier than the summer cheese, when the cows are eating flowers,' Martial explains.

The cheese is heated in a *caquelon* (an enamel pot heated over a small stove), and mixed with dry white wine for added flavour, and potato starch to make sure it doesn't separate. Once the cheese is melted, chunks of bread are dipped in with long forks. Tradition dictates that anyone who drops their bread in the cheese will be issued a forfeit, as owner Thierry explains. 'Each table tends to decide the penalty: it could be to take off a piece of clothing, act the clown, have a drink or sing a song... there are lots!'

FONDUE DE BEAUFORT
Beaufort cheese fondue

Serves 4

Preparation and cooking time:
10–30min

880g (31oz) Beaufort cheese
400ml (14fl oz) dry white wine
20g (¾oz) potato starch
2 baguettes of crusty bread
green salad, to serve
balsamic vinegar, to serve

1 Grate the cheese finely and place in the *caquelon.*

2 Pour the wine over the cheese and then add the potato starch.

3 Cut the bread into cubes.

4 Ten minutes before ready to serve, place the *caquelon* on the hob/hot plate on a medium heat and keep stirring with a wooden spoon. When the cheese has melted, bring to the boil for one minute, then transfer to the gas stove to serve for continual heat.

5 Serve with a green salad drizzled with balsamic vinegar.

*'When there's not much cheese
left, you can crack an egg into the
caquelon and it makes something
like a cheese omelette.*

Martial Vuillemin

TARTE AU CITRON
Lemon tart

*Menton is known
for its lemons,
thanks to its
annual Fête du
Citron, when
thousands of citrus
fruits adorn floats,
sculptures and
decorations all
over town. At Le
Petit Port, Nicole
Lardello uses the
fruit in her tarte
au citron, which
is adored by locals
and visitors alike.*

Chef //
Nicole Lardello
Location //
Le Petit Port, Menton

The striking thing about the tarte au citron at the tiny restaurant Le Petit Port is its size. Layered with sweet pastry, a simultaneously sharp and sweet lemon filling, and then piles of cloud-like meringue on top, it's enormous. Its creator, Nicole Lardello, believes there should be no short measures. 'It's not a criticism, but in other restaurants the tarte au citron is hardly anything, and that's why I think people come here. I just make a tarte, and I'm not thinking about the costs or whether it's too expensive to make, I just serve what is the right amount. The meringue isn't traditional, but people like it.'

The tarte is one of many desserts that Nicole makes for the century-old restaurant, which she runs with her charismatic brother Gaby and his wife Lisa. 'It's a very old restaurant, the water used to come up to the front, that's why it's called Le Petit Port. We have lots of regulars. It's a family restaurant, people feel at home here,' she says. The last stop before you cross the border, Menton has a decidedly Italian air about it, with a rambling maze of yellow and orange houses piled up next to the sea. There are a number of tropical gardens found around the town, so it's no surprise that citrus fruits grow well here and local lemons are the pride of the town.

'There's a big difference between Menton lemons and other lemons. The smell is special and you can even eat the skin,' says Nicole. 'There are lemon groves all around town in the gardens. My cousin has one, my neighbour does too.' The fruit is celebrated every February at the spectacular Fête du Citron, which takes over the town for two weeks and features about 145 tonnes of fruit being turned into enormous sculptures, carnival floats and decorations. 'So much work goes into it, it's magnificent,' says Nicole.

TARTE AU CITRON
Lemon tart

Serves 8–10

Preparation and cooking time:
2hr 15min (not including 1hr
refrigeration time)

For the pastry

500g (1lb) flour, plus extra for rolling
  pastry
200g (7oz) caster sugar
250g (9oz) unsalted melted butter
2 tbsp olive oil
5 egg yolks

For the filling

1L (1¾pt) milk
8 egg yolks
280g (10oz) sugar
4 tbsp cornflour
zest & juice of 4 lemons

For the meringue topping

8 egg whites
100g (3½oz) sugar

1 Preheat the oven to 180°C (350°F).

2 To make the pastry base, place the flour, sugar and butter in a food processor or mixer and blend until it forms breadcrumbs. Add the oil and egg yolks and blend again until it forms a ball of dough.

3 Roll the dough out on a lightly floured surface with a rolling pin, then press it into a 30cm (12in) tart tin with your hand, and then prick with a fork. Bake in the oven for 20 minutes. Leave to cool.

4 In a saucepan, warm the milk and add the other filling ingredients, whisking the mixture until it thickens. Pour into the cold pastry case and smooth with a spatula. Leave to cool in the fridge for an hour.

5 Prior to serving, make the meringue topping by whisking the egg whites with the sugar until they stand in firm peaks.

6 Smooth the meringue onto the tart with a palette knife, giving it a wave-like texture. Then, with a kitchen torch, brown the edges. Alternatively, place under a hot grill until the meringue starts to brown.

'My uncle was a top chef at the Hôtel de Paris [in Monaco] during the 1950s. I was always with him when I was little. It's him who made me want to cook. It's not a "job" for me, it's a passion.'

Nicole Lardello

CRÊPES SUZETTE

Flambéed crêpes with orange butter sauce

The iconic dessert crêpes suzette was invented by chance in 1895 at Monte Carlo's Café de Paris. More than 120 years later, it is still the restaurant's signature dish, with its sweet crepes flambéed via a heady dose of Grand Marnier next to diners' tables.

The creation of crêpes suzette goes down in history as one of French gastronomy's most famous tales. The most popular story goes that in 1895, the Prince of Wales – the future King Edward VII of England – was dining at the Café de Paris in Monte Carlo, Monaco, but things didn't go to plan, as the restaurant's current head chef Franck Lafon explains: 'The chef wanted to create a special dessert, but when he poured the alcohol into the pan, it burst into flames. The Prince really liked it and asked what the dessert was called. The chef quickly created a name and said, "Princely crêpes." The Prince said, "No, that won't do," and as he was there with his *copine* [girlfriend], he said, "We'll call them Crêpes Suzette." And from then on, that's what the dish was called.'

Other stories about the dessert's origins, and the identity of Suzette, do exist but Franck asserts that the best-known is from the Café de Paris. While exact details of the story have been lost in time, it's unlikely that Suzette – whoever she was – would have expected the dessert to still be so popular more than 100 years later. But the Café de Paris is dedicated to recreating the spectacle of its creation with the use of a special trolley that harmonises perfectly with the restaurant's belle époque decor, which features stained-glass panels and cosy booths with brass fixtures and fittings. 'We prepare the crêpes and other ingredients in the kitchen, but it's always flambéed by the waiter. People see it being done on the next table and ask for it. Lots of places don't prepare it in front of the clients, because it takes a lot of time and you need space,' he says. 'The secret is to have good products: good oranges, Grand Marnier (nothing else) and good butter. You can't do a "light" version!'

Chef //
Franck Lafon
Location //
Café de Paris, Monte Carlo

CRÊPES SUZETTE
Flambéed crêpes with orange butter sauce

Serves 4

Preparation and cooking time: 1hr 30min

1 orange
1 lemon
150g (5¼oz) flour
2g (¾oz) finely ground salt
150g (5¼oz) sugar
4 eggs
1 vanilla bean
30ml (1fl oz) curaçao liqueur
500ml (17½fl oz) milk
50g (1¾oz) butter + 100g (3½oz) butter
8 sugar cubes
100ml (3½fl oz) orange juice
50ml (1¾fl oz) lemon juice
30ml (1fl oz) cognac
100ml (3½fl oz) Grand Marnier
sprinkle of sugar, to serve

1 Grate the zest from half the orange and half the lemon, juice the flesh and set the juice aside. Reserve the remaining peel.

2 In a bowl, mix the flour, salt, sugar, eggs, vanilla, curaçao and milk. Sprinkle with a pinch of the orange and lemon zest, and then whisk the batter until it is smooth.

3 Pour the mixture through a conical sieve into another bowl to eliminate lumps, then let the batter rest for 1 hour.

4 Melt the 50g of butter in a small to medium-sized pan and cook until it is golden brown, then pour in a ladleful of batter, turning the pan until the batter covers the base. Cook for 30 seconds on each side until lightly golden brown. Repeat with the remainder of the batter, then set the crêpes aside.

5 Rub sugar cubes on the remaining orange and lemon peel.

6 Melt the 100g of butter and sugar cubes in a pan to create a caramel, then pour in the lemon juice and orange juice and another teaspoon of orange zest.

7 Place the crêpes in the juice in the pan and soak, then fold the crepes into quarters. Add cognac and Grand Marnier to the pan.

8 Flambée and sprinkle with sugar before serving.

RECIPE SOURCES

NORTHERN FRANCE

1 **Loïc le Bail**, Hôtel Brittany, Blvd Sainte-Barbe, Roscoff (pp10–13) www. hotel-brittany.com +33 298 69 70 78

2 **Gaël Ruscart**, L'Insolite, Hôtel de France, 4 rue Jean Jaurès, Douarnenez (pp14–17) www.lafrance.dz.com +33 298 92 00 02

3 **Charles-Henry de Valbray**, Château de Saint Paterne, 4 rue de la Gaieté, Saint Paterne (pp18–21) www.chateau-saintpaterne.com +33 233 27 54 71

4 **Régine Boidin**, Le Mirlibut, Étainhus, near Le Havre (pp22–5) www. chefchezvous76.com +33 612 42 15 26

5 **Mickaël Reydellet**, Boulangerie La Parisienne, 52 blvd Saint Germain, Paris (pp26–9) www.boulangerielaparisienne. com +33 143 54 48 72

6 **Laurent André**, Café de la Paix, 5 place de l'Opéra, Paris (pp30–33) www.cafedelapaix.fr +33 140 07 36 36

7 **Myriam Frances**, Crêperie Au Vieux Quimper, 20 rue Verdelet, Quimper (pp34–7) www.creperieauvieuxquimper. fr +33 298 91 31 34

8 **Anne Bourbeau**, Les Petits Matins Bleus (pp38–41) now closed

9 **Franck Quinton**, Le Manoir du Lys, Route de Juvigny, Bagnoles-de-l'Orne (pp42–5) www.manoir-de-lys.com +33 233 37 80 69

10 **Fabrice Gwizdak**, Maison Gwizdak, 19 rue Raugraff, Nancy (pp46–9) www.gwizdak.fr +33 383 32 12 30

11 **Jean-Pierre Hocquet**, Le Train Bleu, 1st floor, Gare de Lyon, Place Louis Armand, Paris (pp50–53) www.le-train-bleu.com +33 143 43 09 06

12 **Alain le Guillou**, Locronan (pp54–7) www.kouignamann-locronan.fr +33 298 91 70 04

13 **Freddy Pommier**, Hôtel du Tribunal, 4 place du Palais, Mortagne-au-Perche (pp58–61) www.hotel-tribunal.fr +33 233 25 04 77

14 **Jordan Fouchet**, Manoir de Surville, 82 rue Bernard Petel, Surville (pp62–5) www.manoirdesurville.com +33 761 61 44 55

15 **Julien & Masako Guérard**, Restaurant Pommeraie Vire, L'Auverre, Route de Flers, Roullours Vire (pp66–71) www.restaurant-pommeraie-vire.com +33 231 68 07 71

16 **Stéphane Zins**, La Boîte à Madeleines, La Louvière, Commercy (pp72–5) www.madeleines-zins.fr +33 329 91 40 86

17 **Pierre Saugrain**, Le Fontaine de Mars, 129 rue Saint-Dominique, Paris (pp76–81) www.fontainedemars.com +33 147 05 46 44

18 **Thomas Croizé**, Le Jules Verne, Restaurant Tour Eiffel, Avenue Gustave Eiffel, Paris (pp82–5) www.lejulesverne-paris.com

19 **Magesh Arumugam**, Les Deux Magots, 6 place Saint-Germain-des-Prés, Paris (pp86–9) www.lesdeuxmagots.fr +33 145 48 55 25

CENTRAL FRANCE

20 **Armelle Krause**, Le Clos aux Roses, 2 rue du Lavoir, Chédigny (pp92–5) www. leclosauxroses.com +33 247 92 20 29

21 **Yacinthe de Geyer**, Château de la Bourdaisière, 25 rue de la Bourdaisière, Montlouis-sur-Mer (pp96–9) www. labourdaisiere.com +33 247 45 16 31

22 **Christophe Hay**, La Maison d'à Côté, 17 rue de Chambord, Montlivault (pp100–103) www.lamaisondacote.fr +33 254 20 62 30

23 **Luc Filoé**, Le Montrachet, 10 place du Pasquier de la Fontaine, Puligny-Montrachet (pp104–107) www.le-montrachet.com +33 380 21 30 06

24 **Gilles Bérard**, Ma Table en Ville, 50 rue de Strasbourg, Mâcon (pp108–11) www.matableenville.fr +33 385 30 99 91

25 **Roland Chanliaud**, La Maison du Colombier, 1 rue Charles Cloutier, Beaune (pp112–5) www.maisonducolombier.com +33 380 26 16 26

26 **Hedwige de Valbray**, Château des Briottières, Champigné (pp116–9) www.briottieres.com +33 241 42 00 02

27 **Stéphane & Nathalie Oudot**, La Cimentelle, 4 rue de la Cimentelle, Vassy-les-Avallon (pp120–3) www.lacimentelle.com +33 386 31 04 85

28 **Cécile Riotte**, Le Vaudésir, 84 rue de Lyon, Avallon (pp124–7) www.restaurant-levaudesir.com +33 386 34 14 60

29 **Lionel Freitas**, Olivier Leflaive, 10 place du Monument, Puligny-Montrachet (pp128–31) www.olivier-leflaive.com +33 380 21 37 65

30 **Marie-Eugénie Dupuy**, La Ferme de Marie-Eugénie, 225 allée de Chardenoux, Bruailles (pp132–5) bnb.lafermedemarieeugenie.fr +33 385 74 81 84

31 **Flavien Ferrand & Christiane Mason**, Maison Bigot, 2 rue Nationale, Amboise (pp136–9) +33 247 57 04 46

32 **Jean-Paul Cousin-Martin**, Les Lichonneux de Tarte Tatin, Lamotte-Beuvron (pp140–43) stephanevaladou.wixsite.com

33 David Gasnier, Anjou Golf & Country Club, Rue Normandie Niémen, Champigné (pp144–7) www.anjou-golf. com +33 241 42 01 01

34 Franck Houdebine, Domaine du Moulin Cavier, Le Croix Cadeau, Avrillé (pp148–51) www.hotelmoulincavier.com +33 241 42 30 45

35 Franck Dépériers, La Petite Boulangerie, 1 place Saint-Félix, Nantes (pp152–5) www.lapetiteboulangerie.fr +33 240 74 36 38

36 Stephanie Moreau, Moulin des Ruats, 23 rue des Iles Labaumes, Vallée du Cousin, Avallon (pp156–9) www. moulindesruats.com +33 386 34 97 00

37 Guillaume Royer, Abbaye de la Bussière, Route Départmentale 33, La Bussière-sur-Ouche (pp160–63) www. abbayedelabussiere.fr +33 380 49 02 29

SOUTHWEST FRANCE

38 Vincent Arnould, Le Vieux Logis, Trémolat (pp166–8) www.vieux-logis. com +33 553 22 80 06

39 Stéphane Andrieux, Château de la Treyne, La Treyne, Lacave (pp170–75) www.chateaudelatreyne.com +33 565 27 60 60

40 Nicolas Magie, Le Saint-James, 3 place Camille Hostein, Bouliac (pp176–9) www.saintjames-bouliac.com +33 557 97 06 00

41 Bruno Grand-Clément, Hôtel de la Plage, l'Herbe le Canon, Lège-Cap-Ferret (pp180–83) www.hoteldelaplage-cap-ferret.fr +33 556 60 50 15

42 David Arruabarrena, La Tantina de Burgos, 2 place Beaurivage, Biarritz (pp184–7) +33 559 23 24 47

43 Michel Guérard, Les Prés d'Eugénie, Eugénie-les-Bains (pp188–93) www. michelguerard.com +33 558 05 06 07

44 Alain Lacoste*, Le Colombier, 14 rue Bayard, Toulouse (pp194–9) www.restaurant-lecolombier.com +33 561 62 40 05

45 Anne France, Château de la Grèze, Brivezac, near Beaulieu-sur-Dordogne (pp200–203) www.chateaudelagreze. com +33 555 91 08 68

46 Marie-Claude Castagné, Moulin à Huile de Noix, Route de Saint-Céré (pp204–207) www.moulin-martel.com +33 565 37 40 69

47 Sébastien Antoine, La Terrasse Rouge, 1 château la Dominique, Saint-Emilion (pp208–11) www. laterrasserouge.com +33 557 24 47 05

48 Flavie Coutin, Miremont, 1bis, Place Clémenceau, Biarritz (pp212–7) www. miremont-biarritz.fr +33 559 24 01 38

SOUTHEAST FRANCE

49 Florence Périer, Le Café du Peintre, 50 boulevard des Brotteaux, Lyon (pp220–23) www.lecafedupeintre.com +33 478 52 52 61

50 Sophie Agrofoglio, A Buteghinn'a, 11 rue du Marché, Nice (pp224–7) www.abuteghinna.fr +33 493 92 28 22

51 Steeve Bernardo, Chez Pipo, 13 rue Bavastro, Nice (pp228–31) www.chezpipo.fr + 33 493 55 88 82

52 Jo Issautier, Lou Balico, 20/22 avenue Saint-Jean-Baptiste, Nice (pp232–5) www.loubalico.com +33 493 85 93 71

53 René Bérard, Bastide des Saveurs, Hostellerie Bérard, 6 avenue Gabriel Peri, La Cadière-d'Azur (pp236–9) www.hotel-berard.com +33 494 90 11 43

54 Thierry Crovara, Hôtel La Mas des Grès, Four à Chaux-Isle sur Sorgue (pp240–3) www.masdesgres.com +33 490 20 32 85

55 Joseph Viola, Daniel et Denise, 156 rue de Créqui, Lyon (pp244–9) www.danieletdenise.fr +33 478 60 66 53

56 Virginie Acchiardo & Gianluca Toselli, Restaurant Acchiardo, 38 rue Droite, Nice (pp250–53) +33 493 85 51 16

57 Michel Mattei, Le Clos du Père Louis, Quartier des Bonnaux, Collobrières (pp254–7) www. leclosduperelouis.com +33 494 48 04 21

58 Michel Leydet, Le Miramar, 12 quai du Port, Marseille (pp258–63) www.lemiramar.fr +33 491 91 10 40

59 Christophe Renaud, La Coquillade, Le Perrotet, Gargas (pp264–7) www.coquillade.fr +33 490 74 71 71

60 Gisèle Angelloz-Pessey, Auberge du Croix, 1 582 Le Croix, Le Grand Bornand (pp268–71) www.aubergeducroix.com +33 450 68 62 84

61 Martial Vuillemin, Chez Pépé Nicolas, Saint-Martin-de-Belleville (pp272–5) www.chezpepenicolas.com +33 609 45 28 35

62 Nicole Lardello, Le Petit Port, 4 rue Jonquier, Menton (pp276–9) +33 493 35 82 62

63 Franck Lafon, Café de Paris, Place du Casino, Monte Carlo (pp280–83) www. montecarlosbm.com +377 98 06 76 23

* Since the time of writing, chef Alain Lacoste has passed away. We include his recipe for cassoulet here with the kind permission of his widow Françoise.

INDEX

Published in August 2017 by Lonely Planet Global Limited
CRN 554153
www.lonelyplanet.com
ISBN 978 17865 7794 8
© Lonely Planet 2017
Printed in China   10 9 8 7 6 5 4 3 2 1
Written by Carolyn Boyd
Photographed by River Thompson

Managing Director, Publishing Piers Pickard
Associate Publisher & Commissioning Editor Robin Barton
Art Direction Daniel Di Paolo
Layout Designer Mariana Sameiro
Illustrator Louise Sheeran
Copyeditor Karyn Noble
Cartographers Julie Dodkins, Wayne Murphy
Print Production Larissa Frost, Nigel Longuet

River Thompson is a food and travel photographer based in London and France: www.riverthompson.co.uk

Carolyn Boyd is a freelance writer, specialising in French travel, gastronomy and culture. She was editor of the *FRANCE* Magazine between 2006 and 2016. Visit carolynboyd.net and follow her on Twitter @carolynboyd and Instagram @carolyncboyd.

From Carolyn: The biggest thank you goes to my husband Toby, and my parents Helen and Ian, and my in-laws Carolyn and Keith who held the family fort during my many dashes to France. A heartfelt thank-you to all the chefs, cooks, bakers and proprietors who gave up their time to help with the project. Thank you to the many tourist offices who helped us, in particular Alison Weatherhead at Normandy Tourism (normandie-tourisme.fr). Also: Loire Valley (valdeloire-france.com), Pays de la Loire (enpaysdelaloire.com), Nantes (lvan.fr), Lorraine (tourisme-lorraine.fr), Meuse (tourisme-meuse.com), Burgundy (burgundy-tourism.com), Biarritz (www.tourisme.biarritz.fr), Aquitaine (tourisme-aquitaine.fr), Provence Côte d'Azur (tourismepaca.fr), Nice (nicetourisme.com), Var (visitvar.fr), Savoie Mont-Blanc and Les Aravis (savoie-mont-blanc.com), Lyon (lyon-france.com), Corrèze (tourismecorreze.com). Also to Brittany Ferries (brittanyferries.com) and Voyages SNCF (voyages-sncf.com). I'd also like to thank the following for their hospitality: Châteaux et Hotels Collection (chateauxhotels.co.uk), Sawdays (sawdays.co.uk), Hôtel Brittany (hotel-brittany.com), Château des Briottières (briottieres.com), Château de Chenevière (lacheneviere.com), Roxanna McDonald in Chédigny (loire-chateau.fr), Château de la Treyne (chateaudelatreyne.com), Le Vieux Logis (vieux-logis.com), Les Pres d'Eugenie (michelguerard.com), La Coquillade (coquillade.fr), L'Hostellerie Bérard (hotel-berard.com), Relais 12 Bis (relais12bis.com) and Sally Lecky-Thompson. I'm grateful to editor Karyn Noble for her patience, good humour and fantastic support.

Lonely Planet offices

AUSTRALIA
The Malt Store, Level 3, 551 Swanston Street,
Carlton VIC, 3053 Australia
Phone 03 8379 8000

UNITED KINGDOM
240 Blackfriars Road, London SE1 8NW
Phone 020 3771 5100

STAY IN TOUCH lonelyplanet.com/contact

USA
124 Linden St, Oakland, CA 94607
Phone 510 250 6400

IRELAND
Unit E, Digital Court, The Digital Hub, Rainsford St,
Dublin 8, Ireland

Paper in this book is certified against the Forest Stewardship Council™ standards. FSC™ promotes environmentally responsible, socially beneficial and economically viable management of the world's forests.

TECHNIQUES IN HUMAN GEOGRAPHY

PETER TOYNE
Lecturer in Geography,
University of Exeter

and

PETER T. NEWBY
Lecturer in Geography,
Middlesex Polytechnic

Macmillan Education

First published 1971
Reprinted with corrections 1972
Reprinted 1974, 1976
Published by
MACMILLAN EDUCATION LTD
Houndmills Basingstoke Hampshire RG21 2XS
and London
Associated companies in New York Dublin
Melbourne Johannesburg and Delhi

Printed in Great Britain by
BUTLER AND TANNER LTD
Frome and London

DuH
T

copy 4

Acknowledgements

The publisher and authors would like to
thank Robert Turner, Rodney Fry and Pat
Gregory for drawing the diagrams, Andrew
Teed for providing most of the photographs,
Meridian Airmaps Ltd for permission to
use Fig. 1.3, Aerofilms Ltd for per-
mission to use Fig. 1.5, the Institute of
British Geographers for permission to use
Fig. 3.39, and Messrs Nelson Ltd for
permission to use Figs. 3.28 and 3.36.

Contents

Introduction

'A mighty maze, but not without a plan.'
Pope: *Essay on Man*

Geography has always been primarily concerned with location — the one aspect of human and economic activity which other cognate disciplines have tended, very largely, to ignore. At first sight, the location of human and economic activity may well appear to present just as mighty a maze to the geographer as man's life did to Pope, but just as the writer was able to discern some semblance of order in life, so the geographer has increasingly been able to discover a certain degree of order in location.

The search for such order has, however, only been made possible by a change in approach to the subject. The traditional viewpoint that geographical phenomena were unique, philosophically contradicted the view that similar locational patterns might be found in different areas, and led to voluminous descriptions of unique regions at the expense of the recognition of any similarities which they exhibited. It was not until the 1950s that the view of the uniqueness of geographical phenomena was seriously questioned and attention began to turn towards the recognition of pattern and order in the location of human activity.

However, it rapidly became apparent that if locational patterns were to be recognised with any degree of accuracy the former subjectivity of mere verbal description would need to be replaced by more precise and objective methods of measurement and analysis. The collection of appropriately quantified data thus became vital and, in turn, new techniques for the accurate processing and presentation of that data had to be adopted. The search for order was, therefore, accompanied by a 'quantitative revolution' in which the use of geographical techniques for the collection, processing and presentation of data became essential.

The collection of geographical data has always involved the use of both documentary sources and field surveys, but the recognition of the usefulness of sampling these data sources has been one of the most profitable developments in geographical techniques, as will be seen in Section 1 of this book.

One of the main difficulties caused by the quantitative revolution has been the necessity of processing data by statistical methods. Many geographers have met the prospect of using mathematical or statistical techniques with great alarm because it is difficult to imagine any subject other than mathematics more readily dropped at the earliest opportunity. Fortunately, however, although the ways in which data may be statistically processed are many and varied, most of them are relatively straightforward and demand only a very elementary ability for mathematics; as will be seen in Section 2, the methods by which summaries, comparisons and the significance of conclusions may be made from the data involve little more than clear thinking.

Diagrams and maps have always occupied a place of central importance in the visual presentation of geographical data. Indeed, many geographers have been nurtured on the idea that no study is really geographical unless it contains a map! Whilst this particular view may be debatable, the usefulness of diagrams and maps can hardly be denied and they are still the main technique by which geographical data is portrayed, as will be seen in Section 3.

As with all revolutions, the attempts to quantify and experiment with new analytical techniques have not been without their critics, many of whom felt that geographers were beginning to quantify just for the sake of it, and to lose sight of the ends to which these means were being applied. There can be little doubt, however, that despite its inevitable birth pangs the 'quantitative revolution' has not only opened up many new and exciting lines of enquiry, but has also renewed interest in many of the more central themes of human geography, as will be seen in Section 4. Many of the locational patterns which have been identified are readily recognisable at a local level and several topics can thus be pursued locally on a small yet highly rewarding scale. Some of the problems, difficulties and implications of the search for order can, in fact, best be learnt by attempting local analyses of locational characteristics. A number of such topics are suggested in connection with the locational studies reviewed in Section 4. These local studies use, in various combinations, the geographical data techniques outlined in the first three sections of the book and demonstrate some of the problems which arise in attempting to disentangle the locational maze of human and economic activity.

It will be seen that, despite all the obvious changes which have been introduced, the ultimate aims of geographical studies remain hardly altered: the description of the form of human and economic activity and its geographical variations is only made more accurate and reliable by the use of refined data techniques and the systematic search for order. To that extent, the old French dictum seems singularly pertinent:

Plus ça change, plus c'est la même chose.

1 Data Collection

In the final analysis no study can ever be more accurate or reliable than the data upon which it is based. It is important, therefore, that the data used in any study be collected by accurate methods from reliable sources and that it be as precise and detailed as the sources will allow. In geographical studies (as with most others) it is highly unlikely that the necessary data will be found in only one source; more often than not the relevant material has to be pieced together from several different sources whose reliability may vary considerably, with the result that the accuracy of the study may be diminished. Similarly, it is often necessary to base the study on only a sample of the phenomenon being investigated and, unless that sample is properly chosen, inaccurate conclusions may be drawn.

The basic data for any study may be collected either from various documents (Section 1A) or from first-hand surveys (Section 1B), but the reliability of either of these information sources is notoriously difficult to assess. In the case of documentary sources it is rare to find any direct reference to the accuracy of a particular document and there is the attendant temptation to imagine that once something appears in print it must be treated as correct. This is particularly true of statistical documents and inventories, many of which may be based on incomplete information in the first instance: thus, the published results of questionnaires often appear to be detailed and accurate but, unless the survey is a legally compulsory one, there is no guarantee that all the respondents will co-operate or that all the answers given are entirely correct.

When first-hand surveys are conducted, it is essential that the same attention to accuracy and reliability be paid, especially when samples are taken. If, for example, we were to make a study of the religious and political beliefs of a group of students, we could quite easily 'cook the books' to show

whatever we wished. Consider an extreme case: suppose there were 250 students to be sampled and we wished to show that religious heretics with conservative beliefs were not in such a minority as some people might think. If we were to include all the people known to be of this particular persuasion in our sample, and to survey relatively fewer other students, we could easily prove the point. Although this result would be nothing less than dishonest, it could be arrived at quite accidentally and unintentionally unless the data for sample studies is collected by properly defined procedures. It follows, therefore, that if a survey is to be accurate it must be based on truly representative information (Section 1C).

1A DOCUMENTARY SOURCES

Much of the data used by the human geographer is derived from documentary sources, though the information content of such documents varies considerably. Maps and aerial photographs, for example, potentially contain a great deal of data relating both to the physical and human landscape whereas the various statistical censuses, timetables and directories usually refer to more limited aspects of one particular phenomenon.

1A 1 Published Statistics
For many geographical studies, published statistics are often less useful than data collected from other sources because the information required for any particular study is not quite the same as that which has already been published. In addition, many of the published statistics are not available at a sufficiently small scale; it frequently happens in geographical studies that the published statistics refer to urban districts,

1

rural districts or parishes when detail is required about a suburb, village or farm. In such cases, the available data can only serve as a guide or adjunct to information collected elsewhere.

Most published statistics have been collected by official government departments, and Her Majesty's Stationery Office has published a series of *Guides to Official Sources* such as the population census, the census of production and all the various statistics on the labour force, local government, agriculture and food and social security. Several of these guides are particularly useful since they describe the statistics which are available from the past; thus, for example, *Guides to Official Sources No 6: Census of Production Reports* (HMSO, 1963) describes the census as it was carried out between 1907 and 1960.

Apart from these *Guides*, there has not been a short and comprehensive account of official statistical sources since a survey made in 1957 by Kendall. This survey is, however, useful since many of the sources referred to remain unchanged and, of course, it is a good guide to the sources which relate to the period preceding the late 1950s.

More up-to-date information on official sources may be found in *Government Publications* which comes out every year, and which contains a note of every document published by or on behalf of the Government. This information can be further supplemented by the quarterly publication *Statistical News,* in which details of future surveys and progress reports on current surveys can be found. A synopsis of documentary and statistical sources dealing with the social environment was, for example, contained in *Statistical News No 8* (Beltram, 1970).

1A 1a Population and housing statistics

The census of population is one of the more important sources of information for studies in human geography because of the wealth of detail which it contains. It is basically hierarchical in structure with the local information, for parishes in rural areas and for wards in urban areas, being grouped together successively to form county reports and national summary tables. Its value is also enhanced since it has been published every ten years since 1801 (with the exception of 1941 when there was no census owing to the war) thereby facilitating studies of the changing pattern of population.

Although the census is known as the 'Census of Population' its title is somewhat misleading because in addition to detailed population statistics *per se* it also contains a great deal of information on housing and household arrangements. Naturally, the content changes from time to time but, in general, the statistics on the population itself relate to its size, density, age, marital condition, birthplace and nationality, while the data on housing and households usually includes details of tenure, number of rooms and the availability of sanitary facilities.

Not all the information is available for the smallest census districts (parishes and wards) and this is often one of the major drawbacks of the census for local studies. In recent years at this scale, the number of persons (males and females counted separately) is given together with figures on the density of population (persons per acre), the number of private households and the population they contain, the number of structurally separate dwellings, the total number of rooms occupied and the average number of persons per room.

More detailed information on the age-sex structure of the population is given only for counties, local authority areas (county boroughs, municipal boroughs, urban districts, rural districts), conurbation centres and new towns. Similarly, a detailed analysis of the age-sex structure of the population under the age of 21 is given for these larger areas. The birthplaces and nationalities of the population are given only for counties, county boroughs, urban areas of 50 000 population or more, and new towns.

Similarly, most of the detailed information on housing is given only for the larger administrative areas. Thus, the number of people living in houses of different sizes, the number of people per room, and the number of buildings and households which have certain sanitary facilities (hot and cold water taps, fixed baths and water-closets) is given only for counties, local authority areas, conurbation centres and new towns. Yet more detailed analyses of certain aspects of dwelling structure and household tenure [the number of people living in owner-occupied, rented (furnished or unfurnished), or other accommodation] are available only for counties, conurbation centres, new towns and urban areas with a population of more than 50 000.

Other information is additionally available from the Registrar General who may provide unclassified material at a cost. It is possible, for example, to purchase data on migration within, into and out of Scotland based on the results of a sample census taken in 1966 and giving details of migrants by sex, age, marital status and socio-economic group. For more detailed information the cost rises proportionately, and data extraction only becomes feasible for industrial and commercial firms or research institutions.

The census does have its disadvantages, particularly relating to the lack of detailed information given at a very local level; in addition, several other problems arise from the lack of homogeneity in size and composition of the administrative units, the consequent incompatibility with socio-economic structures and the instability of administrative boundaries (Robertson, 1969).

In addition to the census of population, the Registrar-General also publishes detailed statistics on certain specific aspects of the population: the *Quarterly Returns* are published four times a year, the *Statistical Review for England and Wales* once a year, and the *Decennial Supplement* every ten years. All three give details of mortality and birth statistics by sex, age and area, though the *Quarterly Returns* tend to give special reports such as the mortality tables for Greater London and the infant mortality tables for the regions and large towns which were published in No 477.

Further details of housing conditions, though only on a regional basis, may be found in two quarterly publications, *Housing Statistics* and *Local Housing Statistics*, which give changes in the number of public and private dwellings and their construction costs

by region and by conurbation. Certain special surveys have been conducted in selected areas dealing with the condition, tenure, gross value, amenities and cost of repair of the dwellings; thus, for example, in 1970 such data was published for the Merseyside and Tyneside conurbations. Other similar surveys, have been made of housing conditions in the West Midlands and in South East Lancashire.

1A 1b Industrial and employment statistics

Every five years the government takes a census of production and the results are reported in the *Annual Abstract of Statistics*, the *Monthly Digest* and *Trade and Industry*. The questions asked of every firm relate to the number of people employed, stocks at the beginning and end of the year, capital expenditure for the year, sale of products by quantity and value, and the total annual production. The major disadvantage of this census is that the data is presented by industries and not by local areas. However, Volume III of the Census does contain a summary of the information arranged on a regional basis for England and on a national basis for Scotland and Wales. This data is therefore useful as a source of national and regional norms against which details of local industrial characteristics collected from other sources may be compared. If data from the census of production is to be used in this way it will be necessary to become acquainted with the Central Statistical Office's 'Standard Industrial Classification' which was revised in 1968. This particular industrial classification may also be useful as an alternative to preparing one's own classification of commercial and industrial enterprises for local studies.

The nationalised industries also produce a statistical description of their year's work which may provide a useful background to a personal study. For example, the *Digest of Energy Statistics* published by the Department of Trade and Industry contains information about demand for various types of power by different kinds of industries; in 1967, for instance, it described natural gas fields and transmission pipes, and analysed the operation of coal mines and productivity in National Coal Board areas. Again the drawback with such surveys is that they rarely analyse at a local level, and can therefore only be used as a starting point for most geographical studies. The reports issued through the National Economic Development Councils and the Councils for various industries all suffer from the same difficulty; and only if there is a concentration of a particular industry in one locality, does it become possible to relate developments in that industry to the local economy.

Fig. 1.1 CLASSIFICATION OF OCCUPATIONS

CLASS		TYPE
I		professional non-manual
II	A	intermediate manual
	B	intermediate non-manual
	C	intermediate agricultural
III	A	skilled manual
	B	skilled non-manual
	C	skilled agricultural
IV	A	partly-skilled manual
	B	partly-skilled non-manual
	C	partly-skilled agricultural
V		unskilled manual

The Department of Trade and Industry also carries out a census of distribution and other services on much the same lines as the census of production. This census gives information about the number of retail and wholesale establishments, their turnover and the number of people they employ, in each of the major urban and rural districts of the counties of Great Britain. It can often be useful in local studies of the geography of retailing (see Section 4C).

The main source of employment statistics is the *Employment and Productivity Gazette*, which is published every month and contains a national review of the numbers employed in various industries as well as a review of wages in selected industries. More useful for local studies is the *Monthly Digest of Statistics* which gives employment statistics on a regional basis.

Further information on occupations and unemployment at a national level and for the regions and conurbations can be found in the Registrar-General's *Economic Activity Tables*. The Manpower Research Unit also produces specialised reports dealing with particular aspects of the labour situation, such as the one in 1968 which analysed the rise in office employment.

Just as the standard industrial classification provides a useful system of analysis for commercial and industrial enterprises, so the Registrar-General's office publication *Classification of Occupations* may be helpful in describing the occupational distribution of any given area. The method of grouping the population by occupational types has been in use since the 1911 census of population as a means of compressing the wide variety of occupational types into a smaller number of more manageable broad categories (fig. 1.1). A more refined classification system of occupational types which takes into account the status a person has in his employment (whether he holds a position of responsibility such as a foreman or manager) was introduced in 1951 and was extensively amended in 1961. Its aim is to group together people whose social, cultural and recreational tastes are much the same, by using occupational and employment status as indicators (fig. 1.2).

1A 1c Agricultural statistics

An overview of agriculture can be found in the *Annual Abstract of Statistics* or in the *Monthly Digest of Economic Trends*, but the most useful primary source of published data for enquiries into the local agricultural economy has been the *Annual Spring Price*

Fig. 1.2 A CLASSIFICATION OF SOCIO-ECONOMIC GROUPS

GROUP	DESCRIPTION
1	Employers and managers in central and local government, industry, commerce, etc., in large establishments who either employ, plan, or supervise in non-agricultural enterprises over 25 people.
2	As group 1, but in enterprises of less than 25 people.
3	Professional workers self-employed in occupations needing qualifications of degree standard.
4	Professional workers who are employers in occupations needing qualifications of degree standard.
5	Intermediate non-manual workers, ancillary to the professions and in occupations whose qualifications require less than degree standard. They do not perform supervisory or planning rôles.
6	Junior non-manual workers in clerical work, sales work, non-manual communications etc., and not in a supervisory or planning capacity.
7	Personal service workers (e.g. food, drink, clothing).
8	Foremen and supervisors.
9	Skilled manual workers.
10	Semi-skilled manual workers.
11	Unskilled manual workers.
12	Self-employed non-professional workers in occupations not requiring training of degree standard and with no other employees than family.
13	Farmers (employers and managers).
14	Farmers (self-employed).
15	Agricultural workers.
16	Members of the armed forces.

Review which established the level of agricultural subsidies for the coming year.

The Ministry of Agriculture Fisheries and Food has published a series of maps of farming types (Ministry of Agriculture Fisheries and Food, 1969) which are based upon a sample of the farmers' returns in some eighty different crop groups and forty different livestock groups. The maps reflect the extent of cultivation of a particular crop or occupation by a particular animal within a 10 km grid square.

In Northern Ireland there has been a series of *Reports on the Agricultural Statistics of Northern Ireland* which give comprehensive reviews of the state of agriculture, and include data on acreage, yields, expenditure, output, numbers of livestock, income and farm labour. The eighth report covered the years 1961–67 and was published in 1969.

The annual reports of the Forestry Commissioners also contain information likely to be of use in a rural survey, with detailed data on the extent of public plantations and afforestation. In addition, the Forestry Commissioners have carried out censuses of woodlands, and the results are available at a county level. More recently, the Forestry Commission has published information on the main forested and afforested areas (Edlin, 1961, 1964, 1969; Rouse, 1964).

The Ministry of Agriculture's *Farm Classification in England and Wales* may be helpful in describing the rural economy of any given region, in just the same way that the standard industrial classification and the classification of occupations may be used in the analysis of industry and employment.

Many statistics are available for certain periods in the past, and these are amply reviewed in an HMSO publication *A century of Agricultural Statistics in Great Britain 1866–1966* (HMSO, 1968). Particularly useful, however, is the survey of English and Welsh farming which was carried out during the Second World War (HMSO, 1946), and which contains statistics related to employment, holdings, capital, types of crop and production, for each of the counties.

1A 1d Transport statistics

Every year the Ministry of Transport publishes statistics on the relative importance of the rail, road, and air services. The information includes the numbers of vehicles and mileage covered, details of all road accidents, the number of vehicles with a road fund licence, and estimates of traffic and expenditure.

An important source is British Rail's *Annual Report* which, along with occasional special reports (such as the Beeching Report) can often be fitted into a local or regional context to give useful information on traffic flows and profitability.

Information about journeys to work is contained in the Registrar-General's *Economic Activity Tables* which analyse the means of transport, the distances covered, and the characteristics of the people who make the journeys. Unfortunately, however, the information is usually in a rather too general form to be very useful at the local level. Like so many other published statistics, therefore, they can only be used as a comparative yardstick and general check.

1A 1e Unofficial statistics

Unofficial statistics are not usually regarded as a primary data source since they rarely refer to local areas. Their main importance, as with some of the official statistics which we described above, lies in the way in which their information may be used to substantiate conclusions based on other information.

Certain industries and individual firms publish their own unofficial statistics often through their trades associations or house magazines. The motor industry, for example, does this on an annual basis, while the Iron and Steel Association publishes a set of statistics every month. Similarly, The Times' *Quarterly Review of Industry* often includes general statistics related to various industries. The house magazines of certain major firms also generally include some statistics usually related to output, sales or turnover; in this respect, though they are difficult to obtain, the house journals of the leading stores may be particularly useful, especially in studies of retailing.

Technical and professional journals may also publish processed data. For instance, *The Economist* has produced a series of reports over the period 1965–68 on the regions of Britain. The value of such reports lies not only in the statistics which are presented, but also in the topics investigated, the problems which are analysed, and the conclusions which are reached.

1A 2 Unpublished Statistics

Some data may, for one reason or another, remain unpublished, but more often than not it is used as the raw material from which other statistics and information are compiled: information from small collecting units, whether they be firms, individuals or small geographical entities, is added together to present a wider statistical picture. For this reason, unpublished statistics are often the best source of information available for local studies, since the small collection units are, almost inevitably, small-area units. Their main disadvantage, however, is that they are relatively inaccessible to all except those who are engaged on advanced research, though in certain circumstances such information may be released upon enquiry or request to the collecting authority.

The Department of Employment and Productivity, for instance, collects data on employment and unemployment for each of the employment exchange areas, and it may be that under certain circumstances such localised information would be made available. Similarly, industrial information may also be available in the returns which individual firms make for the census of production, or in the returns which are made by the factory inspectors (employed by Her Majesty's Factory Inspectorate). In addition to these possible sources there may be various reports and other information presented by government ministries, departments or boards, or by committees within individual firms which are intended for limited internal circulation. Very often, however, the original returns to censuses are confidential, as, for instance, are the returns which shopkeepers make for the census of distribution and other services conducted by the Department of Trade and Industry. In such circumstances, the information will not be released.

One very helpful source of information is provided by the 'Census of Population Enumerators' Handbooks' which, after a period of 100 years, become available for inspection. Since these are the documents on which individual household responses are noted, a very detailed analysis of population in the nineteenth century can be obtained (Armstrong, 1968).

Local planning authorities, surveyors' departments and engineers' departments often carry out their own surveys in connection with certain future developments and do not publish all the results. Many planning departments, for example, have data on the spheres of influence of the towns for which they are responsible. Other information which they often possess includes traffic flows, urban and rural land-use surveys, and surveys of recreation (especially if there is a National Park in the planning authority's area). Surveyors' and engineers' departments often carry out studies of re-housing schemes and redevelopment plans. Most of these studies can be consulted in the office of the department concerned. The same is also true of statistics relating to rateable values, which are used as an indicator of land values; most treasurers' departments or rating offices will make the rateable-value books available for inspection. Rateable values are one of the most common sources of information about urban land values for several reasons. Firstly, they are completely accessible. Secondly, they go back through time, enabling the changes in land values to be analysed, and thirdly, they reflect certain characteristics such as the location, size, and function of the building. Their application to urban surveys has been outlined by Davies *et al.* (1968), and their usefulness in local studies will be outlined in Section 4C 2c.

For agricultural studies it may be possible to gain access to the returns which every farmer is required to make each year. The National Agricultural Advisory Service groups the farm returns into N.A.A.S. districts which are, for many purposes, sufficiently small to be useful for local studies — there are, for instance, twenty-five such districts covering the counties of Devon and Cornwall. The data may be obtained either through the local office of the Ministry of Agriculture, or directly from a sub-branch of the National Agricultural Advisory Service, if there is one locally.

Often associated with universities are

Agricultural Economics Services [formerly known as the Provincial Agricultural Economics Service (PAES)] which are further sources of unpublished data. The local director is unlikely to release base statistics, but he may make certain conclusions available in the form of reports meant for restricted circulation. Again, where information has been given in confidential returns, that information will not be released because confidential categories must be maintained.

Before approaching any of these 'unofficial' sources, the study problem must have been formulated in precise terms, so that the appropriate authority can be asked specifically for relevant information. In this way, the time of officials is not wasted and the success of later surveys is not jeopardised.

1A 3 Maps

Published maps are often an invaluable source of quantitative information. Topographical maps contain details of both the physical and human landscape from which may be abstracted basic information relevant to any particular study, whilst many other maps are published which contain information on specific themes.

The Ordnance Survey produces topographical maps of Great Britain at three different scales (1:10 560; 1:25 000; 1:63 360) each of which contains information on the location and form of settlements, communication networks, relief, drainage, and even administrative boundaries. Most of the 1:10 560 maps represent an area of 25 sq km, while the 1:25 000 maps (of which there are 2 027 sheets in the 'provisional' series) represent an area of 100 sq km, and the 1:63 360 maps (of which there are 189 sheets) each represent an area of 1 800 sq km. In addition to these three scales there are plan maps which are particularly useful in the analysis of urban morphology and function (see Sections 4B and 4C). Plans at the 1:1 250 scale are available for most towns with a population of more than 20 000, and the 1:2 500 plans cover the whole of Britain with the exception of moorland and mountainous areas.

Naturally, the amount of detail shown diminishes as the scale of the map decreases; thus, for instance, field boundaries and the location of individual houses become progressively more generalised until they are no longer shown on the 1:63 360 scale. Hence, the more local or the more detailed the study, the more relevant will be the larger scale maps.

Quite apart from their obvious usefulness in terms of map interpretation, such maps can be used to abstract information about the location and form of the physical and human landscape. In physical geography they are particularly useful in morphometric analysis and in the analysis of drainage basin characteristics, both of which involve measurements from the map (Morisawa, 1968; Chorley, 1957). Similarly, in human geography, measurements of field shapes sizes and boundaries, the number and orientation of communication links and the location and form of settlements can all be obtained from an appropriate scale topographic map (see Section 4C).

In addition to these topographical maps, the Ordnance Survey also produces a series of thematic maps most of which are at a scale of 1:625 000. Unfortunately, most of these maps portray information relating to the 1940s and 1950s and may therefore be of rather limited value; thus, for instance, the distribution of coal and ironfields is shown for 1940, the electricity supply areas for 1946, the gas and coke industry for 1949, and although there is a map showing population change between 1951 and 1961, most maps of population refer to the period 1921–47. Similarly, the maps of local accessibility at this scale are based on a survey of bus linkages between villages and urban centres in the period 1947–50. Nevertheless, such maps may well provide a useful starting point for a particular study.

A series of archaeological maps is also produced, three of which (Southern Britain in the Iron Age, Ancient Britain and Monastic Britain) are at the 1:625 000 scale, and two (Roman Britain and Britain in the Dark Ages) are at the 1:1 000 000 scale.

The Ordnance Survey also publishes maps on behalf of the Institute of Geological Sciences and the Soil Survey of England and Wales. Geological maps at a scale of 1: 63 360 are available for practically the whole of Britain (only parts of the Scottish Highlands and North Devon are not covered) and more detailed maps at the 1:10 560 scale are published for some of the coalfields. The actual manuscript maps at the 1:10 560 scale are available for inspection at the Museum of the Institute of Geological Sciences. In comparison, the coverage of soil maps is limited mainly to Scotland and Wales and at the 1:63 360 scale only.

A partial cover of land use maps of Britain is also available, 110 such maps at the 1:25 000 scale having been prepared.

Another source of map evidence is the local planning authority which, by law, has to produce plans of future developments. Maps are periodically revised to keep abreast of changes in policy, and these are always available for inspection. These maps, at a 1:10 560 scale, summarise information on industrial, commercial, retail, and residential functions as they exist and as they are proposed, population density in residential areas, open spaces in towns, mineral workings, ancient monuments, and the location of areas which are to be comprehensively redeveloped. Rural planning authorities produce much the same sort of map on a smaller scale, showing built-up areas, industrial areas, agricultural areas, green belts, mineral workings, areas of landscape value, recreational areas, together with proposed developments and changes.

1A 4 Aerial Photographs

Aerial photographs can be used for much the same interpretative purposes as maps, and can be used to add detail to map analysis. They possess the advantage that they show everything of the human and physical landscape, whereas maps only show selected aspects of this landscape. Photographs can be obtained from such companies as Hunting Air Surveys, Meridian Airmaps, from the R.A.F. and the Department of the Environment which may dispose cheaply of old coverage, and from local bodies such as a planning department, a university or a college of education.

There are two types of aerial photograph: obliques (fig. 1.3) which are taken when the camera is used at an angle less than 90° to the earth, and verticals (fig. 1.5) which are taken when the camera is at an angle of 90°. Both suffer from disadvantages in the representation of scale. On obliques, scale is not constant from the foreground to the background, and this produces the effect known as 'fore-shortening', while verticals suffer from scale distortion due to the configuration of the land. Obliques, however, are advantageous in that they present a 'plastic' impression of topography directly, whereas with vertical photographs a 'plastic' impression can only be obtained with special equipment and after special training.

Despite this extra effort, verticals are used more often than obliques in investigations, largely because their 'plastic' impression is much more amenable to analysis. With vertical photographs nothing is hidden by superimposition, as can happen with obliques when a large feature in the foreground masks smaller features behind it. In addition, vertical photographs are directly comparable with maps, and can be used with accuracy to add detail to maps, while the particular type of 'plastic' impression serves to reduce, in visual terms, the scale distortion which is known to exist.

The 'plastic' impression which is created is known as stereovision and is exactly the same as the three-dimensional picture which our eyes normally see. Each eye, however, sees a slightly different image: the left eye sees more of the left face of a figure, while the right eye sees more of the right face of a figure. The existence of these two images can be demonstrated by rapidly opening and closing each eye alternately: any object in central view appears to change position. The two slightly different images are fused together in the brain so that both the left

Fig. 1.3 AN OBLIQUE AERIAL PHOTOGRAPH: Canterbury, Kent

and right faces of a figure can be seen simultaneously, thereby creating three-dimensional vision.

The same effect can be produced mechanically by using vertical photographs. As the survey aircraft is flying on course, the shutter of the camera is operated at pre-specified intervals. In the time between each picture being taken, the aircraft flies over a certain distance, and so only a proportion of the objects appear on the photograph sequence. This proportion is known as the overlap (fig. 1.4), and it is this overlap which provides the basis for stereovision. The left hand side of the overlap pair has a slightly different image of the objects from the right hand side of the pair due to the distance

flown by the aircraft and these correspond to the images seen by the left and right eyes respectively (fig. 1.5). Using a piece of equipment known as a stereoscope, an object which is found on both photographs is brought into coincidence by optical means and is seen as a three-dimensional, 'plastic' image. The basis of the stereoscope is shown in fig. 1.6. A and B are the overlapping pair of photos, with the lens of the stereoscope above each. As we look through the lenses, an object X is located on each photograph (the location of the object is shown by the light rays travelling upwards from A and B to the lenses). The effect of the lenses, however, is to bend the light rays and apparently place the object between the pair of photographs. When this happens, the images from both photographs are said to have fused, and the fused image has exactly the same qualities as any object that we see in everyday vision. Thus, the function of the stereoscope is to produce a single image from two widely separated aspects of an object, one with the quality of a left image, and one with the quality of a right image, in order that the image can be 'taken apart' by the eyes, the left eye seeing more of the left face of the image and the right eye more of the right face, and fused again in the brain to

produce a three-dimensional effect.

The ability to see aerial photographs in three dimensions enhances their usefulness, especially in the greater degree of detail which is an aid to the interpretation of features. With sufficient skill one can discern agricultural and urban land-uses, urban morphology, communication types, topography, vegetation and even evidence of soil and geological type and structure. The interpretation of these features is based upon an analysis firstly of colour tones which vary from black, such as an expanse of deep

Fig. 1.4 THE OVERLAP: the shaded area represents the part of the two photographs which is identical, and it is this overlap which is used to produce stereoscopic vision (see Fig. 1.6.) Best results are obtained with a fifty per cent overlap

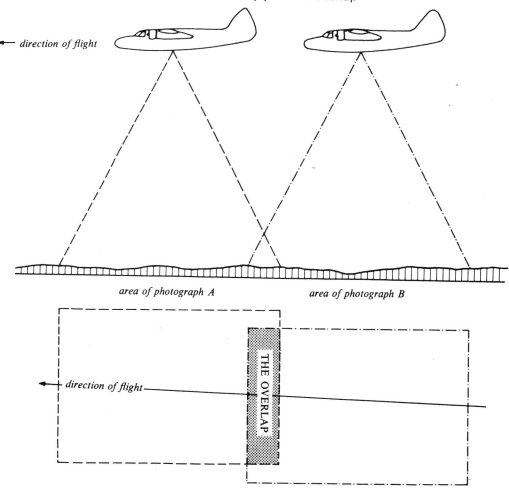

← *direction of flight*

area of photograph A   *area of photograph B*

THE OVERLAP

← *direction of flight*

Fig. 1.5 A STEREO-
PAIR OF AERIAL
PHOTOGRAPHS:
Chipping Sodbury,
Gloucestershire
(copyright Aerofilms
Ltd)

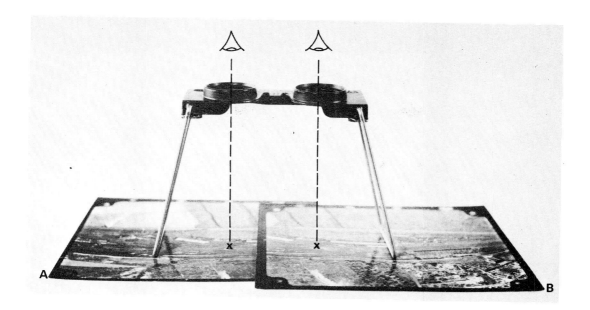

Fig. 1.6   THE STEREOSCOPE: The object *X* in the overlap portion of photographs A and B appears 3-dimensionally to the observer. Simple stereoscopes, such as the one illustrated in the upper diagram, are available at modest cost; more sophisticated stereoscopes, such as the mirror stereoscope illustrated in the lower diagram, allow more of the photograph to be analysed at any given time

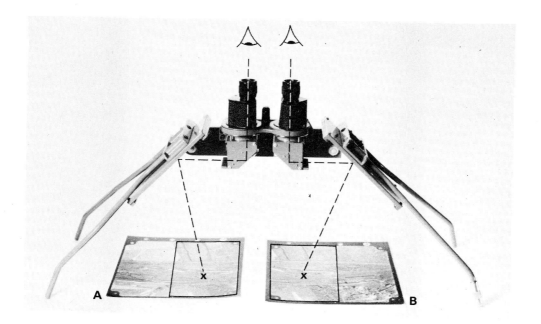

water, through to light grey, such as a newly-mown hay field; secondly, of textures which range from a smooth even surface, such as a wheat field, to an irregular mottled effect, such as deciduous woodland; and thirdly, of the lengths of shadows in order to determine the approximate height of objects and the size of well-known objects, giving an idea of the area covered by the photographs.

It is impossible, within the confines of this book, to describe fully the techniques of aerial-photograph interpretation. They can be learnt only from studies of pairs of photographs in conjunction with an instruction manual. Their use, in local studies, lies in the fact that they are excellent three-dimensional models of reality, and consequently such things as change over time, different land uses and their relationship with a topographic control are easily perceptible. Further details of air photographs and their interpretation may be found elsewhere (Dickinson, 1969; Spurr, 1960).

1A 5 Timetables and Directories

Timetables for public service vehicles can be used to abstract information relating to route structure, journey times and frequency of service. They are available at a reasonable price from local bus companies and from British Rail. The information can be substantiated by more data, such as the number of passengers carried or the number of tickets issued. The data can be used to study connectivity, establish spheres of influence, and generally build up a picture of accessibility around larger urban centres (see Section 4D 3).

Directories, ranging from the popular town guides to the detailed descriptions contained in such volumes as Kelly's Directories, can be one of the most valuable sources of information, particularly in urban studies. Town guides tend to place more emphasis on the social basis of the town concerned, and contain only very general information on its commercial and industrial structure;

most directories, however, give detailed enumerations of houses, inhabitants of residential buildings and the industrial, commercial, and retail structure of the town (Davies *et al*, 1969).

1A 6 Historical Sources

In many cases, a study will gain in depth if the historical background to the present situation is described; indeed, it may be found, after an exploratory analysis, that the most important aspect of a particular phenomenon is its general evolution. In such circumstances, a working knowledge of source materials which describe past periods is essential.

Many of the official and unofficial statistics which we described earlier (Sections 1A 1 & 1A 2) are available for a number of years in the past. The census of population is a good example of this, in that it goes back to 1801. Other sources may not stretch so far back, but despite this obvious limitation and the added difficulty that there have normally been changes in the boundaries of the collection areas, we can still use these sources to present a picture of the situation at particular times.

Generally speaking, data has only been collected on an extensive scale in the twentieth century, as the government has taken an increasingly larger part in the economic life of the country. The best way to discover what is available is to consult the volume entitled 'Government Publications' for the year concerned. Official statistics have only been collected regularly with a view to analysis and presentation since the late eighteenth century. The majority of the returns describing land use, farm size, and production for the nineteenth century are now lodged in the Public Record Office in London, or in the Home Office Papers, and so are inaccessible to most people. However, it is worth enquiring at the Record Office in large towns and county towns to see if any copies of these returns exist for the local area. As an alternative to researching into these primary sources various academic journals should be consulted to see if the data for the local area has been analysed.

In addition to agricultural statistics there may be others in the County Record Office and local archives which present a picture of the major towns of the country. For example, there might be a description of the rates for having a stall in the market, and the total amount of such dues, all of which indicate the prosperity of a place. There may be information referring to road tolls, or the records of licencing magistrates showing the importance of road hauliers. The variation is such that only personal enquiry will reveal just what exists in any given region.

In addition to the information formally preserved in the County Record Offices, there exists another extensive and largely untapped source of information in the Parish Registers. Prior to the official registration of births, deaths and marriages, records were kept in the churches concerned. These may be inspected by agreement with the local vicar as an aid to enquiries into such things as family size, infant mortality, life expectation and average age of marriage. An interesting use of Parish Registers has been demonstrated by Perry (1969).

There are also secondary historical sources, which differ from primary sources in that the picture they present is basically a verbal descriptive one. These are likely to be more accessible since archives are wary of loaning valuable historical documents, while more than one copy of these secondary sources was printed.

Agriculture was particularly well documented in the nineteenth century. At the turn of the eighteenth century the Board of Agriculture commissioned a 'General View' of the agriculture of each English county. In addition to these official descriptions, various private people wrote about their journeys (e.g. William Cobbett's *Rural Rides*). The state of agriculture in Britain is also described in the agricultural journals of the time, such as the *Annals of Agriculture* and the *Journal of the Royal Agricultural Society*.

Descriptions of the industrial state of the nation were not collected on a large scale, and consequently it is impossible to generalise about sources. The most likely source of information is the local reference library or archive collection, for such descriptions as there were, were often published privately. There is a general lack of primary sources for industry, due to the destruction of records after a certain period has elapsed, or to firms going into liquidation, and to a lesser concern with paper work in the first place. As a result, locally held secondary sources are often the main source of industrial information for the local area.

In studying patterns of change, one of the most important sources available are maps from different periods. For towns such maps can be found in such books as *The Beauties of England and Wales*, the 'Victoria County History' series and local histories. In some places, town plans may have been produced relatively early in the nineteenth century. The early editions of the Ordnance Survey are also most useful and often there are also privately produced maps of various areas in the eighteenth and early nineteenth centuries. The tithe maps, and maps commissioned to show the extent of private estates, are particularly useful in historical studies of land use. Most of these early maps are available in County Records Offices, but particularly useful in this respect is the re-printing of the complete first edition of the 1:63 360 Ordnance Survey Map of Great Britain. Ninety-seven sheets covering England, Wales and Scotland are now available (published by David & Charles of Newton Abbot, Devon).

It will also be found that past editions of both timetables and directories are often available, and these, too, can be very useful in reconstructing the past. Trade directories, for example, have generally been produced since the early part of the nineteenth century, and since they list all the business activities of the settlements of different regions, they can be used to build up a picture of a region's commercial structure at various times in the past (Morgan 1967).

The last important secondary source is the study of books and journals dealing with a particular topic. The writings of other people can crystallize one's own conclusions and help put personal findings in a wider context. In addition, these journals may present data which can be useful in one's own study. These sources can usually be found in the local collection of a public library.

EXERCISES

1 Make a list of all the data sources mentioned in this section which are available for your local area. Indicate where these may be obtained.
2 For what purposes is each scale of Ordnance Survey map best suited?
3 How can aerial photographs be profitably used in a local study?
4 Classify the following occupations by social class and by socio-economic group as defined by the *Classification of Occupations* (figs. 1.1 & 1.2): fisherman, miner, engineer (electrical), cabinet maker, publican, chemist, laboratory assistant, agricultural machinery driver, estate agent, porter, bricklayer, fabric dyer, actor, cook, bus driver, glass process worker, gardener, municipal engineer, blacksmith, precision instrument maker, company director, draughtsman, telephone operator, shoe repairer, valuer, maid, clerk, stevedore, weaver, auctioneer, shop assistant, chimney sweep, architect, groundsman, cashier, typist, fireman, railway inspector, gas welder, schoolteacher, street vendor, railway guard, office cleaner, M.P., printing press operator, dock labourer, motor mechanic, waiter, hairdresser, civil service executive officer, university lecturer, window cleaner, medical practitioner, postman, tailor, radio mechanic, warehouseman, nurse, insurance broker, garage proprietor, sportsman, journalist, crane operator, brewer, electrician, painter, bricklayer's labourer, policemen, barman, caretaker, judge, ward orderly, salesman, surveyor, personnel manager.
5 Assess the comparative value of topographical maps and aerial photographs as sources of quantitative geographical data.

FURTHER READING

Armstrong, W. A. 'The interpretation of the Census Enumerator's books for Victorian towns' in Dyos, H. J. (ed), *The Study of Urban History* (Arnold, 1968).

Beltram, G. 'Methods of surveying categories of people presenting special problems and needs.' *Statistical News* No. 8.

Chorley, R. J. 'Illustrating the laws of morphometry.' *Geological Magazine*, 94 (1957), pp. 140–50.

Davies, W. K. D., Giggs, J. A., Herbert, D. T. 'Directories, Rate Books and the commercial structure of towns.' *Geography*, 53 (1968), pp. 41–53.

Dickinson, G. C. *Maps and Air Photographs* (Arnold, 1969).

Edlin, H. D. (ed), *New Forest* (For the Forestry Commissioners: H.M.S.O., 1961).

Edlin, H. D. (ed), *Dean Forest and the Wye Valley* (For the Forestry Commissioners: H.M.S.O., 1964).

Edlin, H. D. (ed), *Snowdonia* (For the Forestry Commissioners: H.M.S.O., 1969).

H.M.S.O. (1946), *National Farm Survey of England and Wales*.

H.M.S.O. (1968), *A Century of Agricultural Statistics in Great Britain, 1866–1966*.

H.M.S.O. (1969), *Sample Census 1966, Great Britain: Commonwealth Immigration Tables*.

Kendall, M. G. *Sources and Nature of the Statistics of the United Kingdom*, Vols I & II, (Oliver and Boyd, 1957).

Ministry of Agriculture, Fisheries and Food, *Type of Farming Maps of England and Wales*, (H.M.S.O., 1969).

Mitchell, B. R. *Abstracts of British Historical Studies*, (Cambridge, 1962).

Morgan, M. A. 'South-west England' in Mitchell, J. B., *Great Britain — Geographical Essays*, (Cambridge, 1967).

Morisawa, M. *Streams, Their Dynamics and Morphology*, (McGraw-Hill, 1968).

Perry, P. J. 'Working class isolation and mobility in rural Dorset 1837–1936: a study in marriage distances' *Transactions of the Institute of British Geographers*, 46 (1969), pp. 121–42.

16

Robertson, I. M. L. (1969): 'The Census and research: ideals and realities', *Transactions of the Institute of British Geographers*, 48 (1969), pp. 173–85.

Rouse, G. D. (ed.) *The New Forest of Dartmoor*, (For the Forestry Commissioners: H.M.S.O., 1964).

Spurr, S. H. (1960): *Photogrammetry and Photo-Interpretation*. (Ronald, 1960).

1B SURVEYS

In section 1A we dealt with information which could be collected from documentary sources, and we suggested where such information could be found. Very often, however, not all the information we may need can be gleaned from such sources, and it becomes necessary to make a direct survey for our own particular study. Such surveys will involve making certain direct observations in the field and/or asking appropriate people certain questions.

1B 1 Observation

The most common form of direct field observation is that of 'land use mapping'. From an early age most geographers will be familiar with making maps of agricultural land use, but these are but one type of land use map. Similar surveys can be made in either a rural or an urban context, and it is important that we distinguish between them because they call for mapping at different scales. Rural land use is best mapped at the 1:10 560 or 1:25 000 scale because the land parcels are large and a fairly extensive coverage is needed. Urban land plots, on the other hand, are smaller in size; there is more information per unit area, and therefore the coverage is smaller, and, thus, the best mapping scale is 1:2 500.

The framework within which the survey is performed is important. Each function can either be mapped as unique, and a classification built up afterwards, or an existing classification can be used and the results compared with already published informa-tion. Many classifications of land use have been devised, in fact probably almost every study has devised its own appropriate classification. When making a particular study, therefore, it may be helpful to see what kind of classifications have previously been used and to use or adapt one of them. Thus, for instance, in a local study of agricultural land use, the Ministry of Agriculture's *Farm Classification in England and Wales* (see Section 1A 1c) might be used in conjunction with the land use classification established by the Land Use Survey of Great Britain (Coleman & Maggs, 1964); in a study of the industries of a given region, the standard industrial classification adopted by the Central Statistical Office (see Section 1A 1b) could similarly be employed; in the analysis of retail and urban land uses, the scheme used by Murphy (1966) or one of the many other classifications (Bartholemew, 1955; Diamond, 1962; Mayer & Kohn, 1967) could be adopted.

Naturally, land use mapping can be a laborious and time-consuming occupation. In order, therefore, to minimise the effort involved, it may be useful to make a sample of the whole area (see Section 1C).

1B 2 Questionnaires and Interviews

In certain circumstances it becomes necessary to collect information by means of questionnaires and interviews. As has already been shown, published information is not always available at a scale which is appropriate for the particular study being undertaken; in many studies it is necessary to have data either relating to individual people, firms or establishments, or to areas smaller than those for which information is already published. Similarly, it is very often useful to collect people's opinions, reasons, or motives in order that the locational patterns of human activity be correctly understood. Indeed, since the location of human activity is largely the result of man's decisions involving his own personal choices and preferences, no analysis of location can ever be really complete without some attempt to describe the motives and choices of the decision maker.

Questionnaires and interviews become necessary, therefore, when published data and other sources do not refer to the appropriate scale, or when reasons, motives, and opinions need to be assessed in order to explain locational patterns.

In a survey of industrial land use, for example, it may be necessary to find answers to such questions as the length of time that each factory has occupied its site, the reasons for its original location and any subsequent alterations, the extent to which management is satisfied with the site, and the origin and destination of its raw materials, labour and products. With such information a picture of the industrial geography of a local area can be built up (Braithwaite, 1968; Keeble, 1969).

Activity systems are also elements of land use and, as such, have patterns which can be mapped and analysed. Obvious examples of such systems are 'the various journeys made by the public to work or to shop. In analysing such behaviour patterns, the only source of information is the person who is making the particular kind of movement, and so interviews and questionnaires once more become essential: it may, for instance, be useful to ascertain not only how far people travelled but their method of transport, the frequency of their visits and their reasons for using particular shops or shopping centres.

The main source of such information is, obviously, going to be 'people', and the problem becomes one of how to extract the information required from people who may not wish to answer questions. This means that we have to know how to construct a questionnaire, and how to put the questions.

1B 2a The form of the questionnaire

The form of the questionnaire is affected by various factors:

(i) the first of these is the willingness of the subject to divulge information. If questions are of a personal nature, people are going to be reticent about giving an answer. Consequently, in this sort of situation a questionnaire cannot really consist of a series of YES/NO answers. Therefore, one has to use an interviewing technique to 'lead' the subject to give the answer during the course of conversation. While data *is* obtained using this method, it is very difficult to analyse by virtue of the fact that it is given in conversation.

(ii) the second factor which has to be considered is the need for useful information to emerge from a survey. The easier basic data is to analyse, the more apparent will be any picture and the more valid any conclusions which are drawn. In considering this factor, by far the easiest questionnaire to analyse is one in which all the answers consist of putting a tick in the relevant box, for all that is needed is to go through the questionnaire replies marking down the total number of responses to each part of the questionnaire.

(iii) the third factor follows on from what we have just said. While the 'box' questionnaire is the easiest to analyse, it is also very difficult to construct. Without fairly elaborate pre-testing, we cannot be sure that the questions are always those most relevant to the problem, and there is always the possibility that the questions can be phrased in such a way that the subjects may misunderstand them. In addition, the rigid form of the questionnaire leaves the interviewer with no scope for probing into an answer. It is always worthwhile, at the end of an interview, to engage the subject in conversation on a particular aspect of the questionnaire in order to make sure that the subject has understood the questions and answered accordingly, and to obtain more material (which, in this case, is easier to analyse than a questionnaire based wholly upon conversation, since there is already the basic framework on which to hang the replies).

There are, therefore, two extremes in questionnaire techniques. On the one hand, there is the personal interview in which the interviewer has a series of guide questions which he uses to lead the subject to give an answer, while on the other hand, there is the rigid questionnaire filled in by the subject without any need for the interviewer to be there. The personal technique is adaptable to individual subjects, and, using his skill, the interviewer can usually get most people to take part and can get to know what they really think. However, the possibility of bias in the phrasing of questions always exists, and in general the technique is one which should only be used by skilled interviewers. Because of this, and because of the ease of analysis, most people tend to use a more rigid form of questionnaire, but this too has its disadvantages. If the questionnaire has to be completed by the respondent himself, such as with a postal questionnaire or one left at an address for later collection, there is, apart from the possibility of misinterpretation, the likelihood that when it is seen not to be an official questionnaire it will be condemned to the waste paper bin. As might be expected, many people adopt a mid-course, putting the subject's responses into a rigid framework, but asking the questions personally, so that they can explain what is wanted if the subject does not understand.

1B 2b What to include

In constructing a questionnaire we need to know three types of information:

1   Information which locates the interview and respondent.
2   Information which tells us about the respondent.
3   Information about the respondent's attitudes or actions.

1 If we were carrying out an interview in depth, it would have to take place in surroundings to which we could return, if necessary, at a subsequent time. The reason for this is that on analysing our responses we may find that some of them are completely out of character with what we should expect, and if the investigation is to be thorough we need to know the reasons for this. We have to interview, again, the subject who made the responses, and so we must have a means of checking on our subjects. We must know their names and their sample number, if we gave them one, their addresses, their sex, and to check that we re-interview the right person in a family, their relationship to the head of the household. Finally, we have to know the circumstances in which the first interview took place, the date, the time and the location, because it is always possible that a subject's replies may have been influenced by the strangeness of the surroundings, or by the presence or absence of other people. For example, if the interview took place at 7.00 p.m. in a family house, then we would expect the respondent to be aware of the fact that the majority of the family were present, and this may affect his replies.

With this information we can return to the subject to find out whether he misunderstood, whether external influences made him give a wrong answer, or whether he gave a true answer — in which case the interviewer can probe further.

The other use for this information is to indicate the time period over which all the interviews were conducted. If this were too long, then there may have been a time variable which influenced people's responses, so that instead of interviewing in one time period we were interviewing in several, thereby taking several subsamples.

However, if the interview was carried out in less formal surroundings, such as a street, then it would be inadvisable, for several reasons, to take down the same degree of personal detail. Firstly, it is time consuming and street interviews have to be short or people become angry at being kept standing. Secondly, the demand for such personal details appears to contradict any statements which may be made about anonymity, and the interview may be refused. This is a problem which may appear with the household interview, but in the circumstances it is easier to overcome by explaining the possible need for subsequent interviews.

2 It is essential that the respondents form a good cross-section of the study group, so that we have sufficient information from which to deduce the relationship between the sample and the whole population. This aspect is further developed in Section 1C. The information that is required is generally concerned with the social background of the subject, and usually includes such things as his age, when he finished his education, his marital status and details about the family unit (the size and composition) in which he is living or in which he was brought up. Other information is usually sought on the subject's occupation (and for this the Registrar-General's classification which we mentioned earlier can be used), which, together with the type of dwelling and whether or not it is owned, provide good indicators as to that person's socio-economic status. Again, the degree of detail varies depending upon the location and type of interview. Some data, such as age, can be based upon the interviewer's assessment.

Information of this nature is needed because past studies have shown that a person's actions and attitudes can be influenced by his material existence. Because of the personal nature of much of this data, the interviewer should note down the observable features (such as the external appearance of the dwelling, and, if invited inside, the furnishings, or, if the survey is a fairly random street selection, the appearance of the subject). This will often save having to ask too many embarrassing questions about the subject's standard of living or income, which, because they are embarrassing, are likely to contain a greater proportion of error in the replies.

3 The collection of data on actions, attitudes and opinions is the most crucial part of the questionnaire, since it is upon the analysis of this section that the conclusions are based. Thus the questions should be influenced by the fact that the data has to be coded and analysed. They should be simple, and only those directly relevant to the problem should be included.

Generally speaking, it is much easier to collect information on facts than on opinions. The type of geographic fact which might be investigated using the questionnaire technique is: 'Where did you go for your holidays last year?', 'Where do you shop for various types of goods?', 'Which shop have you just come from?', 'Where do you live and where do you work?' In these cases the answers are merely entered into the appropriate columns. However, if we were surveying people's origins, delimiting a town's sphere of influence, testing the tendency of different classes of clientèle to visit different shops, or finding out how often farmers visit a market, we would have to be careful how the questions were phrased so that there was not a whole range of replies, each person giving the location of his own home, and putting in his own terms how regularly he visits a certain shopping centre; (e.g. 'a couple of times a week'; 'several times a month'; 'two or three times a year'; 'first time for a couple of years', and a host of other replies which are equally difficult to codify). To make sense of this data requires a great deal of extra effort, when in fact the problem need not have arisen. Instead of saying: 'Where do you come from?', we could say: 'Do you live

a In the town of X
b Within one mile of X
c Between one and five miles of X
d Between five and ten miles of X
e Elsewhere'?

Similarly, we could say: 'Do you visit X

a More than once per week
b Once per week
c One to three times per month
d Less than twelve times per year'?

In this way the data is comparable throughout the sample. The type of error outlined above is one of the most common made by people who are relatively inexperienced in questionnaire construction and technique, and to ensure that one does not fall into it or any other errors, one should get several friends to complete the questionnaire, ask them if they had any difficulties, and see if their responses can be analysed easily.

Collecting people's opinions is a much more hazardous task. When a person is asked what they think of something, they reply that the problem has never struck them, or that they do not know what you are talking about, or that they think it is not your concern. In situations such as these, skill as an interviewer comes to the fore, because it is essential that the majority of people, through one's approach, give an answer that reflects their true opinion.

In what sort of opinions are we, as geographers, interested? It is difficult to give a whole list, but we can indicate types of problem in which an analysis of opinions can play an important part in drawing conclusions. For instance, the obvious extension to the question 'Where did you go for your holidays last year?' is '**Why** did you go there for your holidays?' In asking such a question we are, in fact, asking the subject to enumerate the qualities of a particular place. We could follow this up by asking the subject if he would have preferred to have gone elsewhere, and we can use the answers to measure the competing attractions of various types of holiday area. We are also interested in people's attitudes to their environment. For example, we can ask people in blocks of flats if they like living there, or we can enquire of someone who travels a long way to work if he would prefer to live nearer to his work or work nearer to his home. Other facts about which people have important opinions are distance and the weather. What one person may think of as a long distance, may appear reasonable, or short, to another. We may find that people think a particular distance is longer or shorter than it actually is, or that the weather is not sufficiently cold to take precautions about heat loss from houses, when, in fact, such precautions could result in an appreciable saving in heating costs. That is, we have to determine people's attitudes to aspects of the physical environment, because it is upon these attitudes that people base their actions. Similarly, we may want to study one group's attitude towards another. For instance, do people living in slums think that the civic authorities are doing enough to alleviate their condition, and what is the opinion of owner-occupiers as they are the ones who will have to pay for improvements? All these attitudes affect the way in which people behave, and consequently they are important factors to consider when describing patterns of behaviour.

There are various ways in which we can get people to give their opinions on a particular problem, or their attitudes to a particular feature:

(a) We can merely ask them what they think about the problem. This type of question is known as the 'open-ended' type and has the disadvantage that the replies, because they will be very different, are very difficult to analyse.

(b) We can ask the subject a direct question and give him a choice of replies, with instructions to mark the one with which he agrees most. We could ask the question: 'Do you think that the council spends enough on the upkeep of the roads?', giving the subject a choice of 'yes', 'no' or 'don't know' (fig. 1.7). The technique can be extended so that the replies reflect the attitude more closely by re-phrasing the questions thus: 'Whom do you think should pay for the upkeep of the roads?'

  (i) 'I think that the council should pay out of the general rates.'
  (ii) 'I don't see why I should pay since I don't drive.'
  (iii) 'I think drivers should pay in relation to the size of their vehicle.'
  (iv) 'I think people should be responsible for the road surface in front of their premises.'
  (v) 'I think the burden should fall upon the central government.'

(c) We can also ask the subject to rank a set of alternatives. We might say, 'The council has the following schemes under consideration: new council offices; rehousing slum dwellers; renovation of old people's houses; replanting of parks; purchase of snow moving equipment. Which three schemes should it tackle first, and in what order?' Using this technique we can estimate competing attractions.

(d) The subject can also be asked to rate his attitudes on a scale which runs from one extreme of the attitude to the other. For example, the instructions might read: 'Mark your attitude to the statement below on the scale provided':

The effect that high rise buildings has on social contacts is:

Very good	No effect	Very bad
Increases contacts and develops neighbourliness		Decreases contacts and inhibits neighbourliness

NAME OF FIRM..   DESCRIPTION OF ACTIVITY........................ ....

1 Below you will find a list of factors which can be used to evaluate site satis-
   faction and the attractiveness of the South-West as an industrial location.
   Please indicate any factors which have proved to be less than satisfactory.
   Any factors *NOT* marked will be assumed to be satisfactory.

a	availability of land		k	links with other firms
b	buildings		l	links with schools, colleges, etc.
c	distance from raw materials		m	labour turnover
d	distance from major markets		n	climate
e	availability of labour		o	personal reasons (please specify)
f	roads		p	other factors (please specify)
g	railways			
h	port facilities			
i	air service			
j	workers' transport			

2 Did the firm consider any other location

    a. in the South-West?   YES ☐   NO ☐

    b. elsewhere?   YES ☐   NO ☐

    If YES to b., please specify ....

3 Was the local authority of assistance
   in establishing you at your site?   YES ☐   NO ☐

    If YES, please specify...

4 Do you find the area provides sufficiently
   for your needs in

    a. retail facilities?   YES ☐   NO ☐

    b. recreation and entertainment?   YES ☐   NO ☐

Fig. 1.7 QUESTIONNAIRE : to evaluate industrial site satisfaction

As an alternative, we could reduce the scale to a series of points. If there were three check marks they would represent 'good', 'no effect' and 'bad'; five check marks introduces the qualifiers 'very good', 'good', 'no effect', 'bad' and 'very bad'. We can have a seven, nine, even ten-point scale, but we must remember that the larger the number of choices the more error is introduced into people's responses — one man's 'fairly good' might be another's 'quite good'. The danger is one of having so many check points in the scale that there are not sufficient easily distinguishable adjectives to describe them.

1B 2c Layout of questionnaire

Once the technique of data collection has been decided, the next problem is the way in which the questions are laid out. The questions themselves should be concise, simple and crystal clear, especially if the interviewer is not going to be present to help the subject out of any difficulties. In addition, the questions should avoid any connotations, for strong feelings affect answers because people are wary about being heard to voice extreme opinions. Therefore terms with political, religious and social connotations should be avoided. For instance, a person should never be asked what class he thinks he is, unless people's attitude to class is being tested.

We are now in a position to put the questions on to paper. At this point we gain from being concise, for people are much more willing to answer a short questionnaire. However, we must be careful not to waste any advantage that this confers by having a poor layout, for not only does this increase the questionnaire's apparent length, it also tends to create a sense of confusion. It is much better if the format is attractive and easy to appreciate. If the questions are set out in easily distinguishable columns or rows, the subject does not have to search for the next question in the series. The concepts of questionnaire layout and construction are dealt with more fully in Goode and Hatt (1952), Oppenheim (1966), Young (1966), and Archer and Dalton (1968).

1B 2d Interviews

The essence of interviewing is tact, both in what is said and done. If people are being interviewed in their own homes, you should go there with a letter of introduction, explaining who you are, where you are from, and the aim of the project. At this stage the interviewer should stress that once the information has been collected it is for presentation purposes, completely anonymous, and for educational use only. Work through the questions methodically, noting the answers on the recording schedule and explaining away any difficulty without giving away any clue as to the answer required. (The term 'recording schedule' is used if the answers to the questions are noted by the interviewer. If the answers are recorded by the respondent, the term 'questionnaire' is used.) Never make any response or show any expression to the answers, and, at all costs, avoid 'talking down' to the subject — this is the easiest way to lose any goodwill that has been built up. When all the questions have been completed, thank the subject for taking part (so as to retain his goodwill) since he may be needed to take part in a follow-up survey.

EXERCISES

1   You are going to do a small study, in your home area, about people's movements (where they go shopping, how often they go, etc.). Design a questionnaire which would be suitable for this enquiry.
2   Design a questionnaire for use in a study of farming in a given region. (You will need to find out *more* than just what is grown where: what kind of questions will it be necessary to ask?)
3   Try out your questionnaire on 'movements' with your fellow students.

FURTHER READING

Archer, J. E. and Dalton, T. H., *Fieldwork in Geography*, ch. 6 (Batsford, 1968).
Bartholemew, H., *Land-use in American*

Cities, Appendix B, pp. 147–157 (Harvard, 1955).

Braithwaite, J. L., 'The post-war industrial development of Plymouth: an example of the effect of national industrial location policy.' *Transactions of the Institute of British Geographers* No. 45 (1968), pp. 39–50.

Coleman, A. A. and Maggs, K. R. A., *Land-Use Survey Handbook:* THE SECOND LAND-USE SURVEY (1964).

Diamond, D. R., 'The central business district of Glasgow' in *I.G.U. Symposium in Urban Geography*, *London 1960*, pp. 525–534 (Gleerup, 1962).

Goode, W. J. and Hatt, P. K., *Methods in Social Research* (McGraw-Hill, 1952).

Keeble, D. E., 'Local industrial linkage and manufacturing growth in Outer London', *Town Planning Review* No. 40 (1969), pp. 163–188.

Mayer, H. M. and Kohn, C. F. (eds.), 'Urban land-use surveys and mapping techniques.' Section 9 in *Readings in Urban Geography* (Chicago University Press, 1967).

Murphy, R. E., 'The American city: An Urban Geography', ch. 11, *Urban Land-Use Maps and Patterns* (McGraw-Hill, 1966).

Oppenheim, A. N., *Questionnaire Design and Attitude Measurement* (Heinemann, 1966).

Young, P. V., *Scientific Social Surveys and Research* (Prentice-Hall, 1966).

1C SAMPLING

Alice: 'Where shall I begin, your Majesty?'
King: 'Begin at the beginning; and go on to the end, then stop.'
Lewis Carroll

In collecting information from documentary sources or by means of surveys, there is always a temptation to collect every last shred of evidence and to amass a huge volume of statistics related to the topic being studied. This 'magpie' complex, reminiscent of the King's advice to Alice, seems particularly to have affected geographers, not only in the past, but also more recently with the advent of the 'quantitative revolution' which has encouraged the search for more and more statistics. Naturally, it is not always possible to obtain 'complete' information, whereas, at other times, far too much detailed information seems to be available. In geography, the problems created by this dilemma are magnified because so much emphasis has traditionally been laid on the study of regions or areas. In order to study any aspect of human behaviour in a spatial context it seems necessary, at least initially, to collect information for the whole of the area under study. But in fact, of course, this proves to be almost impossible both in terms of time and effort, and the result is that some alternative shorter way of obtaining information about the 'typical' characteristics of a given area has to be found.

One way of circumventing the problem is by making 'case studies' of small areas or of individuals thought to be typical of the whole population. Thus, for example, in studying the agriculture of a particular region, two or three farms thought to be characteristic of farming in that area might be selected for detailed study, and every aspect of their organisation investigated. The conclusions which can be reached about farming in the region will depend entirely on how typical the few farms really are, and, inevitably, there is more than a strong probability that they will not be entirely characteristic. In a very significant sense this method is rather like putting the cart before the horse: it assumes that a typical condition is already known and then tries to prove it by selecting biased examples. Thus, for instance, it may be thought that the average university student is a long-haired, protesting, immoral layabout, and the point can be proved by making a case study of three or four such students; whether this is really the correct conclusion is, however, somewhat open to question!

Basically, this method of approach is a very elementary kind of sampling procedure, and is often referred to as **purposive sampling**. Although in detail it is wide open to criticism, its objectives are undeniably sound; that is, if a sample can be taken which is *truly* representative of the total population, any conclusions which may be inferred from the sample will, in all probability, hold for the total population. The big problem, of course, is to find a reliable method of taking the sample which is not open to the kind of criticism already levelled against purposive sampling.

Naturally, there is no one universal method which can be applied to any given situation: in certain circumstances, it may be that a **systematic sample** would be appropriate, in others a **random sample** might give rise to a more reliable set of data, whilst in another situation it might be necessary to employ a **stratified sample.** In geographical studies of areal distributions, the decision is further complicated by the question of whether to take the sample at points, along lines, or by quadrats. A wide range of alternative sample designs is, therefore, available (Cole and King, 1968; Gregory, 1963; Yates, 1965).

Once the appropriate sample design has been chosen, the size of the sample has to be determined. Ideally, the sample should be as small as possible so that time and effort may be minimised, but it must still be large enough to yield representative and reliable results. Similarly, what may be a suitable sample size in one situation may be totally inadequate in another. The time that is available for the study will also affect the size of the sample which may be taken. The greater the time available, the larger can be the sample size, but also more time could be spent in making a more sophisticated sample design which usually allows the sample size to be reduced. On the other hand, if the population is stratified into a large number of categories, the size of the sample is likely to be increased since an efficient sample has to be taken from the smallest category and this means, in turn, that the size of sample in all the other categories has to be increased. Finally, of course, a large sample in geographical terms may mean collecting data from a large area, and this again will have to be set against the amount of time available for the study.

Despite all these general problems which may influence the size of sample in a very general way, it must not be forgotten that accuracy and reliability are more important than the time factor, otherwise the sample will be little better than a purposive 'case-study'. There are, in fact, advanced statistical techniques which can be used to indicate the ideal sample size. The procedure, which is explained in detail in Section 2C 4, is based on the results of a pilot survey. Knowledge of the sample standard deviation allows us to calculate the standard error, and from this we can determine the number of items to be sampled in order that the sample population mean approximates, within defined limits, to the true population mean with a given probability of success.

1C 1 Systematic Sampling

From what we have already said about the different kinds of sample design, it will be appreciated that there are several varieties of systematic sample according to whether points, lines or areas (quadrats) are being considered and whether the population has an areal distribution or not. In all such designs, however, the items selected from the parent population are chosen, as their name suggests, in a systematically regular way.

If we were studying characteristics with no reference to their geographical location, the sample items could be chosen by counting every nth item in the total population. For instance, in making a sample of the size of settlements in a given region, we might select every tenth settlement from the complete alphabetical list of settlements; or similarly, in taking a sample of customers at a grocer's store we might interview every fifth customer coming out of the shop. The actual number of items to be selected would, of course, have been previously determined by the method outlined in Section 2C 4. Thus, when a systematic sample is made of a non-areal distribution, the sample items are drawn at regular intervals from the total population.

Precisely the same concept applies in taking a sample of an areal distribution, except that in such cases either points, lines or quadrats may be chosen as the basis. Suppose, for example, that we were sampling the distribution of land use within a given area (fig. 1.8), and that it had been found necessary by the methods described in Section 2C4 to take twenty-five sample items. The first, and most obvious, way of selecting these twenty-five items might be to construct a grid so that twenty-five inter-section points would be regularly distributed over the map of the study area (fig. 1.8A). The type of land use which occurs at each of the twenty-five points would then be noted and this information would form the basic information for our study.

Instead of selecting twenty-five points, we may have decided to make a linear sample over the same area. In this case, a series of lines (or transects) would be set out at regular intervals over the area (fig. 1.8B) and the relative proportions of the different kinds of land use along each such transect would be recorded. Such transect lines may be drawn horizontally, diagonally, vertically or in any direction across the study area, provided that they are drawn at *regular* intervals. Some of the factors which affect the efficiency of this technique, such as the fragmentation of the distributional features, have been studied by Haggett and Board (1964), but this technique is one of the most accurate that is available to the geographer in relation to the time spent on the enquiry (Haggett, 1965, p. 199).

Finally, we may have chosen to sample a series of quadrats rather than points or lines. In this case, twenty-five sample areas would be defined at *regular* intervals (fig. 1.8C) and the proportions of different land use in each area calculated.

Despite the relative simplicity of these systematic techniques, there is a very real danger that they may pick out regular variations in phenomena and thus bias the result. Hence, in our example of selecting every tenth settlement from a list of all settlements, it is more than likely that too many small villages would be chosen; likewise, in our grid of land-use sampling points, it may well happen that many of the points coincide with every occurrence of a land-use type which, in reality, forms only a small proportion of the total land use of the area. In either case, the sample would not

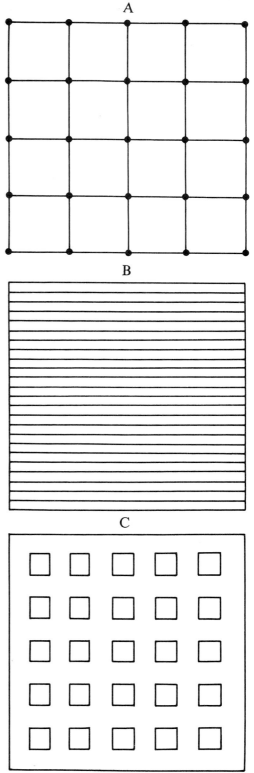

Fig. 1.8 ALTERNATIVE METHODS OF SAMPLING: A—25 point locations; B—25 transects; C—25 areas (quadrats)

have been a truly representative one. It is for this reason that *simple* systematic sampling techniques such as these are rather un-reliable.

1C 2 Random Sampling

One way in which it might be possible to obviate some of the difficulties inherent in systematic samples is to select the items from the total population in a random way. In fact, random methods of sampling are really based on the 'laws of chance', the same laws that enable us to lose money at roulette or dice. We lose money at these games because we cannot determine the next number that is going to be spun or thrown. In making a random sample we are effectively trying to ensure that any particular item will not be selected (just like the roulette wheel). In other words we try to select the sample items rather like we might select our eight draws on the football pools — almost like sticking a pin in the list! Thus, for instance, in selecting a sample of customers at a grocery store we might continue to pick the next person who comes along after the previous interview has finished until enough people have been interviewed to complete the required sample size. Similarly, we might even try to select items from a list by drawing out the number of the item from a hat containing all the numbers in the set.

Normally, in establishing a random sample we make use of a rather more refined method of selecting the items, based on a sequence of already published random numbers which have usually been drawn by a computer playing an electronic game of dice. These tables of random numbers (see fig. 1.9) are printed in blocks of four digits, but each individual digit is drawn, at random, from the series 0–9. We can understand this more easily if we imagine the computer playing with a ten-sided dice which is thrown four times. Each throw results in a number from nought to nine, which forms one of a block of four digits. Since each of these numbers is drawn at random we can combine blocks of digits or parts of these blocks into a 2, 3, 4, 5, 6, 7, 8 figure random

Fig. 1.9 TABLE OF RANDOM NUMBERS

2360	0839	7626	8142	2074	0049	6163	2495
1807	8874	2653	2696	5824	7736	4482	1700
6057	3237	3931	1073	0953	4182	4328	3367
1581	6623	6572	2962	5905	5837	3394	0996
2980	5273	0016	1507	3261	1585	0168	2529
4126	4260	8651	3164	9543	0990	7591	7586

number and so on *ad infinitum*. The tables can be read either horizontally or vertically the sequence of numbers will still be randomly occurring.

These random numbers can then be used to select items either from an areal distribution or a non-areal distribution. In the case of a non-areal distribution, instead of choosing every *n*th item in the list as we did in the systematic sample, we could select on the basis of a series of randomly chosen numbers. Thus, if we used the random number tables set out in fig. 1.9 and read horizontally, the first ten selections in a list containing 1 000 items would be numbers 236, 008, 397, 626, 814, 220, 740, 049, 616, 324 on the list, whereas had we been choosing ten items systematically, we should have chosen items 100, 200, 300, 400, 500, 600, 700, 800, 900, 1 000.

Similarly, in the selection of items in an areal distribution, we could choose the appropriate co-ordinates, lines, or quadrats by means of random rather than systematic co-ordinates. Using the sequence of numbers displayed in fig. 1.9 as a basis for establishing six figure grid references, the first twenty-five sample points would be distributed in the random manner shown in fig. 1.10.

These randomly chosen numbers may also be used to locate sample items other than by the use of co-ordinate grid references. For instance, suppose that it is necessary to make a sample of houses in a town. Each road or street is ascribed a number from 0 upwards, and within each street each house is ascribed another number from 0 upwards. Suppose, further, that there are 99 streets and that the maximum number of houses in any street is 897. If, therefore, we select five-figure blocks of random numbers from the tables, we can

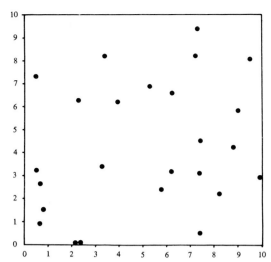

Fig. 1.10 RANDOM SAMPLING OF POINTS: 25 points generated by 6 figure co-ordinates read from a table of random numbers (such as Fig. 1.9)

use the first two digits to indicate the road, and the next three to indicate the house. The first five-figure block of numbers (reading horizontally) is 23600. The first two digits (23) might indicate 'The Mall', and number 600 The Mall might be Buckingham Palace. The next number is 83976. The 83 indicates the street, Park Lane, and 976 the number of the house in Park Lane. However, since there are not 976 houses in Park Lane, the next three-digit number is read from the tables, that is 268. So the chosen house is now number 268 Park Lane. We continue this process until the required sample size is reached.

The advantages of random sampling are that we need not have any prior knowledge about the structure of the population, and yet we can be relatively secure in the knowledge that this type of sample will represent most of the variation in the population. However, the method does fall down in certain circumstances. For example, when we do not know the extent of the population we cannot draw a random sample. For this reason we often take a preliminary sample to give a general idea of the extent and characteristics of the parent population. In addition, there is always the possibility, albeit rather remote, that the laws of chance might work against us and not with us, thus giving us a poor or mis-

leading result, in rather the same way that systematic sampling could select rather biased examples.

1C 3 Stratified Sampling

The only sure way of including representatives of all possible conditions within the sample is to divide the total population down into component parts and to take an appropriate sample from each of the components. This can, of course, only be done when we already have a rough idea of the structure of the statistical population. If, for instance, we were studying the recreational habits of the population of a particular town, it would be logical to assume that people would differ in their behaviour according to their age and sex. In taking a sample of the population it would, therefore, be wise to make sure that the number of people sampled in each age group and sex category was in the correct proportion, and this is done by **stratifying** the sample. Each of the different 'strata' (categories) of the total population is sampled by either the systematic or random methods already outlined.

Clearly the stratification of the sample becomes a little more complicated when we are dealing with area distributions. If we were studying land use within a given region, for example, it would be useful to stratify the sample according to the different geological or soil types in the region. To do this, it is first necessary to measure the extent of each geological (or soil) type. Geology of type 'A' might occupy 10 square km, 'B' might cover 50 square km and 'C' might cover 30 square km (fig. 1.11). If we were going to take a sample of 4 500 points, then these could be allocated in the following way. The total extent of the study area is 90 square km, of which 10 are covered by rock 'A', 50 by 'B' and 30 by 'C'. The 4 500 sample points are then divided according to these proportions

A: $10/90 \times 4\ 500 = 500$ sample points
B: $50/90 \times 4\ 500 = 2\ 500$ sample points
C: $30/90 \times 4\ 500 = 1\ 500$ sample points

All the instances in which we can stratify our sample must fulfil two conditions.

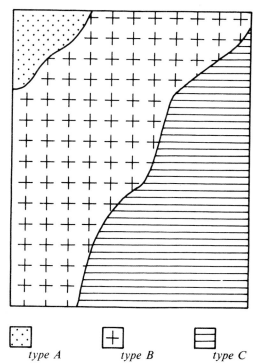

type A   type B   type C

Fig. 1.11 THE BASIS OF STRATIFICATION:
distribution of 3 geological types

Firstly, we have to know the structure of the population before we can do anything; and, secondly, to give an accurate result the strata that we choose must be relatively homogeneous, that is, they should contain little internal variation. Not only is the accuracy of the sample increased by ensuring that no group is omitted and that each group is weighted in proportion to its size, but also the information is easier to collect once the initial groundwork has been done, since the homogenity of the strata means that fewer items are needed in the sample. This point is brought out very well by the changes in the agricultural census of England and Wales. The opportunity was taken to re-structure and rationalise the census so that it would meet the needs of the 1970 World Census. Apart from the re-structuring of the questionnaire, the most important change was in the form of the stratification. By stratifying on the basis of farm type and farm size rather than on the basis of a sample from one-third of the parishes of England and Wales, the number of holdings

questioned was reduced from 80 000 to 30 000 without any significant loss in efficiency. The technique is one which is particularly suitable for geographical research (Wood, 1955).

EXERCISES

1 Take a sheet of a land use or geology map and, over half of it, carry out a series of random samples using 10, 20, 40, 80 and 160 sample points. Why do the results vary? What is the best sample size?

2 Using the same map sheet as in question 1, carry out two of the following samples: random, systematic and linear. Do the sample sizes differ? If so, why? How could the sample sizes be reduced?

FURTHER READING

Cole, J. P. and King, C. A. M., *Quantitative Geography*, ch. 3 (Wiley, 1968).

Dury, G. H., *Map Interpretation* (Pitman, 1960).

Gregory, S., *Statistical Methods and the Geographer*, ch. 7 (Longman, 1963).

Haggett, P., *Locational Analysis in Human Geography*, ch. 7 (Arnold, 1965).

Haggett, P. and Board, C., 'Rotational and parallel traverses in the rapid integration of geographic areas' in *Annals of the Association of American Geographers* (54), pp. 406–410 (1964).

Wood, W. F., 'Use of stratified random samples in Land-Use study' in *Annals of the Association of American Geographers* (45), pp. 350–367 (1955).

Yates, F., *Sampling Methods for Censuses and Surveys* (Griffin, 1965).

29

2 Statistical Manipulation of Data

To many people the very mention of the word 'statistics' is enough to cause instant depression, and many others tend to think of statistics themselves as one of the major plagues of modern civilisation! Nevertheless, most of the information which we collect for geographical studies will be in the form of basic raw statistics. We shall need, therefore, to learn how to process these basic statistics, so that the facts which they contain may be readily recognised.

Suppose that we have made a survey of certain aspects of land use in the hypothetical county of Devwall, and that from both documentary sources and direct field survey we have collected statistics for each of the 67 parishes in the county. These may be a set of data showing the amount of pastureland in each of the parishes, another set showing the amount of arable land, and a third set showing the amount of land above 500 m in each parish. None of these *data sets*, as they are called, would make any immediate sense if they were published in their original unprocessed form, as can be seen in the pastureland data in fig. 2.1.

In the first instance, we need to summarise the information so that salient points can be recognised at once. Thus, it might be useful to know how many parishes had a great deal of pastureland, how many had an average amount, and how many had very little. In order to point to these basic facts, we should have to process the crude figures in such a way that a summary of the information could be effected.

Once we had described the data set in this way, it would be necessary to explain the patterns which we observed. One of the main questions would, inevitably, concern the causes of the patterns. We should need to investigate which factors were important in causing the patterns we had described, and in this process we would undoubtedly find it necessary to compare one set of figures with another. In our land-use study,

for example, the amount of pastureland may be related to the amount of high ground in the parishes, and we should need to find out whether this was really the case. Thus, we should need to compare the two sets of figures (amount of pastureland: amount of land above a certain height).

But, having made such comparisons and conclusions, we should need to know whether these same comparisons and conclusions were really significant ones. Hence, the third stage of the study would involve testing the conclusions for **significance.**

It can be seen, therefore, that the original data sets in the study have to be processed statistically in three basic ways. First, from the data sets **summaries** have to be made; second, certain **comparisons** need to be effected; and third, tests of **significance** have to be applied. These three stages in the processing of the original data sets form the basis for the subdivisions of this section.

The statistical techniques which may be used in these three stages of data processing vary, however, according to the kind of data which is being processed. The figures in a data set (or the **variables** as they are called in the language of statistics) are of two different kinds: these are **discrete variables** and **continuous variables,** the difference between them being very simple.

For instance, the number of students in a class could be 1, 2, 3 ... 25 ... 36 and so on: there could not be 25·5 or 23·2 individuals. In such a case as this the variables can only take certain values — there cannot be 25·5 students in a class. Data which contains variables such as these is called **discrete** or **noncontinuous data,** and the variables are called **discrete** or **noncontinuous variables.**

Noncontinuous data and variables are, patently, very different in their nature from other data and variables which could, theoretically, take any value at all in a given range. For instance, the height of any

Fig. 2.1   AN ORIGINAL DATA SET : % amount of pastureland in 67 parishes of Devwall county

PARISH NUMBER	% PASTURE	PARISH NUMBER	% PASTURE	PARISH NUMBER	% PASTURE
1	34	24	45	46	61
2	48	25	57	47	68
3	50	26	64	48	69
4	66	27	75	49	62
5	70	28	48	50	61
6	70	29	59	51	54
7	72	30	60	52	64
8	62	31	77	53	55
9	56	32	42	54	58
10	61	33	50	55	65
11	56	34	58	56	56
12	45	35	53	57	56
13	37	36	58	58	63
14	48	37	52	59	54
15	35	38	61	60	59
16	52	39	63	61	58
17	54	40	59	62	58
18	61	41	52	63	68
19	54	42	61	64	65
20	54	43	56	65	50
21	65	44	56	66	58
22	58	45	50	67	50
23	58				

person could be 170 cm, 170·1 cm, 170·2 cm and so on. These variables are, in a sense, **continuous** and it is for this reason that data and variables such as these are called **continuous data** and **continuous variables.** Clearly any problem which involves exact *measurement* will give rise to continuous data and variables, whereas *enumerations* will generally give rise to discrete variables. Similarly, any grouped data must be treated as discrete data.

This distinction between continuous and noncontinuous data and variables is a very important one, because the techniques which are available for processing continuous data are very different from those which are available for processing non-continuous data, and should not, indeed, be used for that purpose (and vice-versa).

2A SUMMARIES

There are, in common use, four main methods by which the original data set may be summarised:

1 The data may be **grouped** around certain critically defined values.

2 A **typical** value of the data set may be used to indicate some kind of 'average' condition.

3 The **deviation** of those occurrences which are **not** typical can be measured to show something of the 'scatter' of the distribution.

4 Both the **typical** and the **deviation** can be used together to present an overall picture, in one measure, of both the 'average' and the 'deviation'.

2A1 Grouping Techniques

If you were asked to comment on the examination marks obtained by a group of students in an examination, you would almost intuitively begin by saying that a certain number of people got 70% or more, so many got between 60% and 69%, and so on. In effect, you would be compressing the original data into small groups around certain critical values (in this case, 70%, 60% etc.).

It is precisely this method which is used to group any data set. First of all, meaning-ful **classes** (e.g. 60%–69%) are established, and then the number of observations which occur in that class are counted. Since the original data now appears in grouped form, it is to be treated as **discrete** data.

Each of the classes obviously has an upper and a lower limit: the lower value of the class is known as the **lower class limit**, and the higher value the **upper class limit**. Thus, in the class 60–69%, the lower class limit is 60, and the upper class limit is 69. In certain circumstances, however, we may find it convenient to establish a class which does not have a definite limit at one end; for instance, it may be useful in the case of exam marks to have a class 'below 40%' or another, as we suggested, 'above 70%'. These classes, not being bounded at both ends, are referred to as **open classes.**

The main problem, of course, is to find out which classes appear to be appropriate and meaningful. If, first, we consider the overall distribution of the data set, we may be able to see, by simple inspection, whether there are any 'natural' groupings within the data. This is most easily done by drawing what is known as a **scatter diagram** (fig. 2.2). On a graph we simply plot the number of

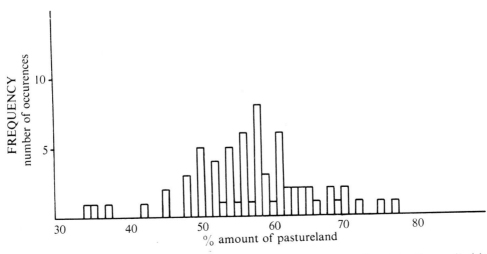

Fig. 2.2 SCATTER DIAGRAM (SCATTERGRAM): pastureland in Devwall (data from Fig. 2.1)

times a particular figure occurs, so that the diagram really shows how the figures are distributed along their **range** (from the lowest to the highest value). Every single figure of the data set is plotted, and then if any obvious groupings occur in the data, they are taken as the **ideal** class limits. It would be wrong to establish a class which breaks up any major grouping, for the essential nature of the distribution would be lost. In our land-use data (fig. 2.2) for example, it is clear that a 'natural' group exists between 50–59%. To divide this down the middle creating a group of 50–54% and another of 55–59% would be both meaningless and irrational. We can also see that other natural groups fall, for example, between 40–49%, between 60–66%, and between 67–70%.

Yet these *ideal* groups have to be reconciled with the fact that the classes established should be of regular size, whether they be in **arithmetic progression** (e.g. 1–2: 3–4: 5–6: 7–8) or **geometric progression** (e.g. 2–4: 5–8: 9–16). Clearly, the natural groupings may not be regular in this sense, and it will be necessary to seek a compromise solution to the situation. For our land-use data, for instance, we could suggest that classes in arithmetic progression of 'less than 39%', 40–49%, 50–59%, 60–69%, and 'over 70%', would be appropriate in that most of the natural groupings follow this sequence.

However, not all the natural groupings follow this sequence: two natural groups of 60–66% and 68–70% are apparent. A compromise has, therefore, to be made, but since most of the natural classes do coincide with the suggested 'arithmetic progression' classes, we may accept this as a reasonable basis of classification.

Having thus suggested a suitable series of classes, it is necessary to bear in mind a second, and very important, consideration. We should not try to establish *too many* classes, for if we do, we run the risk of losing the whole point of the exercise; the salient points of the data would be missed because *detail* would remain instead of the summary which we were trying to establish.

The actual number of class intervals to be established will be partly dependent on the total number of observations in the distribution and also on the 'range' of the data set. As a general guide, it is useful to follow the general 'rule of thumb' that the number of classes should never exceed **five times the log of the number of observations in the data set**. By adopting this procedure, we safeguard against establishing too many classes. Thus, if we had originally 100 observations, the maximum number of classes would be $5 \times \log 100 = 5 \times 2 \cdot 0000 = \mathbf{10}$.

Having established the classes, the number of observations which fall into each class can be tabulated (fig. 2.3), such a table being

Fig. 2.3 A FREQUENCY DISTRIBUTION : % amounts of pastureland (as shown in the original data set Fig. 2.1)

CLASS	ITEMS	CLASS FREQUENCY
<39	34 35 37	3
40–49	48 45 48 45 48 42	6
50–59	50 56 56 57 59 50 58 53 58 52 52 54 58 56 59 54 58 52 54 58 58 50 50 55 56 54 52 58 59 54 56 50 56 58	34
60–69	66 62 61 64 60 61 68 69 62 61 64 65 63 61 63 68 61 61 65	19
>70	70 70 72 75 77	5

called a **frequency table** or a **frequency distribution,** since it shows the frequency of occurrences within each of the classes (i.e. the **class frequency**). More precise methods of establishing appropriate classes are reviewed in Section 3B 1b.

2A 1a Histograms

A more vivid impression of the frequency distribution can be given if, instead of presenting it as a frequency table (fig. 2.3), it is drawn up as a graph. We could, for example, construct a graph showing the class frequency plotted against the class. The horizontal axis of a graph is always referred to as the *abscissa* (or the 'x' axis), and as can be seen from fig. 2.4, it is on this axis that we plot the class. The vertical axis is referred to as the *ordinate* (or 'y' axis) and on this axis the scale showing the class frequency is marked (fig. 2.4). Whenever we draw graphs, the ordinate is the axis which should be used to show the *variable* quantity, or the **dependent variable,** as it is called. The abscissa is used for the **independent variable.** The dependent variable is so called because its size is *dependent* on the other variable. Hence, in constructing a histogram, it is the class frequency which is the dependent variable, and which is plotted on the ordinate or 'y' axis. The scale used on the

ordinate should be chosen with reference to the range of frequencies involved. In this case, the maximum frequency occurs in the interval 50–59 % and is 34: hence the ordinate must range from 0 to 34 (note too, that the ordinate scale must always start from zero). The scale of the abscissa will be determined similarly by the number of classes to be used. Finally the size of the graph (which will also, of course, affect the size of the scale interval) will be affected by similar considerations. The resultant graph must show what it is designed to show effectively, and it is this principle which must be remembered when deciding the size and scale of the graph. It would be of no use, for instance, to present a graph in which the scale was so small that the differences between the frequencies in each class were hardly visible or in which the scale was so large that differences were exaggerated.

When the size and scale have been decided, we can present our information by drawing columns of appropriate lengths to show the number of occurrences in each class (the class frequency). Such a diagram is called a **histogram.** It is drawn as a series of 'blocks' and these blocks indicate that we are dealing with grouped data. Hence, the technique of drawing a histogram is one which is to be reserved for non-continuous (discrete) data, the grouped data upon which it is based being non-continuous. When, however, we have some continuous data or where the groups used are very small so that the continuous nature of the information is not lost, we should use different techniques — which will indicate more effectively the continuous nature of the distribution. In this case, we construct what are called **frequency polygons** rather than histograms.

2A 1b Frequency polygons

The method of drawing these polygons is similar to that already described in the construction of histograms. On the ordinate will be represented the class frequency, on the abscissa the class interval, but in this case the interval will be represented by the **class mark.** (The class mark is the mid-point of the class; thus, in the class 40–59, the class mark is 50). The graph, therefore,

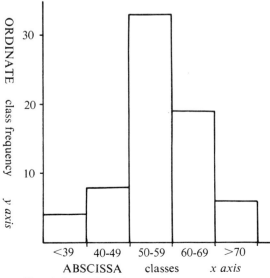

Fig. 2.4 HISTOGRAM: pastureland in Devwall (data from Fig. 2.3)

34

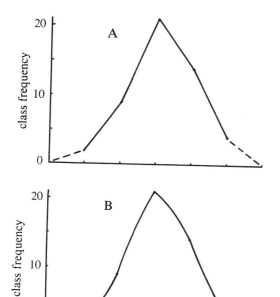

Fig. 2.5 CONTINUOUS DATA: heights of students (cm) in a class: A—frequency polygon; B—frequency curve

already referred to (fig. 2.5A). If this polygon is then 'smoothed out' (i.e. the sharp points rounded off), the resultant line is called a **frequency curve** (fig. 2.5B), but unless this rounding off is done by accurate statistical methods, it is better not to attempt it, but to leave the diagram as a polygon (see Section 3A 1b).

2A 1c Relative and cumulative histograms and polygons

The histogram and the frequency polygon are the methods of expressing the variable nature of the data with which we are dealing, in its simplest form. Two other variations on this theme which show the same thing in a slightly different form can also be useful in our analysis. First, instead of being interested in only the absolute frequency of each class, it may well be that we should like to express the frequency of each class as a percentage of all classes. In our land-use example 9% of all parishes fall in the class 40–49% pastureland, and 51% in the 50–59% group (fig. 2.6). Simply, all we need to do is to work out the frequency of each class interval as a percentage of all the occurrences. The table in which we set out the information is similar to the Frequency Table, except that *actual* frequencies are replaced by *relative* frequencies and, therefore, the resultant table is called a **relative frequency table,** or **relative frequency distribution,** or, occasionally, a **percentage distribution** (fig. 2.6). When the histograms or curves portraying this information are drawn, it is only the scale on the ordinate that is changed to show percentages rather

portrays class frequency plotted against class mark. The impression of the abscissa scale will be, as can be appreciated from fig. 2.5A, of a continuum of values, as opposed to a grouping (non-continuous) as was previously used for the histogram. A point is marked for each class mark/frequency and then each of these points is joined up to form the frequency polygon

Fig. 2.6 A PERCENTAGE DISTRIBUTION: based on the data shown in Fig. 2.3

CLASSES (% of pastureland)	ACTUAL FREQUENCIES (no. of parishes)	RELATIVE FREQUENCIES (% of parishes)
<39	3	4·5
40–49	6	9·0
50–59	34	51·0
60–69	19	28·0
>70	5	7·5

Fig. 2.7 A CUMULATIVE FREQUENCY DISTRIBUTION: based on the data shown in fig. 2.6.

CLASSES (% pasture-land)	CUMULATIVE FREQUENCIES (no. of parishes)
<39	3
<49	9 (3 + 6)
<59	43 (3 + 6 + 34)
<69	62 (3 + 6 + 34 + 19)
<79	67 (3 + 6 + 34 + 19 + 5)

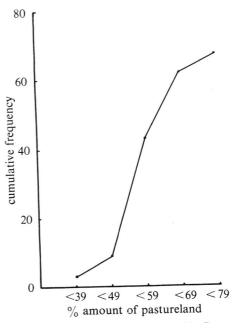

Fig. 2.8 AN OGIVE: pastureland in Devwall (data from Fig. 2.7)

than absolute values. The resultant diagrams are called respectively **relative frequency histograms** and **relative frequency polygons** or **curves**.

The other slightly different portrayal of the same basic information could be to indicate the number of parishes which have, respectively, <40%, <50%, <60%, <70%

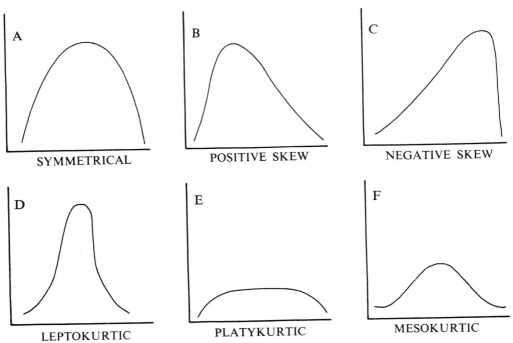

Fig. 2.9 DESCRIPTION OF FREQUENCY CURVES

>80% pastureland. In a sense, this is a cumulative figure, and it is for this reason that a distribution such as this, presented in tabular form, is called a **cumulative frequency distribution** (fig. 2.7). A graph of this distribution will, clearly, give rise to a cumulative frequency polygon or curve, and this curve is usually called an **ogive** (fig. 2.8).

By the same arguments and methods used to make relative frequency distributions and curves from crude frequency distributions and curves, it is easy to transform ogives to percentage ogives.

All these techniques of grouping data and of presenting frequency distributions and curves are, as can be seen, very valuable in presenting a shorthand 'overall' picture of the variable nature of the data set with which we began. It is usually found that frequency curves for any data set have characteristic shapes. By being familiar with these shapes, we can adopt a further shorthand terminology for the description of the particular distribution with which we are dealing. There are three main *types* of frequency curve: (a) symmetrical (which is the one we shall encounter most) (fig. 2.9A); (b) skewed to the left (called 'positive' skew) (fig. 2.9B); (c) skewed to the right (called 'negative' skew) (fig. 2.9C). These terms, therefore, describe the general *shape* of the distribution, whilst a further description of the 'peakedness' of the distribution can be given by a characteristic called **kurtosis.** A distribution which has a relatively high peak is called **leptokurtic** (fig. 2.9D); one which is essentially flat is called **platykurtic** (fig. 2.9E); and one in between these two extremes, the normal distribution, is called **mesokurtic** (fig. 2.9F).

EXERCISES

1   Using the information given in fig. 2.10, construct
    (a) a frequency distribution,
    (b) a histogram,
    (c) a relative frequency histogram.
2   Using the information given in fig. 2.11, construct
    (a) a frequency distribution,
    (b) a frequency curve,
    (c) a relative frequency curve,
    (d) an ogive.
3   What do these diagrams show, and how effective are they in summarising the original data?
4   Measure the heights of all the students in your study group, and construct a histogram to portray the information you have collected.

Fig. 2.10   NUMBER OF FOOD SHOPS: sample of 105 settlements, N. France.

4	6	2	1	15	5	4
7	4	1	2	15	2	3
69	3	141	87	2	1	1
20	1	4	13	1	2	5
3	1	3	6	11	1	13
8	5	8	8	3	4	2
30	405	24	15	1	5	2
234	2	4	29	60	8	5
14	18	1	1	2	2	1
5	2	11	2	3	2	2
4	2	6	6	4	36	10
4	16	5	33	63	2	1
4	3	3	9	11	3	3
1	696	5	2	1	2	6
1	10	4	60	17	2	4

Fig. 2.11 PROTEIN CONTENT OF NATIONAL AVERAGE FOOD SUPPLIES PER HEAD

COUNTRY	grams/ day	COUNTRY	grams/ day	COUNTRY	grams/ day
Austria	86·6	U.S.A.	90·6	Columbia	46·1
Belgium	85·0	Ceylon	41·8	Dominican Republic	49·8
Denmark	92·3	China	58·8	Ecuador	45·2
Finland	92·9	India	49·7	El Salvador	58·5
France	98·6	Pakistan	47·8	Guatemala	58·5
Germany	79·7	Israel	85·2	Jamaica	57·9
Greece	94·2	Lebanon	72·0	Mexico	73·0
Ireland	90·2	Mauritius	49·4	Paraguay	66·0
Netherlands	78·2	South Africa	80·4	Peru	58·0
Norway	80·8	Syria	78·0	Surinam	44·5
Portugal	74·2	Turkey	97·5	Uruguay	94·5
Spain	79·9	United Arab Republic	85·5	Venezuela	61·2
Sweden	83·5	Australia	90·1	Japan	72·4
Switzerland	88·2	New Zealand	112·0	Philippines	42·4
United Kingdom	89·3	Argentina	77·2	Jordan	51·6
Yugoslavia	98·8	Brazil	66·8	Libya	52·8
Canada	91·1	Chile	79·4	Rhodesia	75·2

2A 2 Measuring the Typical

If you were asked to say something about Tottenham Hotspur's goal scoring record in any given season, you would probably begin by saying that not only are they a great team, but that they score about two or three goals each match. 'Two or three goals' is a 'typical' score for this team, and we could, therefore, think of '2 or 3' as a typical value of a data set containing a list of the number of goals scored in each and every match of the season.

How would you have selected that typical value of '2 or 3'? You may have thought that this was the number of goals which was most frequently scored, or you may have worked out some kind of mathematical 'average' score. Either method would be valid, and it is these same methods which are employed in analysing *any* data set. We may, therefore, either

1 Select the most frequently occurring value or

2 Calculate some form of 'average' value in order to express a 'typical' figure for the data set.

2A 2a The mode

The technical name given to 'the most frequently occurring value' is the **mode.** It is derived from the French expression 'à la mode' which means 'fashionable'; since the 'most fashionable' usually becomes the 'most frequently occurring', it is not difficult to see why this word is used.

All we need to find now is the 'most frequently occurring value' of the data set. We have already talked about 'scatter diagrams' which, it will be recalled, show how many times a particular value occurs in a data set (fig. 2.2). From these diagrams, therefore, we can see at a glance which is the most typical value (i.e. the mode). In the land-use example (fig. 2.2), it is clear that 58% occurs most; thus we could say that the typical parish has 58% pastureland, or, in more technical terms, that the modal value of pastureland in Devwall parishes is 58%.

If we have already grouped the data set into some form of frequency distribution so that the data is now effectively **discrete** data, we can still find a **modal value** of the data set. Patently, on a histogram or frequency polygon the 'peak' of the distribution represents the 'most frequent' class. We can simply refer to that class as the mode, but since it is a whole *class value* (e.g. 50–59%), rather than a single figure, it is wise to differentiate between the two kinds of value. The mode of a histogram is usually, therefore, referred to as the **modal class value.** In fig. 2.4 for instance, it can be seen that the 'peak' on the histogram corresponds to class 50–59%; the **modal class value** is then 50–59%. For similar reasons, when we talk of the mode on a frequency polygon, we give it a different name: in this case, because the polygon plots class frequency against *class mark*, we call the mode the **modal class mark.**

Of course, in some data sets, there may be two or more modal values: where this is the

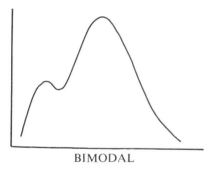

BIMODAL

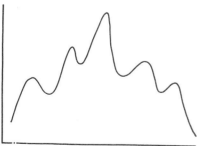

MULTIMODAL

Fig. 2.12 BIMODAL AND MULTI-MODAL DISTRIBUTIONS

case, we call the distributions respectively **bimodal** and **multimodal** distributions (fig. 2.12), and we shall need to quote the corresponding number of modal values.

2A 2b The average

It is surprising how most of us find no difficulty at all in talking about 'averages', yet we mostly claim to be hopeless at figures. In fact, we use the term 'average' rather frequently, and also rather loosely.

None of us would have much difficulty in working out the average number of times we saw our girl or boy friend in a week. If we were doing it accurately, we would make a list of the number of dates we had had for each week since we had been going out with the person in question, add all these figures up, and divide the total by the number of weeks. Now if we translate this description into the more technical language which we have introduced, we could say that the list of 'number of dates per week' is the 'data set' of the study. To work out the 'average' we would add up each of the figures in the data set, and divide that total by the number of figures in the set.

This kind of 'average' is called, more properly, the **mean** (or **arithmetic mean**) of the data set. There is another, very different, way of calculating the 'average', which we call the **median,** and it is simply because the two methods are different that we need to call them by different names. We shall see how to calculate the median later.

The description which we have just given of the mean is really quite a mouthful. It is often difficult to describe in words how to calculate different figures, and this can be a bit of a nuisance. In order to simplify matters, we may adopt a kind of 'shorthand' terminology. In fact, shorthand symbols are used for each of the words in the description, and so, if we are to make use of this simplifying device, we must become conversant with the accepted shorthand form.

There are three basic shorthand symbols which we need to know:

1 In statistics, the word 'figure' (or 'variable') is perhaps the most commonly employed. So our shorthand begins with

'figure'. The symbol for 'figure' is x.

2   The sign for 'add up' ('the sum of') is conventionally the Greek capital letter, Sigma, Σ.

3   The number of figures in a data set is represented by the letter n (which stands for 'number').

Having established the shorthand symbols, we may now re-write our earlier definition of the 'mean' which was given as 'the sum of each of the figures in the data set, divided by the number in that set'.

Substituting symbols for words, therefore,
'the sum of all the figures in the data set' $= \Sigma x$
'divided by' $= \div$
'the number of figures in that set' $= n$

Hence, the mean $= \dfrac{\Sigma x}{n}$.

Normally, we denote the mean by a little line above the figure x ($\bar{x}$), which we call a 'bar': thus, $\bar{x}$ (pronounced 'x bar') is the symbol for the mean.

Let us now calculate $\bar{x}$ for the land use data in fig. 2.1.

$$\Sigma x = 3821 \qquad n = 67$$
$$\bar{x} = \frac{\Sigma x}{n} = \frac{3821}{67} = 57 \cdot 0\%$$

The other kind of 'average' to which we have already referred, is the **median.** If we arrange the data set so that the highest value is at the top of the list, and all the figures follow by rank to the smallest value, the figure which falls half-way down the list will be the median of the data set.

Hence, with the land-use data set, the median value will be found by arranging the 'pastureland' values in descending order from the highest (77%) to the lowest (34%) (as in fig. 2.14), and then taking the figure which comes half-way down the list. In this example we are concerned with a data set which contains an *odd* number of figures (67), so that the figure exactly half-way down the data set is figure number 34; that is, 58%. But suppose we had a data set containing an *even* number of figures. There would not be a figure which occurred *exactly* half-way down the list, so how would we find the median? For instance, suppose

Fig. 2.13   RANKED DATA SET: student heights

STUDENT NUMBER	HEIGHT (cm)
1	185
2	180
3	175
4	172
5	170
6	170
7	167
8	165
MEDIAN	171

we had a data set showing the height of eight students (fig. 2.13). There is no actual figure which divides the list into two parts, so we must calculate one. Patently, the half-way point occurs *between* students 4 and 5 (i.e. 170 and 172 cm). The mid-point between the two figures will be given by the arithmetic mean of the two figures: in this case, $\bar{x}$ will be 171 cm and it is this figure which we quote as the median of the data set.

EXERCISES

1   Calculate (a) the mode,
              (b) the mean,
              (c) the median,
    of the data sets presented in figs 2.10 and 2.11.

2   Calculate the mode, mean and median of the heights you collected for Exercise 4 of Section 2A 1.

2A 3 Measuring Deviation

Whilst it may be useful to describe the data set by some 'average' measure, there remains the problem of describing the remainder of the population which does not correspond to this one value. It is all very well to describe land use by suggesting that the average (mean) amount of pastureland is 57%, but there are many parishes where the amount is different from this. Some have much more, others have far less. How then may we measure this 'deviation from the average'?

Perhaps the most obvious way would be to describe the difference between the parish with the most pastureland, and that with the least. In this example, the greatest amount of pastureland is 77%, the smallest is 34%, so we could say that the **range** is from 34% to 77%. But this tells us nothing about *how many* parishes are near to the average, or how many are below the average. What we need is something which will measure the deviation of parishes from the average value, in terms of some handy **deviation value.**

We have shown how there are two main methods of expressing the average: the arithmetic mean and the median. It follows

Fig. 2.14 CALCULATION OF VARIANCE AND STANDARD DEVIATION: original data from Fig. 2.1

Col. 1 x	Col. 2 $(x - \bar{x})$	Col. 3 $(x - \bar{x})^2$	Col. 1 x	Col. 2 $(x - \bar{x})$	Col. 3 $(x - \bar{x})^2$	Col. 1 x	Col. 2 $(x - \bar{x})$	Col. 3 $(x - \bar{x})^2$
77	+ 20·1	404·01	60	+ 3·1	9·61	54	− 2·9	8·41
75	+ 18·1	327·61	59	+ 2·1	4·41	54	− 2·9	8·41
72	+ 15·1	228·01	59	+ 2·1	4·41	53	− 3·9	15·21
70	+ 13·1	171·61	59	+ 2·1	4·41	52	− 4·9	24·01
70	+ 13·1	171·61	58	+ 1·1	1·21	52	− 4·9	24·01
69	+ 12·1	146·41	58	+ 1·1	1·21	52	− 4·9	24·01
68	+ 11·1	123·21	58	+ 1·1	1·21	52	− 4·9	24·01
68	+ 11·1	123·21	58	+ 1·1	1·21	50	− 6·9	47·61
66	+ 9·1	82·81	58	+ 1·1	1·21	50	− 6·9	47·61
65	+ 8·1	65·61	58	+ 1·1	1·21	50	− 6·9	47·61
65	+ 8·1	65·61	58	+ 1·1	1·21	50	− 6·9	47·61
64	+ 7·1	50·41	58	+ 1·1	1·21	50	− 6·9	47·61
64	+ 7·1	50·41	57	+ 0·1	0·01	48	− 8·9	79·21
63	+ 6·1	37·21	56	− 0·9	0·81	48	− 8·9	79·21
63	+ 6·1	37·21	56	− 0·9	0·81	48	− 8·9	79·21
62	+ 5·1	26·01	56	− 0·9	0·81	45	− 11·9	141·61
62	+ 5·1	26·01	56	− 0·9	0·81	45	− 11·9	141·61
61	+ 4·1	16·81	56	− 0·9	0·81	42	− 14·9	222·01
61	+ 4·1	16·81	56	− 0·9	0·81	37	− 19·9	396·01
61	+ 4·1	16·81	55	− 1·9	3·61	36	− 20·9	436·81
61	+ 4·1	16·81	54	− 2·9	8·41	34	− 22·9	524·41
61	+ 4·1	16·81	54	− 2·9	8·41			
61	+ 4·1	16·81	54	− 2·9	8·41			
			$\Sigma(x - \bar{x})^2 = 4\,771.77$					

that the methods of establishing deviation values will vary according to the measure which was used to evaluate the average.

2A 3a Deviation from the mean

A very simple way of assessing the amount of deviation from the mean within the whole set of data, is to find out by how much each individual occurrence deviates from the mean and then add up each of these individual deviations. These individual deviations can be tabulated alongside the original figures in the manner shown in fig. 2.14, and the total sum of the deviations indicated at the foot of that column. The difference between the mean and each value may be either positive or negative, but since we wish to know how much *overall* deviation there is in the data, we may ignore the question of whether the individual deviations are positive or negative. The **total deviation,** therefore, is the sum of the differences between each figure in the data set and the mean value of that set, irrespective of sign: in our shorthand, which we explained in the preceding section, that is:

$$\Sigma |x - \bar{x}|$$

(the vertical brackets are the symbols for 'ignore the sign').

However, although *ignoring* the sign is convenient, it is not correct, mathematically. We therefore need to find some mathematically correct way of removing the sign of the individual deviations, or, in mathematical terminology, of **standardising** the deviations.

We can all remember from first form mathematics that a plus times a plus is a plus ($+ \times + = +$), and that a minus times a minus is a plus ($- \times - = +$). If, therefore, we multiply every figure by itself (i.e. square it), we shall always end up with a *positive* figure. ($-6 \times -6 = +36: +6 \times +6 = +36$). And so, in order to standardise the deviations in our data set by correct mathematical means, all we do is to square the individual deviations.

The sum of these squares differences will then be the **total deviation squared.** In our shorthand, this becomes:

Total deviation squared = $\Sigma(x - \bar{x})^2$

Now, if we divide this sum by the number of observations in the data set (i.e. by *n*), we shall have calculated the 'mean squared deviation from the mean'. This is rather a mouthful and a new term is employed to describe this — the **variance** of the data set.

Hence the **variance** $= \dfrac{\Sigma(x - \bar{x})^2}{n}$

In calculating the variance it is necessary to tabulate, first of all, the individual deviations (as in fig. 2.14 col. 2), square them (fig. 2.14 col. 3), then add them up and substitute this value in the formula just given above. In terms of the land-use data it can be seen that the variance (fig. 2.14):

$$\frac{\Sigma(x - \bar{x})^2}{n} = \frac{4771 \cdot 77}{67} = \mathbf{71 \cdot 22}$$

What we are really wanting to find however is not the mean **squared deviation** but simply the mean deviation. Thus, if we take the square root of the squared deviation, we shall have calculated the 'standardised' mean deviation. This also reintroduces the feature of the negative and positive nature of the deviations, since the square root value of any number can be, by definition, either positive or negative — the root of 4 is ± 2: of 16 is ± 4 etc.

This 'standardised mean deviation from the mean' is referred to as the **standard deviation** of the data set, and is usually indicated by the small Greek letter, sigma σ, though, occasionally, the small letter 's' is used to denote the same thing. Hence:

$$\sigma = \sqrt{\frac{\Sigma(x - \bar{x})^2}{n}}$$

Using our example once more:

$$\sigma = \sqrt{\left(\frac{\Sigma(x - \bar{x})^2}{n} \right)} = \sqrt{71 \cdot 22} = \mathbf{8 \cdot 44}$$

Since the **variance** is the **standard deviation squared,** and since 'standard deviation' is written as 'σ', we can adopt a new sign for **variance**, σ^2. As can be seen from our example of land use, the number of calculations necessary to find both σ^2 and σ is rather great, and if we were dealing with a bigger data set, the amount of calculation would be just too much. The laborious part of the calculation is that of finding each individual deviation, squaring it, and then summing the total. Fortunately, it is possible to manipulate the formulae algebraically, so that in the end fewer calculations are necessary, and these revised formulae then take the form:

$$\sigma = \sqrt{\left(\frac{\sum x^2}{n} - \bar{x}^2\right)}$$

and

$$\sigma^2 = \frac{\sum x^2}{n} - \bar{x}^2$$

Where only *grouped* (i.e. **discrete**) data are available as a basic information source, these methods of calculating σ^2 and σ cannot be used, and further manipulations of the formulae are necessary. Full accounts of all these algebraic modifications will be found elsewhere (Gregory, S. 1963).

2A 3b Deviation from the median

The median was obtained by establishing the midpoint of the data set arranged in decreasing order of size. Now if we divide the list into two further halves, we shall find that we have four equal parts, each containing 25% of all the figures in the data set. These new lines are called **quartiles**, because they divide the list into four parts. The quartile at the top end of the arrayed values is referred to as the **upper quartile**, and the one at the lower end, the **lower quartile**. Clearly, these new quartile dividing lines will enclose the central 50% of all the occurrences. The difference between the upper and lower quartile values is known as the **inter-quartile range (IQR)**.

Now let us calculate the IQR for our land-use figures. We have already tabulated the values in descending order from highest to lowest (fig. 2.14). The median, as we have already seen is 58%. Having found the median of the 67 values in the data set, we next divide the first 33 figures into two equal parts; hence figure number 17 in the list (62%) is taken as the upper quartile. By the same procedure we find that the lower quartile is 52%. Hence, the IQR = 10% (62% – 52%).

This process of dividing the range of the data set into quartiles is just one case of a quite general scheme for dividing up a distribution into such **quantiles.** It is equally feasible to divide the range into as many parts as are felt to be necessary to demonstrate a particular point. Hence, if there were ten divisions, we should be creating **deciles**; if eight, **octiles**; if six, **sextiles**; and so on. This method of quantile division of the list serves, therefore, as another method of describing the dispersion of the data set.

EXERCISES

1   Using the information in figs. 2.10 and 2.11.
    (a) construct the quartiles;
    (b) find the values of **i** the upper quartile,
              ii the lower quartile;
    (c) find the Inter-Quartile Range;
    (d) calculate Variance;
    (e) calculate Standard Deviation.
2   For the student heights data which you have collected for Exercise 4 of Section 2A 1, calculate the same characteristics as those in Exercise 1 above.
3   Which method of measuring deviation appears to you to be the most useful, and why?

2A 4   The Overall Picture

It should be apparent by now that measures of the typical and measures of deviation are both necessary for a complete description of any data set. Simply to say that the mean amount of pastureland in Devwall is 57% is all right, but it means more if the extent to which there is a deviation from that mean can be indicated also. Hence, an 'overall' picture of the data set could be given by saying that the mean is 57% and the standard deviation is 8·44.

If we further relate these two figures together as a kind of ratio, we are able to express more effectively, in one combined measure, the overall variability of our data set.

We find too, that there are certain features about the mean and the deviation from the mean which are repeated for many different data sets, so that we can talk of a 'normal' data set or, more technically, a **normal distribution.** Such a distribution has certain properties which are important for our later studies.

2A 4a Combined measures

Two measures which combine central tendency and dispersion estimates are available.

First, there is one which is based on the median and the quartiles. If we express these as a ratio and divide the Inter-Quartile Range by the median value and then multiply by 100 we shall obtain what is called the

$$\textbf{index of variability} = \frac{\text{IQR}}{\text{median}} \times 100\%$$

In the case of our land use data the index of variability $= \dfrac{10}{58} \times 100 = 17\%$

Secondly, in precisely similar ways, we may arrive at an index based on the relationship of the standard deviation to the mean.

This index is called the **coefficient of variation,** and is denoted by the letter V.

$$V = \frac{\text{standard deviation}}{\text{mean}} \times 100\% = \frac{\sigma}{\bar{x}} \times 100\%$$

Substituting our land-use data in the formula it is seen that

$$V = \frac{8\cdot44}{57\cdot00} \times 100 = 14\cdot8\%$$

It is important that we understand precisely what these indices really mean. After calculating the coefficient of variation, we find that $V = 14.8\%$. What does this mean?

A moment's reflection will make it clear that if the standard deviation of the marks had been less, then the V value would have been less. Conversely, had the standard deviation been larger, V would also have been greater. Since standard deviation is a measure of the average amount of deviation from the mean, it follows that if this value is great in relation to the mean, many of the occurrences do not approximate very closely to the average (i.e. that the figures are highly dispersed). If, on the other hand, the standard deviation is small in relation to the

mean, there is not such a large 'dispersal' of the figures. Therefore, the lower the V value, the more the overall population approximates to the mean, and this being the case, from what was said in Section 2A 1c, the distribution will be very 'peaked' around the mean (Leptokurtic). In a sense, therefore, V measures 'Kurtosis' (see Section 4B 2).

Of all the methods of describing the central tendency and dispersion of data sets, it is the mean and the standard deviation which are most frequently employed, since, in general, they can be used as the basis of more refined analytical techniques whereas the others cannot.

2A 4b The normal distribution

From what we have said, it can be seen that the mean and standard deviation together will describe the overall shape of our frequency distribution or frequency curve. It was pointed out earlier (Section 2A 1c) that frequency curves tend to have certain characteristic shapes, and that the 'symmetrical' type (fig. 2.9A) is the one which

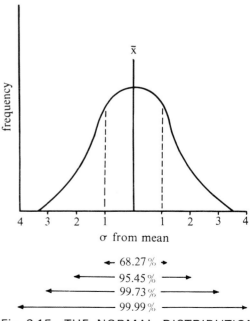

Fig. 2.15 THE NORMAL DISTRIBUTION

44

we shall normally encounter most. For this reason, the 'symmetrical' type is also called the **normal curve,** or, if it is in the form of a frequency table, the **normal distribution** (occasionally referred to as the **gaussian** distribution).

The normal curve is one which looks like that in fig. 2.15, and which has certain characteristic properties, notably:

1 The distribution is symmetrically placed around the MEAN value.

2 The maximum extent of the curve will normally be contained within a distance of ± 4 standard deviations from the mean value. Of course, this is not always the case and so we say that 99·99% of all occurrences will be within this distance, thus allowing for an occasional case (i.e. 1 in 10 000 cases) where the range may be greater. In other words, we could say that it is '99·99% probable that occurrences will fall within the range of 4σ of the mean'.

3 Similarly, it is found that:
68·27% of all occurrences will be within a distance of $\pm 1\sigma$ of the mean,
95·45% of all occurrences will be within a distance of $\pm 2\sigma$ of the mean,
99·73% of all occurrences will be within a distance of $\pm 3\sigma$ of the mean.

Ideally we could calculate the percentage number of points which would fall within any given distance of the mean (quoted in terms of σ), and in most elementary statistical tables a table which shows these 'percentage points of the normal distribution' will be found (Lindley and Miller, 1966, Table 2).

By the same reasoning as that in point 2 above, we could equally say that with the **normal curve** there is a
68% probability that the occurrence will occur within a range of $\pm 1\sigma$ of the mean.
95% probability that the occurrence will occur within a range of $\pm 2\sigma$ of the mean.
99% probability that the occurrence will occur within a range of $\pm 3\sigma$ of the mean.

Note that we have 'rounded off' these figures for the sake of brevity.

It is these notions which form the basis of deciding the size of samples which need to be taken in any study, as we shall demonstrate in Section 2C 4; they also provide the background for understanding certain problems about the reliability or significance of certain data, as we shall show in Section 2C. It is, therefore, important that these principles are clearly understood, for a great deal of statistical analysis is based on them.

EXERCISES

1 Using the information in figs. 2.10 and 2.11 respectively, calculate:
   (a) the index of variability
   (b) the coefficient of variation.
2 Calculate these same indices for the data on student heights (collected for Exercise 4 of Section 2A 1).
3 What, precisely, do these indices show?

2B COMPARISONS

We are all very used to making comparisons: our everyday language is full of them ('How does the price of butter compare with the price of margarine?'); so is the language of poetry ('Shall I compare thee to a summer's day?'). Despite the often heard comment that 'comparisons are odious', there should be little reservation in making comparisons in geography, because they are of a similar nature to those which we make elsewhere everyday.

There are, basically, three different kinds of comparison which we are likely to use in geographical studies. First, there are those comparisons which are *purely descriptive*. Geographers have always been particularly good at making simple descriptive comparisons. Much of geographical writing involves the comparison of two or more different regions from the point of view of their physical features, land use and human occupance. Indeed, it could be argued that some of the greatest geographical writing ever produced went under the name of 'comparative regional geography'. This type of descriptive comparison is outlined in Section 2B 1.

The second kind of comparison is one which is made in order to explain, at least *by inference*, certain characteristics which have already been described. For instance, if we were making a study of performance in an examination, we would need to explain why each candidate got the marks he did. To do this, we would need to think of all the factors which might be important in causing the distribution of marks obtained. This would be the difficult part of the study, for we would need to think very carefully of all the possible factors which might be involved. In this particular example, we would probably suggest that among the factors involved would be (a) the IQ, (b) the social background, and (c) the attitude to work of each candidate. Each of these three factors are effectively what we might call **dependent variables** because examination performance is thought to be dependent upon them.

We should then test to what extent these dependent variables were related to examination performance, and this we could do by comparing each candidate's examination performance with his rating on each of the dependent variables. Thus we should compare examination marks with (a) IQ rating, (b) some measure of social background, and (c) some measure of attitude to work. Having made these comparisons, we would be able to indicate the way in which the variables appeared to be related and then, *by inference*, we would be able to suggest which factors were important in explaining the examination performance achieved. Similarly, in geography we usually need to explain the patterns which we describe. For instance, in our study of land use in the various parishes of Devwall county, we found that the amount of pastureland varied considerably between the parishes ($V = 14 \cdot 8\%$ — Section 2A 4a). Patently, if the study is to be at all worthwhile we should next need to ask why there was such a variation in pastureland amounts. As with the question of examination performance which we mentioned above, we should need to sort out those factors which we thought to be important in causing the pattern we described. Again, this would be the difficult step in our study, for we should have to take

care to sort out those factors which *logically* appeared to be important; there is, of course, no guarantee that we would have thought of every factor. In the end, we should probably decide that the following factors were among the more important ones in determining the amount of pastureland in the parishes:

1 Attitude of farmers.
2 Soil type.
3 Climate.
4 Wealth of farmer.
5 Government aid.
6 Height of land.

These six variables would form our **dependent variables.** In order to see whether and to what extent they were related to the amount of pastureland, we could compare each of the parishes' pastureland amount with its score on each of the variables in turn. If, for example, those parishes which had large amounts of pastureland also had considerable tracts of high land, and vice-versa, we could probably infer that the amount of high land was a factor in determining the type of land use. The comparison between the two variables allows us to infer an explanation of a phenomenon, hence we shall refer to these kinds of comparison as **inferential explanatory comparisons**; and we shall describe them in detail in Section 2B 2.

The third type of comparison is also 'explanatory' in nature, and involves comparing some theoretical data with the actual data available. This comparison we shall refer to as the **theoretic explanatory comparison**. It will be discussed further in Section 2B 3.

2B 1 Purely Descriptive Comparisons

Describing the differences or similarities between two data sets is not an easy task. Let us consider, as an example, the difficulties which arise in comparing the amount of pastureland in a sample of ten parishes in each of two regions. There would be two data sets, one for each region, which we could set out side by side as in fig. 2.16. In

Fig. 2.16 CALCULATION OF MEAN AND STANDARD
DEVIATION : % pastureland in 10 parishes of region X
and 10 parishes of region Y

	DATA SET X (region X)			DATA SET Y (region Y)	
PARISH NUMBER	X	X^2	PARISH NUMBER	Y	Y^2
1	15	225	1	60	3 600
2	20	400	2	53	2 809
3	25	625	3	47	2 209
4	30	900	4	42	1 764
5	35	1 225	5	59	3 481
6	40	1 600	6	62	3 844
7	38	1 444	7	48	2 304
8	33	1 089	8	56	3 136
9	24	◆576	9	57	3 249
10	22	484	10	54	2 916
	$\overline{X} = 28 \cdot 2$ $\sum X^2 = 8\ 568$			$\overline{Y} = 53 \cdot 8$ $\sum Y^2 = 29\ 312$	

$$\sigma_x = \sqrt{\left(\frac{\sum x^2}{N} - \overline{X}^2\right)}$$

$$= \sqrt{\left(\frac{8\ 568}{10} - 795 \cdot 24\right)}$$

$$= 7 \cdot 85$$

$$\sigma_y = \sqrt{\left(\frac{\sum Y^2}{N} - \overline{Y}^2\right)}$$

$$= \sqrt{\left(\frac{29\ 312}{10} - 2\ 894 \cdot 44\right)}$$

$$= 6 \cdot 08$$

order to differentiate between these two data sets, we shall refer to the one set as 'data set X', and the other as 'data set Y'.

We would begin our comparison, no doubt, by comparing the 'typical' amount of pastureland in region X with the typical amount in region Y. As we have seen in Section 2A 1, there are several ways of measuring the typical, of which the most widely used is the 'mean' value. Hence, we shall first calculate the sample mean pasture land for the two regions: region X has a mean amount of 28·2 % pastureland, whereas region Y has 53·8 %. We can also say something about the deviation of both sets of data: for instance, the standard deviation of region X (σ_x) = 7·85, and that of region Y(σ_y) = 6·08 (fig. 2.16). We should, no

doubt, then be tempted to say that region X is different from region Y because the means and standard deviations of the two regions are different from each other.

It will be clear that great care needs to be taken when describing the two data sets together, for whilst it might appear, for example, that the two 'sample means' are very different figures, and that therefore there is a difference between region X and region Y, this difference may be more apparent than real. In any case, one might ask, how big a difference between the two data sets must there be for there to be a 'significant' difference between them? This is a problem to which we shall return later (Section 2C 1).

This, then, is the simplest form of comparison — a pure description of similarities or differences between any two or more data sets related to the same topic. In this case, the topic was 'amount of pastureland', but whatever it is, the important point is that this kind of comparison of two examples of the same subject is NOT an explanation of anything. We may, therefore, call this kind of comparison a **pure description.**

EXERCISE

Make a comparison of the number of food shops found in settlements of 8 000 to 12 000 population in Yorkshire and Northern France (data in fig. 2.17).

Fig. 2.17 NUMBER OF FOOD SHOPS: 15 towns in Yorkshire and 15 towns in Northern France

YORKSHIRE		NORTHERN FRANCE	
town number	number of shops	town number	number of shops
1	45	1	28
2	32	2	27
3	39	3	34
4	63	4	26
5	38	5	34
6	44	6	42
7	49	7	38
8	53	8	44
9	61	9	49
10	41	10	28
11	39	11	31
12	49	12	36
13	53	13	38
14	52	14	31
15	50	15	42

2B 2 Inferential Explanatory Comparisons

It was said earlier that a comparison between dependent and independent variables can often lead to an **inference** of cause and effect. In our land-use study, for example, we suggested that the amount of pastureland in a parish may be related to the amount of high ground (land over 500 metres) in that parish. How can we determine whether this is the case or not?

First, we should need to see how the data sets vary with respect to each other; hence the analysis begins by setting out the two data sets side by side (fig. 2.18). It can be seen at a glance that, in general, the amount of pastureland increases as the amount of high land increases, so that we could say that there is some degree of **correlation** between the two data sets. The correlation is not perfect for, if it were, *every* parish with an 'above average' amount of high land

Fig. 2.18 AMOUNT OF HIGH GROUND AND PASTURELAND: 12 parishes of Devwall

PARISH	DATA SET X % of land above 500 m	DATA SET Y % amount of pastureland
Crofton	26	37
Hornby	30	46
Backwell	33	48
Mere	36	49
Norton	54	50
Bentley	46	54
Throapham	52	56
Lidyard	58	62
Morchard	65	65
Bishopston	68	67
Gunnymead	70	74
Woodbury	74	79
	$\overline{X} = 51$	$\overline{Y} = 57$

would have an 'above average' amount of pastureland; in fact, as can be seen even from a brief visual inspection of the data sets, this is not the case at all. How, then, can we measure accurately the **degree** and **form** of correlation between two data sets? There are four major ways of showing statistically such correlations: firstly, we may calculate the **co-variance** of the data sets; secondly, we may calculate what is called a **correlation coefficient** for discrete or continuous data; thirdly, the correlation coefficient may be calculated in a different way for ranked data; and fourthly, we may show the correlation's form graphically by drawing what are called **regression lines**.

2B 2a Co-variance

We have just said that in our land use study, the correlation between pastureland and high ground was not perfect because not every parish which was above average in terms of pastureland amounts was above average as far as high ground was concerned. This method of comparing the two data sets is, in fact, the one which underlies the statistical calculation of co-variance: we may measure the extent to which the data sets co-vary in terms of their mean values and their deviations.

The first step, therefore, is to calculate the *mean* value of each data set, and then to measure the deviation of each parish away from the mean of each set.

In comparisons such as this, where we are trying to see if one variable is related to the other, we need to establish which of the variables is the **dependent** one and which is the independent one. Patently, in our current example, 'the amount of pastureland' is to be treated as a dependent variable, since, if our assumptions are correct, it is dependent on the amount of high ground. In order to distinguish between the two data sets, the one which is being considered as dependent is referred to as data set Y, the other, the independent, as data set X. (This convention stems from the other convention mentioned in Section 2A 1a that on a graph the dependent variable is plotted on the Y axis, whereas the independent is plotted on the

Fig. 2.19 CALCULATION OF CO-VARIANCE: based on data in Fig. 2.18

PARISH	DEVIATION data set X $(X - \overline{X})$	DEVIATION data set Y $(Y - \overline{Y})$	PRODUCT $(X - \overline{X})(Y - \overline{Y})$
Crofton	− 25	− 20	500
Hornby	− 21	− 14	294
Backwell	− 18	− 9	162
Mere	− 15	− 8	120
Norton	3	− 7	− 21
Bentley	− 5	− 3	15
Throapham	1	− 1	− 1
Lidyard	7	5	35
Morchard	14	8	112
Bishopston	17	10	170
Gunnymead	19	17	323
Woodbury	23	22	506

$$\Sigma(X - \overline{X})(Y - \overline{Y}) = 2\ 215$$

$$\frac{\Sigma(X - \overline{X})(Y - \overline{Y})}{N} = \frac{2\ 215}{12} = 184 \cdot 58$$

X axis. Hence, the dependent variable and its data set are referred to as data set Y).

The mean of data set Y (amount of pastureland) may be calculated and then the deviation of each parish away from that mean $(y - \bar{y})$ may be measured and entered in a further table (fig. 2.19). Similarly $\bar{x}$ and the values of $(x - \bar{x})$ may be calculated and entered in the same table.

We find, of course, that some parishes are above average in both data sets (i.e. $x - \bar{x}$ and $y - \bar{y}$ are both positive), while some are below average in both (i.e. $x - \bar{x}$ and $y - \bar{y}$ are both negative). There are also those (e.g. Norton or Throapham in fig. 2.18) which are above average on one score and below average on the other. But to go through the whole list quoting every single parish in turn is a very long-winded affair and, indeed, we cannot immediately see to what extent the dependent and independent variables are related. Somehow, therefore, we need to compress our data once more so that we can quote one single figure which will describe both the **extent** and the **direction** of *all* the parishes' deviations together.

The direction of the deviation is easy to indicate.

We saw in Section 2A 3a that multiplying signs involves changing the sign. Thus, $+ \times + = +$, $- \times - = +$ and $+ \times -$ or $- \times + = -$. If we use this notion in our attempt to describe how these two data sets vary with each other (co-vary), we can indicate all those cases where both figures are in the same relationship with a $+$ sign, and all those where they are inverse (one above, one below average) with a $-$ sign. Hence, all we need to do in order to express the relationship of the deviation of each pair of observations (pastureland and height) is to multiply the deviation in set X by the

deviation in set Y, taking care to note the signs. For instance in fig. 2.19 it can be seen that the deviation of Norton parish is -21, which tells us that it is above average on one, below on the other, whereas the deviation of Morchard parish is $+112$, which means that in both observations it is either above or below average.

If we go on to add up all these deviations, subtracting when the signs are $-$, we shall arrive at a figure which will indicate the *sum* of the *product* of the deviations ($\Sigma(x - \bar{x})(y - \bar{y})$). In order to find the mean of any value, as we have shown before, all we have to do is to divide by the number of items involved (n). Hence, to find the MEAN sum of the PRODUCT of the DEVIATIONS we divide $\Sigma(x - \bar{x})(y - \bar{y})$ by n; i.e.

$$\frac{\Sigma(x - \bar{x})(y - \bar{y})}{n}$$

where $n =$ the number of **pairs** of observations (i.e. the number of parishes).

Fig. 2.20 CALCULATION OF CO-VARIANCE: amount of arable land and height in 12 parishes of Devwall

PARISH	DATA SET X % land over 500 m	$(X - \bar{X})$	DATA SET Y % of arable land	$(Y - \bar{Y})$	$(X - \bar{X})(Y - \bar{Y})$
Crofton	26	-25	63	20	-500
Hornby	30	-21	57	14	-294
Backwell	33	-18	52	9	-162
Mere	36	-15	51	8	-120
Norton	54	3	50	7	21
Bentley	46	-5	46	3	-15
Throapham	52	1	44	1	1
Lidyard	58	7	38	-5	-35
Morchard	65	14	35	-8	-112
Bishopston	68	17	33	-10	-170
Gunnymead	70	19	26	-17	-323
Woodbury	74	23	21	-22	-506

$$\bar{X} = 51 \qquad \bar{Y} = 43 \qquad \Sigma(X - \bar{X})(Y - \bar{Y}) = -2\ 215$$

$$\frac{\Sigma(X - \bar{X})(Y - \bar{Y})}{N} = -184{\cdot}58$$

This value is referred to as the **co-variance** of the data sets [i.e. co(mbined) variance]. In this particular case the co-variance is +184·58 (fig. 2.19). What does this show? Short answer — it shows us, in one measure, something of the *relationship* between the two sets of data in combination. It is important at this point to realise that the co-variance value can be either a positive or negative value, depending on whether the two data sets under consideration vary in the *same* direction or not. If both vary in the same direction (as in fig. 2.19) (i.e. an increase in pastureland is associated with increased height), then the value will obviously come out POSITIVE (as it does here). However, if the two data sets vary in an INVERSE sense, then the values will be NEGATIVE. For instance, if we were dealing with percentage of arable land compared with height (fig. 2.20), we could see that the values in set Y decrease as the values in set X increase. The result is that the co-variance comes out as a negative figure ($-184·58$) (as can be seen in fig. 2.20). This is an important point to which we shall return a little later: if the relationship between set X and Y is in the *same* direction, co-variance is $+$, if the relationship between set X and Y is in the *opposite* direction, co-variance is $-$.

2B 2b The product moment correlation coefficient

We saw in Section 2A 3a, that any data set has a deviation which can be measured by the standard deviation (σ). Hence, where we are comparing two data sets, X and Y, one further measure of the deviation of each data set is this same standard deviation. We can calculate two values of σ: one for data set X (σ_X), the other for data set Y (σ_Y). If we then multiply the one by the other ($\sigma_X \sigma_Y$) we have a further measure of the combined deviations of the two data sets.

Hence, we find that when we are trying to see if two data sets X and Y are correlated, there are two different kinds of deviations which may be calculated. First, there is the co-variance which, as we have seen, measures the deviations of the two data sets *together and at the same time*;

second, there is the standard deviation which measures the deviations *irrespective of each other*. If we compare these two measures with each other (by expressing the one as a proportion of the other), we shall be able to tell how far the two data sets are related to each other. If the co-variance and the combined standard deviations are the same value, there will obviously be a high degree of similarity between the two data sets; if the two measures are not the same, then the correlation is less, and the more dissimilar they are, the more marked the absence of correlation. Since we are going to express one measure as a ratio of the other, we shall arrive at one simple figure which will indicate the extent of the correlation. This figure is indicated by the small letter 'r', and is known as the **product moment correlation coefficient** (or, sometimes, as the **Pearson correlation coefficient,** after the statistician, Pearson, who devised it) and is given by the formula:

$$r = \frac{\text{co-variance of data sets } X \text{ and } Y \text{ taken in pairs}}{\text{standard deviation of data set } X \text{ multiplied by standard deviation of data set } Y}$$

or, in statistical shorthand

$$r = \frac{\Sigma(x - \bar{x})(y - \bar{y})/n}{\sigma_X \quad \sigma_Y}$$

From what we have just said about how this figure is derived, it follows that values of r will occur in the range $+1$ to -1.

The sign, positive or negative, indicates whether the relationship is in the same direction or in an inverse direction. We saw in Section 2B 2a that where the two data sets vary in the same direction, the co-variance value comes out positive.

The values of standard deviation are always, as we saw in Section 2A 3a, positive or negative. Hence, the value r will be positive when the relationship between the two data sets is in the same direction. Where, however, the two data sets vary in INVERSE relationship (as in fig. 2.20), co-variance is negative, hence r is negative.

Perfect correlations will, therefore, be indicated by $+1$ and -1. As the correlation becomes less perfect, so the r value decreases towards 0, which occurs when there is NO correlation between the two data sets. The nearer the r value is to $+1$ or -1, the more perfect is the correlation.

In general, for convenience, the following critical values are taken to describe the different degrees of correlation:

Values of $\pm \cdot 700$ to $1 \cdot 000$ show
　　a high degree of association
$\pm \cdot 400$ to $0 \cdot 700$ show
　　a substantial relationship
$\pm \cdot 200$ to $0 \cdot 400$ show
　　a low degree of correlation
$\pm < \cdot 200$ show
　　a negligible relationship.

Now let us see how our two examples work out. First consider the 'pastureland' example. We have already calculated **co-variance** which is $+184 \cdot 58$ (fig. 2.19). Standard Deviation can be calculated by the method outlined in Section 2A 3a. (*As a revision exercise, work these out*). These are calculated as

$$\sigma_X = 16 \cdot 01$$
$$\sigma_Y = 12 \cdot 12$$

Substituting in the formula

$$r = \frac{\Sigma(x - \bar{x})(y - \bar{y})/n}{\sigma_X \; \sigma_Y} = \frac{184 \cdot 58}{16 \cdot 01 \times 12 \cdot 12} = +\mathbf{0 \cdot 95}$$

This means that there is a high degree of association between the amount of pasture-land and height above 500 metres, and that as height increases or decreases so does the amount of pastureland.

On the other hand, in the example dealing with arable land (fig. 2.20) it was shown that the co-variance was $-184 \cdot 58$ (Section 2B 2a). Hence, with the Standard Deviation being

$$\sigma_X = 16 \cdot 01$$
$$\sigma_Y = 12 \cdot 12 \quad \text{(as before)}$$

we find that

$$r = \frac{-184 \cdot 58}{16 \cdot 01 \times 12 \cdot 12} = -\mathbf{0 \cdot 95}$$

This means that there is a high degree of association between the amount of arable land and height above 500 metres, but that as height *increases*, the amount of arable land *decreases*.

Hence, it can be seen that correlation coefficients are a convenient shorthand way of expressing both the type and degree of association between two variables.

EXERCISE

From a study of agricultural land use in an area to the east of Dartmoor, it appeared that the amount of land given over to rough pasture varied according to altitude. Show to what extent these two phenomena are correlated (fig. 2.21).

Fig. 2.21　LAND USE AND HEIGHT:
　　　　　8 sample farms

farm number	height (metres)	% of rough pastureland
1	400	0
2	500	6
3	600	16
4	700	34
5	800	58
6	900	80
7	1 000	90
8	1 200	95

2B 2c The Spearman rank correlation coefficient

Although the calculation of the Pearson correlation coefficient (r) is a simple procedure, it is a rather lengthy one. It will be noted, too, that it can only be calculated for data which is in *absolute* values (e.g. *amount of high ground*). Very often, of course, we may not have sufficient time at our disposal to calculate r values in the manner we have just described; similarly, we do not always have data in absolute values, but in some other form, such as a list of items ranked in terms of their *relative order*. For example, examination results are not infrequently published as a list of names showing the relative position of each candidate (e.g. 1st Smith, 2nd Jones, 3rd Hughes . . .). Such a data set is what is called, in statistical language, a **ranked data set,** and the data is simply called **ranked data.** In order to differentiate between this kind of measurement and the kind which gives rise to discrete or continuous data such as we have used so far, two terms are employed: ranked data is said to be data on an **ordinal scale**; discrete and continuous data occurs as a **nominal scale.** Data on an ordinal scale is, effectively, **discrete data,** and so, from what we said earlier, different statistical procedures have to be used (Siegel, 1956).

Hence, where time is limited, or where the data which is available is in ranked form, we shall need to use another method to calculate whether or not a correlation between two data sets exists. There are, in fact, several slightly different techniques for comparing the ranks of two data sets, one of the best known and most widely employed being the **Spearman rank correlation coefficient** (called Rho ρ). This is one of the 'non-parametric' tests which, as we shall

explain in Section 2B 3b, often use ranks rather than actual numbers. In order to show that this correlation coefficient has been calculated by a different method from 'r', the letter 's' is normally written as a subscript to 'r' ('s' for Spearman). Hence, r_s refers to the Spearman rank correlation coefficient.

The basis of calculating r_s is the comparison of *differences in rank* of each item in the two data sets. Thus, as a starting point, we shall need to list the two data sets side by side so that the differences in rank may be easily worked out. As an example, let us rework the data relating to the twelve parishes in Devwall county. The rank of each parish in terms of (a) its amount of pastureland and (b) its amount of high ground, is entered into the table (fig. 2.22) (the parish with the greatest amount of pastureland is given first rank (1)). Then the difference of rank in the two data sets can be worked out, and we call the difference in rank the 'd' value. Thus the 'd' value for Norton parish

Fig. 2.22   CALCULATION OF d^2: based on data in Fig. 2.18

PARISH	Column 1 RANK in amount of pastureland	Column 2 RANK in amount of land >500 m	Column 3 difference col 1/2 (d)	Column 4 d^2
Crofton	12	12	0	0
Hornby	11	11	0	0
Backwell	10	10	0	0
Mere	9	9	0	0
Norton	8	6	2	4
Bentley	7	8	-1	1
Throapham	6	7	-1	1
Lidyard	5	5	0	0
Morchard	4	4	0	0
Bishopton	3	3	0	0
Gunnymead	2	2	0	0
Woodbury	1	1	0	0
		$\Sigma d^2 = 6$		

is $+2$, while that for Bentley is -1. Some parishes have the same rank on both scores, and their 'd' value is, consequently, 0.

Notice that some parishes have positive 'd' values while others have negative 'd' values. We have seen why it is necessary to 'remove the sign' when calculating values showing deviations (Section 2A 3a), and again it is necessary to do so here. Hence, we shall need to square the 'd' values, thus giving d^2 as in column 4 of fig. 2.22. It is these 'd' values which are then used in the following formula in order to calculate r_s (note that the technique is precisely that used before, based on calculating differences in the two data sets which are being compared):

$$r_s = 1 - \frac{6\Sigma d^2}{N^3 - N}$$

where d^2 = differences in rank squared

N = number of items being compared.

In our land-use example (fig. 2.22), we see that $\Sigma d^2 = 6$, and that the number of items being compared (N) is 12. Hence, substituting in the formula above, it is shown that

$$r_s = 1 - \frac{6 \times 6}{12^3 - 12} = +\mathbf{0.98}$$

From what we said earlier about r values (which applies equally to r_s values), we may say that there is a strong positive correlation between amount of pastureland and high ground.

Sometimes, however when we put the individual items of the data sets into rank order, we may find that two or more of the items *share the same rank*. For instance, suppose we were carrying out a study of the relationship between agricultural employment in villages and the distance of those villages from large cities, and we had finally drawn up a table showing the rank of each village relative to the others with respect to

Fig. 2.23 CALCULATION OF d^2: parishes' ranks in agricultural employment and their distance from a major town

PARISH	RANK in agricultural employment	RANK in distance from town	d	d^2
Crofton	1	12	-11	121
Hornby	2 = (2·5)	11	-8.5	72·25
Backwell	2 = (2·5)	10	-7.5	56·25
Mere	5	9	-4	16
Norton	4	7	-3	9
Bentley	7	6	1	1
Throapham	6	8	-2	4
Lidyard	8	3 = (4)	4	16
Morchard	10	3 = (4)	6	36
Bishopston	9	3 = (4)	5	25
Gunnymead	11	2	9	81
Woodbury	12	1	11	121
			$\Sigma d^2 = 558\cdot5$	

(a) number of people employed in agriculture and (b) the distance of that village from the large city, as in fig. 2.23. Here it can be seen that Hornby and Backwell parishes are 'second equal' in terms of employment (i.e. both have the same percentage of the population employed in agriculture), and that Bishopton, Morchard and Lydyard are all 'third equal' with respect to the distance from the city (i.e. they were all the same distance away). Such occurrences as this are known as **tied ranks.**

Before we can calculate r_s, it is necessary to give an actual numerical value to the tied ranks. In fact the *middle value* of the tied ranks is ascribed to each of the tied ranks for purposes of our calculations. In our example it can be seen that of Hornby and Backwell which share rank 2, one would have been rank 2, the other rank 3. So the middle value of these two tied ranks is 2·5, and this is the value we ascribe both to Hornby and Backwell. Similarly, of Bishopston Morchard and Lydyard which share rank 3, one would have been rank 3, another rank 4 and another rank 5. The middle value of these three tied ranks is 4, and it is this value which we ascribe to each of these three parishes in our calculation of r_s (shown in brackets in fig. 2.23).

Let us now calculate r_s using these 'tied rank' values: it can be seen that $\Sigma d^2 = 558\cdot5$ and $N = 12$; substituting in the r_s formula, therefore:

$$r_s = 1 - \frac{6 \times 558\cdot5}{12^3 - 12} = -0\cdot95$$

Hence there is a strong negative correlation between agricultural employment and distance from the major city (i.e. as proximity to town decreases, agricultural employment increases).

As can be readily appreciated, this method of calculating is both more rapid and less accurate than the Pearson method and this is reflected in the actual r_s value calculated. For instance, the r value for pastureland and height was $+0\cdot95$, the r_s value was $+0\cdot98$, yet both use the same basic information. The difference is simply a reflection on the different method used.

EXERCISE

A study has been made of the turnover and the number of shops in various London shopping centres, and it is thought that

Fig. 2.24   TURNOVER AND NUMBER OF SHOPS:
selected London suburbs

SHOPPING AREAS	RANK in turnover	RANK in number of shops
Central London	1	1
Croydon	2	2
Kingston	3	7
Brixton	4	6
Bromley	5	10
Ilford	6	4
Peckham	7	5
Lewisham	8	28
Wood Green	9	16 =
Clapham	10	13
Sutton	11	15
Hounslow	12	23
Ealing	13	21
Woolwich	14	29
Kilburn	15	12
East Ham	16	16 =
Streatham	17	19
Harrow	18	9
Holloway	19	25
Hammersmith	20	22
Tooting	21	18
Walthamstow	22	3
Wembley	23	24
Richmond	24	11
Bexleyheath	25	20
Fulham	26	26
Catford	27	30

perhaps the turnover of these areas is related to their number of shops. Show whether there is such a correlation between turnover and number of establishments (data in fig. 2.24).

2B 2d Regression

Correlation coefficients, such as those described in Section 2B 2b and 2B 2c, indicate the extent to which two variables are related. From r and r_s values, for instance, we can say more accurately whether the two variables show a high degree of association, a substantial relationship, a low degree of correlation or even a negligible relationship. Frequently, however, we may wish to know more than just the extent of the relationship; the *form* of that relationship may also be of interest. For example, having shown that the amount of pastureland is correlated with the amount of high ground in a parish ($r = +0·95$), it would be useful to know *what amount* of pastureland is related to what height. (If a parish had, say, 50% of its area over 500 metres high, how much of its area would be in pastureland?).

In fact, the form of the relationship may

be shown quite easily by means of a graph. We saw earlier (Section 2A 1a) that a graph shows the relationship between two variables, and that we normally plot what we call the **dependent** variables on the ordinate, or Y axis, while the independent variable is plotted on the abscissa, or X axis. Let us now, therefore, plot the information about pastureland and heights for each of the parishes on such a graph.

First, we need to decide which is the dependent and which the independent variable. Clearly pastureland is dependent on height, so that 'amount of pastureland' is the dependent variable and is plotted on the Y axis (fig. 2.25A).

It can be seen from this graph that the general form of the relationship between the variables follows, more or less, a straight line (called a **linear relationship**). This straight line shows the 'average' trend of the relationship; if we know the precise form of this 'average' trend we can begin to answer the question which we asked above, namely, 'What amount of one variable relates to what amount of the other?'

In this particular example, we could almost

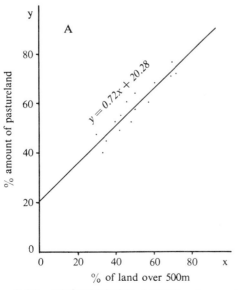
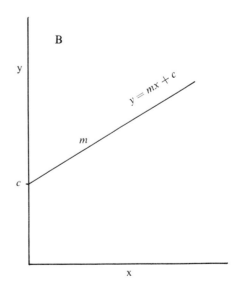

Fig. 2.25 REGRESSION LINES: A—pastureland and heights (data from Fig. 2.18); B—the general form of the line

draw in such a line by eye, but in order to be more accurate we should normally calculate mathematically the exact position of this average line. Such lines are called **regression lines,** and they describe, as we have suggested, the 'best fit' line through a series of points on a graph.

A straight line on any graph clearly describes the relationship of the values of the Y axis (ordinate) to those of the X axis (abscissa). A value of Y is related to a value of X, but the overall form of this relationship is also reflected in the position and slope of the line. Hence, if we are to know how Y values are related to X values, we shall need to take account of the position and slope of the average 'best fit' line going through the actual points. Generally it is found that the relationship of Y to X is given as

$$y = mx + c$$

where 'm' is a measure of the slope of the line and 'c' describes the position of the line on the graph by giving the point at which the line cuts the Y axis (fig. 2.25B).

Once m and c are known for a given relationship, it is easy to see how we would calculate what amount of Y (pastureland in our example) is related to what amount of X (height). Given a particular height (X), Y could easily be calculated by substituting the specific figures in the formula $y = mx + c$.

However, before we can do this, we need to calculate m and c. For both of these there are formulae which enable us to find their values.

We can calculate m by substituting in the formula

$$m = \frac{\Sigma xy - (\Sigma x)(\Sigma y)/N}{\Sigma x^2 - (\Sigma x)^2/N}$$

where N = the number of pairs of observations. And, similarly, we can find c by substituting in the formula

$$c = \bar{y} - m\bar{x}$$

So first of all, in order to find m or c, we must calculate Σx, Σy, Σxy, Σx^2, $\bar{x}$ and $\bar{y}$. All except Σxy were calculated earlier when we were calculating r (fig. 2.14), so this does not involve a great deal more labour!

In this particular example, the following values were calculated

$\Sigma x = 612$	$\Sigma x^2 = 34286$
$\Sigma y = 684$	$\bar{x} = 51\cdot0$
$\Sigma xy = 37099$	$\bar{y} = 57\cdot0$

Substituting, therefore, to find m:

$$m = \frac{37099 - 34884}{34286 - (612)^2/12} = \mathbf{0\cdot72}$$

Then, to find c:

$$c = 57 - 0\cdot72 \, (51\cdot0) = \mathbf{20\cdot28}$$

We are now in a position to use our formula $y = mx + c$, to draw in the regression line. We have calculated m and c, so in this example the regression line is described by

$$y = 0\cdot72x + 20\cdot28$$

In order to locate the line on the graph, we calculate the two values of y
  (a) the value of y when x is the 'mean' of the x data set ($\bar{x}$)
  (b) the value of y when x is any other value.
Thus, in our example, where the value of $\bar{x}$ is $51\cdot0$,

$$y = (0\cdot72)(51\cdot0) + 20\cdot28 = \mathbf{57\cdot0}$$

We shall calculate the other value of y when x is, say, 72. Hence,

$$y = (0\cdot72)(72\cdot0) + 20\cdot28 = \mathbf{72\cdot12}$$

It is these two pairs of values ($y = 57\cdot0$ when $x = 51\cdot0$ and $y = 72\cdot12$ when $x = 72\cdot0$) which we then plot on our original graph (fig. 2.25A), and, as can be seen, this line passes like an average through the middle of the array of dots on the graph. Note, too, how it crosses the Y axis at a value of $20\cdot28$ — i.e. the value of c. It is normal to indicate on the regression line the form of the equation which it represents — thus, we print on the line in this example, $y = 0\cdot72x + 20\cdot28$ (fig. 2.25A).

However, in certain circumstances it is necessary to use not the ordinary graph paper (on which we have been so far plotting regression lines), but either semi-logarithmic or log-log paper (see Section 3A 1e). In such cases either or both of the axes used for the graph will be on a logarithmic scale. It is

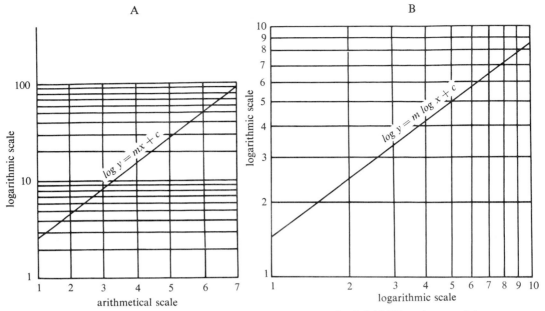

Fig. 2.26 REGRESSION LINES AND LOGARITHMIC SCALES: A—semi-log paper; B—log-log paper

necessary, therefore, when calculating the form of the regression line, to use the appropriate *logs* rather than the original figures.

In general we can say that

1 When we are using semi-log paper, the X axis will be the normal arithmetical scale, and the Y axis will be the logarithmic scale. Hence, all the calculations which involve 'y' values will have to be made using the *logs* of the y values. Thus, in this case, the final form of the regression line will be written

$$\log y = mx + c \quad \text{(fig. 2.26A)}$$

2 When we are using log-log paper, both x and y values will be measured in terms of the log values and so the form of the regression line will be written

$$\log y = m \log x + c \quad \text{(fig. 2.26B)}$$

In Section 4 we show how these semi-log and log-log regression lines can be calculated.

Hence, given any value of x, it is possible to estimate the value of y — provided this average relationship holds.

This then is a regression of y relative to x (or 'y' on 'x' as it would have been desig-

nated in statistical terms). Now what have we done? You will remember that we started by saying that we wanted to find a line which would show a kind of 'average relationship' of the points on the graph, and that is precisely what we have achieved. We have put our line through the middle of the points in such a way that the distances of all the points from this line are at a minimum. (We have 'minimised' the distance of the line from each of the points.) Now, in this case so far, we have measured the 'y' values relative to the 'x' values. In other words, we have *minimised* the distances in a vertical sense on the graph. Thus, the vertical distances of the points from the line are at a minimum. The measure of this distance was calculated in our formula by 'squaring' the distances so as to remove the signs — note the number of 'squared' values in our formulae for calculating m — and it is for this reason that the method of fitting the line to the points is known as the method of 'least squares'.

It is equally possible to calculate a regression line of x on y which would measure the 'least squares' in a horizontal direction, and this line will obviously be of

58

a different slope from that of the line y on x, but it will intersect the line of y on x at the mean value point. Thus, for any data set there will be two regression lines — one which predicts y from x and one which predicts x from y. Of course, the form of the regression is different in every problem which we consider. In some, the slope of the line will be greater than the one which we have calculated; for others, it will be less. What is important to remember is that the regression line describes the overall form of the relationship between two variables, whereas the correlation coefficient simply describes the extent of the relationship.

We have only considered here simple problems involving two variables. Naturally, we may wish to compare more than two data sets in some studies, and there are methods which enable us to do this. These are called **multiple correlation** methods and **factor analysis.** Further details of these methods, which are beyond the scope of this book, may be found elsewhere (Cole and King, 1968; King, L., 1969).

EXERCISE

Using the information about pastureland and altitude which we used in the exercise at the end of Section 2B 2b (fig. 2.21), calculate and plot on a graph the appropriate regression line.

2B 3 Theoretic Explanatory Comparisons

A slightly different way of explaining the distributions with which we are dealing is one which we might call the **inferential theoretic** method. By this method we compare the *actual* distributions with a distribution which we think *would have* existed had certain conditions been important. This latter distribution is, of course, a theoretical distribution. If the two distributions show the same basic pattern (i.e. if they compare well) we shall know that the factors we assumed to be important in our theoretical distribution will be, by *inference*, important

in the real distribution. This method, however, can only be used where the data set is in **grouped** form (in other words, it is a method for **discrete data** only).

Let us consider an example to show how this method works. Assume that we have collected information about the amount of pastureland in the parishes of Devwall county and we find that the *observed* frequency distribution of farms with more than 50% pastureland plotted against the amount of land 500 metres or more high is as in fig. 2.27. Now it appears, even from a casual inspection, that most farms with more than 50% of their area as pastureland are found in regions with a large amount of their area over 500 metres. We would, intuitively, suggest that height is an important factor in determining the amount of pastureland. But this is a very rough way of analysis — after all, it is purely an intuitive guess that this is the case.

Fig. 2.27 FREQUENCY DISTRIBUTION: 135 parishes with more than 50% pastureland

	% AMOUNT OF LAND OVER 500 m				
	0–20	21–40	41–60	61–80	81–100
Number of Parishes	5	10	10	30	80

2B 3a The null hypothesis

We can, in fact, start to measure the extent of this supposed correlation by setting up a theoretical distribution of farms which would exist, if height were of no importance. If the observed distribution had a similar form to this hypothetical one, then we could say that height was not important. If, on the other hand, it were not like it, then we could say that height probably was important.

It is, therefore, important that we set up a reasonable theoretical distribution, and this theoretical distribution we call a **null hypothesis,** because it is a distribution which would occur if something were not the case.

In our present example, we would set up

Fig. 2.28 EXPECTED FREQUENCY DISTRIBUTION: 135 parishes with more than 50% pastureland based on the null hypothesis that height does not affect the amount of pastureland

| | % AMOUNT OF LAND OVER 500 m | | | | |
	0–20	21–40	41–60	61–80	81–100
Number of Parishes	27	27	27	27	27

the **null hypothesis** that height was not important. If this were the case, then the number of farms found in each height category would be the same. Since there are five height categories here (0–20 up to 81–100), and a total of 135 farms, it follows that we should expect 27 farms in each height group. Thus the *expected* **frequency distribution** would read as shown in fig. 2.28.

2B 3b Comparing the observed with the expected

We are now in a position to compare the observed (O) with the expected (E) frequencies, and this we can do by calculating a quantity which is known as Chi-squared (written χ^2).

It is calculated by adding up the difference between each observed and expected frequency squared and divided by the expected frequency, i.e.

$$\chi^2 = \Sigma \frac{(O - E)^2}{E}$$

We shall find it easy to calculate χ^2 if we set out our data as in fig. 2.29.

This value of χ^2 is in a sense rather like a correlation value (r or r_s) in that it shows how one data set varies from the other, but it makes no immediate sense as a figure in itself. This figure has to be tested to see if the total difference between the two data sets which it represents is significant or not. We shall describe how this may be effected in Section 2C 3.

The Chi-squared test belongs to a series of statistical techniques known as **non-parametric statistics**. These differ from the parametric tests with which we have been mainly dealing in that they are 'distribution free': the parametric tests assume that the data under analysis conforms to the 'normal' distribution, whereas non-parametric tests do not make this initial assumption. Many of the non-parametric tests use not actual

Fig. 2.29 CALCULATION OF CHI-SQUARED: data from Figs. 2.27 and 2.28

| | % AMOUNT OF LAND OVER 500 m | | | | |
	0–20	21–40	41–60	61–80	81–100
Observed frequency (O) (Fig. 2.27)	5	10	10	30	80
Expected frequency (E) (Fig. 2.28)	27	27	27	27	27
$O - E$	– 22	– 17	– 17	3	53
$(O - E)^2$	484	289	289	9	2 809
$\dfrac{(O - E)^2}{E}$	17·93	10·7	10·7	·33	104·04
$\Sigma \dfrac{(O - E)^2}{E} = 143\cdot70$					

numbers but **ranks,** as we have seen with the Spearman rank correlation coefficient (Section 2B 2c) and the Chi-squared test. The reader who wishes to pursue these techniques further is referred to the works of Siegel (1956), Hoel (1960), and Fraser (1957).

EXERCISE

We have collected information about the number of antique shops in towns of 8–12 000 population in southwest England, and we find that most of those towns which have a more than average number of antique shops (5), seem to be those which contain high percentages of retired people. Fig. 2.30 shows the form of this distribution.
(a) Establish a null hypothesis to test the effect of retired people on antique shop distribution
(b) calculate the value of Chi-squared for this data.
This information will be used again later in the exercise at the end of Section 2C 3.

Fig. 2.30 OBSERVED FREQUENCY OF ANTIQUE SHOPS: 28 towns classified according to the percentage of retired people they contain

| | % OF TOTAL POPULATION RETIRED | | | | |
	0–1	2–3	4–5	6–7	8
NUMBER OF TOWNS 8–12 000 population which have more than 5 antique shops	2	4	4	8	10

2C SIGNIFICANCE

We have seen that comparisons may be either descriptive or explanatory, and we have seen how precise statistical methods may help us to make these comparisons in an accurate manner. However, great care must be taken when making such comparisons.

When comparing two data sets of the same phenomenon, we need to be certain that any differences or similarities between the two sets could not have occurred by chance. It is just possible, for instance, that, had we chosen different parishes for our pastureland study, the figures may not have shown the same difference at all, even though they may have been sampled properly by methods such as those which we outlined in Section 1C. Similarly, there is a very real danger that we may be misled by correlation coefficients which appear to be so precise. It is possible, for example, that under certain conditions the correlation may have occurred by chance. The figures in our data set may just happen to have been the right ones to bring about a correlation. For instance, in our land-use example it may be that the sample parishes which we have used just happen to yield a set of figures which produce a correlation; whereas, if we chose another set of parishes in the region, even assuming our sampling technique to be correct, no correlation may occur at all. In this case, it would have been mere chance that the correlation had come out the first time.

It is necessary, therefore, to find a method of testing our comparisons to see whether they *could* occur by chance, and whether they really are **statistically significant.** If a comparison is statistically significant, we mean that the apparent comparison could not have occurred by chance.

Since the comparisons which we can make are of different kinds, so too are the methods which we can employ to establish whether those comparisons are significant or not. Hence, the three different methods of comparison which we outlined in Section 2B have specific tests of significance which may be applied to them. Pure descriptive comparisons may be tested by calculating the **standard error of the difference** and using the 'students' t **test'**; inferential explanatory correlations are tested by the students' t test (modified) and by the fitting of **confidence limits** to regression lines; inferential theoretic explanations are tested by several tests, of which the best known is χ^2 tested against degrees of freedom.

2C 1 Significance in Purely Descriptive Comparisons

The basic factor which underlies the whole need for tests of significance is one which we have just mentioned above, notably the fact that in our *sample* we may, by chance, have chosen just those figures which when manipulated statistically suggest that there is some significant difference between them.

When we compared two data sets which were different examples of the same characteristic (e.g. the land use in parishes of two major regions), we began by comparing the *means* of the two data sets (Section 2B 1). Now, since both data sets were only *samples* of the total population, we were here also dealing with **sample means.** The big problem, therefore, in assessing whether the difference between the two sample means is significant or not, is really one of knowing whether the **true means** (i.e. the means of the **total population**) would differ to the same extent as the sample means.

2C 1a Standard error of the mean

Each sample mean figure is liable to some error, because it is only a calculation based on a sample. This error can in fact be estimated quite simply by using the formula which will calculate what we call the **standard error of the mean** (the name 'standard' comes from the fact that the standard deviation (σ) is used in its calculation), and is found by dividing the standard deviation by the square root of the number of items in the sample.

i.e. $$\text{S.E.}\overline{X}. = \frac{\sigma}{\sqrt{n}}$$

where n = number of items in sample.

It will be recalled from Section 2A 4b that in a normal distribution there is a 68% probability that any figure will occur within a range of $\pm 1\sigma$ of $\bar{x}$, a 95% probability that it will occur within a range of $\pm 2\sigma$ of $\bar{x}$ and a 99% probability that it will occur within a range of $\pm 3\sigma$ of $\bar{x}$. Hence, it follows that the **true mean** of any population will be equal to the sample mean, ± 1, 2 or 3

standard errors of the sample mean with, respectively, 68%, 95%, 99% levels of probability. This we can write in our short-hand as follows

$$\overline{X} = \bar{x} \pm \frac{\sigma}{\sqrt{n}} \quad \text{with 68\% probability}$$

$$\overline{X} = \bar{x} \pm \frac{2(\sigma)}{\sqrt{n}} \quad \text{with 95\% probability}$$

$$\overline{X} = \bar{x} \pm \frac{3(\sigma)}{\sqrt{n}} \quad \text{with 99\% probability}$$

2C 1b Standard error of the difference

Now when we are comparing *two* sample means, it is obvious that each sample mean is subject to a standard error. Hence in data set X, we can see that there will be a standard error of $\bar{x}$ (S.E.$\bar{x}$), and in data set Y, a standard error of $\bar{y}$ (S.E.$\bar{y}$). In our land use example, these figures are, respectively,

$$\bar{x} = 28{\cdot}2\%; \text{S.E.}\bar{x} = \textbf{2}{\cdot}\textbf{48}$$
$$\bar{y} = 53{\cdot}8\%; \text{S.E.}\bar{y} = \textbf{1}{\cdot}\textbf{92}$$

The big question, as far as the difference between $\bar{x}$ and $\bar{y}$ is concerned, is whether this difference is significant or not. Again, for the same reasons already explained with reference to each data set's sample mean figure, the difference between these two sample means is also liable to some error. We need, therefore, to calculate the **standard error of the difference** between these sample means (i.e. S.E.$\bar{x} - \bar{y}$).

2C 1c Probability levels

Just as the standard error of the mean has certain probability characteristics, so does the S.E. of the difference. Thus we can say that there is a

68% probability that $\text{S.E.}\overline{X}. - \overline{Y}$

$$= \text{S.E.}(\bar{x} - \bar{y}) \pm \left(\frac{\sigma_x}{\sqrt{n_x}} + \frac{\sigma_y}{\sqrt{n_y}} \right)$$

95% probability that $\text{S.E.}\overline{X} - \overline{Y}$

$$= \text{S.E.}(\bar{x} - \bar{y}) \pm 2 \left(\frac{\sigma_x}{\sqrt{n_x}} + \frac{\sigma_y}{\sqrt{n_y}} \right)$$

99% probability that $\text{S.E.}\overline{X} - \overline{Y}$

$$= \text{S.E.}(\bar{x} - \bar{y}) \pm 3 \left(\frac{\sigma_x}{\sqrt{n_x}} + \frac{\sigma_y}{\sqrt{n_y}} \right)$$

In other words, if the difference of the sample means $(\bar{x} - \bar{y})$ is greater than $2 \times$ the standard error of the difference, that difference is probably significant (there is only a 5% chance that it could have occurred by chance); if it is greater than $3 \times$ S.E. of the difference, then it is almost certainly significant (i.e. only a 1% chance of occurring by chance). This, in fact, gives us our standard 'shorthand' connection of *levels* of significance.

If there is a 95% level of probability that this would not have occurred by chance (there is a 5% chance that it *would* have occurred by chance), then the difference is **probably significant.**

If there is a 99% level of probability that this would not have occurred by chance (1% chance that it *would* have occurred by chance), then the difference is **significant.**

If there is a 99·9% level of probability that this would not have occurred by chance (0·1% chance that it *would* have occurred by chance), then the difference is **highly significant.**

In our particular example we have seen that the actual difference $(\bar{x} - \bar{y}) = 25·6 \%$ S.E. of difference $= 4·40$. Hence, we may safely conclude, since $(\bar{x} - \bar{y})$ is greater than 3 times the S.E. of the difference, that there is a highly significant difference between the two regions in terms of the amount of pastureland.

2C 1d Student's 't' test

It will be appreciated, however, that this is a rather rough and ready method of assessing the levels of probability. We have been dealing only in terms on 1, 2 or 3 standard deviations, but if we divide the difference between the sample means by the S.E. of the difference we shall get a more accurate measure of how many times greater than the S.E. the actual value is. This method is known as **students' *t* test,** and the index which we have just calculated as '*t*' ('Student' was the pen name of the mathematician Gosset, who first described this '*t*' distribution). Hence

$t = \dfrac{\text{the difference between the sample means}}{\text{S.E. of the difference between the sample means}}$

In our example, therefore, 't' $= \dfrac{25·6}{4·4} = \mathbf{5·81}$

This value of 't' is then looked up in a series of tables or on a graph, to show the % probability of this occurring by chance (just as we did before in the less refined method). In these tables (Lindley and Miller, 1966, Table 3) or on the graph, t values are plotted against 'degrees of freedom'. Degrees of freedom are simply a statistical convention relating to the number of items in samples, and are given as the **number of items in the sample minus 1.** Where, as here, we are dealing with 2 samples, then the degree of freedom is the number of items in *both* samples minus 2. Hence, in our example, where we have 2 data sets each with 10 occurrences, the degrees of freedom are $20 - 2 = 18$.

We are now in a position to see whether the difference is significant or not. Reading off $t = 5·82$ against 18 degrees of freedom, we see that the difference between the two regions (X and Y) could have occurred by chance in only 0·1% of all cases, and that, therefore, there is a 99·9% probability that the difference is significant. The difference is, therefore, **highly significant.**

EXERCISE

Using the information given in fig. 2.17, show to what extent there is a significant difference in the number of foodshops found in towns in Yorkshire and Northern France.

2C 2 Significance in Correlation and Regression

The methods available for testing the significance of correlation coefficients and regression lines are similar to those outlined in the previous section, and are necessary for precisely the same reasons.

63

2C 2a Students' 't' and 'r' values

Having calculated correlation coefficients, we need to know whether these could have occurred coincidentally for the reasons outlined in the preceding section. The method which we use for testing the significance of a correlation coefficient is the **students' 't' test,** although the formula for calculating 't' in this case is different from that used in the preceding section. The formula involves the use of the correlation coefficient (r) and the 'degrees of freedom' once more, and is written

$$t = \frac{r \sqrt{(n-2)}}{\sqrt{(1-r^2)}}$$

where $n-2$ are the 'degrees of freedom' and r the correlation coefficient.

In our pastureland example (Section 2B 2a), we saw that the correlation between amount of pastureland and amount of land over 500 metres came out $r = +0.95$. The number of occurrences in the data set 'n', $= 12$. Hence

$$t = \frac{0.95 \sqrt{10}}{\sqrt{(1 - (0.95)^2)}} = \mathbf{9.62}$$

As before, this value of t is read off against the 'degrees of freedom' (in this case 10) to ascertain the level of probability of this correlation occurring by chance.

In this particular example it will be seen that with $t = 9.62$ and 10 degrees of freedom, we are well within the 0.1% probability level. This means that there is only one chance in 1 000 that this correlation would have occurred by chance, and so it is 99.9% probable that the correlation is a significant one. Using the terminology established earlier, the correlation may be described as **highly significant.**

This same 't' test may be used for either of the correlation coefficients which we examined in Sections 2B 1a and 2B 1b — i.e. the Pearson Correlation Coefficient or the Spearman Rank Coefficient, and the levels of probability of the coefficient occurring by chance are the same as those which we outlined earlier in Section 2C 1c.

EXERCISE

How significant is the correlation which was calculated in the exercise at the end of Section 2B 2b (data in fig. 2.21)?

2C 2b Standard error and regression lines

Regression lines, too, whether they be y on x or x on y, are only 'best estimates', and again we need to show the 'levels of probability' that these could or could not have occurred by chance. This we can do by calculating the **standard error** of the estimates. The formula for this, when the regression is y on x, is

$$Sy = \sigma y \sqrt{(1 - r^2)}$$

where Sy = Standard Error of y.

For our regression using the land-use example (Section 2B 2b)

$$Sy = 12.2 \sqrt{(1.0 - 0.95^2)} = 3.775$$

This figure is then used to establish 'confidence limits' around the regression line. We showed earlier (Section 2A 4b) that, with a normal distribution, there is a 68% probability that actual values will differ from the mean by no more than $\pm 1\sigma$; a 95% probability that they will differ by no more than $\pm 2\sigma$; and a 99% probability that they will differ by no more than $\pm 3\sigma$. Since our Standard Error (Sy) was calculated using σ, these same probability properties will hold for it as for the standard deviation. Thus there is a 68% probability that the points near our regression line will not be further away from the line than at a distance of ± 1 Standard Error (in this case of ± 3.775 units on either side of the line); a 95% probability that they will be no further than $\pm 2Sy$; and a 99% probability that they will be no further away than $\pm 3Sy$.

If we therefore draw a pair of lines at the appropriate distance away, we can represent these limits of probability (the 'Confidence Limits') on our graph. In our example, we find that $Sy = 3.775$, so we draw a line 3.775 units above the regression line and another one 3.775 units below the regression line. This confidence limit will be that of 1 Sy. By the same processes we can establish other confidence limits at distances of 2 Sy and 3 Sy away from the regression line (fig. 2.31). We would not normally leave all three confidence limits on the graph, but simply indicate the 2 Sy or 3 Sy (i.e. 95%–99%) level.

EXERCISE

On the graph which was drawn to show the regression line between pastureland and altitude (exercise at end of Section 2B 2d), plot the 95% and 99% confidence limits (data set in fig. 2.21).

2C 3 Significance in Theoretic Explanatory Comparisons

We saw in Section 2B 3 how Chi-squared could be calculated to show whether the observed occurrence of a phenomenon corresponded in any way to a distribution which might, theoretically, have been anticipated if certain factors had not been important.

Once more, we need to know whether the differences between the observed and expected values (which χ^2 measures) could be the result of chance or not. So, again, we need to test the significance.

The value of χ^2 is then looked up in a table showing the percentage points of the χ^2 distribution: just as 't' values are read off against 'degrees of freedom' to assess the significance of differences between two means, so the χ^2 value is read off against the appropriate 'degrees of freedom' to show whether the difference between the observed and expected distribution is significant (Lindley and Miller, 1966, Table 5).

In our particular example, it can be seen that $\chi^2 = 143 \cdot 7$ against 4 degrees of freedom $(n-1)$ is well within the limit and that there is a 0·1% probability of this value occurring by chance. Therefore, the null hypothesis on which the comparison was based could only occur by chance once in a thousand occasions. Hence, there is a 99·9% probability that the observed differences are *not* the result of a

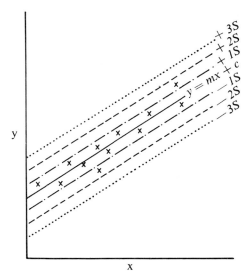

Fig. 2.31 REGRESSION LINES AND CONFIDENCE LIMITS

chance occurrence, and that the differences are statistically highly significant.

The fundamentally important task in calculating χ^2 is that of making the correct null hypothesis and of ascribing the correct 'expected' values for the distribution. Thereafter, care must be taken with the interpretations, as it is all too easy to get lost in a language which deals with double negative statements such as 'there is a 0·1% probability that the null hypothesis could not have occurred by chance'.

EXERCISE

Using the initial data and the null hypothesis established for the problem described in the exercise at the end of Section 2B 3, show whether the percentage of retired people is a statistically significant factor in explaining the distribution of antique shops (fig. 2.30).

2C 4 The Size of a Sample

Implicit in all our testing of significance has been the assumption that the samples we

65

use in any study should have been properly drawn. We have already described (Section 1C) the ways in which samples should be made, but we must now consider the important question of how large the sample should be.

In Section 2C 1a, we showed how a 'sample mean' has a 'standard error' which can be calculated by means of the formula

$$\text{S.E.}\bar{x} = \frac{\sigma}{\sqrt{n}}$$

and which enables us to estimate, with various levels of probability, the limits of the **true** mean ($\bar{x}$) of the whole population from which the sample was drawn. Knowing that we can calculate S.E., it becomes apparent that we could also judge how large a sample would be necessary to give us a **true** mean to within given limits. If we knew, from a very small sample, what the standard deviation and sample mean were likely to be, we could decide what sort of S.E. we would be willing to accept as being reasonable. We may decide in our land-use example that for region X we need to take a sample which would enable us to estimate at the 95% probability level the true mean to within $+$ or -4% of the sample mean. How large a sample do we need to take to estimate to this level of probability?

We saw earlier that $\text{S.E.}\bar{x} = \frac{\sigma}{\sqrt{n}}$.

This may be re-written to give $n = \frac{(\sigma)^2}{d}$.

The desired $\text{S.E.}\bar{x}$ is, we have just decided, to be within $+$ or -4% of the sample mean at the 95% level — i.e. $2x\ \text{S.E.}\bar{x} = 4\%$, therefore S.E. must $= 2\%$.

Knowing S.E., therefore, and also knowing from our initial survey (fig. 2.16) that $\sigma = 7.85$, we can calculate what size sample, n, is necessary.

In our particular example, therefore,

$$n = \left(\frac{7.85}{2.0}\right)^2$$

$$n = \mathbf{15.41}$$

Hence, it would be necessary to sample at least 16 farms from the mean population in order to arrive at the degree of accuracy which was suggested.

Hence, determining the appropriate size of sample is a two-stage process. A small sample is made first in order to get an impression of the standard deviation of the population, and thereafter, when n is calculated, the full scale survey is mounted.

FURTHER READING

Cole, J. P. and King, C. A. M., *Quantitative Geography* (Wiley, 1968).

Fraser, D. A. S., *Nonparametric Methods in Statistics* (Wiley, 1957).

Gregory, S., *Statistical Methods and the Geographer* (Longmans, 1963).

Hoel, P. G., *Elementary Statistics* (Wiley, 1960).

King, L. J., *Statistical Analysis in Geography* (Prentice-Hall, 1969).

Lindley, D. V. and Miller, J. C. P., *Cambridge Elementary Statistical Tables* (C.U.P., 1966).

Siegel, S., *Nonparametric Statistics* (McGraw-Hill, 1956).

Spiegel, M. S., *Statistics* (Schaum, 1961).

3 Visual Representation of Data

Having processed the raw data set which has been collected from various sources, the next step may be to present that data in some visual form. The figures contained in a data set will refer either to time, space or to both. It follows, therefore, that the method of portraying the data set will initially be determined by which of these aspects is to be described. If we wished to show the spatial distribution or location of the characteristic being studied, we should inevitably begin by portraying the information in map form. On the other hand, if the data referred to only one location we should not be concerned with any spatial variation, and our presentation would be restricted to the use of various diagrams without a spatial context.

3A DIAGRAMS

There are, of course, many different ways of presenting the basic data in diagrammatic form, but it will not matter how accurately sampled or processed that data is if we do not choose the correct method for its portrayal. As we shall see, it is important that we understand not only the uses of different diagrams, but also their misuses and abuses.

Basically there are two main kinds of diagram: first, there are various graphs, and second, there are many different symbols, both of which are extensively used in studies of human geography.

3A 1 Graphs

The simplest kind of graph is one which is used to locate the position of a given characteristic with respect to any two variables represented by the two axes of the graph, the abscissa and the ordinate (Section 2A 1a). On the abscissa (or Y axis) is plotted the dependent variable whilst the independent variable is represented on the ordinate (or X axis). Each of the points which locate the items in the study is then joined together to form a 'polygon' or curve (fig. 2.5) and an immediate visual impression of the data set is given. There are, however, many modifications which can be made to this simple graph in order to show more complicated relationships though it is important to remember that if the scales of the axes are not properly chosen the slope of the curves produced will be distorted, thereby giving an erroneous impression of the data. Great care is needed in the construction and interpretation of even the most simple graph.

3A 1a Cumulative graphs
Cumulative graphs, of which the ogives described in Section 2A 1c are an example, are mainly used to show the amount and rate of change of various characteristics over

Fig. 3.1 PRODUCTION OF THREE BRANDS OF WASHING POWDER

BRAND	OUTPUT BY YEAR OF PRODUCTION									
	1	2	3	4	5	6	7	8	9	10
X	20	40	60	80	100	120	140	160	180	200
Y	100	110	121	133	146	161	177	195	214	235
Z	100	181	245	294	330	355	371	380	384	385

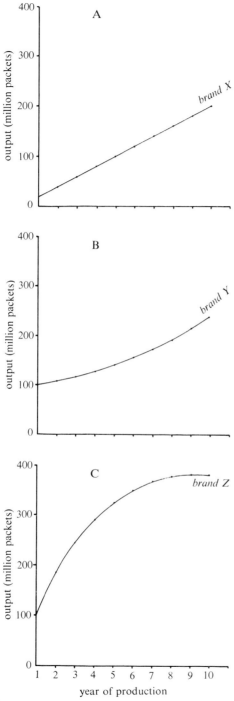

time. A great deal of care, however, needs to be taken over their interpretation since there is a vast difference between the *rate of change* and the *amount of change* in any given situation.

Consider, for example, the consumption of three brands of washing powder over a ten year time period (fig. 3.1). In the first year of production 20 million packets of brand *X* are sold, compared with 40 million packets in the second year, 60 million in the third year and so on — each year there is a constant increase of 20 million packets in the *amount* of production. Over the same period, brand *Y* washing powder is also increasing in production but in this particular case the *amount* of increase is, in fact, increasing annually, whereas production of brand *Z* powder whilst increasing, is doing so by a *decreasing* amount in each successive year. If these figures are plotted cumulatively on a graph it can be seen that when the *amount* of increase is constant between each period the production curve takes the form of a straight line (fig. 3.2A) whereas an increasing amount of increase has a slope which becomes increasingly steeper (fig. 3.2B) and a decreasing amount of increase has a slope which becomes progressively less steep (fig. 3.2C).

However, although there is a constant *amount* of increase in the production of brand *X*, it is clear that the *rate* of increase is in fact decreasing. The increase in production between year 1 and year 2 is from 20 million to 40 million packets, which is obviously a 100% increase; between year 2 and year 3, production again rises by 20 million units from 40 million to 60 million packets, but this time the increase of 20 million units is only 50% of the original production in year 2 (40 million packets). Progressively, in fact, the *rate* of increase of production is gradually decreasing, so that between years 9 and 10 the increase is only 11·1%. Brand *Y*, however, whose production was seen to be increasing by an increasing *amount* is, in fact, increasing only at a constant *rate*; an increase in production from 100 to 110 units in the first two years represents a 10% increase in both *amount* and *rate*, but the increase between the ninth

Fig. 3.2 PRODUCTION OF WASHING POWDER (data from Fig. 3.1) : A—brand *X*; B—brand *Y*; C—brand *Z*

Fig. 3.3 CUMULATIVE PERCENTAGE DISTRIBUTION: growth of City of Exchester

DATE	ACTUAL AREA OF CITY (sq m)	PERCENTAGE OF 1970 AREA
1670	2 500	2·5
1720	4 000	4
1770	8 000	8
1820	14 000	14
1870	35 000	35
1920	80 000	80
1970	100 000	100

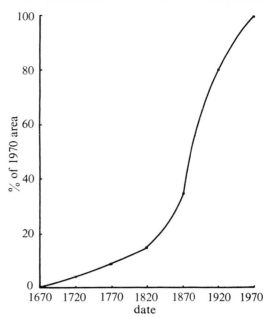

Fig. 3.4 CUMULATIVE PERCENTAGE DISTRIBUTION: growth of City of Exchester (data from Fig. 3.3)

and tenth years from 214 to 235 units, whilst in *amount* much greater than in the first period, is still only a 10% *rate* of increase. In describing the shape of curves, therefore, the dangers associated with the use of the terms 'amount of increase' and 'rate of increase' and the implications of each must be realised before they are used. (See also Section 3A 1e.)

Apart from this straightforward type of cumulative graph which simply plots the actual amounts of production of one variable on the ordinate against time on the abscissa, successive amounts of production expressed as *proportions* of the final total amount of production can also be plotted in a similar manner. For example, from a survey of architectural styles and map evidence we could make an estimate of the size area of a town at various time intervals up to the present day. If the sizes of the town at all dates in the survey are then expressed as a percentage of the maximum size and the resultant data is plotted graphically, a per-centage cumulative graph results (figs. 3.3 and 3.4).

A similar technique, but relating two variables together, is employed in the construction of **Lorenz curves.** If, for example, we were studying the output of two firms over a period of years we could, for each firm, express each year's production as a percentage of the total cumulative production over the whole time period (fig.

3.5). Both of these resulting values would then be plotted together by drawing two axes (representing, respectively, the production of firm *A* and firm *B*) and dividing both

Fig. 3.5 CUMULATIVE PERCENTAGE DISTRIBUTION: growth in output of two firms

YEAR	OUTPUT OF FIRM A each year's output as % of 1970	OUTPUT OF FIRM B each year's output as % of 1970
1961	10	5
1962	30	10
1963	50	15
1964	60	20
1965	65	30
1966	70	45
1967	75	65
1968	80	90
1969	90	95
1970	100	100

69

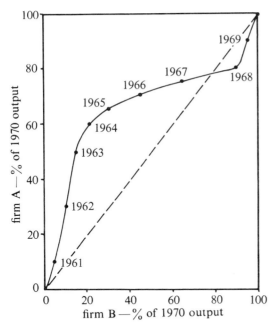

Fig. 3.6 LORENZ CURVES: growth in output of two firms (data from Fig. 3.5)

firm are used as the first pair of co-ordinates. These are then added to the production percentages for the second year and these form the next set of co-ordinates. This process continues until the last year, when both firms' cumulative production will be 100%.

Lorenz curves are interpreted in a special way. If the proportion added each year was the same for both firms, then the trace line would lie at 45° from the origin, and it is against such a trace line that the actual result is compared. If the line is above the trace, then the firm on the vertical axis is growing at a faster rate than the firm on the horizontal axis, whereas if it is below the 45° trace, then it is growing at a slower rate than the firm on the horizontal axis. The extent to which it is above or below the 45° trace shows the extent to which one of the firms dominates the other in terms of growth rates (fig. 3.6). Clearly, such curves can be valuable in comparing the growth of any two features such as the growth of population in two parishes, the growth in employment in two regions, the production of two crops in two areas. Alternatively, they can be used to great effect in relating various characteristics to the area which they occupy,

into percentages (fig. 3.6). Each firm's yearly production is expressed as a proportion of total production accumulated over the entire period. The production percentages of each

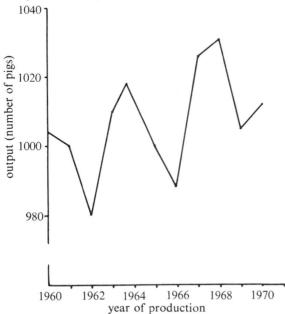

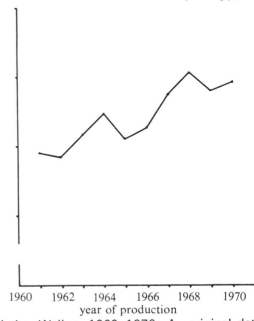

Fig. 3.7 SMOOTHED GRAPH; pig production in Nether Wallop, 1960–1970: A—original data (Fig. 3.8); B—smoothed data, based on the 3 year running mean (Fig. 3.8)

thereby giving some measure of locational concentration or dispersal (Section 4A 2).

3A 1b Smoothed graphs

When information in a time series is plotted graphically, it may be apparent that despite the smaller yearly variations a general trend seems to emerge. For instance, in fig. 3.7A, which shows the output of pigs from a farm at Nether Wallop between 1960 and 1970, it looks very much as though despite the annual fluctuations pig production is, *in the long run*, generally increasing. Clearly it would be useful if a curve could be extrapolated which would indicate this general trend. In fact, this can be done by calculating and plotting on the graph a value known as the **running mean** which shows the mean of several values over a given period of time. Thus, if we examined the pig production not for each year individually but for a series of years at a time, we could calculate a new 'long run' average. For instance, suppose we considered pig production for periods of three years at a time (fig. 3.8); production for each of the years in 1960, 1961 and 1962 ran at 1 014, 1 000 and 980 pigs respectively, hence the mean figure for this period is 998 pigs: in the period 1961, 1962 and

Fig. 3.8   CALCULATION OF THREE
YEAR RUNNING MEAN :
pig production in Nether Wallop,
1960–70

YEAR	ANNUAL PRODUCTION	3 YEAR MEAN
1960	1 014	
1961	1 000	998
1962	980	997
1963	1 010	1 003
1964	1 018	1 009
1965	1 000	1 002
1966	988	1 005
1967	1 026	1 015
1968	1 031	1 021
1969	1 005	1 016
1970	1 012	1 018

1963 production ran at 1 000, 980 and 1 010 pigs giving a 3-year mean of 997 pigs: in the period 1962, 1963 and 1964 production was 980, 1 010 and 1 018 pigs giving a 3-year mean of 1 003 pigs. In this way we could calculate the 3-year mean figure for each successive moving period. If these new 3-year means were plotted on a graph using the central year of each group as the co-ordinate on the abscissa, the long-run trend of production would emerge (fig. 3.7B).

Of course, we may have chosen any size of time period, not just a 3-year one. We may, perhaps, have chosen to calculate a 5-year or any other number of years (*n*-year) moving or running mean. In fact, the number of values for which the moving mean is calculated will be influenced by the periodicity of the irregular fluctuations which need to be smoothed.

The main disadvantage of this technique is the possibility that an up-turn may be inverted into a down-turn or vice-versa, and that there may also be a lag between the smoothed up or down cycles and the actual up or down turn. This is more likely to happen when there is a rapid change from low values to high values. These disadvantages can be overcome by applying a weighting function to each section of the smoothing series by means of the binomial expansion (Holloway, 1958).

3A 1c Compound graphs

Sometimes it may be necessary to compare graphically two or more *dependent* quantities at the same time and in such circumstances compound graphs are particularly useful. The different dependent quantities are each represented by a curve on the graph but the curves are either superimposed on top of each other or, for the sake of clarity, one is placed above the other in a cumulative way. If, for example, we had collected data on the total gas production of a given country for a series of years, and had been able to get figures of the relative production of various forms of gas (coal gas, oil gas and natural gas), we could usefully construct a compound graph to show the relative production of each sector (figs. 3.9 and 3.10). The largest identifiable sector is first

Fig. 3.9 PRODUCTION OF GAS : Great Britain, 1958–68

TYPE OF GAS	PRODUCTION (million therms)										
	1958	1959	1960	1961	1962	1963	1964	1965	1966	1967	1968
coal	2355	2215	2237	2213	2163	2123	1959	1769	1633	1432	1036
oil	69	152	217	240	357	553	847	1227	1724	2188	2532
natural	6	12	13	13	17	21	60	271	265	480	1062
total	2430	2379	2467	2466	2537	2697	2866	3267	3622	4100	4630

plotted on the graph and above it is plotted the cumulative production of the two largest sectors, then the three largest and so on. In this particular example, coal gas is clearly the largest sector and is therefore plotted first: the next trace line shows the combined production of coal- and oil-gas, and the third line shows the total production of all three forms of gas. The difference between this type of compound graph and those where the different sectors are superimposed is shown in fig. 3.10B.

3A 1d n-dimensional graphs

Very often, the data which has been collected for any study can be divided into a number of different sub-categories: for example, employment data might be divided into industrial, agricultural and service employment, thereby creating three such classes, whereas the agricultural production of a given region might be divided into five classes such as pigs, cattle, poultry, oats and rye. In such cases, the different classes can be effectively portrayed by the use of *n*-dimensional

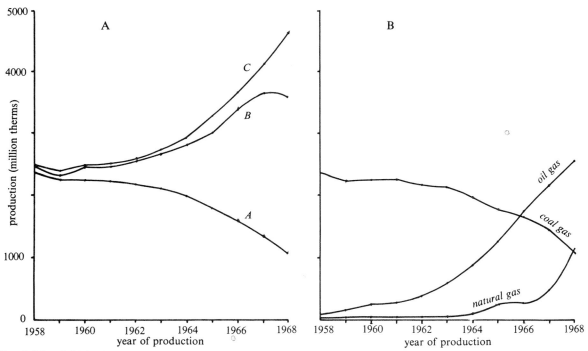

Fig. 3.10 COMPOUND GRAPHS, production of gas (data from Fig. 3.9) : A—data plotted cumulatively for each sector : line A is the largest sector (coal gas), line B represents the two largest (coal gas and oil gas added together) and line C represents the combined production of all three forms of gas ; B—each sector plotted separately and superimposed

graphs (*n* indicating that any appropriate number of dimensions (variables) can be used).

The simplest of these graphs, which enables three classes to be presented, is the triangular graph (fig. 3.11). This is constructed by drawing an equilateral triangle and dividing the three axes into percentage scales with the top end of one scale on one axis forming the bottom end of the scale on the next axis. Each point is located by constructing a trilinear co-ordinate parallel to the next side: thus, in fig. 3.11 which shows employment in agriculture, industry and services, the 'agriculture' percentage is drawn in parallel to the 'industry' axis, the 'industry' percentage is drawn parallel to the 'service' percentage, and the 'service' percentage is drawn in parallel to the 'agriculture' axis.

There are other, more common forms of three-dimensional graph such as block

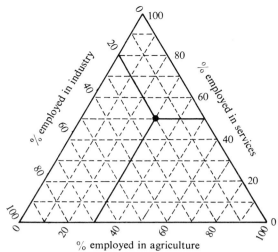

Fig. 3.11 TRIANGULAR GRAPH: each point is located with reference to the 3 axes: the point shown on this graph represents a region with 30% of its population employed in agriculture, 20% in industry and 50% in services (such graph paper is normally referred to as triangular co-ordinate paper)

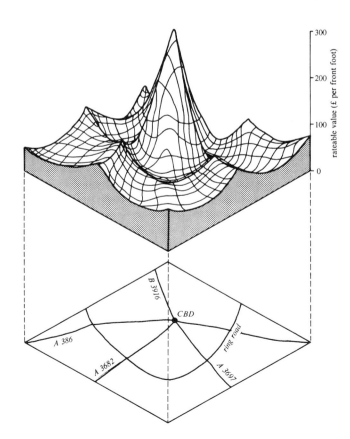

Fig. 3.12 URBAN LAND VALUE SURFACE: the vertical scale is used to indicate the value of land; notice how land values are highest at the centre of the town, along the major roads into the centre, and at the points where the ring road intersects the main roads (see Section 4C.2c)

73

diagrams which portray a frequency or value in one dimension with location marked in the other two dimensions. Thus, for example, land values in a town or population density in a given region could be presented as such an *n*-dimensional graph with the horizontal planes specifying location and the vertical axis portraying the actual values (fig. 3.12). A detailed account of the techniques by which block diagrams are constructed has been given by Lawrance (1968).

Where more than three subclasses of data are available one of the most effective means of presentation is the **star diagram.** Any given number of classes can be plotted as respective radii from a central point, the length of the radii being proportional to the quantity being portrayed. If the end points of the radii are then joined up, a polygonal graph, which looks rather like a star, will result. Normally, these graphs are drawn so that the *areas* represented by each of the

variables are proportional to each other; for this reason, the scale along each of the radii is calculated in terms of a square root progression. This is done by marking a point 1 scale unit from the origin on each radius (or axis) and calculating all further lengths along the axes in square root multiples of this first scale unit. Thus, the second point is not located at a distance of $2 \times$ the first scale unit, but at a distance of $\sqrt{(2 \times \text{the first scale unit})}$; likewise, the third point is located at a distance of $\sqrt{(3 \times \text{the first scale unit})}$ from the origin. Hence, with a scale unit of 1 cm, the first point is located 1 cm from the origin, the second point at 1·41 cm ($\sqrt{2}$ cm) and the third at 1·73 cm ($\sqrt{3}$ cm). If we used an ordinary arithmetic scale instead of this square root scale, the areas contained within the second point on the radii would be more than double the area contained within the first point, thus destroying any element of comparability.

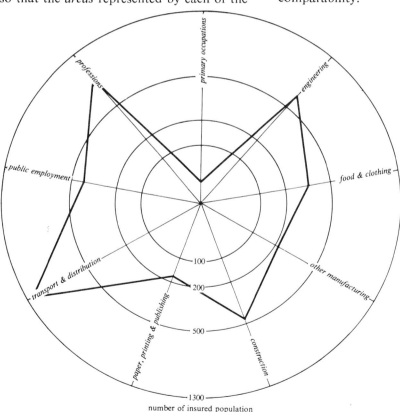

Fig. 3.13 STAR DIAGRAM: employment in Greater London (data from Fig. 3.14); with 9 employment sectors to be portrayed, 9 radii each 40° apart are constructed and an appropriate scale along them is chosen. (The graph paper which is used to draw these diagrams is normally known as 'polar co-ordinate' paper)

Fig. 3.14 EMPLOYMENT IN GREATER LONDON : June 1966

OCCUPATION	NUMBER EMPLOYED (thousands)
Primary occupations	12·3
Engineering	685·8
Food & Clothing	300·3
Other manufacturing	176·3
Construction	297·9
Paper, printing, publishing	188·5
Transport & Distribution	1 163·9
Public & Local authority employees	424·3
Professions	7 55·9

Any number of data sets may be plotted by this method, with the obvious limitation that the number of radii should not be so great as to make the diagram incomprehensible. It can be appreciated, for example, in fig. 3.13 that with 9 radii the diagram is beginning to appear rather cluttered.

In general, star diagrams are particularly effective for the portrayal of employment data (figs. 3.13 and 3.14), the economic base of a particular area and even the attitudes of different groups of people to specific problems. Thus, for instance, the attitudes of various socio-economic groups to living in different parts of a town could be sampled by questionnaire and the average attitude of each group presented as one axis of the star diagram.

3A 1e Logarithmic and semi-logarithmic graphs

In certain instances it may be necessary to transform data by plotting it on logarithmic or semi-logarithmic (also known as log-normal) graph paper. This differs from normal graph paper in that the scale increases at a geometrical rather than arithmetical rate (fig. 3.15A). The scale on ordinary graph paper is usually divided into inches and tenths of an inch. On logarithmic paper the scale increases at a constant rate of 10, and is divided into 'cycles', the difference between the beginning and end of each cycle being ten times greater than the previous cycle. Thus, if the first cycle on logarithmic paper runs from 0·1 to 1·0, the second will run from 1·0 to 10, the third from 10 to 100, the fourth from 100 to 1 000 and so on (fig. 3.15A).

Semi-logarithmic paper differs in that only the scale on the ordinate is logarithmic, the abscissa having the normal tenth-inch divisions (fig. 3.15B).

There are three main circumstances in which these special types of graph paper may be useful:
1 When the range of data is very large: a logarithmic scale tends to 'compress' the values because the cycles successively increase by a factor of 10.

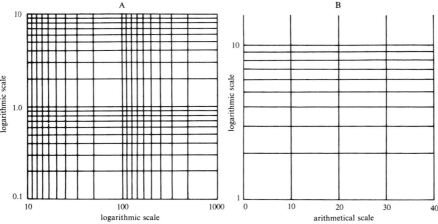

Fig. 3.15 LOGARITHMIC SCALES : A—log-log paper on which the scale of both axes is in geometrical progression ; B—semi-log paper on which one scale is in geometrical progression and the other in normal arithmetical sequence. The arithmetical scale may be drawn in British Imperial or metric units. Any interval range may be chosen for each 'cycle'

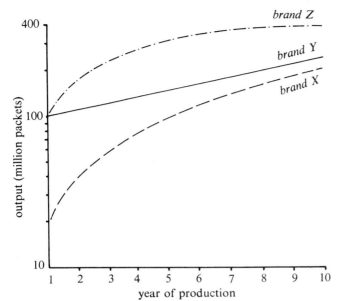

Fig. 3.16 RATES OF CHANGE, washing powder production (data from Fig. 3.1): on semi-logarithmic paper a constant rate is indicated by a straight line (as is the case in this example with brand *Y*)

Fig. 3.17 STEEL EXPORTS : U.K. 1946–66

YEAR	EXPORTS (million tonnes)	YEAR	EXPORTS (million tonnes)
1946	1·80	1956	1·40
1947	1·35	1957	2·75
1948	1·50	1958	2·65
1949	1·35	1959	3·05
1950	2·55	1960	2·40
1951	2·05	1961	3·45
1952	0·80	1962	3·00
1953	1·50	1963	2·80
1954	2·40	1964	2·70
1955	1·45	1965	3·95
		1966	3·40

2 When there is more data at one end of the range of a distribution than at the other: because the scale is increasing progressively, the upper end is relatively more 'compressed' than the lower end.

3 When *rates* of increase in a data set, rather than the *amounts* of increase are to be portrayed: we saw earlier (Section 3A 1a) that the rates of increase are more difficult to portray than the actual amounts of increase. If the original values of a data set are plotted successively on logarithmic paper in time series, the resulting curves indicate the *rate* of change rather than the amount. The greater the slope of such curves, the greater is the rate of change between the points which constitute the form of the line (fig. 3.16).

EXERCISES

1 Using the data shown in fig. 3.17, construct a small graph and show the long-run trend by computing a 3-year running mean. How different would be the form of a 5-year or 2-year running mean?

2 Portray the data shown in fig. 3.18 by any appropriate graph and justify your choice of method.

Fig. 3.18 STEEL CONSUMPTION : U.K. 1958–66

INDUSTRY	railways	motors	coalmining	engineering	shipbuilding	construction
	Million tonnes consumed					
1958	1·05	1·75	0·65	2·40	0·98	1·88
1959	0·75	2·20	0·60	2·49	0·75	1·97
1960	0·70	2·45	0·62	2·55	0·74	2·63
1961	0·72	1·85	0·61	2·51	0·62	2·75
1962	0·63	2·07	0·50	2·47	0·58	2·51
1963	0·49	2·30	0·53	2·63	0·77	2·53
1964	0·48	2·50	0·53	2·95	0·65	2·98
1965	0·50	2·51	0·48	3·02	0·66	3·10
1966	0·47	2·53	0·48	2·95	0·66	2·80

3A 2 Symbols

Most data can be represented in symbolic form, the size of the symbol being proportional to the quantity portrayed. There are three main kinds of proportional symbol: the simplest, pictorial symbols, portray the data by appropriate symbolic pictures of the items to which the data refers, but more precise symbols whose area or volume is proportional to the quantity portrayed are also used.

3A 2a Pictorial symbols

Pictorial symbols are usually drawn to look like the variable they are representing. For example, the volume of a country's car production may be symbolised by a series of cars, the total number of which represents the total car production; similarly, wheat production could be represented by symbolic wheatsheaves.

The principle underlying the construction of such symbols is simple: an appropriate value for one of the symbols is first worked

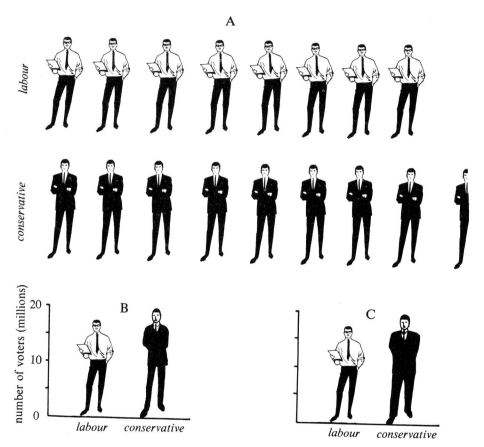

Fig. 3.19 PICTORIAL SYMBOLS, Labour and Conservative voters: A—one symbol represents 2 million voters; B—height of symbol proportional to number represented; C—height of symbol proportional to number represented but width distorted to make Conservative voters apparently much more numerous

out and then the total value to be portrayed is represented by an equivalent number of symbols. Clearly, part-symbols may also be necessary. Thus, for instance, if we wished to portray the number of people voting Conservative and Labour at a General Election, we must first decide how many actual voters would be represented diagrammatically by one of our symbolic people. Suppose that 16 million people voted Labour: we might decide to make one 'symbol' person equal to 2 million voters, and therefore we should need to draw 8 symbols to represent the 16 million people. But suppose that 17 million people voted Conservative: using the same scale as before, we should need to draw $8\frac{1}{2}$ symbolic people (fig. 3.19A).

An alternative method to this is to make the agreed symbol proportional in size to the quantity it is supposed to represent. Thus, in the 'voting' example, we may make the height of our pictorial voter proportional to the number of Conservative and Labour voters respectively (fig. 3.19B). The obvious danger of using such a method, however, is that it is quite possible to give a false impression of the real scale of values by drawing the symbols altogether proportionately larger rather than on the chosen scale alone. Thus, in the 'voting' example, as can be seen in fig. 3.19C, although the difference is, in fact, being recorded on the vertical scale alone, when the whole symbol is adjusted the difference can be exaggerated, one way or the other. Such manipulation is, of course, not altogether unknown in the popular press.

3A 2b Areal symbols

There are three main kinds of symbol which are commonly used to portray data in proportions relative to the size of their area: the circle, the square and the rectangle.

It has already been shown that the construction of multi-dimensional graphs which portray quantities proportionally to area are based on the square root scale, because it is only by this method that the areas themselves will be proportional. For the same reason, all area symbols are based on a scale involving the square root of the

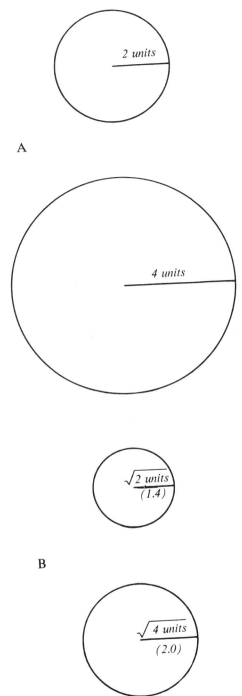

Fig. 3.20 PROPORTIONAL CIRCLES: A—the second circle is drawn with a radius twice that of the first circle, but its area is more than 4 times as great; B—when the second circle is drawn with a radius twice the root of the first circle, its area is exactly double

variable being considered rather than on its actual value.

This principle can be clearly seen in the construction of proportional circles: if two units of a variable were represented by a circle whose radius was two units long, then, if the size of the circle was based on the actual values, four units of a variable would be represented by a circle of radius four units, and that circle would be more than twice the area of the first (fig. 3.20A). If, on the other hand, the circle was constructed with a radius equal to the square root of the actual values, the areas of the resulting circles would, in fact, be proportional to each other: in this particular example, the area of the second circle would be twice that of the first (fig. 3.20B).

The radii of the circles, then, must be drawn to a scale based on the square roots of the actual values. Patently, however, the scale itself must be chosen with respect to the normal considerations of the appropriate size and range of values. Naturally, the range in size of the circles should not be excessive, not only because of the difficulty in comparing and interpreting them, but also because of the sheer technical problem of constructing either very small or very large circles.

Thus, suppose that we were trying to show pictorially the number of substandard houses in two different parishes of a given area. In parish A, there were 2 500 such houses, and in parish B, 3 600. Clearly we first calculate the square roots of the respective numbers, and use them as a basis for establishing the proportional length of the respective circle's radii. Thus, the radius of the circle for parish A must be 50 units long, and that for parish B must be 60 units long. So that the circles will be neither too small nor too large, we finally decide that the actual constructional scale shall be 1 unit of radius will equal 3 mm. Thus, circle A will have a radius of 150 mm (50 × 3 mm) and circle B will be 180 mm radius (60 × 3 mm).

The basis upon which proportional squares are constructed is much the same as for proportional circles. The amount of the variable is square rooted for the same reasons as the proportional circle and this is then converted into scale terms. The resulting value is then used to construct a square of that dimension. Thus, had we wished to present the substandard housing data in terms of squares rather than circles, we should construct for parish A a square 150 mm × 150 mm, and for parish B a square measuring 180 mm × 180 mm.

Strictly speaking, we should adopt the same technique for constructing rectangles. Let us suppose that the first rectangle we construct has to have an area of 25 square centimetres. We can represent this by a whole variety of rectangles, for example 12·5 cm × 2 cm, 10 cm × 2·5 cm, 6·25 cm × 4 cm, or a host of others. If we choose to represent this first statistic, which in scale terms is 25 square cm, by a rectangle 12·5 cm × 2 cm, then this gives us a ratio of breadth to length of 1:6·25. Ideally, every other rectangle we subsequently construct should have sides of the same ratio of 1:6·25. This, however, is rarely done as it involves too many computational steps. More often we compare rectangles in respect of their height or length, that is, we alter the shape of the figure by keeping a constant width across the base and lengthening or shortening the figure to give the correct area. The same conventions, however, are retained in respect of basing the figures upon square rooted values.

It is important to note that proportional circles, squares and rectangles should not be used together to illustrate any one set of data. This is simply because it is very difficult to compare similar areas included in a different shape: although a 5 cm × 5 cm square and a 12·5 cm × 2·0 cm rectangle contain the same area, most people would, on visual impression, imagine the square to be the larger shape. Thus, for instance, if circles are to be used, rectangles and squares should not also be used to illustrate some of the figures.

3A 2c Volumetric symbols

Three-dimensional symbols whose volumes are proportional to quantity portrayed may also be used to represent data pictorially, but whereas the two-dimensional area symbols were constructed on a scale in proportion to the square roots of the basic data, the construction of proportional spheres, cubes and columns is based on the cube roots of the basic data.

Proportional spheres are constructed by taking the cube root of the crude value to be portrayed, converting it into scale terms (as was done in the construction of proportional circles) and using that value as the radius (r) of the shape to be constructed. Thus, if the scale value were 3, a diameter of twice that length, 6 units, would first be drawn (fig. 3.21A). A half-ellipse is next drawn around this diameter to represent the equator in perspective (fig. 3.21B). At 90° to the original diameter, and midway along it, another diameter is constructed and an ellipse drawn around it (fig. 3.21C). The next step is to construct a circle of radius r, so that the two ellipses are completely enclosed by it (fig. 3.21D). Lines of latitude are then drawn in parallel to the first ellipse, and lines of longitude are drawn in as proportional ellipses in the same plane as the second ellipse. Finally, the original construction lines (the initial diameters) are erased, thus leaving a completed sphere (fig. 3.21E).

Proportional cubes are constructed in a similar manner; the cube root of the value to be portrayed is converted to scale terms and this resulting value (x) is used to construct a regular cube in isometric projection (i.e. a cube which has all sides of equal length, with opposite sides parallel to one another and vertical sides perpendicular to the horizontal). The cube is usually drawn edge on, showing two vertical faces and the top horizontal surface in projection. The angle between the retreating base lines and the horizontal should be 30° (fig. 3.22). Further refinements of the techniques of drawing in perspective will be found elsewhere (Clutterbuck, 1966; Barnes & Tilbrook, 1962).

Proportional columns are simple three-dimensional extensions of proportional rectangles. As with the rectangle, the ratio between the sides of the proportional column is not constant, and it is the height of a column of fixed base dimensions that is varied to create visual impressions of physical quantity. The cube root is again the quantity which is expressed in scale terms.

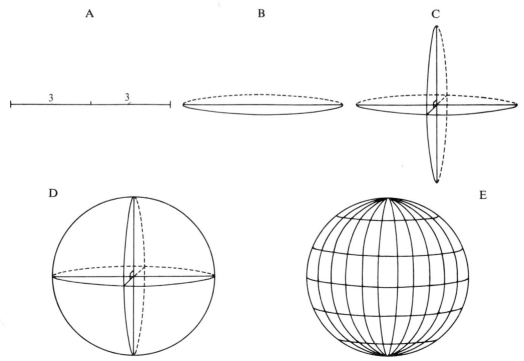

Fig. 3.21 STAGES IN THE CONSTRUCTION OF A PROPORTIONAL SPHERE

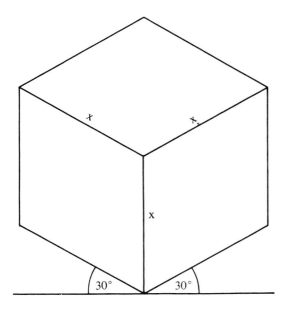

30° 30°

Fig. 3.22 CUBE IN ISOMETRIC PROJECTION

In constructing proportional columns, the measurements of the base are first decided upon, and then a column representing the cube root of the absolute value is drawn in. Thus, for example, if the cube root of the value we wished to portray was 90, and the base of the column was 3×3 units, the height of the column would clearly be $90 \div 3 \times 3$, that is 10 units. These figures are then used to construct an isometric column of base 3×3, 10 units high.

The choice of which symbol to use is very much a personal one. Generally speaking, however, circles, squares and rectangles are preferable to volumetric and pictorial symbols because least error is associated with them. This error comes from two sources: firstly, in construction, it is more difficult to draw a volumetric symbol, and consequently there are more chances of making a mistake; and secondly, in interpretation, flat two-dimensional symbols are less prone to optical illusion and misinterpretation than symbols which attempt to portray volumes. The main advantage of volumetric symbols is that they compress a data set more than areal symbols, and so enable the data to be portrayed without the symbols overlapping.

3A 2d Divided proportional symbols

The relative importance of a number of variables within any total situation may be shown quite effectively by dividing the symbol which represents the 'total situation' into a number of segments proportional in size to the importance of each variable considered. For instance, if we had made a study of employment in a parish of Devwall county, the *total* number of people employed (the 'total situation' referred to above) could have been represented by any of the methods already described (pictorial, areal or volumetric symbols); we may, however, also have collected information about the number of people employed in different sectors, such as the primary occupations (agriculture and extractive industry), secondary occupations (heavy engineering, light engineering, manufacturing), tertiary occupations (retailing and other service industries) or other occupations, and this information could be portrayed by dividing the chosen symbol into appropriate parts.

Generally, the areal symbols are the best means of showing the relative importance of such sectors because they are the easiest

A

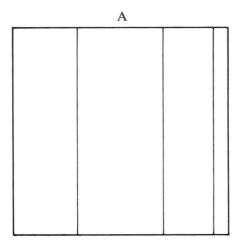

B

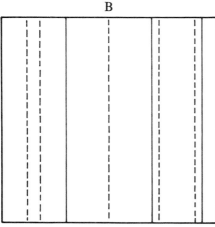

C

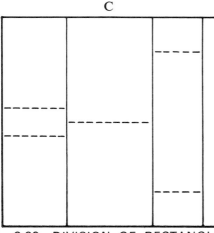

Fig. 3.23 DIVISION OF RECTANGLES:
A—division into major sectors; B—vertical
division into subsectors (indicated by
broken lines); C—horizontal division into
subsectors (indicated by broken lines)

both to construct and interpret. Divided rectangles, squares and circles are, therefore, commonly used for this purpose, and the basis of construction is the same for them all. In each case, the area of the total symbol is taken to represent 100%, and then each of the contributing variables is worked out as a percentage of that total area. Thus, for instance, suppose that a total of 100 000 people were employed, and that of these 31 000 were in primary, 42 000 in secondary, 22 000 in tertiary and 5 000 in other occupations: whatever symbol is chosen to represent the total employment, it would have to be divided into four segments, accounting respectively for 31%, 42% 22% and 5% of the *total* area. Rectangles and squares could be easily divided into these proportions simply by measuring the division according to the length along one side of the symbol (fig. 3.23A).

Further subdivisions within the major sectors may be constructed by similar methods: thus, *within* the primary sectors of our employment example, we may wish to portray the proportions employed in agriculture and the extractive industries, and to do so we should simply calculate the appropriate area to be represented, and represent it by dotted lines *within* the area of the major segment to which it belongs. There are, however, two ways of dividing the major division of the rectangle or square: either the divisions may be made vertically (as were the original ones in this example) or horizontally (fig. 3.23B/C).

The division of circles into proportional segments is effected by calculating the proportions in terms of the degrees of a circle. Clearly, a segment representing 25% of the total circle would cover 25% of 360°, that is 90°, but for more complicated percentages it is not so easy to make such a rapid calculation in the head, and the following formula may be used:

$$d = \frac{V \times 360}{T}$$

where d = the angle of the sector in degrees, V = the actual amount of the variable to be portrayed and T = the grand total (or 'total situation'). Thus, in order to calculate the

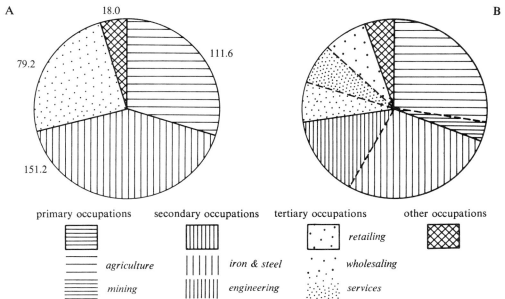

A 18.0 79.2 111.6 151.2

B

primary occupations   secondary occupations   tertiary occupations   other occupations

		retailing
agriculture	*iron & steel*	*wholesaling*
mining	*engineering*	*services*

Fig. 3.24 DIVISION OF CIRCLES: A—major sectors; B—subsectors included (note how variations on the shading scheme for the major sectors are used to identify subsectors)

angle of the 'primary occupations' sector in our employment example, $V = 31\ 000$, $T = 100\ 000$ and therefore

$$d = \frac{31\ 000 \times 360}{100\ 000} = 111 \cdot 6°$$

The respective proportions of the other sectors are found to be $151 \cdot 2°$, $79 \cdot 2°$ and $18°$. The total circle is then divided according to these angles (fig. 3.24A).

Further subdivisions of the circles may be made in precisely the same way: thus, for instance, with 27 000 people employed in agriculture and 4 000 in the extractive industries, these two sectors would be represented by segments of respectively $97 \cdot 2°$ and $14 \cdot 4°$ and dotted lines may be used to place these sectors *within* the primary sector to which they relate (fig. 3.24B).

Divided proportional symbols are particularly useful in comparative studies, since they are proportional to each other in overall size and their internal divisions are also directly comparable one with another. Thus for instance, in comparing two towns in terms of the geographical origins of their populations we may decide to use propor-

Fig. 3.25 COMPARATIVE SYMBOLS, proportional rectangles: population of two towns by place of birth

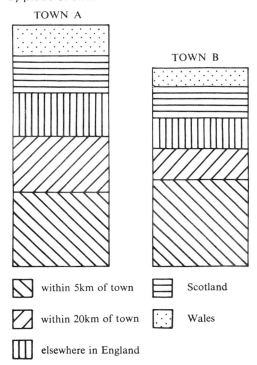

TOWN A

TOWN B

	within 5km of town		Scotland
	within 20km of town		Wales
	elsewhere in England		

tional rectangles to depict any differences or similarities between them, as is shown in fig. 3.25. Proportional squares or circles may equally have been used with just the same effect. The fact that one town is larger than the other is immediately apparent, and a direct visual impression is gained not only of actual numbers of the different 'immigrants' but also of their *relative* importance in each of the two towns.

In order that this comparability is not made too difficult, it is important that the different sectors being portrayed always appear in the same order on the diagrams. The order should be determined on logical grounds: in the employment example which we have used, it may be decided to plot the different sectors either alphabetically or in hierarchical order (primary, secondary, tertiary and then 'other') or in rank order (from largest to smallest). If the rank order is used, then the same rank order must be used for each different case. When divided circles are used, the categories should be plotted from 0° through to 360° in a clockwise direction.

Volumetric symbols (spheres, cubes and columns) are not often used for purposes of division because of the difficulties involved in dividing a three-dimensional representation accurately, and the associated difficulties of interpreting such divisions correctly. Some of the interpretational problems are demonstrated in fig. 3.26A–D, where four different ways of dividing a cube into four equal parts are shown. There is little to choose between the first three alternatives (fig. 3.26A–C) as they all suffer from the same disadvantages. The overall outline tends to be lost in a series of parallel lines and the end face is emphasised to the detriment of the other divisions. This latter point also makes it unattractive visually. The fourth alternative (fig. 3.26D) again suffers from the disadvantage that the corner nearest the observer is over-emphasised and, in addition, the shapes on the top of the cube should be different if they are meant to be seen in perspective as equal divisions of an isometric cube.

EXERCISES

1 Using the data given in fig. 3.18, construct an appropriate series of composite symbols. What factors influence your choice and to what extent does this method of presentation differ from the compound graph which was drawn previously?

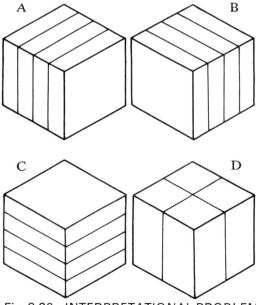

Fig. 3.26 INTERPRETATIONAL PROBLEM OF VOLUMETRIC SYMBOLS: all four alternative methods of division tend to distort or over-emphasise one sector

Fig. 3.27 FOREIGN LABOURERS: selected European countries, 1970

COUNTRY	NUMBER OF FOREIGN WORKERS	PROPORTION OF TOTAL WORKFORCE
Germany	424 787	4·9%
France	255 781	5·6%
Netherlands	36 174	1·7%
Belgium	27 475	4·8%
Luxemburg	7 814	19·6%
Italy	5 180	0·2%

2 Show how you would portray the data given in fig. 3.27 for publication
  (**a**) in a popular newspaper.
  (**b**) in a technical journal.

3B THEMATIC MAPS

The main concern of the geographer is to analyse the spatial distribution and variation of various phenomena, and maps related to specific themes are one of the main devices by which such analysis can be presented in visual form. Naturally, the kind of information which is available for any particular study will in part determine the kind of map which can be drawn, and it is particularly important in this context to distinguish between data which refers to areas and that which relates to a given point location. Equally, the fact that some mapping techniques appear to present the data at a point rather than through an area is just as significant. But quite apart from this consideration, two main kinds of thematic maps can be identified: **symbol maps** are used to portray distributions either at points or within areas, and **line maps** are used to show various relationships *between* points or areas. Whatever the type of map, its main purpose is to convey information *effectively*; maps should not, therefore, be over-complicated or ornately beautified, but should be examples of attractive cartography, neatly drawn, and with clear notation (Board, 1967).

3B 1 Symbol Maps

A wide range of techniques is available for presenting information relating to areas or points. In a way, however, this distinction between area and point is an elusive one since it is clear that what may at one scale be considered an 'area' may, at another, be more appropriately considered as a point. Thus, for example, the size of a settlement's population really relates to an area (that of the whole settlement), but on a 1:63 360 map, the settlement could effectively be thought of as a point and the size of its population portrayed as such cartograph-

ically. In general, therefore, it is necessary to decide according to the scale of the map whether the available data would most appropriately be portrayed with reference to an area or to a point. In addition to this problem, some of the techniques which are available give the visual impression that the data refers to an area, whilst others make it appear to relate to a point. Thus, chorochromatic and choropleth maps refer visually to areas ('choros' is Greek for 'area'), whilst maps using dots and other proportional symbols appear to refer to given point locations.

3B 1a Chorochromatic maps

Chorochromatic maps are among the easiest of all maps to produce. They are non-quantitative and simply portray the presence or absence of a particular characteristic over a given area. Such maps, therefore, are mainly used to portray the location of different kinds of land use. The area under each particular use is either coloured- or shaded-in, and for this reason chorochromatic maps are sometimes known as 'colour-patch' maps.

It is important that the shades or colours used be carefully chosen: different shades should be clearly identifiable from each other so that there is no confusion in the interpretation of the map (fig. 3.28). It may, however, be necessary to find sub-varieties of a similar shade or colour in order to represent sub-categories of major classifications. For instance, in mapping industrial, commercial and retail land uses in an urban area, we may have decided to use yellow, red and green to depict respectively the three main land uses; if we then wished to distinguish between food, household and fashion shops within the retail category we should either use three different shades of green or else superimpose on the basic 'retail' green, line shadings of three different styles.

3B 1b Chloropleths

The construction of choropleth maps is a three stage process: firstly, the entire data set has to be broken down into meaningful classes; secondly, the resulting classes have

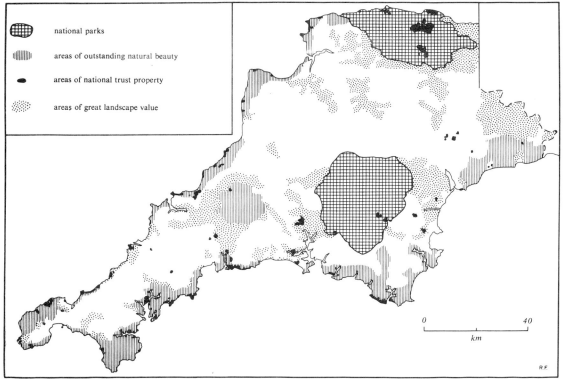

Fig. 3.28 CHOROCHROMATIC MAP: conserved area of southwest England (from Shorter, Ravenhill & Gregory, South West England, p. 51)

to be related to the data collection areas; and finally, the classes have to be portrayed correctly in cartographic form. In other words, choropleth maps are little more than the spatial extension of histograms, in which a data set is grouped into classes which are then plotted in map form, by area.

The classification of the data is the most important of the three stages. Several techniques are available for constructing class boundaries, and, in choosing that which is most suitable for the sample data set, certain factors should be borne in mind. In the first place, there should be a logical relationship between the classes which should be capable of being expressed in mathematical terms. Secondly, the classes should be reasonably equal in size either in terms of the class interval or of the number of data units in each class. Lastly, it is preferable that there should be no vacant classes.

As we have already seen (Section 2A 1a),

class intervals may be established by constructing a scattergram from which any 'natural breaks' in the protrayed distribution are used as the basis of the class intervals (fig. 2.2). It often happens, however, that such 'natural breaks' are not apparent from the scattergraph. In such cases, the *number* of classes to be established must be determined by the general rule that **the number of classes must not exceed 5 times the logarithm of the observations**: the actual class intervals, however, can be determined by more precise methods than those outlined in Section 2A 1a according to whether the rank-size distribution of the observations follows a straight-line or a curvilinear relationship. In order to establish which of these two relationships hold, the data is ranked from highest to lowest value, and the rank of each value is plotted graphically against its actual value (fig. 3.29).

If a *straight-line* relationship between rank and size is apparent, the class intervals may

86

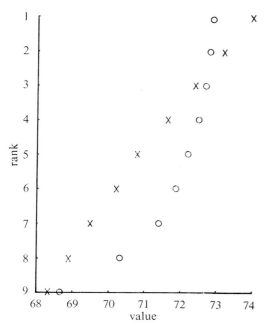

Fig. 3.29 RANK-SIZE DISTRIBUTION: the data indicated by crosses follows a straight-line relationship whereas the data indicated by dots is more nearly curvilinear

be established either according to the number of observations in the data set or according to its range.

The first alternative is to plot an equal number of *observations* per class. In such a case, the total number of observations (N) is divided by the number of classes to be established (C) in order to find out how many observations there should be in each class. The first N/C ranked observations constitute the first class, the second N/C ranked observations constitute the second, and so on, until all the classes are filled with the same number of observations. If, for example, there were 90 observations to be divided into 6 classes, there would clearly be 15 observations per class: the first 15 ranked observations would then form the first class, the next 15 the second class, and so on, up to the last class which would contain the observations between 76 and 90.

Alternatively, classes of equal range could be established. In this case, the range of the observations (R) is divided by the number of classes (C). For example, if the data set had a range of 80 (from 1 and 80) and 8

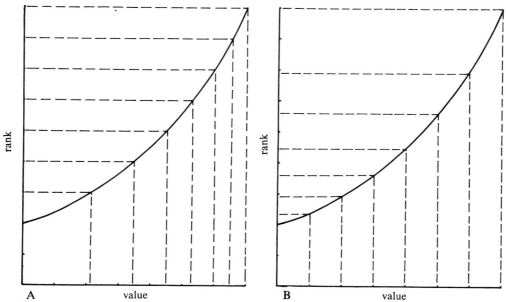

Fig. 3.30 CURVILINEAR FUNCTIONS AND CLASS INTERVALS: A—equal number of observations (ranks) per class; B—classes of equal range (values)

classes were to be established, each class would include a range of 10 and the class limits would be 1–10, 11–20, 21–30, 31–40, 41–50, 51–60, 61–70, 71–80.

These first two techniques are, as we have said, appropriate if the rank-size function approaches a straight-line relationship, rather than a curvilinear function. If these first techniques were used to group a curvilinear function, then certain problems would arise: an equal number of observations per class would result in progressively smaller classes being established (fig. 3.30A), whereas if the classes were of equal range, the number of observations per class would become progressively greater or smaller (fig. 3.30B).

If the relationship between rank value and absolute value is *curvilinear*, then it is better described by a progression, either geometric or arithmetic. The suitability of a geometrical progression in describing the curve can be tested by plotting the dependent (absolute) values on a logarithmic scale on the vertical axis (see Section 3A 1e). If the resulting curve is a straight line, or nearly a straight line, then a geometrical progression is suitable. The first step is again to decide upon the *number* of classes to be established, using the usual '5 × log number of observations' rule. Let us assume that in our data set there are 40 observations ranging in value from 1 to 80: it would thus be necessary to establish 8 classes (5 × log 40). The next step is to calculate the class boundaries and to do this we subtract the logarithm of the bottom item of the range from the logarithm of the top item, and divide the difference by the number of classes. In this example, therefore,

$$\text{Log } 80 = 1 \cdot 90309$$
$$\text{Log } 1 = 0 \cdot 00000$$

$$1 \cdot 90309 \div 8 = \mathbf{0 \cdot 23789}$$

This difference is then taken away from the logarithm of the top item, and the anti-logarithm of the result gives the class boundary:

$$\text{Log } 80 = 1 \cdot 90309$$
$$\text{difference}$$
$$\log 80 - \log 1 = 0 \cdot 23789$$

$$1 \cdot 66520 = \mathbf{46 \cdot 259}$$

This process is continued, taking the difference from the logarithm of the top item, which is now 46·259:

$$1 \cdot 66520 = \log \mathbf{46 \cdot 259}$$
$$- \quad \cdot 23789$$

$$1 \cdot 42731 = \mathbf{26 \cdot 748}$$
$$- \quad \cdot 23789$$

$$1 \cdot 18942 = \mathbf{15 \cdot 467}$$
$$- \quad \cdot 23789$$

$$\cdot 95153 = \mathbf{8 \cdot 9435}$$
$$- \quad \cdot 23789$$

$$\cdot 71364 = \mathbf{5 \cdot 1714}$$
$$- \quad \cdot 23789$$

$$\cdot 47575 = \mathbf{2 \cdot 9902}$$
$$- \quad \cdot 23789$$

$$\cdot 23786 = \mathbf{1 \cdot 7294}$$

The logarithm class intervals are, therefore, 0–1·728; 1·729–2·989; 2·990–5·170; 5·171–8·942; 8·943–15·466; 15·467–26·747; 26·748–46·258; 46·259–80·000.

An alternative method of establishing class intervals is to sum the actual number of classes to be established and to divide the range by this sum. Thus, in our example, where eight classes are to be established, the sum of the classes is 36 (1 + 2 + 3 + 4 + 5 + 6 + 7 + 8 = 36). This sum is then divided into the range of the data (80) to give a constant factor (2·222), which is the factor by which class size is increased. The first class is 0–2·222. In the second class the constant factor is doubled (2·222 × 2 = 4·444) and this is added to the upper limit of the first class to give the limit of the second class (2·222 + 4·444 = 6·666). This process is continued with the third class trebling the constant factor, and so on, giving the following class intervals:

$$1 \times 2 \cdot 222 : 0 – 2 \cdot 222$$
$$2 \times 2 \cdot 222 : 2 \cdot 223 – 6 \cdot 666$$
$$3 \times 2 \cdot 222 : 6 \cdot 667 – 13 \cdot 332$$
$$4 \times 2 \cdot 222 : 13 \cdot 333 – 22 \cdot 220$$
$$5 \times 2 \cdot 222 : 22 \cdot 221 – 33 \cdot 330$$

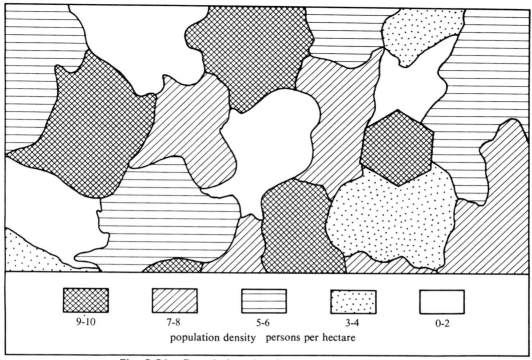

Fig. 3.31 Population density—person per hectare

$6 \times 2 \cdot 222 : 33 \cdot 331 - 46 \cdot 662$
$7 \times 2 \cdot 222 : 46 \cdot 663 - 62 \cdot 216$
$8 \times 2 \cdot 222 : 62 \cdot 217 - 79 \cdot 992$

This last class does not quite reach 80 because of rounding-off errors. So we have to alter the progression slightly so that the last class reads 62·217 to 80·000.

Other progressions can be developed and the choice of which one to use depends on the efficiency with which the progression describes the rank-size relationship.

Once the data has been grouped into classes, the next stage in the construction of the map is to plot the appropriate class value for each of the different areas being analysed. Each class value is represented on the map by a different colour, shading or stippling and it is important that the graduation of colour tone, line shading or stippling should accurately reflect the structure of the class grouping. The intensity of colour tone should reflect the intensity of the category it is meant to portray, and in this respect it is important that the colours of the ranked categories should follow the spectral se-

quence. The same is true of line shading or stippling, using density of the symbol to reflect intensity (fig. 3.31). We can be objective in our choice of density gradients if we base line shading or stippling on an underlay of graph paper. We can put a point at the intersection of every pair of lines or every other pair of lines, or rule every line or every other line, and so on. As an alter-

Fig. 3.32 APPARENT DIFFERENCES IN POPULATION DENSITY

	PARISH	
	A	B
POPULATION IN VILLAGE	250	250
AREA OF PARISH (ha)	100	200
POPULATION DENSITY	2·5/ha	1·25/ha

native, it is possible to buy sheets of stipple or line ruling.

Line ruling or stippling and colour tone can be used together on a map, when more than one variable is involved. Colour can be used to show the different variables (such as types of urban land use) and the line shading or stipple can be used to portray the in-tensity of the variable (such as the rateable value of the building).

Excellent examples of the use of choro-pleth technique of data portrayal can be found in Coppock (1964) and Howe (1970).

Although choropleth maps may appear accurately to show the data upon which they are based, a number of problems are

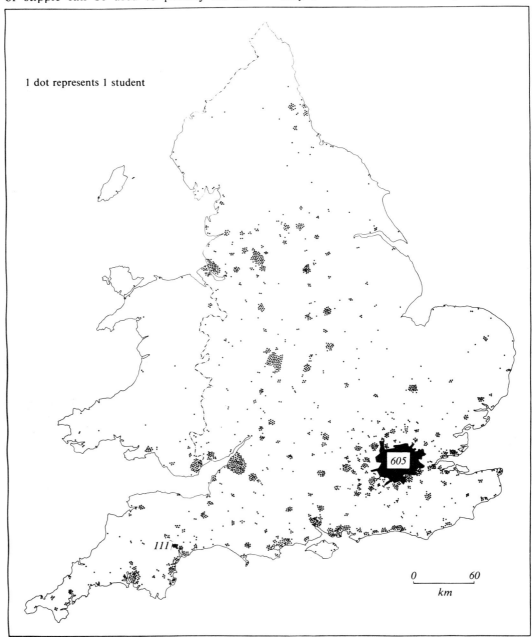

1 dot represents 1 student

605

111

0   60
km

90   Fig. 3.33 DOT MAP: home location of students, University of Exeter, 1969

involved in their interpretation. Usually the data used in their construction refers to administrative areas, such as parishes, which are not all of the same size, and this in turn may affect the actual values used. Consider, for example, two parishes each containing a village of 250 people: parish A contains 100 hectares, parish B, 200 hectares. In terms of population density, parish A appears to have the higher figure but, in fact, this may simply be the result of parish B being a larger parish (fig. 3.32). Great care must, therefore, be taken in the interpretation of such maps unless they are based on information relating to standardised and regular collection areas.

It must also be realised that whatever characteristic is being portrayed does NOT necessarily end abruptly at the boundary shown on the map. All the boundary lines shown on chorochromatic and choropleth maps are, in fact, boundaries of the data collection areas being used, and the value represented within those areas are *average* values for the whole area.

3B 1c Dot maps

The simplest form of symbol which appears to relate to a point location is the *dot*. For every occurrence of a given characteristic, a dot is placed on the map at the appropriate location (fig. 3.33). Naturally, the number of instances when one dot on the map can be used to represent one unit of the variable being portrayed will be relatively rare; normally a representational scale has to be chosen with respect to the total range and geographical distribution of the data.

In fact, the problems involved in choosing the scale are greater than might be imagined at first sight and the only way in which they can be solved is by a process of trial and error. Two things must be avoided if at all possible — excessive clustering of dots in areas where large numbers are to be portrayed and, at the other extreme, insufficient representation in areas with small numbers to be portrayed. The difficulty, however, is that these two extremes are often difficult to reconcile, since the range in the data may be very great.

Associated with this problem is the diffi-

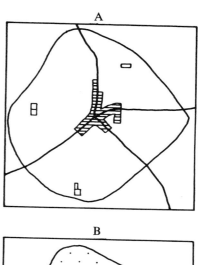

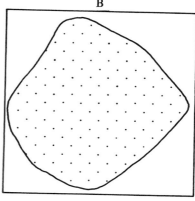

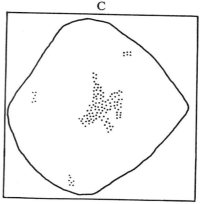

Fig. 3.34 PLACING DOTS OVER AN AREA: A—actual location of settlements in an area; B—an appropriate number of dots representing the population of the settlements may be spaced regularly over the whole area; C—the dots may alternatively be located with respect to the location of the settlements

91

culty of deciding where to locate the dots: when they refer to specific *point* locations difficulty arises if two or more such dots have to be located at the same point. In fig. 3.33, for instance, it is difficult to know which of the dots really does represent the home location of a student, and which does not: given the scale of the map it proves impossible to carry on showing the exact location of each student in urban areas, and, in some cases, the idea of using dots has to be abandoned and a number written in instead. Fig. 3.33 should be an instructive example of how not to draw quantitative maps! Not infrequently, however, dots are used to represent areal data, despite the fact that they really appear to relate to a point. In such cases, difficulty arises in knowing where to locate the dots *within* the area concerned. One alternative is to place the appropriate number of dots regularly throughout the area (fig. 3.34A), but it may be possible to estimate a more meaningful distribution. For instance, if we were plotting the distribution of population by parishes, it

would clearly make more sense to locate the dots as near as possible to the location of the settlements themselves rather than to spread them indiscriminately over the whole area (fig. 3.34B). It can thus be seen that the major problems associated with dot maps are concerned, in one way or another, with the location of the dot. It is important, for academic purposes, that its location should represent something, and from the visual and information point of view it is important that the map should look attractive and convey the right information.

3B 1d Areal and volumetric symbols

Symbols whose area or volume is drawn proportional to the quantity they represent are widely used to show the spatial variations of a data set, either over an area or at a given point but, as was the case with dots, they give the impression, always, of referring to a specific point.

The symbols are drawn in precisely the same way as we have already described

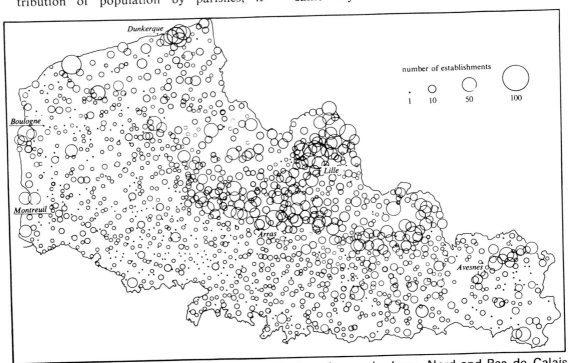

Fig. 3.35 PROPORTIONAL CIRCLES: distribution of grocer's shops, Nord and Pas-de-Calais, France

(Section 3A 2) and are then placed at the appropriate location on the map. The major problem in their use, however, is that their scale must be very carefully chosen with respect to the scale of the map, otherwise a completely uninterpretable map results (fig. 3.35). It is not, in fact, always possible to find an absolutely perfect scale because of the range of data and the scale of the map, and it often happens, as a result, that symbols have to be drawn in with arrows referring to their precise location (fig. 3.36).

EXERCISES

1   Using the 1:63 360 OS map of your local area as a base map, construct a choro-chromatic map of woodland. Compare your classification with the classification adopted by the Land Utilisation Survey. Can you use the Land Utilisation Survey's scheme for your map? Give reasons.

2   Draw a choropleth map of population density for the parishes in your local area. Get the population data from the most recent report of the population census. What map scale will you use and why? Explain your choice of categories and the basis of your shading technique.

3   Draw a dot map of population density for the parishes in your local area and compare it with the choropleth map drawn for Exercise 2. How can you improve the dot map?

4   At what scale would you use proportional symbols to portray population statistics, and why?

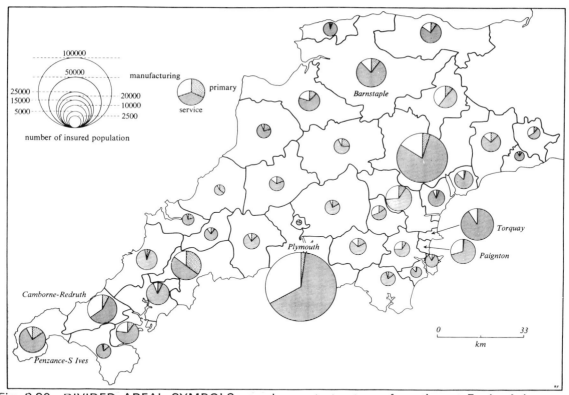

Fig. 3.36   DIVIDED AREAL SYMBOLS: employment structure of southwest England (source: Shorter, Ravenhill & Gregory, South West England, p. 175). Notice particularly that the symbols are normally placed in the centre of the area to which they refer, but that in certain circumstances alternative locations are either more appropriate (e.g. Penzance–St. Ives, Camborne–Redruth) or necessary (e.g. Torquay, Paignton)

93

3B 2 Line Maps

Line maps are used to show the relationships between a series of points or areas. Perhaps the best known are those which show the flow of traffic, population or various commodities between one place and another, either in terms of the actual routes taken (routed flows) or simply in diagrammatic form (desire lines). But line maps may also be drawn to show locations with similar characteristics: isometric lines are drawn to join actual point locations, while isopleths join points which symbolically represent a surrounding area.

3B 2a Routed flows

If the actual route between two points is known, flow lines can be constructed along the very route taken, their width being proportional to the volume of the flow at every point on the route (fig. 3.37). A simple relationship between the width of the line and the volume of the flow is usually chosen (e.g., 10 units of flow may be represented by 1 millimetre) since more complex relation-

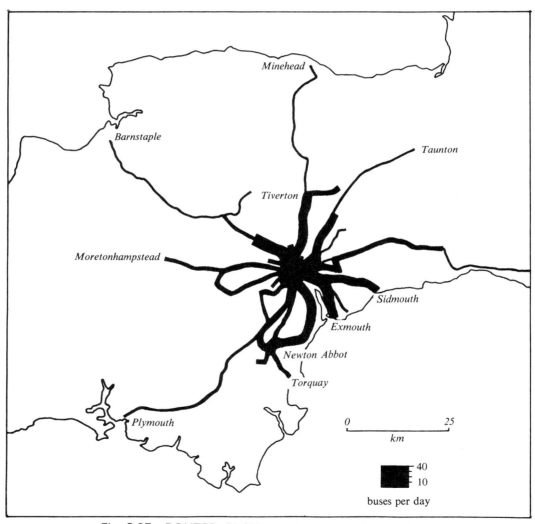

Fig. 3.37 ROUTED FLOW MAP: bus services to Exeter

ships (such as plotting the square root of the flow or its logarithm), which may appear attractive when there is a great range in the volume of the flows, tend to create anomalous visual impressions. For instance, if it had been decided to use the square root value of the flows as the basis for the map, complications would arise in representing two joining flows: a flow of volume one, for example, combined with another flow of volume one to make a flow of volume two, would be represented by two lines of width $\sqrt{1} = 1·000$ joining together to make a line of $\sqrt{2} = 1·4142$. The line representing the combined flows would actually appear to be narrower than the sum of the two flows of which it is composed (fig. 3.38). Thus, while the relationship may be mathematically correct, the result is pictorially undesirable.

A further difficulty in the construction of routed flow maps is that of choosing the appropriate scale for the flow lines relative to the scale of the map. The largest flow must not be so large as to obliterate any other flows, and the smallest flow must be clearly visible. Also, of course, it becomes progressively more arduous to construct thick lines where the actual route is tortuous, and some 'straightening-out' may be neces-

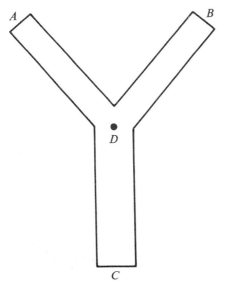

Fig. 3.38 PERCEPTUAL DIFFICULTY IN USE OF ROOT SCALE FOR ROUTED FLOWS: both flows from points A and B to point C are of the same volume and, therefore, the flow from D (where both flows unite) should be twice that of AD or BD. Using the root scale this is patently not the case

sary. This, for obvious reasons, must be kept to a minimum.

3B 2b Non-routed flows

As their name indicates, non-routed flow maps show linkages between points in diagrammatic form as straight lines, either drawn in thickness proportional to the volume of flow, or simply as symbolic links with no reference to the amount of flow. In either case, such non-routed flow lines are usually known as **desire lines** since they indicate a 'desired' flow.

Their main advantage over routed flow maps is that they place the emphasis firmly on the existence of a flow rather than on its precise route, and this can often be very useful since the precise route of certain movements may not always be known. In fact, desire lines were first developed in connection with the movements of urban population from one house to another: in such a context, the route taken becomes irrelevant, if not only difficult to ascertain. Since then, they have been used in a variety of situations but particularly in connection with journeys to work or to shop (fig. 4.45), functional connections between industrial and commercial activities (fig. 3.39) and social linkages in residential areas.

It will be readily appreciated that desire-line maps may be rather difficult to interpret, particularly where the volume of flows or the number of routes is large (figs. 3.39, 4.45). For this reason, alternative methods of flow analysis have been evolved in attempts to identify major flow structures, using matrices. **Matrices** are simply rectangular arrays of numbers arranged in columns and rows, any one entry of which is known as an **element**. Each column and row refers to a point in the study area, places a, b, c . . . i being listed in the same order along the rows as down the columns. The actual volume of flow between each pair of places is then entered in the appropriate cell of the matrix: in fig. 3.40, for example, there are 80 units of flow between Hornby and Cullingford.

The total amount of flow *from* one place to all other places (known as the **out-degree** of the point) is indicated by the sum of the elements in the appropriate row: similarly,

Fig. 3.39   TAXI FLOWS: 24 hour average weekday (GODDARD, 1970).

2000

100

< +100

0   1

km

the total flow **into** one place from all other places (the **in-degree** of the point) is indicated by the sum of the elements in the appropriate column. In order to identify the basic hierarchical structure of the flows, it is first necessary to rank the points in terms of their in-degree. The largest outflow from one point to another is then regarded as the dominant flow from that point, *provided* that flow is to a point of higher in-degree than the point from which it emanates. Points from which the largest flow is to a point of lower in-degree than themselves, are the **nodal,** or **terminal,** points of the structure, and it is upon these points that the desire-line flow structure is based.

Fig. 3.40 shows a matrix of flow structure for ten hypothetical towns, from which it

can be seen that Cullingford, Fordbridge, Stoneleigh and Seaville are all terminal points. The location of the terminal points relative to all the other points is then plotted (fig. 3.41) and the dominant flows are drawn in. The dominant nodal flow structure between the points is thus clearly revealed.

3B 2c Isolines

It is often useful to be able to show points or areas which are similar in some respect, by means of **isolines.** Such lines join together points of equal characteristics, rather like contours join together places of the same height. There are, in fact, many different kinds of isoline of which contours are but one; **isophores,** for instance, join together

96

Fig. 3.40 MATRIX OF BUS SERVICE CONNECTIONS: buses per week between 10 places

from \ to	Hornby	Cullingford	Nutwood	Fulton	Fordbridge	Axmouth	Stoneleigh	Morton	Summerton	Seaville	TOTAL OUT-DEGREE
Hornby	—	80+	20	25	31	7	7	5	20	3	198
Cullingford	*76+	—	50	42	43	10	22	3	16	35	297
Nutwood	10	62+	—	12	52	3	2	7	9	14	171
Fulton	20	84+	2	—	41	8	31	42	22	12	262
Fordbridge	7	42	*51+	22	—	6	10	3	39	34	214
Axmouth	8	12	8	8	3	—	32+	6	2	5	84
Stoneleigh	3	18	7	9	16	*34+	—	12	22	7	128
Morton	4	0	7	2	3	7	1	—	12	46+	82
Summerton	20	31	46	2	9	3	62	4	—	72+	249
Seaville	12	22	4	9	31	4	12	7	*82+	—	183
TOTAL IN-DEGREE	160	351	195	131	229	82	179	89	224	228	1868

* terminal point
+ dominant flow

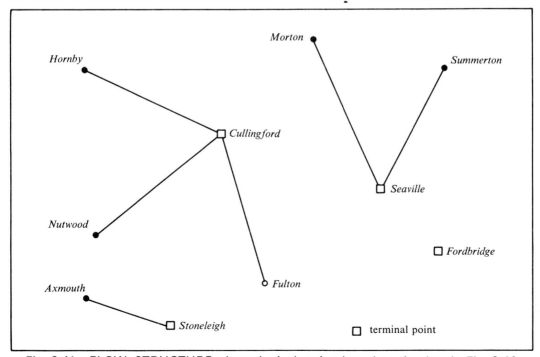

Fig. 3.41 FLOW STRUCTURE: hypothetical region based on the data in Fig. 3.40

points of equal cost charges (such as freight rates from a central point (fig. 3.42A)), **isostades** join together points of similar stages of development (such as building dates), while **isochrones** join together points of similar time characteristics (such as travelling time from a given point (fig. 3.42B)).

The process by which isolines are constructed is similar to that adopted in the construction of choropleth maps. The main problem lies in the choice of the isoline interval which is influenced not only by the range and form of the data set (as it is with choropleth maps), but also by the density of the point locations. This is best understood by considering a contour map, with contours at 50 m, 100 m, 150 m, 200 m and 250 m: five contours are plotted between 50 m and 250 m, but there could equally have been contours at every 25 m, 20 m, 5 m, 1 m,

0·5 m, 0·25 m — in fact, between 50 m and 250 m there is an infinite number of possible contour lines. Yet these are not drawn in, even in the largest scale maps, because there are not enough spot heights, or, as they are sometimes called, 'control points'. Isolines are often interpolated between control points, and there is a limit to the number of isolines that can be interpolated within a given density of control points. If there were only two control points in the study area, there would be enough difficulty in drawing one isoline, let alone an infinite number.

The actual control points should first be plotted on the base map. Data may not always be available for a specific point, and it may be necessary to derive a suitable point location for the purpose of constructing the isoline. This, of course, is always the case when information is available only by areas. In general, the control point should be placed

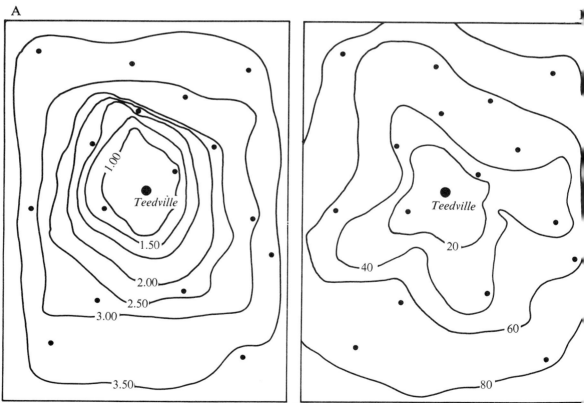

Fig. 3.42 A—ISOPHORES: cost of transport (£ per tonne) of rockery stone from a quarry at Teedville. B—ISOCHRONES: journey times (minutes) from Teedville

in the centre of the area to which the data refers, though in certain circumstances it may be more appropriate to 'weight' the point towards some other location which represents the data more suitably. Thus, for example, if we were constructing a '60% pastureland' isoline, through a series of parishes, the most appropriate point location for the pastureland figure would probably be in the centre of the pastureland area of the parish, rather than in the geographical centre of the parish (fig. 3.43). Isolines which are constructed through derived points such as these are normally known as **isopleths**, to distinguish them from **isometric lines**, which are based on actual point locations (such as spot heights).

Having plotted the control points and gained some idea of their density, the isoline interval can then be determined. As a guide, it is suggested that the number of isolines (classes) should not be more than five times the logarithm of the number of observations, but this can be altered up or down according to the density and distribution of the available control points. The actual isoline (class) intervals can then be determined by the same methods as for choropleth intervals (Section 3B 1b).

The class intervals thus constructed now become isolines that have to be interpolated within the framework of the control points on the base map. The process of interpolation is relatively simple. If, for instance, an isoline of $3x$ was to be interpolated between two control points with values of $2x$ and $4x$ respectively, then the isoline would be drawn exactly half way between the two points, since under normal circumstances isolines are generally interpolated by strict mathematical apportioning. Nevertheless, circumstances do arise in which the location of the isoline appears to be rather difficult to determine. Such 'indeterminate situations' (Mackay, 1953; Haggett, 1965) usually arise when the isoline has to be fitted between four control points. Fig. 3.44A presents such a situation: the population density at four points is shown and it is necessary to fit an isoline of 50 people per hectare through these points. Two solutions are feasible (fig. 3.44B/C), and it may be necessary to choose

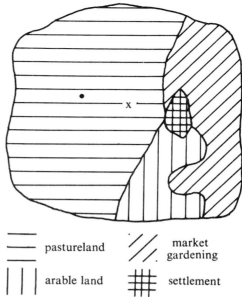

— pastureland   /// market gardening

||| arable land   ### settlement

Fig. 3.43 CHOICE OF CONTROLPOINT: the geographical centre of the parish (marked X) may be chosen to represent the amount of pastureland in the parish, but a point in the centre of the pastureland area itself (marked by a dot) may be more meaningful

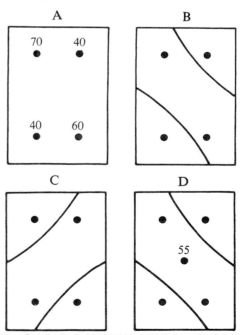

Fig. 3.44 INDETERMINATE SOLUTION: A—location of four control points; B and C—alternative possibilities of isoline location; D—location of a mean midpoint

99

to from	TOWN									
	1	2	3	4	5	6	7	8	9	10
1	0	5	84	88	0	79	59	19	59	42
2	5	0	88	2	18	0	83	86	62	87
3	84	88	0	43	26	92	87	65	75	66
4	88	2	43	0	13	41	25	68	18	0
5	0	18	92	13	0	0	64	0	67	2
6	79	0	26	41	0	0	97	0	1	0
7	59	82	87	25	64	97	0	0	41	63
8	18	86	65	68	0	0	0	0	0	44
9	59	62	75	18	67	1	42	0	0	41
10	42	87	66	0	2	0	63	44	41	0

Fig. 3.45 FLOW MATRIX: bus connections between 10 towns

the one which appears to fit best into the overall pattern of the surrounding area. It is, however, possible to find a solution mathematically by taking the mean value of the four points at a location equidistant from them all (fig. 3.44D).

EXERCISES

1 Draw a flow line map of bus services in your locality; the data can be obtained from local timetables.

2 The matrix in fig. 3.45 shows the number of main road bus connections between ten towns for one week. Using this information, construct a desire line map of dominant nodal flows. The actual location of the ten towns can be chosen in any manner you wish.

3 Discuss the relative advantages and disadvantages of proportional symbols, choropleths and isopleths in portraying data on the following topics, by parishes throughout a given region.
   (a) Density of population.
   (b) Proportions of land under grass, root crops, grains, rough pasture and waste.
   (c) Amount of urbanised land.
   (d) Building density.

4 Fig. 3.46 shows the density of population (people per hectare) in a series of parishes in Devwall county; choose an appropriate contour interval and construct the corresponding isolines throughout the area. Carefully explain your choice of isopleth interval, and describe any other techniques which might have been used to portray the information.

FURTHER READING

Barnes, A. W. and Tilbrook, A. W., *The Theory and Practice of Drawing for Engineers* (E.U.P., 1962).

Chorley, R. J. and Haggett, P., *Models in Geography*. Articles by Board, C. and Garner, B. J. (Methuen, 1967).

Clutterbuck, C. K., *Three-Dimensional Scale Drawing* (E.U.P., 1966).

Coleman, A. and Maggs, K. B. A., *Land Use Survey Handbook*: The Second Land Use Survey (1964).

Coppock, J. T., *Agricultural Atlas of the*

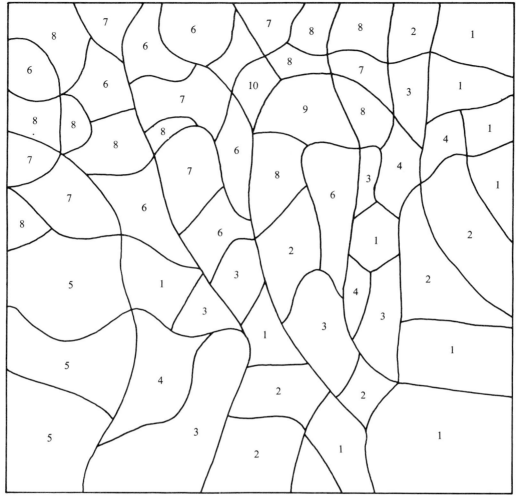

Fig. 3.46 POPULATION DENSITY (people per hectare), Devwall County

British Isles (Felber, 1964).

Dickinson, G. C., *Statistical Mapping and the Presentation of Statistics* (Edward Arnold, 1963).

Haggett, P., *Locational Analysis* (Edward Arnold, 1965).

Haggett, P. and Chorley, R. J., *Network Analysis* (Edward Arnold, 1969).

Holloway, J. L., 'Smoothing and filtering of time and space fields'. *Advances in Geophysics* (1958), 4, pp. 351–389.

Howe, G. M., *National Atlas of Disease Mortality* (Nelson, 1970).

Lawrance, C. J., 'Block diagrams of landscape for terrain classification'. No. 6/66 *Military Engineering Experimental Establishment* (1968).

Mackay, J. R., 'The alternative choice in isopleth interpretation'. *Professional Geographer* (1953), 5, pp. 2–4.

Monkhouse, F. J. and Wilkinson, H. R., *Maps and Diagrams* (Methuen, 1963).

Oxford Economic Atlas of the World (OUP, 1965).

Rosing, K. E., *Computer Graphics. Area* 1, (1969), pp. 2–7.

4 Locational Studies

Location, by definition, is always relative and it is simply because of this that it is possible to find pattern and order in the location of human and economic activity. Since individual locations are separated geographically by distance, they each possess relatively different degrees of accessibility. In turn, because of this difference in relative accessibility, certain locations become more desirable than others, and through a series of agglomerative processes a hierarchical structure of relative locations develops. All locations, like Orwell's pigs, may start equal, but some become more equal than others!

It is hardly surprising, in view of their fundamental rôles in causing relative location that the analysis of distance, accessibility and agglomeration has come to form one of the main themes in the search for pattern and order in location. Such order has been found in a wide variety of situations and at several different scales, but it is particularly in the study of population structure, building form, retailing activity and various types of movement that geographical techniques have been successful in revealing the effects of distance, accessibility and agglomeration.

4A POPULATION

The structure and distribution of population in any given area is fundamentally related to economic and social activity and for this reason studies of population should form an integral part of human geography. It is, however, only relatively recently that the analysis of population has attracted much interest. Many reasons have been suggested for this apparent anomaly (Zelinsky, 1966); among the most important are that reliable statistics have not been universally available and that traditionally in geographical studies more importance was attached to levels of economic production than to the location and development of economic activity.

The two aspects of structure and distribution of population are, of course, mutually inter-related: structure is reflected in distribution and distribution is reflected in structure: thus, maps showing population distribution (such as those described in Section 3B) are really complementary and essential to an understanding of population structure in any given area. The detailed analysis of locational patterns of population structure is, however, still very much in its infancy, but attention is being increasingly directed towards the fundamental relationships which appear to exist between population and geographical space.

4A 1 Structure of Population

The population of a region is made up of several different groups of people which can be identified according to their sex, age, marital status, occupation, religion, language and even nationality. The relative proportions of each of these different groups varies not only from region to region, but also at different periods of time (Clarke, 1965; Johnson, 1967). The effects of such variations are, of course, seen in the human landscape in terms of different building forms and densities, different social areas within settlements and ultimately in the creation of different regional 'character'.

The basic characteristics of population structure are normally illustrated by population **pyramids** (fig. 4.1), the shape of which describes the structure in visual fashion. Thus, for example, predominantly young populations have a rather 'flattened' pyramid with a wide base (fig. 4.1A), whereas 'mature' populations assume a characteristically 'beehive' shape (fig. 4.1B). In fact, it has been shown that different population

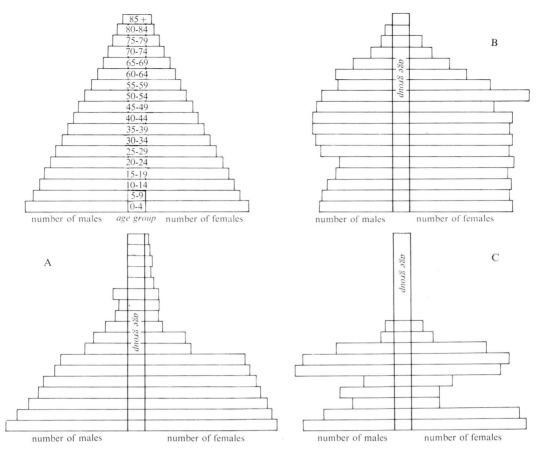

Fig. 4.1 POPULATION PYRAMIDS: the number of males in each age group is indicated on the left, and the number of females on the right side of the diagram. The 'ideal' population structure of a region would have progressively fewer people in each age group, giving rise to a 'pyramid' shape, as in the top left diagram. Other shapes, however, are more characteristic in reality, such as those shown in diagrams A, B and C

structures are associated with different kinds of areas not only within regions as a whole but also within towns (Clarke, 1965). As might be expected, the population structure of a rural area is rather different from that of a town, having fewer young people and proportionately more elderly people: similarly, new housing estates in towns are characterised by population pyramids which are more 'anvil' shaped than triangular (fig. 4.1C), reflecting the large proportion of rather young married couples with one or two small children on such estates.

Alternative methods of expressing popu-

lation structure have also been extensively employed, most of them involving the calculation of some form of ratio. Thus, the **sex ratio** expresses the proportion of men to women in the population at any given time and is simply calculated by the formula

$$\frac{\text{number of males}}{\text{number of females}} \times 100.$$

Various **age ratios** can likewise be calculated to express the importance of any one particular age group in the total population. The choice of the age group can be arbitrary, but it proves more meaningful if

103

it is chosen after a preliminary investigation. For example, in South Devon it is useful to express the aged as a proportion of the total population since it is an important retirement area, and in this case the ratio would be calculated by using the formula

$$\frac{\text{Number of people in age group 65 +}}{\text{Total population}} \times 100.$$

Other age groups would be substituted in this same formula depending on the particular line of enquiry.

Another important measure is the **dependency ratio** which expresses dependent population per 1 000 of the adult population. It is the nearest we can get to measuring the ratio of non-working to working population using Census data, and it is calculated from the formula

$$\frac{\text{Children under 15 + Adults over 65}}{\text{Adults between 15 and 64}} \times 1\ 000.$$

A more dynamic measure of the age structure of a population is found in the **index of ageing** which expresses the relationship between old and young people. It derives a statistic which shows whether or not there are more old than young, and as such can be used to give an indication of whether the population as a whole is becoming younger or older. The formula is

$$\frac{\text{Adults over 65}}{\text{Children under 15}} \times 100.$$

Considerable interest has also been shown in the birth, death and fertility rates, as they vary from area to area. Statistics on mortality are published by the Registrar General, and the crude death rate can be calculated as the number of deaths per 1 000 of the total population:

$$\frac{\text{Number of deaths}}{\text{Total population}} \times 1\ 000.$$

The birth rate is more difficult to determine, since the census of population does not record the actual numbers of babies born in any given period. Unless information can be obtained locally (see Section 1), an estimate has to be made from the table in the census which shows the number of persons in each age-category under 21. The number of 0–1 year olds can then be expressed as a ratio per 1 000 of the total population for the Census area:

$$\frac{\text{Number in age category 0–1 years}}{\text{Total population}} \times 1\ 000.$$

The difference between the crude death rate and the crude birth rate is known as the **natural increase** of population.

Perhaps a more meaningful index than the birth rates calculated from census data is the ratio of young children to women of child-bearing age. This **index of fertility** can be calculated by the formula

$$\frac{\text{Number of children under 5}}{\text{No. of women between 15 and 45}} \times 1\ 000.$$

Although for any region the population structure at any given time may be interesting enough in itself, it is usually even more so when its evolution is traced. This element of change has been variously shown in demographic studies by means of both population pyramids (fig. 4.1D) and the indices of sex, age and fertility already described (Coull, 1967).

The employment structure of the population has also been closely examined and particular attention paid to the distinction between those people who are employed in occupations which bring wealth **into** a given area (**basic** employment) and those which exist to **serve** the existing community (**non-basic** employment). Unfortunately, it is particularly difficult to distinguish between these two different kinds of employment in certain circumstances and it is largely for this reason that such studies have tended to concentrate on individual towns and cities in a rather idiographic way (Isard et al., 1960).

The social structure of the population varies in similar ways to those of its demography. In gathering data on the structure of social systems, two basic techniques have been employed — the interview questionnaire and census data. The interview is the better technique since it can be geared to a specific situation, but it suffers from the disadvantage of the great amount of time spent in collecting the information (see Section 1B 2). In addition to asking questions on a specific topic aimed at highlighting social attitudes, the interviewers are trained to notice features in the house which will reveal more about the attitudes of the respondent (features such as the type of furniture, the internal appearance of the house and the provision of sanitary amenities). The relationships that have been found between attitudes and appearance have been extended to the external condition of the house and garden. Various researchers have found that the general state of the garden, the appearance of the paintwork, and the condition of the pointing and the brickwork and other features can all be correlated with the class of person inhabiting the dwelling. (Big Brother certainly seems to be watching!)

The census of population does contain some useful information on social structure (see Section 1A 1a), but it is usually not on a sufficiently small scale. The more detailed data for enumeration districts can only be consulted in rare instances, and the individual original household returns are strictly confidential.

Despite the difficulties of data collection, a considerable amount of research has been carried out into social structure, though most of it relates to American examples. It has been found, for instance, that socioeconomic status is highly correlated with education, and that there is a strong correlation between income level, rent, occupation and education: fertility and the ratio of men to women are both inversely proportional to socio-economic status (Shevky and, Williams, 1948; Theodorson, 1961; Herbert, 1967). The more advanced techniques of factor analysis have also been used to analyse the structure of social areas. Thus for example, Gittus (1964) has been able to describe the social structure of south-east Lancashire by examining the relationships between age structure, sex ratios, occupancy rates, dwelling structure (as measured by the number of rooms per house) and the provision of sanitation facilities.

The relative concentration or dispersal of the various social classes into different areas may be described, as Timms (1965) has suggested, by the use of an Index of Similarity which is based on the use of location quotients. A location quotient can be used to compare one population characteristic with the total population in terms of its regional distribution; for example, the proportion of males, or of children under 10, or of persons over 65 in part of the study area may be compared with the proportion of the total population in the same part of the study area. Such information is readily available from the Census Reports. Other data can be collected by sample surveys. For instance, the social structure of a town could be sampled by wards and the results compared with the distribution of population by wards. If one ward has 36% of the Registrar General's social class 1 but only 10% of the total population of the town, then obviously this class is concentrated in this ward. This concentration is expressed as a single statistic:

$$\frac{36}{10} = \textbf{3·6}$$

Location quotients below 1 express deficiency in a characteristic, whilst those above 1 show a surplus.

The **index of similarity** is a more general measure than the location quotient since it does not measure anomalies at individual locations but deals with the study area as a unit. It compares the same data sets for which we can use a location quotient using the formula

$$\text{Index of Similarity} = 1 - \frac{\Sigma d}{100}$$

where d is the difference between the 2 data sets. (Either the positive or negative differences can be used since both should be equal).

An example shows the technique in operation. The proportion of the total population and the proportion of social class 1 in 5 wards of a town is shown in fig. 4.2. The positive and negative differences (Σd) both add up to 56 ($+15+3+38$ or $-31+-25$); that is, for wards A, B and D the proportion of social class 1 exceeds the proportion of total population by 56%. This figure is then divided by 100 and subtracted from 1 to give an index of similarity of 0·44. The lower the index, the greater is the dissimilarity between the two data sets.

Fig. 4.2 FIRST STAGE IN THE CALCULATION OF THE INDEX OF SIMILARITY: distribution of population and social Class I, by civil wards

	WARDS				
	A	B	C	D	E
a. % of total population	10	15	30	8	37
b. % of social Class I	25	18	5	46	6
difference (*d*) between a and b	+15	+3	−25	+38	−31

The indices outlined above are useful techniques for summarising distributional qualities, but since they are not true statistical measures of association such as the product-moment correlation coefficient, they are less effective for comparisons of areas through time or space.

Local Study

Aim: To describe the age structure and establish correlations between population structure and social conditions for a given region.

Data source: Population Census.

Method:

1 Define the study area in terms of Census districts.
2 Define age structure in terms of three groups — young, middle-aged and elderly.
3 Add up the total numbers in each age category and express this total as a proportion of the total number of people living in that census district.
4 Construct a three-dimensional graph (see Section 3A 1d) using as co-ordinates the percentages in each age category. Each axis on the graph represents an age category. Starting with the first place, find its co-ordinate on the axis showing the proportion of young people. Construct a line from this point parallel to the next side in an anticlockwise direction. Next find the co-ordinate showing the proportion of middle-aged people. Construct a line from this point parallel to the next side in an anticlockwise direction, and mark where it crosses the first line. Then find the co-ordinate showing the proportion of old people and construct a line parallel to the next side in an anti-clockwise direction. It should intersect at the point already marked. This point represents the location of the first place in relation to the three axes of population structure.
5 Repeat this procedure for every other place.
6 Study the completed graph to see if the points form clusters. If they do, locate the points forming one cluster on the map in order to see if they have any spatial affinities. Repeat this for any other cluster.
7 For each census district calculate or copy from the census the following indices:

(i) population density as

$$\frac{\text{total population}}{\text{area in acres}},$$

(ii) sex ratio as $\dfrac{\text{males}}{\text{females}} \times 1\,000,$

(iii) average change in population since the last census as

$$\frac{(\text{present population} - \text{population ten years ago})}{\text{population ten years ago}} \times 100,$$

(iv) Number of people per room as

$$\frac{\text{number of rooms occupied}}{\text{population in private households}},$$

(v) number of rooms per dwelling as

$$\frac{\text{number of rooms occupied}}{\substack{\text{number of structurally} \\ \text{separate dwellings occupied}}},$$

(vi) proportion of the population at more than $1\frac{1}{2}$ per room.

8 Construct a graph for every combination of pairs of indices. The number of combinations is given by the formula

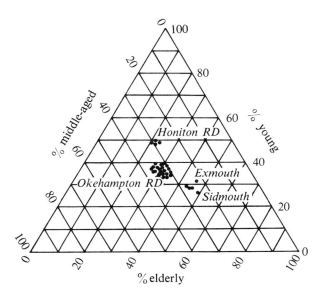

Fig. 4.3 AGE STRUCTURE: urban and rural areas of S. Devon plotted on a triangular graph (such graph paper is normally referred to as 'triangular coordinate' paper)

$$\frac{n(n-1)}{2}.$$

In this case, n is 6 and, therefore, the number of combinations is

$$\frac{6 \times 5}{2} = \textbf{15.}$$

Plot the score of each Census district on each pair of indices as co-ordinates. The number of points on each graph should be the same as the number of Wards in the urban area.

9 Reject those combinations of indices which do not appear to have anything in common, that is those for which the scatter of points does not show a definite trend.

10 For the remaining combinations of indices which do appear to show some relationship, calculate a correlation coefficient.

11 Rank the correlation coefficients and determine a level of significance. Ignore all those coefficients which fall below this level.

Example

Area studied: County of Devon.

The three age categories were first designated as: young — 0 to 24 years;

middle-aged — 25 to 59 years; and elderly — above 60 years. For each administrative division the proportions in these categories were calculated and plotted on a three dimensional graph. It is obvious from the graph (fig. 4.3) that clusters of settlements do exist, and relating the clusters to the map shows that the coastal towns, especially those of east Devon (Sidmouth, Seaton, Budleigh Salterton and Exmouth) have a high proportion of old people showing their importance as retirement areas. The majority of the inland towns form an unstructured cluster, with a fairly even breakdown of population into the three groups, though there are exceptions such as Honiton, Plymouth, Crediton and Tiverton which have a high proportion of young people. In the case of Honiton this can be explained by the existence of an army camp. The rural districts of Devon also tend to form an unstructured group with a high proportion of young people (e.g., Honiton R.D. 38%, Okehampton R.D. 37%).

Next, the 6 indices of population and social condition were calculated for each administrative division, and fifteen graphs were constructed, one for each combination of pairs of indices. Those pairs with no obvious association were rejected and those with some degree of association were tested by a correlation coefficient. The following coefficients were obtained:

Population density and proportion of population living at greater than $1\frac{1}{2}$ per room: $r = 0.78$.

Number of rooms per dwelling and proportion of population living at greater than $1\frac{1}{2}$ per room: $r = 0.66$ (When these indices were transformed on to logarithmic scales, r was increased to 0.70.).

Sex ratio and number of rooms per dwelling: $r = 0.387$.

Sex ratio and proportion of population living at greater than $1\frac{1}{2}$ per room: $r = 0.20$.

Obviously the relationships between the sex ratio, the number of rooms per dwelling and the proportion of the population living at greater than $1\frac{1}{2}$ per room is not yet shown, since no significance could be found in the correlation.

To test the relationship between these variables and social status further, we obtained from the council the number of council house dwellings in each division. These were paired with each of the 6 indices mentioned, and graphs were drawn. Correlation coefficients were calculated for those with the greatest degree of association, and we obtained the following relationship:

Number of rooms per dwelling and the number of council houses:

$$r = 0.81.$$

Watch-points In this example we have established that certain relationships exist between physical factors which can be measured, and we have surmised that these physical factors tell us something about the socio-economic class of the population. We must, however, be careful about pursuing the parallel too far, because the collection areas are too large for us to say anything about them in detail. Having analysed the data at this scale, the next step would be to choose smaller study areas and conduct our own questionnaire survey. The use of census data will bring out macro-variations, but will not tell us anything about the detailed pattern, for which a more detailed survey is required, together with a count of private

dwellings and institutions, so that we know something about the whole occupancy structure of the area.

The data about institutions is important because we should also know about the basis on which the census is based. In Britain, each person is recorded at the place he is at when the census is taken, and not at his usual dwelling, as happens in other countries. Therefore, it is important to know about numbers of institutions, because they can give a spuriously high population for an area.

FURTHER READING

Clarke, J. I., *Population Geography* (Pergamon, 1965).

Coull, J. R., 'A comparison of demographic trends in the Faroe and Shetland Isles'. *Transactions of the Institute of British Geographers* (1967), 41, pp. 159–166.

Gittus, E., 'The structure of urban areas: a new approach'. *Town Planning Review* (1964), 35, pp. 5–20.

Herbert, D. T., 'The use of diagnostic variables in the analysis of urban structure'. *Tijdschrift voor Economische en Sociale Geografie* (1967), 58, pp. 5–10.

Isard, W. *et al.*, *Methods of Regional Analysis* (M.I.T. Press, 1960).

Johnson, J. H., *Urban Geography* (Pergamon, 1967).

Shevky, E. and Williams, M., *The Social Areas of Los Angeles: Analysis and Typology* (California U.P., 1948).

Theodorson, G. A., *Studies in Human Ecology* (Harper, 1961).

Timms, D., ch. 12 in *Frontiers in Geographical Teaching*. Chorley, R. J. and Haggett, P. (eds.) (Methuen, 1965).

Zelinsky, W., *A Prologue to Population Geography* (Prentice-Hall, 1966).

4A 2 Population-Space Relationships

At no scale can the geographical distribution of population be regarded as regular. At the world level, it is clear that there are certain areas of great population concentration (W. Europe has 88 persons per km²) which contrast markedly with vast areas (such as central southern America) which are almost uninhabited; at the national level, the densely populated industrial regions contrast strikingly with the non-industrial areas; at the regional level, population density is always greater in the towns than it is in the surrounding country districts, and within the towns themselves, there are distinct variations in the density of occupance.

However, such variations in population distribution which are apparent from the kind of maps we described earlier (Section 3B), are not without a certain degree of orderly structure. In particular, it has been found that there is a clear relationship between density of population and distance, and that within urban areas there is evidence of distinct 'zoning' of population according to social class.

As distance away from a central point increases, population density, in general, declines (fig. 4.4A). The rate of decline (the 'lapse rate') varies from region to region, but the general form of a negative exponential relationship appears to hold in both urban and rural environments. There have been many studies of the form of the lapse rates for many different regions both in the Western and Eastern hemispheres. Bogue (1949) showed that in the areas immediately surrounding 65 cities in the USA, the rural farm density was about 50 people per km², but that in the areas beyond 650 km from the cities the density had declined to about 10 people per km². In contrast, within cities not only are densities much higher than in rural areas (there is evidence to suggest that population density increases with the size of a city), but also the lapse rates are much greater. Clark (1951) has shown the exact form of the lapse rate for 39 cities throughout the world, and it appears that in general

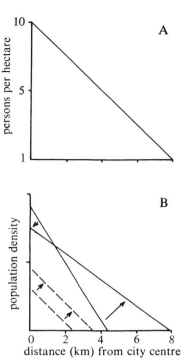

Fig. 4.4 POPULATION LAPSE RATES: A—the normal negative exponential lapse rate; B—changes through time (Western cities black line, nonwestern dotted line)

the density declines by a factor of about 10% for every 8 km from the city centre.

There has also been considerable analysis of the evolution of the lapse rates, and Berry, Simmons and Tennant (1963) have shown that the experience of areas in the western hemisphere is rather different from those of the eastern hemisphere (fig. 4.4B), but it is also true that neither of these two cases represent mutually exclusive experiences since there is also evidence that some 'western' cities' lapse rates followed a pattern more akin to the 'non-western' pattern, and vice-versa. Clearly, there are many different variations but the basic trend of a distance-decay function holds for many regions and cities.

An interesting way of analysing population distribution has been suggested by Stewart (1947) and later modified by Warntz and Neft (1960). The relative proximity of the total surrounding population to any given point (its population 'potential') can be calculated in either of two ways. Stewart

Fig. 4.5 CALCULATION OF POPULATION POTENTIAL

SETTLE-MENT	POPULATION (P)	DISTANCE FROM PLACE A (d)	P/d
A	200	—	200·0
B	400	5	80·0
C	50	10	5·0
D	10	20	0·5
E	40	4	10·0
		$\Sigma P/d = 295\cdot5$	

defined the population potential of a given place as the cumulative product of population and distance at all the surrounding places; it can be calculated from the formula:

Potential of place $= \Sigma p/d$

where p = population at another point

d = distance of that point from A.

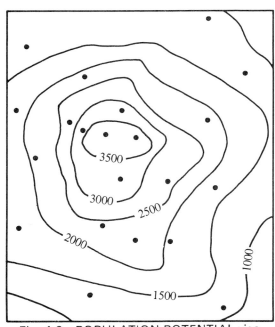

Fig. 4.6 POPULATION POTENTIAL: isopleths are interpolated to join places of the same potential (expressed in 'persons per km'). Such isopleths are also known as 'equi-potential lines'

110

A simple example will show how it can be calculated. The populations of 5 towns are shown in fig. 4.5, which also shows the method of calculation for the potential at place A. This same procedure is repeated to calculate the potential for all the other points in turn and isopleths can then be interpolated from the resultant figures (fig. 4.6).

A variation on this method has been developed by Warntz and Neft and involves the calculation of a **dynamical radius** which is given by the formula:

$$r = \sqrt{\frac{\Sigma(p.d^2)}{P}}$$

where p = population at another place

d = distance of that place from point being measured

P = total population of study area.

Using the same formula as before (fig. 4.5), it can be seen that

$$r = \sqrt{\frac{(400 \times 5^2) + (50 \times 10^2) + (10 \times 20^2) + (40 \times 4^2)}{700}}$$

$$= \textbf{5·3 km}$$

Thus, within a radius of 5·3 km of place A live 91 %

$$\left(\frac{640}{700} \times 100\right)$$

of the total population of the region under study.

The reasons for these variations in population-space relationships are, of course, legion. The large scale relationship which exists between the distribution of population and the exploitation of land and capital resources has long been acknowledged, and it is clear that, in general, a population is found in a particular area because work is, or has been, available there. On a micro-scale, however, the distribution of population is related to the amount of money that various individuals (private and corporate) are willing to bid for the use of a given piece of land, and the amount that they are willing to bid depends on a host of factors not least of which are the physical characteristics of a plot of ground (e.g., gently sloping ground is more suitable for a housing estate than a deeply sloping valley side), the relative location of one plot of ground to others and the ability to pass on costs to the market. In other words, the accessibility of one site relative to other functions is one of the main factors determining the distribution of population. Agglomeration economies are also instrumental in causing population to concentrate itself near to the points which are regarded as most accessible or most desirable. Once a particular site or area is seen to possess some advantage for settlement, its growth is almost self-perpetuating: 'birds of a feather flock together' in this respect so that once a particular area is seen, for instance, to be developing into a high-class, low-density residential zone, it becomes a desirable area for other high-class people who may attempt to move in. In detail, of course, the process

is rather more complicated than this as we shall see later (Section 4C 2b), but the basic notion of different sectors of the population being located with respect to the rents they can afford to bid for different sites remains fundamental (Garner, 1967). Hence, different social classes of the population are located in characteristic zones or sectors within cities.

One of the earliest instances in which this spatial distribution of different social and economic types was described, was in a study of Chicago by Burgess in 1927, who suggested that a city could be thought of as a series of zones produced by outward growth and occupied by specific functions, all of which tended to expand along their outer periphery. Around a central business district he suggested that one could discern a zone that was being invaded by business functions followed by a working class

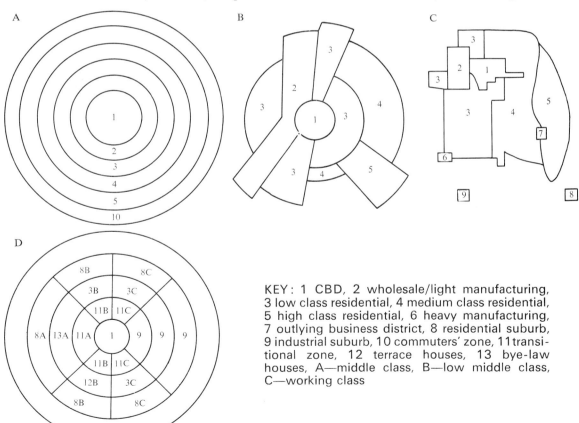

KEY: 1 CBD, 2 wholesale/light manufacturing, 3 low class residential, 4 medium class residential, 5 high class residential, 6 heavy manufacturing, 7 outlying business district, 8 residential suburb, 9 industrial suburb, 10 commuters' zone, 11 transitional zone, 12 terrace houses, 13 bye-law houses, A—middle class, B—low middle class, C—working class

Fig. 4.7 MODELS OF URBAN STRUCTURE: A—concentric zone (after Burgess); B—sector (after Hoyt); C—multiple nucleii (after Harris and Ullman); D—a British city model (after Mann)

suburban zone, and then a higher class suburban zone and finally a commuting zone (fig. 4.7A). In 1939, Hoyt produced a refinement of this model by his inclusion of radii such as arterial roads and suburban railways into the scheme. These radii transform the concentric zone model into a series of sectors of a particular economic or social significance which tend to be self-perpetuating (fig. 4.7B). For example, if a high class residential zone develops near the core, then land values on the outer periphery increase because of the association with a high status area. As a result, only functions which can pass on high costs to the consumer can afford the land, and high class residences are one such function. A third model which comes even closer to reality was suggested by Harris and Ullman (1945). They suggested that urban growth might occur around several minor centres which at one time would have been small villages near to the original town centre. These 'multiple-nuclei' form the nodes around which development occurs either by zones or by sectors, to create the characteristic pattern of differentiated population-space areas (fig. 4.7C). All of these models were designed for American cities, but it appears that the same basic postulates hold for British cities, as has been suggested by Mann (1965) (fig. 4.7D); in either case, it is obvious that the three basic ideas are hardly mutually exclusive and that the structure of urban land use by different sectors of the population is best described by the fusion of all three structural models.

Local Study

Aim: To show population-space relationships of concentration and dispersion using a Lorenz curve, and to analyse the density lapse rate.
Data source: population census.
Method:

1 Delineate the study area in terms of census districts.
2 Calculate the total population and the total area of the study area.
3 Calculate the proportion of the total population living in each census district.
4 Calculate the area of each census district as a proportion of the total study area.
5 Rank the census districts from lowest to highest in terms of their score on (4) above, and for each one note down the associated proportion of the total population living there.
6 Add the two ranked series cumulatively, so that the first pair of readings is composed of the lowest **area** proportion (4 above) and its associated **population** proportion (3 above); the second pair of readings is the lowest and second lowest area proportions and the two associated population proportions, until the last pair of values comprise the accumulated sum up to the largest *area* proportion and the accumulated sum up to the associated *population* proportion, both of the readings being 100%.
7 Use the cumulative proportions as co-ordinates to construct a Lorenz curve, with population on the abscissa and area on the ordinate (see Section 3A 1a, figs. 3.5 and 3.6).
8 Construct a series of concentric circles on a map of the city.
9 Calculate the mean population density for each of the concentric zones.
10 Construct a histogram to show population density against distance from the centre of the city.

Example
Area studied: City of Exeter.

The percentages of the total population living in each of the 17 civil wards which make up the city of Exeter and the areas of the civil wards as percentages of the total area of the city were calculated and then added cumulatively from lowest percentage area to highest percentage area to give the co-ordinates for the construction of the Lorenz curve. Thus, the first pair of co-ordinates are the values for St Mark's, where 5% of the population live in 1·7% of the area. The second pair of co-ordinates are 10·3% of the population living in 3·5% of the area, formed by adding the value for St Mark's and St Matthew's together. This

Fig. 4.8 CUMULATIVE PERCENTAGE DISTRIBUTION: area and population cumulatively added for the 17 Civil wards of Exeter

CIVIL WARD	% OF TOTAL AREA	% OF TOTAL POPULATION
St Mark's	1·7	5·0
+ St Matthew's	3·5	10·3
+ St David's	5·7	14·0
+ Emmanuel	7·9	18·1
+ Polsloe	10·2	24·9
+ Heavitree	12·8	31·2
+ Wonford	15·9	39·1
+ St Leonard's	19·1	45·0
+ Trinity	22·8	50·2
+ Cowick	26·7	56·0
+ Barton	31·6	64·4
+ St Thomas	37·6	68·5
+ Whipton	46·5	76·0
+ Rougemont	58·6	81·5
+ Exwick	70·9	87·3
+ St James'	83·5	93·0
+ St Loye's	100·0	100·0

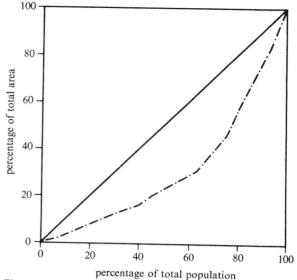

Fig. 4.9 POPULATION-SPACE RELATIONSHIPS: distribution of population in Exeter, shown as a Lorenz curve (data from Fig. 4.8)

process continues until the addition of St Loye's makes both columns total 100% (fig. 4.8). Each pair of values was plotted as co-ordinates, with cumulative population shown on the abscissa and cumulative areas on the ordinate (fig. 4.9).

The actual trace line is compared against a theoretical distribution whose trace line lies at 45° from the origin and which shows a perfectly evenly distributed population. That is, 20% of the population living in 20% of the area; 50% of the population living in 50% of the area, and so on. The degree to which the actual trace line differs from this theoretical trace shows the unevenness of the population distribution, and it is these differences which then need to be explained. For instance, in this case it is clear that there is a marked concentration of population in St Mark's ward, and the reason for

this is that it is largely a working class, terraced housing area. By this method, therefore, the areas of high density are easily identifiable.

The second part of the project was to examine the population density distance-decay function for the city. A series of concentric circles was constructed on a map of the city, the first of which had a radius representing 1 km, and each successive circle was drawn at additional 1 km intervals (fig. 4.10A). The area and population contained within each zone was then calculated and expressed as a ratio of each other. The ratios were then plotted against distance from the city centre as histograms (fig. 4.10B), which clearly show that densities do, in general, decline as distance from the centre increases.

Watch-points The difficult and tedious part of this project is the calculation of population density for each of the zones which are examined. Population data is available only for wards within the city and these wards do not coincide with the concentric zones in our study. There are a number of solutions to the problem, but none of them

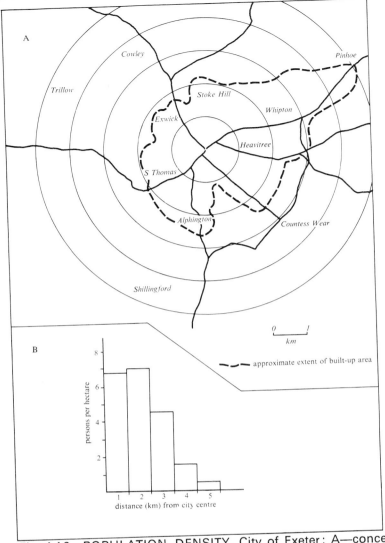

Fig. 4.10 POPULATION DENSITY, City of Exeter: A—concentric zones centred on the peak land value point of the CBD, B—histogram of population density in each of the five zones

will give more than an *approximation* of the area density. Perhaps the simplest method is to work out the area of each ward which falls within each concentric zone, and to multiply that figure by the ward's *mean* population density. The values for each part of the ward falling in each of the zones are then summed and divided by the total *area* of each zone.

The radii of the concentric circles should be chosen with respect to local conditions and availability of time, but clearly the finer the grid the more useful will be the results.

FURTHER READING

Berry, B. L., Simmons, J. W. and Tennant, R. J., 'Urban population densities: their structure and change'. *Geographical Review* (1963), 53, pp. 389–405.

Bogue, D. J., *The Structure of the Metropolitan Community* (Michigan U.P., 1949).

Burgess, E. W. — reprinted in Park, R. E., Burgess, E. W. and McKenzie, R. D., *The City* (Chicago U.P., 1924).

Chapin, F. S. and Pearson, H. S., 'Population densities around the clock' in

Mayer, H. M. and Kohn, C. F. (eds), *Readings in Urban Geography* (Chicago U.P., 1959).

Clark, C., 'Urban population densities'. *Journal of the Royal Statistical Society* (1951), 114, pp. 490–496.

Garner, B., 'Models in urban geography and settlement form' in Chorley, R. J. and Haggett, P., *Models in Geography* (Methuen, 1967).

Harris, C. D. and Ullman, E. L. — reprinted in Mayer, H. M. and Kohn, C. F., *Readings in Urban Geography* (Chicago U.P., 1955).

Hoyt, H., *The Structure and Growth of Residential Neighbourhoods in American Cities* (Washington, 1939).

Mann, P., *An Approach to Urban Sociology* (R.K.P., 1965).

Stewart, J. Q., 'Empirical mathematical rules concerning the distribution and equilibrium of population'. *Geographical Review* (1947), 37, pp. 461–485.

Warntz, W. and Neft, D., 'Contribution to a statistical methodology for areal distributions'. *Journal of Regional Science* (1960), 2, pp. 47–66.

4B BUILDING FORM

The study of building form has traditionally been at the heart of human geography, but recently it seems to have been overshadowed by the more 'functional' studies of settlements and areas. Nevertheless, the analysis of 'townscapes' and the morphological form of settlements in general must still form a necessary part of our subject, since form and function are patently closely inter-related. Indeed, the increasing accent on 'general systems' in the study of the human landscape may well help to rebridge the gap between the two approaches since the success of the systems approach largely depends on placing the emphasis on the inter-relationships between form and function.

Building form has been studied from two slightly different standpoints: on the one hand there are many studies which have analysed the two-dimensional aspects of buildings and their general 'plan' form, whilst, on the other hand, others have tended to concentrate on their three-dimensional architectural form. In either case, increasing use is being made of statistical and classificatory methods in the search for spatial regularities and order.

4B 1 Two-Dimensional Analysis

The study of the distribution of buildings either within towns or in different regions has long been one of the main themes in human geography. For many years, it was largely confined to a consideration of whether the settlements of a given region were 'nucleated', 'dispersed' or of an 'intercalatory' nature (Demangeon, 1908). Intricate explanations related to natural, social or economic conditions were offered to explain the particular form of the building distribution of each region, but the actual method of defining 'nucleation' or 'dispersion' was essentially arbitrary and, certainly, subjective. Similarly, the *extent to which* the buildings or settlements were, or were not, nucleated or dispersed was, except in a very arbitrary way, ignored. Thus, although being perfectly valid, the method of description was vague and imprecise.

More recently, the analysis of two-dimensional building form has employed much more refined methods in order to describe not only the general distributional characteristics of settlements relative to each other, but also the variation in building densities within different areas.

4B 1a Nearest-neighbour analysis

In trying to describe their main distributional characteristics, every building or settlement in a given area may be treated as a **point.** The problem, therefore, of describing location is one of describing the distribution of a series of points in space, and this is by no means easy. How, for instance, can each of the different **point distributions** of settlements shown in fig. 4.11 be described? Probably, we could say that the first series of points (a)

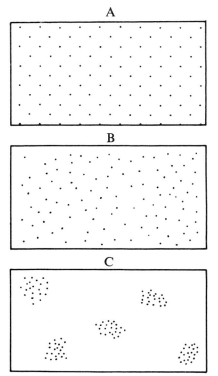

Fig. 4.11 POINT DISTRIBUTIONS: each dot represents one settlement

were more regularly spaced than the second series, (b) and that neither of these were so nucleated (clustered) as the third series (c). But this is not a very accurate description, nor is it an objective one.

It was precisely this problem of the inaccuracy and subjectivity of descriptions based on visual impressions of the point distributions which led to the need to find some new way of analysing such patterns of relative location. The problem was not one which faced geographers alone: botanists, geologists, chemists and many other scientists were all encountering the need to make descriptions of relative location more accurate. It was, in fact, two ecologists, Clark and Evans who first gave a lead in this field in 1954. They evolved a mathematical way of describing the distribution pattern. Their method was to measure the distance between every point and its 'nearest-neighbour', and to substitute these figures in a formula which would give one *figure* to describe the distributional pattern under consideration.

Several versions of this formula have been suggested, some of which may be mathematically suspect (Witherick and Pinder 1972): one that is easy to apply is as follows:

$$R_n = 2\,\bar{D}\,\sqrt{(N/A)}$$

where R_n represents the 'description' of the distribution

$\bar{D}$ = the mean distance between the nearest-neighbours

A = area under study (in same units as $\bar{D}$)

N = number of points in study area.

The values of R_n will occur within the range 0 to 2·15. If all the points were clustered together at only *one* location, R_n would be 0; if all the points were *regularly* distributed throughout the area, R_n would be 2·15; if the points were *randomly* distributed, R_n would be 1·0. Now the advantage of this is obvious: instead of having only three descriptive terms (clustered, regular, random), we now have a continuous description from 0 to 2·15, so that, provided we remember what the 'extreme' values represent, we can describe any distribution numerically. Hence, if R_n was, say, 1·9, we would know that the distribution was tending towards being regular, but not completely so. By this method, our language has been extended and, in the process, greater precision has been added to that language in that we are now less subjective in our description.

This method has been used effectively by geographers in the analysis of settlement distributions (King, 1962; Dacey, 1962), and a summary of this work is given by Haggett (1965).

Local Study

Aim: To analyse the spatial distribution of all settlements in a given area.

Data source: Topographical map of study area.

Method:

1 Measure the distance between each settlement and its nearest-neighbour, and tabulate these distances.

2 Find the mean distance between the pairs of nearest-neighbours.

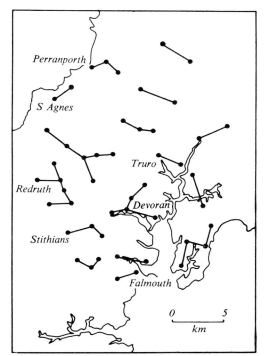

Fig. 4.12 NEAREST-NEIGHBOURS: part of the area near Truro (OS Sheet 190, 1:63360); a line joins each settlement and its nearest neighbour

3 Measure the total area of the study region (in the same units as the distances).
4 Calculate the nearest-neighbour statistic, R_n, by substituting the formula (1) above.

Example

Area studied: A part of central Cornwall (OS Sheet 190, 1:63 360, Truro and Falmouth).

On a transparent overlay sheet of the map, we drew in lines showing the link between each settlement and its nearest-neighbour (fig. 4.12). The length of each of these lines was measured according to the distance it represented, and these 'inter-centre' distances were recorded in tabular form. Next, we measured the total area under study, and found this to be 300 km². (We need this figure for the 'A' value in the formula used for calculating R_n.) The total number of settlements (n) in the study area was 183

(this figure is needed both for working out the mean distance between the nearest-neighbours and, also, for the calculation of R_n).

We now calculated the **mean** distance between the nearest-neighbours ($\bar{D}$). In Section 2A 2b we described how to calculate the mean value:

$$\bar{D} = \frac{\Sigma d}{n}.$$

In this case, therefore, with $\Sigma d = 78.69$ km and $n = 183$,

$$\bar{D} = \frac{78.69}{183.0} = 0.43.$$

Having thus found $\bar{D}$, we can substitute in the formula (1) above:

$$R_n = 2(0.43)\sqrt{(183/300)} = 0.67$$

With $R_n = 0.67$, this meant that the distribution of settlements in this little region was more clustered than regular though, once we were used to it, we could simply have described the distribution in terms of the one figure, 0.67. Having described the distribution, we may then go on to try and *explain* the description.

Watch-points For this study it does not really matter how large or how small an area is chosen; the major problem will probably be that of knowing from what point to measure the distances. Ideally, the inter-centre distances should be measured from the **centres** of each settlement, but this is difficult to do from only map evidence. If the settlement has only **one** church, then take that to represent the centre, or, if there is obviously a main street, take a point half way along that as the centre. Clearly, discretion is necessary!

Arising from this problem will be that of deciding what constitutes a 'settlement'. Do hamlets have to be included, and, indeed, must individual farmsteads be considered? For practical purposes, it will probably be found convenient to define a settlement as a collection of *more than* four or five houses.

117

FURTHER READING

Clark, P. J. and Evans, F. C., 'Distance to nearest neighbour as a measure of spatial relationships in population' *Ecology*, (1954), 35, pp. 445–453.

Dacey, M. F., 'Analysis of central place and point patterns by a nearest neighbour method' *Lund Studies in Geography* (Series B), (1962), 24, pp. 55–75.

Haggett, P., *Locational Analysis in Human Geography*, pp. 231–233 (Arnold, 1965).

King, L. J., 'A quantitative expression of the pattern of urban settlements in selected areas of the United States' *Tijdschrift voor Economische en Sociale Geografie*, (1962), 53, pp. 1–7.

Witherick, M. E. and Pinder, D. A., 'The principles, practice and pitfalls of nearest-neighbour analysis'. *Geography*, Vol. 57, Part 4, November 1972.

4B 1b Size and distance relationships

In any region there is always one very large dominant town or city; then there may be two or three fairly large towns, six or seven slightly smaller towns, and, finally, many villages. In other words, there are few large settlements, but many small ones. It follows from this that if there are only a *few* settlements which are large in a given area, they will be spaced further apart from each other than the many smaller settlements in that same area which will be spaced closer to each other.

Many studies have shown the exact nature of this relationship for different regions. The earliest of them was made in 1933 by Walter Christaller who examined this hierarchy of towns and villages in southern Germany. His empirical findings led him to formulate his 'central place' theory which has had such a great impact on geographical studies of settlements in recent years. Another pioneer in the theoretical approach to the location of settlements, August Lösch (1940) pointed to evidence in the American Middle-West. Settlements were arranged into three size groupings, 300 – 1 000, 1 000 – 4 000 and 4 000 – 20 000 inhabitants, and the distances between the settlements in each group were then measured. Again it was found that there was a strong relationship between size and spacing of the settlements.

Similarly, Brush and Bracey (1955) discovered that in both southwest Wisconsin and southern England, the large towns are about 34 km apart from each other, medium sized towns occur at 12 to 16 km, and small towns are about 6 to 10 km apart.

Thomas (1961), King (1961) and many others have pointed to similar regularities of size and distance in different parts of the world though, of course, the distances separating the various settlements vary from region to region.

The major question posed by this phenomenon is the simple and obvious one of 'Why?'. The answer involves a consideration of the functions of settlements and of their market areas, as we shall see later in Section 4C. Meanwhile, we shall see how the 'size-distance' relationship may be described for any given area.

Local Study

Aim: To investigate the 'size-distance' relationship between settlements in a region.
Data sources: Population census; topographical map.
Method:

1. Construct a histogram to show the number of settlements of given sizes in the study area, and from this establish meaningful classes.
2. List all the settlements which occur in the same size group.
3. Measure the distance between each settlement and its nearest-neighbour *in the same size group*.
4. Calculate the **mean** inter-centre distance between nearest-neighbours for each size group.
5. Calculate the value of R_n (see Section 4B 1a) for each of the size groupings. (This will help to describe the locational pattern of each group of settlements.)

Example

Area studied: County of Devon (OS Sheet 15, 1:250 000).

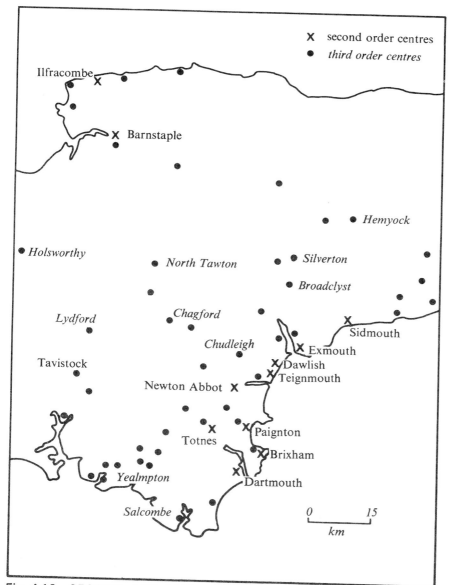

Fig. 4.13 SECOND AND THIRD ORDER CENTRES, County of Devon

From the histogram of settlement sizes it was decided that the most meaningful classes were 1 000–5 000, 5 000–50 000 and 50 000 +. (We have already described in Sections 2A 1a and 3B 1b how such classes should be chosen.) Three lists showing the names of the settlements in each of these three size groups were then prepared. The straight-line distance separating the settle-ments shown on each list were then measured and recorded accordingly, and the mean distances calculated.

It was found that the mean distance between centres of 50 000 or more was 34 km, between centres of 5 000–50 000 inhabitants it was 10 km and between centres of 1 000–5 000 inhabitants it was 6 km.

This, then, describes the form of the 'urban structure' of the region. There are few (3) large settlements, more (12) medium sized settlements and many (74) smaller towns, each at characteristic distances apart. However, if we now plot the distribution of the settlements in each of these three size groups on a map we shall be able to say much more about the characteristic locations of the different sized centres.

Fig. 4.13 shows how the third order centres (1 000–5 000 population) are distributed in Devon. A nearest-neighbour analysis of this pattern yields a value for R_n of 0·37, which means that the settlements of this size are tending to be clustered in their distribution. From the accompanying map we can see, in fact, that they are clustered *around* the larger (second-order) centres — a distribution which seems to be fairly typical of most areas.

By this very simple method, therefore, we are able to point to the salient features of the urban structure in any region. The description so produced, however, needs to be explained. Why, for instance, is there this hierarchical arrangement of settlements and how can we explain the spatial distribution of these settlements in the area under study? Measurement and the statistical manipulation of the data produced is *in itself* of no value, but the patterns which they reveal are very thought-provoking. We see here, very clearly, how statistical processing can be a very great aid in our analysis of geographical patterns.

Watch-points Be careful not to choose too small an area for study on this study. The major characteristics of settlement distribution will not be revealed unless the study area includes a fair number of different sized settlements. You will probably find the County to be the most convenient unit for analysis.

Again, as in the previous local study of nearest-neighbour analysis, take care to measure the 'inter-centre' distances from meaningful points (see 'Watch-points' at the end of Section 4B 1a).

120

FURTHER READING

Brush, J. E. and Bracey, H. E., 'Rural service centres in Southwestern Wisconsin and Southern England', *Geographical Review*, (1955), 45, pp. 559–569.
Christaller, W. (translated C. W. Baskin), *Central Places in Southern Germany* (Prentice Hall, 1966).
King, L. J., 'A multivariate analysis of the spacing of urban settlements in the United States', *Annals of the Association of American Geographers*, (1961), 51, pp. 222–233.
Lösch, A. (translated W. H. Woglom), *The Economics of Location* (Yale U.P., 1956).
Thomas, E. N., 'Towards an expanded central place model', *Geographical Review*, (1961), 51, pp. 400–411.

4B 1c Building density

We have already seen (Section 4A) that there are certain regularities in the spatial distribution of population density. Clearly, the density of building is at least in part a reflection of population density and so we might well expect to find similar regularities in the spatial variations of building density. In fact, building density lapse-rates can be calculated in a similar way to the population density lapse-rates.

The reasons for the spatial variations in building density are, naturally, complex. Historically, the main reason for building at high densities was the pressure on land. This was evident even in medieval towns with, for example, the infilling of burgage plots. (These were plots of land given to the burgesses of a town, often as an inducement to settle in the town.) Once these had been completely built over, the owners began to build upwards. This was done by the simple expedient of adding another storey on to those which already existed, and it was in this way that the overhanging upper storeys developed. We can see the same pressure on the land today (Gottman, 1966). In our city centres the tendency is to build upwards and to exclude functions which are wasteful of space — it is for this reason that parks and car parks, which are central area functions, are found on the fringe of the city centre. Land owners require an adequate return on the money which they have invested, and consequently, buildings are high in central areas, since the more tenants there are on a piece of land, the greater is the return to the property owner. The only constraints to this high density development are the constructional techniques and the possibility of saturating the market with accommodation.

Outside the central area, where property values are lower, the returns per unit area can be lower and, consequently, density can be lower. Nevertheless, both in the past and at the present, questions of cost effectiveness have been major considerations. The process of repeating a house type in the form of a terrace economised in design, in the amount of materials (there was, for instance, only one dividing wall between houses) and in labour costs, since repetition of the same units increased the efficiency of labour. The same considerations are found on housing estates today. A study of house types will show that the number of models is limited and that they are repeated throughout the estate in such a way as to get the maximum number acceptable for the area.

So far, we have tended to look at the problem from the point of view of return on money invested. But, in addition to this, we must not ignore the fact that demand also conditions the density at which we build and live. On the one hand, there has been the developer who, aiming at the greatest return on his capital, has built at the highest density the market can bear; and on the other hand, there has been the 'market' which has been divided up into several categories in terms of effective demand. Generally speaking, the poor have been able to afford less land, and it was partly this conditioning fact which resulted in the back-to-back terraces of the nineteenth century when there were large numbers of poor people in our industrial cities who required housing. Market subdivision is an important consideration to bear in mind at the present time, and has led to the idea that we should pay for what we can afford.

However, in terms of social conscience our society is relatively highly developed and it has grown up with the idea that we should make some concessions to the idea of equality of sacrifice. One of these has been that the poor should not always be relegated to areas with low space amenities. Against this, however, is the fact that the public authorities have to have some return on their capital, and consequently they have to build efficiently. It is partly for this reason that high-rise apartment buildings have been popular. Not only do they occupy little land, but they are also built on a pre-fabricated, modular basis and possess great economies in the provision of public utilities, such as water, electricity and gas.

In addition, sociological research has revealed that people living in slum areas at high densities possess a degree of social cohesion which is unknown elsewhere, and these findings have influenced planning concepts (Wilmot and Young, 1957). An example of this is to be found in Sheffield in the Parkhill development scheme which retains some of the essence of the physical structure of the old terraces: a very high building density, flats which front on to a long pedestrian 'street', which emphasises the unity of the development and overawes the individual flat in the same way that the old terrace houses were overawed by the street, and the retention of the old amenities of local shops, a primary school and public houses.

Planning concepts have also been influenced in the opposite direction, firstly, by market forces and secondly, by behavioural research. There is a school in planning circles which acknowledges the fact that the market can influence greatly the provision of dwellings and amenities. It recognises the fact that most people would prefer to live in a detached house than in a semi-detached house, and in a semi-detached house rather than in a flat. On the open market these preferences are catered for by the development companies and speculative builders, and they have resulted in suburbia as we know it today, where the emphasis is on privacy rather than communal identity. Public development schemes have usually been at a higher density than the private schemes and, since the authorities wanted to get the best value for their money, they often constructed the estates on cheap land at the edge of the town. The other pressure for low density buildings comes from the findings of psychologists and other behavioural scientists. It has been found by psychologists that rats develop frustrations, complexes, become moody and, in some instances, aggressive when they are forced to live in high density conditions. Planners and architects, fearful of the same happening to human society, have, therefore, advocated low density living.

The last factor which we have to consider as an influence on building density is taste or style (see Section 4B 2). The rigid styling of nineteenth century towns was well suited to economies in space, but it provided the basis for a reaction early the following century. Reaction against overcrowding and poor conditions led to a new concept of living — the city in the country. The ideas of the exponents of garden cities have conditioned people's aspirations; but even now there is evidence of a reaction against this in some quarters as concern grows at the rate at which the countryside is being engulfed by our urban expansion.

We have attempted to show some of the factors which have affected building density through time — the physical lack of space in the medieval towns, paralleled by concepts of cost-effectiveness in our building programmes today, ideas of taste, partly affected by physical conditions, and the dialogues that exist in the planning profession. The emphasis has been upon the recent past, because this is of more significance for our towns today, and because many of the things about which we have talked, especially the important concept of cost-effectiveness, can be applied in a spatial dimension.

Local Study

Aim: To describe the spatial variation of urban building density.
Data source: Urban 'plan' map (OS 1:10 560 scale).
Method:
1   Place a transparent overlay on the map and construct a fine grid over the whole area: a 50×50 grid is adequate for one sheet at the OS 1:10 560 scale.
2   Put a sheet of dots (such as Zip-a-tone no. 3) between the transparent overlay and the map. Take several grid squares

Fig. 4.14   CALCULATION OF SPATIAL RUNNING MEAN

ROWS	COLUMNS		
	A	B	C
1	13	12	16
2	12	10	15
3	10	7	11

To the values of the central cell (row 2, column B) are added the values of all the cells which immediately surround it, and the total value is divided by the number of cells. Thus, the mean figure for cell 2B is

$$10 + 13 + 12 + 16 + 12 + 15 + 10 + 7 + 11 = 106$$

$$\frac{106}{9} = 11 \cdot 78$$

The value ($11 \cdot 78$) is then plotted instead of the original value for cell 2B.

at random and count how many dots there are, on average, in each grid square.

3 Work through the map systematically, counting how many of the dots in each cell coincide with buildings.

4 Calculate a spatial running mean using this data. This has the effect of transferring the data into a continuous distribution, which is somewhat easier for mapping purposes. The technique is exactly the same as for a linear moving mean (Section 3A 1b). To the value of a central cell add the values of all cells immediately surrounding it and divide the total result by the total number of cells (fig. 4.14). The resulting mean figure is then plotted instead of the original value for that cell. The procedure is repeated throughout the whole map

with each cell (except those at the periphery) acting in turn as the central cell.

5 Interpolate isopleths on the smoothed density surface, developing first of all an adequate number of classes and an appropriate class interval (as outlined in Section 3B 2c). Finally, convert the isopleth values into percentages so that they show the percentage built-up area.

Example
Area studied: part of the city of Exeter (OS Sheet SX 99 SW 1:10 560).

A 50×50 sampling grid, covering the map with 2 500 small cells, was first drawn over the map sheet. We calculated that for our dot grid, which was a sheet of Zip-a-tone no. 3 shading, there was an average of 35 dots per cell. The number of dots falling on

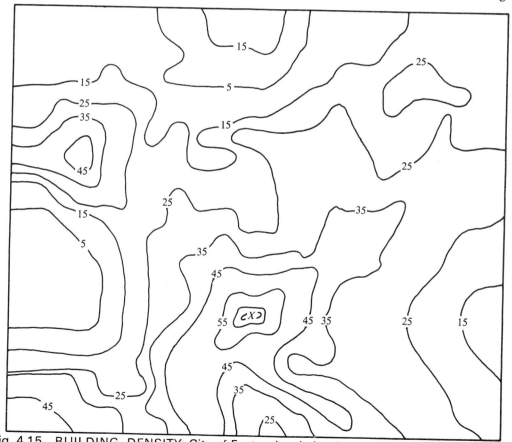

Fig. 4.15 BUILDING DENSITY, City of Exeter: isopleths showing the percentage amount of built-on land. Notice the general decrease in density away from the city centre (marked X on the map)

123

buildings in each cell were counted and the spatial moving mean of each cell was calculated. Isopleths were then drawn in and, as can be seen from fig. 4.15, there is a general tendency for building density to decline with increased distance from the city centre. We can go on to calculate a moving average over a larger area and generalise even more since the map still shows the influence of local anomalies, but this really requires the assistance of an electronic computer. This technique enables us to study variations in building density at various scales and allows us to introduce the techniques of topographic analysis, such as curves of cumulative building density and profiles from the point of highest density to the periphery (see Section 2A 1c). In much the same way, the basic map of cell densities and isopleths can be used as a basis for calculating the lapse rates of building density for various times since about 1800. It is only on the basis of such description that the trends can be evaluated and projected for the purpose of planning decisions.

Watch-points It is better to work with the raw data all the way through the project and only convert to percentages at the last possible moment. Not only is this an economy in effort, it also means that there is less likelihood of making a mistake. Thus, the isopleths should be interpolated from the raw data, and then converted into percentage values.

FURTHER READING

Gottmann, J., 'Why the skyscraper?', *Geographical Review*, (1966), 161, pp. 190–212.
Wilmot, P. and Young, M., *Family and Kinship in East London* (R.K.P., 1957).

4B 2 Three-Dimensional Analysis

One of the main ways in which urban growth and form has been studied is through the analysis of the three-dimensional structure of the town's buildings (Johns, 1965). As a town grows, new building takes place at its periphery and at certain points within the existing built-up area, while renewal of older building also takes place within the urbanised area. Thus, by analysing the three-dimensional morphological structure, some insight into the past evolution of the settlement can be obtained.

In order to achieve this end, many classifications of building morphology have been suggested (Whitehand, 1965). In general, however, most studies have identified different buildings according to their basic constructional characteristics, their design and the materials used in their construction.

From the point of view of construction, buildings can best be thought of as elements within a modular framework. The smallest elements of the module are rooms which are linked together by virtue of ownership. In turn, these 'ownership units' may be linked together to form larger structural units, of which four main types have been recognised. **Discrete blocks** are individual prime building units, such as detached houses, villas standing in their own grounds, or free standing public buildings; they are the equivalent of 'studded townscapes' (Smailes, 1955). **Discontinuous blocks** are characterised by a fragmented building line such as is produced by semi-detached houses or rows of 'town houses'. The essential characteristics of **continuous blocks,** apart from an unbroken facade, is the repetition of the prime building unit. The terrace is the typical example, giving rise to a townscape which has been referred to as 'ribbing' (Smailes, 1955). The last category, of **mixed continuous blocks,** follows on from the way in which we have defined the previous one. In many instances a building line may be continuous, yet the units may not be repeated. The juxtaposition of old and new in our crowded town centres is a good example of this category.

The design of individual buildings has also been used in attempts to analyse townscapes. In Britain there have been four major periods of domestic architecture, of which

124

the earliest was the Gothic style. This was followed in the seventeenth century by the Classical period which, in turn, was followed by the Romantic revival of the nineteenth century. This gave way, after the First World War, to what can loosely be described as the Modern period. Within these general periods, however, there was a great variety of artistic expression, often manifested in the building units employed. It must also be remembered that fashions vary spatially, so that what may have been in vogue in one town at any given period may have been out of favour or unheard of in another.

Early Gothic

The early Gothic style was greatly influenced by the structural techniques of the age. Its finest expression lies in medieval church buildings, but it remains extensively as half-timbered housing. Pressure on the land meant that buildings had to go upwards, and a situation in which buildings had different numbers of overhanging upper storeys crowned by a steeply pitched roof produced a strongly vertical effect (fig. 4.16). This was often echoed by the picture effect of half timbering thrusting upwards. Because of the variety of much old building, and since there are but few examples of each style, it is often sufficient to specify 'Medieval' rather than break it down into sub-groups such as various types of ecclesiastical, Tudor, Dutch and so on.

Classical

With the Renaissance, **classical** concepts of urban life and architecture spread to Britain. Since it is a more recent style than the Gothic, many more examples remain.

The main contrast between Medieval Gothic and the Classical is that the emphasis is on horizontal construction lines and repetition, rather than the vertical of the Medieval townscape. As the Renaissance developed into the Regency, decoration of the buildings became much more apparent, though the underlying horizontal line remained. In addition to this stylistic change, we also have to remember that buildings were constructed for different social classes.

Fig. 4.16 MEDIEVAL BUILDINGS, Exeter: *top*, THREE GABLES, Cathedral Yard said to be 1540; *centre*, TUDOR HOUSES, Stepcote Hill (notice the two overhangs); *bottom*, MOL'S COFFEE HOUSE, Cathedral Close [though the date of this building is 1596, the Dutch style gable end is a later addition (1885)]

The contrast is usually obvious, the smaller buildings, built at a higher density, with little decoration or landscaping being meant for the working classes.

Renaissance ideas on architecture were first adopted in Britain in the seventeenth century and were expressed in the works of Sir Christopher Wren, Sir John Vanbrugh and Inigo Jones. However, it was not until the eighteenth century, the period when Britain was ruled by the House of Hanover, that the style made a large scale impact on our towns.

We can best recognise the styles of the Classical period by comparison. Georgian building is more formal than a great deal of later building, both in its layout and in its architectural expression. It is a more 'pure' form of the Classical than that which was to succeed it. The basic features of the Georgian style, on which later styles were developed, were:

(i) **Symmetry** at every level of construction: symmetry was often rigorously defined as being the repetition of features across each major axis. If we split a Georgian house down the middle, we often find the same number of windows on one side as on the other. If we then take a typical street of such houses, we find that there is an equal number on the left and on the right, and at the top end and at the bottom end. At every level there is this symmetry, imbuing an overall sense of balance and co-ordination (fig. 4.17).

(ii) **Repetition** of the structural features: we saw above that there is symmetry of the planned units about the major axes. This was achieved by the repetition of the housing unit. At the level of the individual house, each one is basically the same as its neighbour. Thus, the decorative and functional features are repeated by the repetition of the housing units.

(iii) **Horizontal line:** this develops from the repetition discussed above. Since each external feature is being repeated, the continuation of that façade in the horizontal emphasises that plane of construction.

Fig. 4.17 *left*, GEORGIAN TERRACE, Barnfield Close, Exeter (c. 1805) ; *right*, LATE GEORGIAN—REGENCY TERRACE, Southernhay West, Exeter (c. 1825)

Because of this, Classical buildings tend to have an overall long, low effect which contrasts with the vertical lines of construction of the Gothic or Romantic revival.

(iv) **Decorative features:** these were less important in Georgian buildings than was the case later on. Little attention was paid to landscaping, in most cases the buildings abutted on the streets, and what little there was was strictly formal — grass with regularly spaced trees often forming a geometrical pattern, in a central square or circus. Decoration tended to be limited to the lower storeys of the house, where it would be seen most, and in this respect the doorway is amongst the most decorative features of Georgian architecture. The door is often framed by two fluted pillars, with a plain lintel over the top. The door itself is usually divided into panels. There may also be a porch supported by a couple of plain, classical columns. In civic buildings of the period, such columns may support a covered arcade. Windows were another feature which changed with the advent of the Georgian style. The non-opening or outward opening leaded glass windows of the previous century were replaced by sash windows which moved up and down. The panes of glass were also larger, in rectangular form, with six or nine panes to a window. The façades may have been decorated by pillars or false pillars (pilasters) which were attached to the wall.

Some of the best examples of the Georgian style of building are to be found in Bath. The basic building form found throughout the town is the terrace and the layout is formal, though less so towards the end of the town's period of Georgian growth as crescents and circuses replaced the terraces and squares in vogue earlier. The same rigidly formal layout and repetitive terrace is found in Craig's development of Newtown, Edinburgh. While these are two of the best examples of this style that can be found in Britain, there are many other more local instances that deserve to be investigated. County towns or small market towns often have an old coaching inn or short terrace based on Georgian concepts of style. With these, however, there is always the possi-bility that the structure of the building is earlier, and that the façade was altered as a result of the great upheaval in style.

The main difference between the Regency concepts of style and earlier Georgian concepts is one of the degree of decoration. The same symmetry, repetition and visual horizontal line remained, but was made more elaborate by a greater degree of design at all levels.

Much more attention was paid to landscaping, both public and private. The importance of buildings in Regency townscapes was decreased with this attention to vegetation, and this is seen at its best at the present day, since most of the trees have now reached a period of full maturity. Only now are we seeing the Regency townscapes as they were meant to be seen. It is interesting to note the effect of Regency landscaping in the creation of 'functional' units — parks and ambulatories were often laid out, and trees were used to separate pathways from roads.

There was a much freer use of classical modes of expression in the buildings, with sometimes a mixture of styles — plain Doric columns being found together with the more elaborate Ionic and the highly fanciful Corinthian. A cornice and pediment were sometimes added to a terrace block, thereby providing it with an overall unity, and the façade was usually textured with the use of fluted pilasters and decorated motifs running the length of the building, dividing one storey from another. During the Regency, ironwork came into its own in terms of design and expression, often being used in porches, canopies, balconies and readily apparent in railings.

A good example of a Regency town is Cheltenham, built for the same recreational and social purposes as Bath. In Cheltenham there is evidence of altered façades, Regency terraces and highly elaborate late Regency villas all set in a very mature, planned landscape. At the other end of the social scale, the major differences are in landscaping and the size of the dwelling units. The poorer people lived in ordinary terraces characterised by their small size, repetition, low angles of roof and a total absence of vegetation, either public or private. Once we care to look for them, however, the same Classical themes of symmetry repetition and the horizontal line form the core of design concepts for these areas as well, and they provide a good introduction to the townscapes of the nineteenth century.

The most conspicuous stylistic innovation of Victorian Britain was in the form of workers' housing. The nineteenth century was a period of great industrial growth which required a great deal of manpower. The designers of workers' housing were influenced, in no small part, by prevailing ideas on design, as well as by the need for efficiency in the use of space. Terraces were not only a cheap way of housing a large number in a restricted area, but they were also typical building styles of Georgian and Regency towns, and these workers' terraces possessed the basic horizontal design structure. The repetition of the same housing units, with the repetition of the individual elements, the windows and the doors,

together with a continuous parapet, little differentiation on the façade of housing units, a roof line parallel to the road and a low angle of pitch of the roof, all emphasised the horizontal rather than the vertical (fig. 4.18).

Decoration of these terraces was limited by economic considerations, but classical motifs can often be discerned around the windows and doors, with fluted wooden doorframes, doors panelled with fluted surrounds, and sash windows with a keystone arch above. These are the most common features, but one may come across others, perhaps a shoe-scraper by the front door or some decoration on the drain gulleys and pipes. While these terraces were the largest scale additions to Victorian towns, they were not the most imposing. During the century the industrialists often ploughed back the profits they had made through the town into civic buildings for the town. These buildings were very much in the Classical idiom — Greek temples trans-

Fig. 4.18 VICTORIAN WORKERS' HOUSING: *left* Roberts Road, Exeter; *right* modern re-furbishing of such terraces can improve their general appearance—East John St., Exeter

ported to industrial town centres. They are usually fronted by very solid columns supporting a triangular pediment. The buildings may be decorated by sculpture which enhances their overall formality.

Romantic

In the latter part of the nineteenth century a reaction set in against the Classical style, which took the appearance of planned informality and individualistic Classicism, and which is usually known as the **Romantic** style.

The importance of the terrace as an economic building unit is demonstrated by the fact that it continued to be built during this period of reaction, but the change in style was reflected in small scale design elements. The pitches of roofs became steeper, chimney pots taller. As the market became able to pay more for its dwellings, so the new design elements became more apparent. Small gables were built on to the façades of the terraces, thus destroying, in part, the horizontal line which was the basic visual element of the Classical terrace, and replacing it by the vertical line of the Gothic. This was emphasised by steeply pitched porches above the doorway, pointed and serrated edges to the roof parapet, the use of different coloured bricks placed vertically to form an arch above the window, and the fact that these were dwellings for the middle classes was apparent from the small front gardens.

The extremes of reaction to Classicism were seen in the designs for the richer classes. This reaction was always individualistic, either reverting to 'fairy-tale' Gothic, with pointed turrets, long windows with a pointed arch at the top and steeply pitched eaves (fig. 4.19A), or to Italianate innovations, square and stocky, using building materials to provide colour and texture on the surface. Because they were usually built for the rich, these styles are often found as villas set in their own grounds (fig. 4.19B).

The most important aspect of the Romantic

Fig. 4.19 ROMANTIC STYLE: *left*, fairy-tale Gothic style, slightly modified—Montifiore House, University of Exeter; *right*, Italianate style—Reed Hall, University of Exeter

reaction was the development of the Garden City style. The concept of a Garden City originated as a philanthropic venture to rectify the evils of nineteenth-century industrial housing (Howard, 1960). The houses were in the cottage style, usually two storeys, with the upper one formed by a sloping roof, and were generally built in a highly landscaped environment, with trees planted on the roadside verges and hedges isolating the gardens and houses from the outside world. Good examples of this style are found in Bournville, built at the bequest of the philanthropist George Cadbury, and Letchworth, the first of the products of the modern town planning profession.

Modern

The period after the First World War has produced several important trends in style. The most important of these in areal terms is the degradation of the Garden City concept into 'suburbia', the detached and semi-detached houses built in one or two forms and repeated throughout the extent of a housing estate. These were generally built for middle-class house buyers, and much of the space was given over to private uses — only a limited amount was set aside for public recreation and circulation. The cottage style remained the basis, but it became transformed by the opulence of the materials used in its construction, and was influenced by the ideas of an articulate market, resulting in the development of the bungalow and chalet styles.

At the lower end of the social scale, the style was adopted by public housing authorities, but, because of lack of money, the appearance of the houses and estates tended to be spartan, with landscaping and decoration as residuals whose expense was met only after the more important task of housing the people was completed. However, more land was devoted to accessibility and public recreation. More recent local authority architects have been innovating in the layout of estates.

Fig. 4.20 BAUHAUS STYLE: often this style was adopted and adapted quite markedly as can be seen in these two examples; *left,* St Loye's Hotel, Exeter; *right,* housing in Jennifer Close, Exeter

The major innovation in style this century stems from Germany and the Bauhaus school of design. This style of architecture was 'avant-garde' in the 1930s, and it was in the fifteen or so years after that most of the pure examples were built. The most obvious feature of the style is the continuity of form, especially in the horizontal. The buildings appear to 'flow' round corners, with the angular junction replaced by a smooth curve. Flats built between the wars often show this to good effect, as the balconies flow around the outside and unite the building. Other indicators of Bauhaus styling are flat roofs, windows at the corners of buildings (often a dozen or so panes of glass set in an iron frame) and a disposition to paint the buildings white or cream. If anything, the Bauhaus style showed the impact of new materials on building style (fig. 4.20).

Pressure on land and the need to keep scale economies in mind has led to the development of the skyscraper block. It is difficult not to recognise these, by virtue of their block form, their great size towering over the surrounding townscape and, more recently, their very free use of glass. The better buildings can be seen as an extension of Bauhaus principles, the unity of the building, curving façades and, more especially, the use of glass to give it a light and airy appearance.

In addition to modern developments in style, the twentieth century has also been a period of imitation, in much the same way as the nineteenth century. Industrial towns built their civic buildings in the more pure Graeco-Roman form. Imitation has not always been the result of a lack of ideas; in many cases it has been the product of real sympathy with the town, getting the 'feel' of it, seeing what is actually there and trying to get the new to blend in with the old. 'Neo' styles are often found in city centres, partly as a result of fabric and functional deterioration to a point at which it pays to replace the buildings, and partly as a result of war damage.

Finally, the different materials used in the construction have also been used in the analysis of morphological features.

Mud and Plaster

In certain rural areas where building materials are poor, it is still fairly common to find houses built of stones and rubble held together by mud and straw, and faced with a type of plaster. This is generally known as 'cob'. It is, however, relatively rare in urban areas, except in some medieval buildings.

Wood

This is rarely used now as a visible structural material — the only period when it was used extensively for this purpose was the medieval, in the half timbered frame houses of the time. It is, however, still used as the structural basis for the roof and floors, and as external decoration.

Stone

As a category, this is more important than wood. Because the usage of stone is often very local we can only give the following general guide. Chalk is rarely used as a medium, only a few examples exist in Kent. Limestone has been much more popular, and, if the building is old, may be highly weathered which will provide a clue to identification. Local igneous rocks such as granite, metamorphic rocks or hard sedimentary rocks such as millstone grit, may have been used. In some areas it is still common to find houses whose walls have been hung with slates, or with tiles.

Bricks

In terms of actual usage this will be the largest category, since the majority of houses built since 1800 have been built in brick. Bricks were once made out of local clays and used locally, but nowadays this is less true. However, various types of clay do produce different coloured bricks. The clays of the Bovey Basin near Newton Abbot produce a white/yellow brick, while the red clays of East Devon produce a deep red brick. In North London a pale yellow brick is found, while South of the Thames various shades of red brick are found. Local variations in types of brick certainly exist all over the country. The majority of houses are roofed by tiles which are made from the same clays as bricks, or, if modern, by tiles made from cement and artificially coloured.

Industrial materials

Industrial building materials are becoming increasingly important because they represent economies of scale and, consequently, cheaper construction costs. Cement blocks are amongst the most used of industrial materials, but are rarely seen as they are usually covered by such things as pebble dash or a plaster-type finish. Pre-stressed concrete has been used increasingly in the post war period, mainly in the construction of large blocks of flats and skyscraper office blocks. A recent innovation in building design is the use of industrial sections, usually in concrete. They have been much used in blocks of flats, where there is one size and shape for the floor and others for the walls.

Once the buildings have been classified in this manner, their distributional characteristics can be analysed to present a model of the stages of building development over time. As with so many other geographical themes, there has been a tendency in the past simply to present distributional maps of morphological types without examining their basic characteristics. Such maps should only be the starting point and information sources for further analyses.

Local Study

Aim: To analyse the spatial characteristics of morphological building form.
Data source: Field survey.
Method:
1 Using a classification of morphological form such as that outlined in fig. 4.21, classify every building in the study area. It will probably be most useful to make a series of transects through the study area.
2 Measure the distance between the centre of each building and the end of the transect nearest the centre of the study area.
3 For each building type, calculate the

Fig. 4.21 A CLASSIFICATION OF BUILDING FORM

	FORM	CODE
STRUCTURES	Discrete blocks	1
	Discontinuous blocks	2
	Continuous blocks	3
	Mixed continuous blocks	4
STYLES	GOTHIC	G
	CLASSICAL (C)	
	Georgian high class	Cgh
	Georgian low class	Cgl
	Regency high class	Crh
	Regency low class	Crl
	Victorian high class	Cvh
	low class	Cvl
	civic	Cvc
	ROMANTIC (R)	
	Gothic high class	Rgh
	Italianate high class	Rih
	cottage middle class	Rbm
	terrace middle class	Rtm
	terrace low class	Rtl
	MODERN	
	neo-	MN
	suburbia — middle class	Msm
	suburbia — low class	Msl
	Bauhaus	MB
	block over four storeys	ME
MATERIALS	Mud and plaster	P
	Wood	W
	Stone	S
	Brick	B
	Industrial	I

mean and standard deviation distance from the centre.

4 For each pair of building types, test the respective mean and standard deviation for significance using student's *t* test (Section 2C 1d).

Fig. 4.22 BUILDING STYLES AND DISTANCE FROM CITY CENTRE

STYLE	MEAN DISTANCE (in metres)	STANDARD DEVIATION
modern neo-Georgian	110	50
Bauhaus	280	90
Georgian High class	610	120
Suburban Middle class	990	510
Terrace Middle class	1040	820
Gothic High class	1050	850

Example

Area studied: City of Exeter.

A series of transect routes through the city were chosen so as to give a representative cross-section of the morphological styles of the City. One such transect ran for 1 600 metres from the city centre (as defined by the methods outlined in Section 4C 2c), and six building styles were observed: Georgian High Class (Cgn), Gothic High Class (Rgn), Terrace Middle Class (Rtm), Suburbia Middle Class (Msm), Bauhaus (MB) and Modern Neo-Georgian (MNCg). The distance of every building from the city centre was then measured (the measurement being taken to the mid-point of each building's frontage). The mean distance (and its standard deviation) of all the buildings of each style was then calculated (fig. 4.22). It follows from what we said earlier (Section 2A 3a) that the standard deviation can be used as a simple measure of the locational patterns of the building styles: those styles which have a high standard deviation relative to their mean distance will be those which are not grouped together at a 'characteristic' distance from the city centre whereas those whose standard deviation is small tend to 'group' around the mean distance and are, therefore, more nucleated in their distribution. The standard deviation can, in this way, be used as an alternative to the calculation of nearest-neighbour statistics, though it is, of course, much less precise. In our particular example it was found that the standard deviations were low in the Neo-Georgian, Bauhaus and high-

class Georgian styles, and so it can be concluded that these three building styles *tend* to be grouped together at characteristic distances from the city centre.

The next step was to see whether the locations of the different building styles were significantly different from each other. Thus, for example, whilst it may appear that the neo-Georgian buildings (110 m from the city centre) are located at a different distance from those of the Bauhaus style (280 m from the centre), it may well be that these differences are more apparent than real. In order to test whether these differences were statistically significant, student's t test was employed (see Section 2C 1d), each pair of building styles being tested in turn. The results indicated that the locations of the neo-Georgian, Bauhaus and Georgian class buildings differed significantly from those of other styles. The significance of the differences between the locations of the other three styles was open to more doubt. For instance, with 42 Middle class terrace units and 25 Middle class suburban units, the value for t was just under 2·00 which, with 65 degrees of freedom, is barely significant at the 5 % level. In the same way, the value for t between Middle class suburban and high class Gothic with 36 degrees of freedom was 2·1 which, while just significant at 5 %, is well below the 1 % level, while the value for t between Middle class terrace and High class Gothic with 53 degrees of freedom did not reach the 5 % level.

Having thus discovered which building

styles were associated with characteristic locations for each of the transects, we were then able to describe rather more precisely the general form of building within the city.

Watch-points This technique is a relatively easy one to put into operation and so there are few points of difficulty to note. The main thing is to appreciate the basis of the classification which is being used, and this may require more reading about architectural style to supplement the contents of this section. Rather than analyse the visual aspects of the landscape, as we have done with our stylistic classification, the emphasis could be placed upon the date of construction of the buildings.

Having obtained the results, it may be worthwhile attempting to generalise them in terms of the urban structure models which we outlined in Section 4A 2. Elements of all three models will probably be evident.

FURTHER READING

Howard, E., *Garden Cities of tomorrow* (London, 1960).

Johns, E. M., *British Townscapes* (Arnold, 1965).

Sheppard, J. A., 'Vernacular buildings in England and Wales: a survey of recent work by Architects, Archaeologists and Social Historians' *Transactions of the Institute of British Geographers*, (1966), 40, pp. 21–37.

Smailes, A. E., 'Some reflections on the geographical description of townscapes' *Transactions of the Institute of British Geographers*, (1955), 21, pp. 99–115.

Solomon, R. J., 'Procedures in townscape analysis' *Annals of the Association of American Geographers*, (1966), 56, pp. 254–268.

Whitehand, J. W. R., 'Building types as a basis for settlement classification' in Whittow, J. B. and Wood, P. D., *Essays in Geography for Austin Miller* (Reading U.P., 1965).

4C RETAIL AND SERVICE OUTLETS

Over the past twenty years or so, the geography of retailing and service industries has come to form one of the main themes in human geography. Its origins are traceable to the work of Walter Christaller, a German geographer who published a study entitled 'Die zentralen Orte in Süddeutschland' (Central places in Southern Germany) in 1933. This study, interestingly enough, was basically on the theory of the size, spacing and functioning of settlements, and it was here that the now familiar concepts of k-values, hexagonal trade areas and lattices were first advanced. In 1940, August Lösch published his modification of Christaller's ideas in 'Die raumliche Ordnung der Wirtschaft' and there then followed a number of empirical studies which sought variously to verify or nullify these basic theoretical ideas (see Appendix, pp.179–182).

The empirical work itself has covered a wide variety of topics ranging in scale from studies of regional systems of central places (e.g. Thorpe and Rhodes, 1966) to monographs of individual cities (e.g. Berry, 1963). It is rare indeed, in geographical studies, that theory has generated so much enthusiasm!

4C 1 Regional Patterns

The relationship between the various settlements of a given region has been particularly well studied in America, though there is also a quite extensive bibliography of English examples as well (Berry and Pred, 1961).

Interest has focussed mainly on the hierarchical structure of settlements in a given region in general, and on the size of settlements relative to the number of functions they perform and the number of establishments they contain, in particular.

4C 1a Number of functions

Several studies have been made of the precise relationship between the size of settlements and the number of retail and service functions they contain. It is found, for most

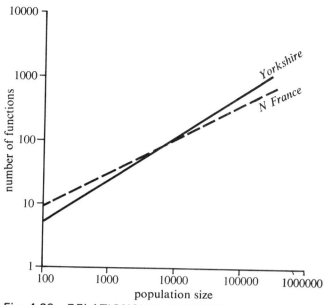

Fig. 4.23 RELATIONSHIP BETWEEN NUMBER OF FUNCTIONS AND THE SIZE OF SETTLEMENTS: Yorkshire West Riding and Nord and Pas de Calais Departments, France

parts of the world, that there is at least a substantial correlation between the two variables (e.g. King, 1962; Berry and Garrison, 1958). For instance, the product moment correlation coefficient (r) between settlement size and the number of functions is 0·89 for the West Riding of Yorkshire, and 0·78 for the northern coalfield of France (fig. 4.23).

The precise nature of the overall relationship between the two variables, as measured by a regression line (Section 2B 2d), does, of course, vary from region to region. In some areas, the regression line is steep (as, for example, is the case in the West Riding of Yorkshire) while in others the line has a more gentle slope (as in northern France), indicating the differences between regions in the rate of duplication of functions and, consequently, in the overall nature of the distribution of services (fig. 4.23). In general, however, settlements in all regions tend to follow the general rule of an exponential rate of increase of function proportional to size.

Since the regression line shows an 'average' condition, as we explained in Section 2B 2d,

it serves as a useful yardstick by which to measure the relative provision of services in the settlements of any given region.

Local Study

Aim: To show the relationship between the size of settlements and their functions.
Data sources: Population Census; published information (Trade Directory or Board of Trade's Census of Distribution and other Services); field survey.
Method:
1 Define the area for study: it will be necessary to choose quite a large area in order to get a representative cross-section of all sizes of settlement.
2 Measure the number of different functions performed by each settlement. This may be collected either from the Board of Trade's 'Census of Distribution and other Services' for your county or a local trade directory (such as Kelly's). Alternatively, you may make a survey yourself of all the services provided by the settle-

135

ments in the study area, or you may be able to use the Board of Trade Census as a starting point and survey only those settlements which were not included in the published report.

3 From the census of population, estimate the population sizes of each settlement.

4 Using the method described in Section 2B 2b, calculate the correlation coefficient of the two data sets ('number of functions' and 'size of settlement'), taking care to decide properly which data set represents the dependent (y) variable and which is the independent (x) variable. (In this example, the independent variable should be 'size of settlement'.)

5 Having calculated 'r', make a regression analysis of the data using the technique outlined in Section 2B 2d. It will be necessary to use log-log graph paper (see Section 3A 1e).

6 Describe the results of the analysis, pointing to the salient features of the distribution of functions in the study region.

Example

Area studied: The Exeter region.

Having defined the region, we tabulated all the information relating to population and numbers of functions and made a simple correlation analysis of the two data sets. It was found that $r = +0.88$.

Next, the information was plotted graphically on log-log paper. The **range** of functions (data set y) was from 1 to 300, and the range of population (data set x) from about 100 to 80 000. It was decided to make a 3 cycle × 3 cycle graph so that on the x axis the cycles would go from 100 to 1 000; 1 000–10 000; 10 000–100 000; and on the y axis from 1 to 10; 10–100; and 100–1 000. Each settlement was represented on the graph and the 'best fit' regression line was calculated. As can be seen from fig. 4.24, the relationship between population size (x) and number of functions (y) is given by the equation

$$\log y = 0.6433 \log x - 0.7136.$$

Using this information we were then able

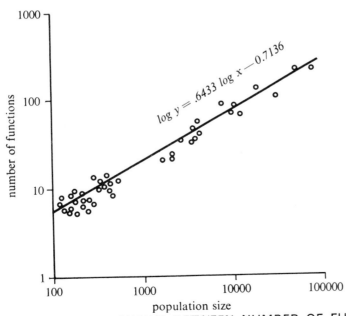

Fig. 4.24 RELATIONSHIP BETWEEN NUMBER OF FUNCTIONS AND THE SIZE OF SETTLEMENTS: Exeter region

136

to describe which settlements occurred above the regional average, and which below, and also to describe the overall character of the increase of services with settlement size.

Watch-points Since this exercise involves the use of log-log graph paper, care must be taken when calculating the regression line. In Section 2B 2d we showed that, with log-log graphs, the calculation of '*m*' and '*c*' is based on the *logarithms* of the actual values of *x* and *y*, and that the form of the regression is expressed as

$$\log y = m \log x + c$$

This means that the calculated values of log *y* have to be 'anti-logged' before they can finally be plotted on the graph.

It may well be necessary, because of time limitations, to survey only a *sample* of the settlements in the study area. It is important, as we stressed in Section 1C, that the correct *kind* of sample is made. For this exercise you may decide that some form of stratified sample would be the most appropriate since it is important that the different town sizes be represented in their correct proportions.

FURTHER READING

Berry, B. J. L. and Pred, A., 'Central place studies: a bibliography of theory and applications', *Regional Science Research Institute, Bibliography* Series no. 1, (1961).

Berry, B. J. L. *et al.*, 'Commercial structure and commercial blight', *University of Chicago Department of Geography Research Papers*, (1963), 85.

Christaller, W. (translated Baskin, C. W.), *Central Places in Southern Germany* (Prentice Hall, 1966).

Lösch, A. (translated Woglom, W. H.), *The Economics of Location* (Yale U.P., 1956).

Thorpe, D. and Rhodes, T. C., 'The shopping centres of the Tyneside urban region and large scale grocery retailing', *Economic Geography*, (1966), 42, pp. 52–73.

4C 1b Number of establishments

Just as there is a general increase in the number of functions with the size of a settlements, so there is an increase in the total number of business establishments which perform those functions. As we would also expect, the exact form of the relationship between size of settlement and the number of business establishments it contains differs from region to region. This general tendency, however, conceals many differences (between various functions) in the number of establishments they can support in different sized places. Berry and Garrison (1958) were the first to describe this relationship in detail with their study of 52 different services in 33 settlements of Snohomish County (USA).

Having plotted on a graph the relationship between the number of establishments of each service type (*N*) and the population of the centre (*P*) they were able to analyse, for each of the 52 services, the precise form of the relationship. In particular, they were able to analyse the variation between different services in the average minimum population that was necessary for the support of each service. This 'minimum population' is known as the **threshold size** of a particular service, and can be easily estimated from the graph showing the relationship between *P* and *N*, for it is the value of *P* where *N* = 1.

It was found that some services, as we might intuitively guess, require a larger population for their support than do others, and for the first time it was known rather more precisely just how many people were, on average, required before a particular service could be provided in a settlement. Thus, for example, it was found that 196 people were required for the support of one filling station, 380 people for a physician, 729 for a florist and 1 214 for an undertaker (Berry and Garrison, 1958).

Later workers, particularly Haggett and Gunawardena (1964), have tried to find a more refined method of estimating the threshold size of different functions, using a modified Reed–Muench technique to calculate the **median population threshold.** They found, for example, that in southern Ceylon the median threshold population for co-op stores was 663, while for post offices it was 950, and for dispensaries, 1 277.

Not only are we able to be more precise about the threshold population required for the support of a particular function, but we may also examine, from the same graphs, the differing rates of duplication of various functions. We tend, intuitively, to think that if, for example, 196 people are needed to support one filling station, it will need twice that number of people to support two filling stations, three times that number for three stations, and so on. However, this is just not the case. In fact, as Berry and Garrison (1958) have shown, the rate of duplication of services is different for each service: some are duplicated more rapidly than others, as we might expect. Furthermore, there are regional differences in these relationships.

The reasons for these variations are largely economic. No business can survive if it cannot attract sufficient custom, and the minimum necessary custom varies from business to business, as we have seen. This is largely due to the factors of supply and demand. Some businesses deal in commodities which require a very heavy level of investment and for which individual demand is not frequent (e.g. furniture). In such a case, it would be necessary to attract trade from a large number of customers, so that the total demand would be sufficient to meet the investment costs. On the other hand, some businesses deal in commodities requiring less total investment, but for which individual demand is frequent and steady (e.g. groceries). These businesses could, therefore, survive by supplying a relatively smaller number of people. However, beyond the threshold level each business will try to attract more custom. If that additional custom is sufficiently large, the original premises may become too small and extensions will have to be made. Naturally, often due to historical factors of site, some business premises may be physically unable to expand. In such a case, some other firm may take this opportunity to 'tap' some of the surplus custom, provided there is enough to meet the 'threshold' needs, and it will

establish another outlet for similar commodities. The opportunity for competition, therefore, underlies the rates of duplication of business establishments.

Local Study

Aim: To describe the relationship between the number of establishments of various service types and the population of the centres in which they are found.

Data sources: Population Census; published information (trade directory or the Board of Trade's Census of Distribution and other Services); field survey.

Method:
1 Decide which kind of function you wish to study (preferably choose a fairly common service (e.g. grocer) and a fairly rare one (e.g. undertaker) so that you have a reasonable contrast).

2 Follow the general method outlined for the local study in the previous section (4C 1a), but this time measure the number of establishments of each kind of service you are analysing.

3 Having calculated the correlation coefficients and the regression equations, compare and contrast the results for each of the services you have studied, by drawing up a table showing the **threshold size** of each service and the mean population required for the support of 2, 3, 4 ... *n* establishments of each function. From this you should be able to say something about the rates of duplication of services.

4 The analysis so far could be only the starting point for many other interesting topics. For instance, you could estimate theoretically how many establishments of a particular kind a place of a given population should have, on average. You could then compare this theoretical estimate with the actual number found in a place of that size, and try to explain the differences.

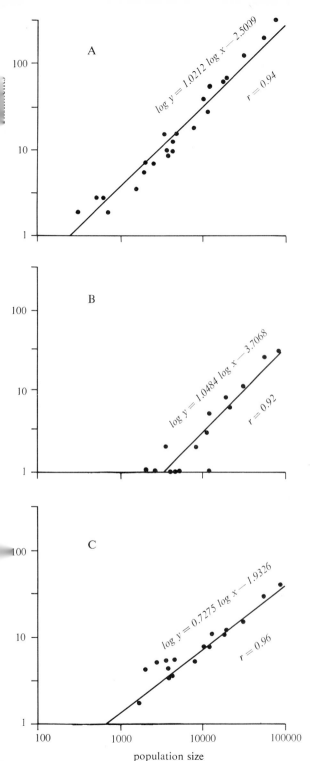

Example

Area studied: Exeter region (grocery stores, furniture stores and chemists).

Having collected the basic data from the Census of Population, Kelly's Directory and our own fieldwork, we plotted the relationship between population size and the number of establishments for each settlement on log-log graph paper. We then calculated both the product moment correlation coefficient (r) and the regression equation for each of the 3 service types. As can be seen in fig. 4.25 the equations are as follows:

for chemists
$$\log y = 0.7275 \log x - 1.9326 \quad r = 0.96$$
for grocers
$$\log y = 1.0212 \log x - 2.5009 \quad r = 0.94$$
for furniture stores
$$\log y = 1.0484 \log x - 3.7069 \quad r = 0.92$$

From these formulae and from the graphs themselves, we can derive the information shown in fig. 4.26. Patently, grocery stores have the lowest threshold requirements (260), chemists have higher requirements (580) and a furniture store needs about 3 350 people for its support. However, if we next examine the rates of duplication of these facilities, it can be seen that there is some variation between them, which is, of course, reflected in the different slopes of the regression line (see Section 3A 1e). These differences then require explanation.

Watch-points The difficulties and problems involved in this study are the same as for those detailed for the previous study (Section 4C 1a).

Fig. 4.26 POPULATION REQUIRE-
MENTS OF THREE FUNCTIONS

NUMBER OF ESTABLISHMENTS	Grocery store	Chemists	Furniture store
1	260	580	3 350
2	510	1 400	6 600
4	1 020	3 500	13 000
8	2 080	8 600	25 000
16	4 200	21 000	48 000

population size

 g. 4.25 RELATIONSHIP BETWEEN NUMBER
ESTABLISHMENTS AND THE SIZE OF SETTLE-
:NTS, Exeter region: A—grocery stores; B—
niture stores; C—chemists

FURTHER READING

Berry, B. J. L. and Garrison, W. L., 'A note on central place theory and the range of a good', *Economic Geography*, (1958), 34, pp. 304–311.

Haggett, P. and Gunawardena, K. A., 'Determination of population thresholds for settlement function by the Reed–Muench method', *Professional Geographer*, (1964), 16, pp. 6–9.

4C 1c The functional hierarchy

In Section 4B 1b we saw that there appears to be a 'size-distance' relationship between the settlements of a given region. In the last two sections we have pointed to certain regularities that exist between the size of a place and the number of functions it performs and the number of establishments of various kinds which it contains. If we now consider these three relationships together, we shall be able to understand better the spatial distribution of settlements and functions.

In summary, the regularities so far outlined are that in any given region

a there will be many small settlements spaced relatively close to each other, but few larger settlements spaced relatively far apart.

b small settlements perform few functions but larger settlements perform more functions.

c some functions have low threshold requirements while others have high threshold requirements.

If we now examine the distribution of each of the different functions in turn, we shall find that those functions which have low threshold requirements are those which are found in practically every settlement of a region. Those functions, however, which require a large population in order to be economically viable obviously cannot survive in the many small settlements of a region. Such 'high threshold' services will, therefore, be located only in the larger settlements, where their threshold requirements can be met. Thus, we find that the distribution of functions is very closely related to the distribution of population. There emerges, therefore, a further regularity in the location of retail and service outlets, and it is this regularity of functions which is known as the 'urban hierarchy'.

There have been many attempts to describe the character of the urban hierarchy for several different regions. Many of the earlier studies distinguished between the various settlements of a region on the basis of the functions which they performed, often in a more or less arbitrary way. For example, Bracey (1962) distinguished between 1st, 2nd and 3rd order villages in central southern England on the grounds that 1st order villages had at least 20 shops, 2nd order villages had 10, and 3rd order villages had 5. Similarly, Brush (1953) distinguished between 234 central places in southwestern Wisconsin on the basis of the number of retail and service units they contained, and identified a hierarchy of hamlets, villages and towns. Smailes (1946) used a 'trait complex' based on the presence or absence of banks, Woolworths stores, secondary schools, hospitals, cinemas and weekly newspapers to identify the urban hierarchy of England and Wales. On this basis, the towns of England were graded into 5 types: major cities, cities, major towns, towns and sub-towns.

Having thus distinguished between the settlements, it was possible to describe what functions appeared to be typical of each level of the hierarchy. In a sense, however, this was rather like putting the cart before the horse, since the basis of the classification was arbitrary. Nevertheless, these early studies were extremely useful in pointing the direction for later work, which has attempted to establish rather less subjective bases for the classification of settlements. Berry and Garrison (1958) applied various tests based on a form of nearest-neighbour analysis, and significance was tested by means of a Chi-squared analysis. By this method, three classes of settlement were identified in Snohomish County (USA). Later work has shown how cluster analysis and factor analysis may also be used to define the urban hierarchy more objectively on the basis of the functions which are typical of different settlements (Berry, Barnum and Tennant, 1962).

The urban hierarchy, then, is largely determined by the factors of supply and demand: a service cannot exist unless there is sufficient demand at a particular location to meet the costs of production of that service. This simple fact has been demonstrated in a theoretical way by Walter Christaller (1933) and August Lösch (1940). Their 'k-values' which were used to generate a theoretical settlement pattern were really little more than simple measures of threshold populations for different functions. Supply and demand functions are not, by any means, the only factors in explaining the character of the urban hierarchy, but that they are basic to the understanding of the pattern is undeniable.

Local Study

Aim: To demonstrate the difficulty of identifying, objectively, meaningful tiers of settlements and functions and to give some insight into the characteristics of the urban hierarchy.

It will be obvious from what has been said already that, while the subjective approach to the identification problem is not an ideal one, the results do enable us to see something of the characteristics of functional location. On the other hand, the refined statistical procedures required to achieve greater objectivity are not only more advanced than the basic techniques which we have outlined in Section 2, but are also likely either to be very time-consuming or to require the facilities of a computer. For these reasons, we shall limit our example to a consideration of the subjective approach and try to analyse which functions appear to be typical of which settlements. Those who wish to pursue the statistical procedures involved in the 'quantitative' approach are

referred to the published works of Clark (1956), Clark and Evans (1954) and Berry and Garrison (1958).

Data sources: Population Census; published data (trade directory of the Board of Trade's Census of Distribution and other Services); field survey (all previously collected for the two preceding local studies).

Method:

1 Using the graph of 'functions-population' which was prepared for the study at the end of Section 4C 1a, try to identify any obvious groupings of settlements (tiers) and label those *A, B, C*, etc. . . .

2 Construct a matrix showing the names of the settlements in the study area along the **rows**. (The settlements should be ranked from highest to lowest in order of their position on the graph, and heavy lines drawn in the matrix to indicate the 'groupings' of settlements which you have identified.) (fig. 4.27) Rank the functions according to their threshold population, and enter them along the **columns** of the matrix from left (lowest rank) to right (highest rank) (fig. 4.27). (See Section 4C 1b for the calculation of threshold population.)

3 Make a study of the data displayed (pay attention to such questions as (*a*) do the functions show any marked differences as between main settlement 'groups' which you established? (*b*) what combination of functions are most typical of which groups of settlements? (*c*) are there any settlements which seem to be 'abnormal'?).

4 On a map of the study area, plot the different settlement tiers, and then make an analysis of this distribution.

Example

Area studied: South Devon.

From a graph showing the relationship between size of settlements and the number of functions they performed, five types of settlement (respectively referred to as types *A, B, C, D,* and *E*) were identified subjectively. In this particular example (fig. 4.28A) the groupings seem apparent enough, particularly when it is recalled that the graph is

Fig. 4.27 A DATA MATRIX : number of establishments of each function in all settlements of a given region

SETTLEMENTS		Grocer	Butcher	Confectioner	Greengrocer	Hairdresser	Cobbler	Ironmonger	Clothier	Baker	Doctor	Dentist	Chemist	Furniture	Bookseller	Fishmonger	Cinema	Architect
GROUP A	Hornby	28	12	6	9	14	6	5	12	8	14	6	7	6	3	3	2	3
GROUP A	Blackwell	34	10	14	8	12	7	4	10	9	18	7	4	8	2	3	1	4
GROUP B	Sharow	17	5	8	4	3	2	2	4	1	5	3	3	2	1			
GROUP B	Merbeck	13	9	5	6	7	3	1	6	4	4	4	3	1				
GROUP B	Surrision	14	7	6	2	6	4	1	5	2	6	3	5	1				
GROUP B	Reedville	15	6	7	4	4	3	2	7	4	3	3	6		1			
GROUP B	Fryton	8	4	9	6	2	1	1	5	1	2	2	2	1				
GROUP C	Brookley	2	1	2														
GROUP C	Teedtown	2																
GROUP C	Caton	3		1														
GROUP C	Firbeck	1																
GROUP C	Woodbury	2		1														
GROUP C	Nutwood	2																

FUNCTIONS — ← Low threshold — High threshold →

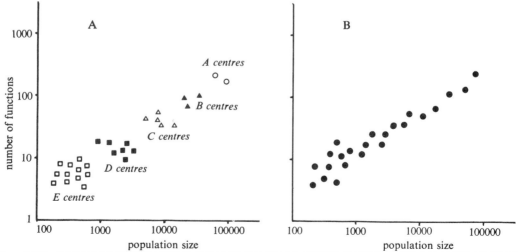

Fig. 4.28 THE IDENTIFICATION OF FUNCTIONAL TIERS IN THE URBAN HIERARCHY : A—Exeter region—5 tiers can be recognised quite distinctly ; B—hypothetical region where a continuum appears and where it is consequently difficult to identify any 'breaks' in the sequence

142

drawn on log-log paper so that the scale is distorted progressively to the top right hand corner. Of course, had we been dealing with a much larger area there would have been many more points on the graph and it would then have appeared as if the settlements were distributed on a continuum rather than in distinct clusters (fig. 4.28B). In such a case, only the more refined techniques which are mentioned earlier would be able to distinguish meaningful 'breaks' in the continuum.

A matrix (similar to the one outlined in fig. 4.27) was next constructed to show the number of establishments of the different functions in each settlement, so that we could see which functions were typical of each level of centre.

Using both the graph and the matrix, we were then able to make a detailed analysis of the urban hierarchical structure of the region. The class A centres (Exeter and Torquay) both had about 200 functions and populations in excess of 50 000, and, though differing slightly, they contained a full range of all possible functions. The 'B' centres (Paignton, Exmouth, Newton Abbot) had populations between 18 000 and 30 000 and performed 125–135 functions. The functions which they did not perform were largely those having high threshold requirements (e.g. poster advertising contractors). Class C centres (Tiverton, Teignmouth, Sidmouth, Dawlish) perform fewer functions (65–85) and have lower populations (7 000–12 000) and characteristically do not offer some of

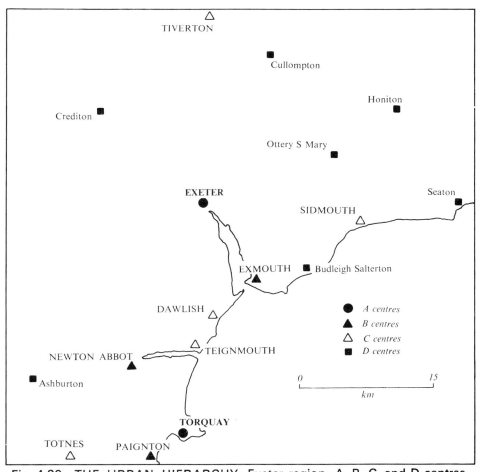

Fig. 4.29 THE URBAN HIERARCHY, Exeter region, A, B, C, and D centres

the high threshold services which were offered in 'B' centres (e.g. department stores).

It was also interesting to see that the number of establishments of each functional type varied according to the grade of centre, and particularly with respect to the high threshold services. Thus, for example, Exeter (Grade A centre) had fourteen furniture stores whereas Exmouth (Grade B centre) had only three. Similar comparative analysis of functions, establishments and settlements could be effected for each of the functions and grades of centre.

The geographical distribution of the various levels of centre was next plotted on a map (fig. 4.29). From this it was clear to see how the provision of services varied spatially and in accordance with the distribution of population. Notice particularly the difference between the inland and coastal areas of the region. A, B and C centres (with the exception of Tiverton) are all coastal or estuarine towns; in this area, there is, therefore, a greater range of goods and services offered more frequently (in a spatial sense) than in the inland area. People living in the settlements of the inland area, therefore, will tend to have far less choice of shopping centres and have to travel greater distances more frequently in order to find the higher order services than people living in settlements nearer the coast. The location of settlements of different functional order will clearly affect the spatial behaviour of the population, and this is a theme which we shall take up again in Section 4D.

Watch-points The most difficult part of this project will undoubtedly be the identification of the settlement 'clusters' from the graph. Pay particular attention to the fact that the graph is drawn to a logarithmic scale.

FURTHER READING

Berry, B. J. L. and Garrison, W. L., 'Functional bases of the central place hierarchy', *Economic Geography*, (1958), 34, pp. 145–154.

Berry, B. J. L., Barnum, H. G. and Tennant, R. J., 'Retail location and consumer behaviour', *Papers and Proceedings of the Regional Science Association*, (1962), 9, pp. 65–106.

Bracey, H. E., 'English central villages: identification, distribution and function', *Lund Studies in Geography* Series B, (1962), 24, pp. 169–190.

Brush, J. E., 'The hierarchy of central places in Southwestern Wisconsin', *Geographical Review*, (1953), 43, pp. 380–402.

Clark, P. J., 'Grouping in spatial distributions', *Science*, (1956), 123, pp. 373–374.

Clark, P. J. and Evans, F. C., 'Distance to nearest neighbour as a measure of spatial relationships in population', *Ecology*, (1954), 35, pp. 445–453.

Haggett, P., *Locational Analysis in Human Geography*, ch. 5 (Arnold, 1965).

Smailes, A. E., 'The urban mesh of England and Wales', *Transactions of the Institute of British Geographers*, (1946), 21, pp. 1–18.

Vince, R., 'A description of certain spatial aspects of an economic system', *Economic Development and Cultural Change*, (1955), 3, pp. 147–195.

4C 2 Intra-Urban Functions

Studies of the characteristics of urban commercial structure have been concerned, in general with three major themes; first, there have been attempts to define an intra-urban hierarchy, more-or-less on the lines of the inter-urban hierarchy which we described in Section 4C 1; second, there has been great interest in the commercial core of large urban settlements, the so-called 'central business district' (CBD); and third, there has been considerable analysis of land and property value patterns within the urban area. All three themes are, of course, interrelated, and no analysis of the retail geography of an urban area could be complete without a consideration of them all. However, the number of 'complete' retail geographies so far produced is very small, for the obvious reason that research into any one of the themes is a very detailed, costly and time-consuming matter. Most analyses of intra-urban commercial structure are for American cities, such as those by Berry (1963) and Garner (1966), both of which deal with the city of Chicago; British examples are, in comparison, few in number. Not only this, but, as Haggett (1968) has pointed out, 'we continue to rely rather heavily on information from the top-twenty of the world cities'.

4C 2a The intra-urban hierarchy

In most towns, shops and services can be found in more than one shopping area. Even in the smallest town it is possible to recognise a central business district, where most of the shops and services are located, and one or two other places where there may be either one or two shops close to each other, or even just a street-corner shop on its own. Generally speaking, the larger the town, the greater will be the number of business centres which arise to serve the population. Not only does the number of business centres increase in this way, but there is also a change in the character of those centres. Certainly, some will be larger than others and offer a greater, if not different, range of goods and services than the others. Some may be a kind of street-corner shopping centre whilst others may be developed along major roads (called **ribbon centres**). Not only this, but the character and range of services provided in the central business district itself also changes according to the overall size of the urban settlement. In general, therefore, the larger the town, the greater will be the complexity of its business structure.

Some of the earliest, and probably best known, work on the commercial structure of cities was that by Berry, Tennant, Garner and Simmons (1963) relating to the metropolitan area of Chicago. For this city, they found that there is a hierarchy of business centres which is made up of five different levels:

1 Isolated convenience stores and street-corner developments.
2 Neighbourhood business centres.
3 Community business centres.
4 Regional shopping centres.
5 The Central Business District.
The kinds of shops and services associated

with each of these levels has been described elsewhere (Berry et al., 1963), from which it is apparent that the metropolitan intra-urban hierarchy is, in many ways, rather like the progression from village, through 'town', to 'city' in the general hierarchy of a region which we have described earlier (Section 4C 1).

Work on British cities has revealed the existence of a similar intra-urban hierarchy. Smailes and Hartley (1961), for example, point to a three tiered hierarchy below the CBD in Greater London:

A Regional centres (e.g.; Brixton, Kingston).
B Suburban centres (e.g.; Eltham, Wembley).
C Minor suburban centres (e.g.; Shepherds Bush, Hendon).

More recently, Thorpe and Rhodes (1966) have identified a four-fold hierarchy, below the level of CBD, in the Tyneside conurbation, which is described as comprising:

A Major centres.
B Suburban centres.
C Small suburban centres.
D Neighbourhood centres.

As before, each centre contains a different range of goods and services according to its importance.

It will be noted that in the English examples, the equivalent of the lowest level of the American intra-urban hierarchy, the 'corner-shop' centre, has not been considered.

Studies of the intra-urban structure of smaller towns and cities than the large metropolitan (provincial) centres reveal that the range of shopping centre types is less, the smaller the town. Hence, in a small market town such as Ripon, with a population of 10 000, there is a CBD, but only a few 'corner-shops' elsewhere throughout the city: in a city of more moderate population, such as Exeter (80 000 population), however, there are distinct suburban shopping centres in addition to the CBD and the corner stores.

Each of these different centres performs a different rôle: its range of services being a reflection of the size and characteristics of the area which it serves.

It is interesting to note also that the size of establishments of each function varies according to the level of hierarchy in which they are found. In the CBD, the functions are usually performed in larger establishments than their equivalent in a suburban shopping centre. In fact, in general, shops increase in size according to the level of centre. Thus, a grocer's shop at the street-corner level is likely to be smaller than one in a suburban shopping centre which, in turn, is smaller than a grocery supermarket in the CBD.

The reason for this is, of course, related to the volume of business which the shop may be expected to attract. In general, businesses in the CBD can expect to attract a greater trade from a larger area, and hence their premises will be bigger.

Local Study

Aim: To identify the main characteristics of intra-urban shopping centres.
Data sources: Population census; field survey.
Method:
1 Make a survey of the number and type of business premises in each of the suburban shopping centres in the study area (excluding the CBD and isolated 'corner' stores).
2 Estimate the size of population served by each centre. To do this, calculate the size of the trading area of the centre (see Section 4D 3) and multiply it by the estimated mean population density of the area.
3 Construct graphs and calculate the regression lines to show the relationship between population served and the number of establishments and functions in each of the centres.
4 Repeat steps 1 to 3 of the project outlined in Section 4C 1c.

Example
Area studied: Devon towns of greater than 15 000 population.

Having made our survey of the number and types of business premises in the suburban shopping centres of Devon towns, we delimited the sphere of influence of each centre. This was done by asking shoppers in each centre their place of residence, plotting this information on a street map and then drawing in the maximum extent of the centre's influence (see Section 4D 3 for

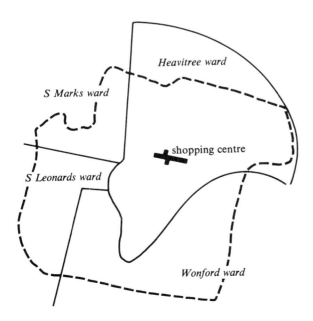

Fig. 4.30 RELATIONSHIP BE-TWEEN SHOPPING CENTRE TRADING AREA AND CIVIL WARDS, Heavitree, Exeter: trading area indicated by broken line, ward boundaries by continuous lines

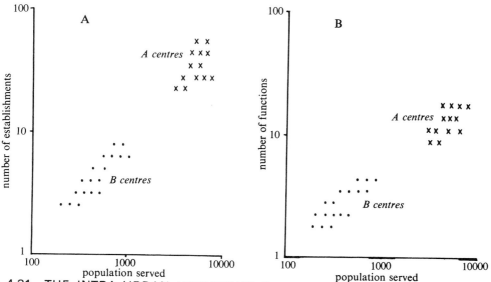

Fig. 4.31 THE INTRA-URBAN HIERARCHY, Devon towns larger than 15 000 population : A—relationship between number of establishments and the size of population served ;
B—relationship between number of functions and the size of population served

further details of this method). The total population contained within this area was then estimated: first we calculated the average density of population of each of the wards in which the defined area was located and then multiplied this figure by the area of the shopping centre's sphere of influence. For example, as can be seen in fig. 4.30, the sphere of influence for the Heavitree (Exeter) shopping centre included mainly the ward of Heavitree, but also parts of Wonford, St Leonard's and St Mark's wards. The population densities of these wards were 26·8, 22·8, 16·8 and 25·0 persons per acre, hence the mean density of population for these wards was 21·6 persons per acre. The area of the Heavitree shopping centre's trade was found to be 152 acres, hence the estimated population for the centre was 3 283.

We were then able to plot the graphs showing the numbers of establishments and the number of functions plotted against population size for each of the shopping centres (fig. 4.31 A and B). In both of these graphs, two distinct 'groups' of centre are apparent; in one group of centres (marked A in fig. 4.31 A and B) the total number of functions ranges from 9 to 20, the total

number of establishments ranges from 20 to 120, and the population served ranges from 2 000 to 8 000. In the other group (marked B in fig. 4.31 A and B) the number of functions ranges from 2 to 6, the total number of establishments ranges from 3 to 8, and the population served ranges from 300 to 1 000. The type A centres we shall call major suburban centres, the type B centres we shall call minor suburban centres. Next, we calculated the mean population served by the major centres and we found this to be 4 480, whereas, making the same calculation for the minor centres, we found that their mean population was 590. Similar calculations for both types of centre showed that the major centres had an average number of 14 functions and 60 establishments. We then tested these mean figures for both types of centre to see whether they were statistically significant, using the student's t test (Section 2C 1d), and we found that the differences in all cases were significant at the 95% probability level.

Having thus found that there were, in fact, two distinctly different kinds of suburban centre in the region, we went on to analyse which functions were typical of which centre. This we did by drawing up a matrix (similar to the one used in Section 4C 1c) which showed the shopping centres ranked from highest to lowest along the rows, and the functions listed from those occurring most frequently to those occurring least, along the columns.

From this matrix it was quite clear that '*B*' centres typically contained grocers, green-grocers, butchers and confectioners, whereas '*A*' centres would offer, in addition to these services, functions with higher threshold requirements, such as newsagents, chemists, jewellers, ironmongers, hardware stores, public houses and drapers.

Watch-points It must be remembered that the population served by each centre is no more than a rough estimate: too much reliance must not, therefore, be placed on the results of the survey, which can only serve as a guide.

In calculating the population served by each centre, the population density was expressed in acres (British imperial unit of area). This is in accordance with the practices of the census of population from which the density figures were obtained.

FURTHER READING

Berry, B. J. L. *et al.*, 'Commercial structure and commercial blight', *University of Chicago Department of Geography, Research Paper*, (1963), 83.

Garner, B. J., 'The internal structure of shopping centres', *Northwestern University Studies in Geography*, (1966), 12.

Haggett, P., 'The spatial structure of city regions', Centre for Environmental Studies, working paper 6: *The future of the city region* (1968).

Smailes, A. E. and Hartley, G., 'Shopping centres in the Greater London area', *Transactions of the Institute of British Geographers*, (1961), 29, pp. 201–213.

Thorpe, B. and Rhodes, T. C., 'The shopping centres of the Tyneside urban region and large scale grocery retailers', *Economic Geography*, (1966), 42, pp. 52–73.

4C 2b Functions in the central business district

The central business district is, as we have already said, the major shopping and commercial zone of a city, and it offers the greatest range of goods and services of any of the business centres found in a city. The actual physical limits of the CBD are not always easy to define. Sometimes it is obvious where the CBD ends because there may be a park or some other break in land use (CBD to other functions), but more often the CBD 'merges' into some adjacent area of a different character.

Many methods have, nevertheless, been used in attempting to delimit the CBD. Most of them involve the calculation of some form of land use index. Murphy, Vance and Epstein (1955), for instance, devised a Central Business Intensity Index (CBII) and a Central Business Height Index (CBHI), which could be calculated for each block of buildings; only those blocks which had a CBII of 50% or more and a CBHI of one or more could be considered as belonging to the CBD. The difficulty in applying this method directly to an English city is simply that 'blocks' of buildings do not exist, and so some careful modification is necessary.

Alternatively, the rateable values of all the properties in the area have also been used to define the CBD. Having established a Peak Land Value Intersection Point (PLVIP) (see Section 4C 2c), it may be possible to delimit the CBD by assuming that those premises whose rateable value is less than a certain percentage of the rateable values of the premises at the PLVIP do not belong to the CBD. Murphy (1966) suggests 5% as representing the limit in American cities (see Section 4C 2c).

It is not, however, easy to devise an objective method of delimiting this area and, indeed, a useful project would be to look into this particular problem.

Within the CBD, however, the precise range of services offered varies according to the size of the city itself. In a small market town of 10 000 the CBD would contain several food shops (such as grocers), together with certain clothing and household shops; it would not, however, contain any department stores or large furniture shops or any functions which could be described as 'high order' (Section 4C 1b). Only a large city would contain such high order functions in its CBD. In a sense, therefore, we can think of CBD's varying in their range of goods according to some hierarchical structure based on their size.

Further, the CBD's of larger cities tend to contain what we may call 'specialised functional areas'. Banking, insurance and linked financial concerns are often found together in a distinct 'financial core' area. Other functions similarly tend to locate in such specialist districts. In large American cities Berry has recognised the existence of furniture districts, exotic market areas, entertainment districts, printing districts, and automobile rows (where new- and used-car dealers are located). In fact, even in the smallest market town some tendency to such functional grouping of services will be evident, though the tendency becomes more marked the larger the town. The reason for this is simple; there is usually an advantage

to be derived by two or more competitors from locating near to each other. At first sight, this proposition appears to be something of a contradiction, but there is a very logical explanation for it. Imagine a large beach, uniformly peopled, on a not-too-sunny day. Many of the sunbathers want an ice cream, so a single ice cream vendor would obviously set up his stall in the middle of the beach. A queue develops and he does a roaring trade. Imagine now, that another ice cream vendor comes along, sees the queue, and decides to 'cash-in' on the market. Where will he locate? — patently, very close to the original vendor because there he can 'tap' the queue. It is for reasons similar to this, therefore, that shops of a similar kind will try to find locations close to each other. Once they are so established, the advantages for the customer also become apparent — in particular, it is easier for the customer to 'shop around'. Hence, in any CBD, there will be some evidence of the functional grouping of like or linked services into distinct locations (fig. 4.32).

Fig. 4.32 GROUPING OF SIMILAR FUNCTIONS, Exeter High Street: between 50 and 100 m distance from the PRVP is a characteristic group of clothing shops—*from left to right*, The Skirt Shop, Woodleys (shoes), Dolcis (shoes), Dormar fashions, Kendall (rainwear), Ernest Jones (jewellery), Lennards (shoes). Notice, too, the location of financial offices on the first and second storeys

It follows from what we have just said, that there will be characteristic locations for each kind of shop. Ladies fashion stores, for instance, tend to locate near the centre of the CBD, while car showrooms and supermarkets occur near the CBD edge. The main factor influencing such site selection practices is the rent the shop is willing to pay for a particular site, and how this operates in detail we shall examine in the next section (4C 2c).

The location of the different kinds of function in the CBD was first studied by Murphy, Vance and Epstein (1955). For eight American cities (Tacoma, Grand Rapids, Worcester, Sacramento, Salt Lake City, Phoenix, Tulsa and Mobile) they analysed the CBD's land use both vertically and horizontally. The results are interesting because they demonstrate how different functions are found in different characteristic locations within the CBD. First, they divided the CBD into four 100 yard (91 m) walking zones from the centre (as defined by the PLVIP), and second, the amount of space which was occupied by each function in each of these four zones was tabulated in rank-order form. From this table it was possible to see which functions were found characteristically in which zones. For instance, following the same method in Exeter, it is found that most food shops are found in zone 1 (up to 100 yards walking distance from the PLVIP), whereas most household shops are found in zone 3 (fig. 4.33). Having discovered this pattern, we then need to explain it.

Local Study

Aim: To analyse the location of CBD functions.
Data sources: Field survey; plan map of central area (O.S. scale 1:1 250).
Method:
1 Make a land use map of the central business area, and try to define the CBD's precise boundary.
2 Establish a point from which to measure the distances of each shop type. This could probably be chosen quite simply if you know the town well. The point should be some 'central point' around which all the CBD seems to revolve. (In many towns this is the point where people tend to congregate, i.e. where pedestrian flows are at their maximum.) Precise methods of defining such a point have been used in most studies, however, and the best known and most widely used method is that of calculating the point which has the greatest average land value (Murphy, Vance and Epstein use the PLVIP; modified techniques can be used for British cities — see Section 4C 2c).

Fig. 4.33   FUNCTIONAL LOCATION IN EXETER
Based on the techniques outlined by Murphy et. al. (1955) ; ranked data (e.g. 1 indicates zones in which greatest number of establishments of a given function are located).

FUNCTION	DISTANCE FROM PRVP (yards)			
	0–100	101–200	201–300	301–400
food stores	1	2	3	4
clothing stores	3	1	2	4
household stores	4	3	1	2
variety stores	2	4	1	3
financial offices	4	1	3	2
Public offices	1	2	—	—

3   Map the distribution of each shop of a given type; either each kind of shop (e.g. grocers, butchers, ironmongers) or just groups of functions (e.g. food shops, household shops) may be analysed.

4   Using the modified nearest-neighbour analysis (outlined in the worked example) test to see if the distribution of functions is uniform, random or clustered.

5   Measure and tabulate the distance from the central point to each establishment of each given function; calculate the mean distance for each function, then test the difference between the mean values of each function for significance using the student's t test.

6   Offer explanations for the patterns you discover.

Example

Area studied: The CBD of Exeter.

First of all we calculated the Peak Rateable Value Point by the method outlined in the next section (4C 2c), and located it on the map of the central area. We next plotted on the map the location of seven business types (food shops, household stores, clothing shops, variety (departmental) stores, financial offices, public offices and medical services) (fig. 4.34). Even from simple inspection it appeared that most of the functions were found at one particularly characteristic location; clothing shops, for instance, seemed to be located between about 50 and 100 metres of the PRVP. Closer inspection showed that some of the functions appeared to be more 'grouped' than others. How then, could we describe the locational characteristics of these six functions without being too subjective? Perhaps we could use the nearest-neighbour technique once more, since it measures, objectively, the extent to which a distribution is grouped, uniform or random?

The distribution of shops along a street, with which we are dealing here, is conceptually the same thing as a distribution of points along a line. It has been shown (Burghardt, 1959; Dacey, 1960) that in order to test such a distribution for characteristics of grouping or randomness, it is necessary to use a modified version of the nearest-

Food   Financial Offices

Clothing   Public Offices

Household   Medical

Variety   Vacant

Fig. 4.34 LOCATION OF SEVEN TYPES OF BUSINESS, Exeter High Street

neighbour method, which compares the proportion of 'reflexive pairs' of nearest-neighbours in the actual distribution with the number of reflexive pairs which could be expected in a theoretically random distribution. A 'reflexive pair' is simply two points which have each other as their

151

nearest-neighbours. It is also possible to distinguish between second-nearest-neighbours, third-nearest, nth nearest-neighbours, and again, for each of these 'orders' of pairs we can identify any reflexive pairs.

It has been shown that the proportion of nth order reflexive pairs in a distribution will vary according to whether the whole series of points in the distribution are uniformly spaced, randomly spaced or grouped together (Clark, 1956). There will be a proportion of $(\frac{2}{3})^n$ reflexive pairs of order n, if the distribution is **random**; there will be more than $(\frac{2}{3})^n$ reflexive pairs of order n, if the distribution is **uniform**; and there will be less than $(\frac{2}{3})^n$ reflexive pairs of order n, if the distribution is **grouped**. For example, in terms of first order reflexive pairs (i.e. places whose first nearest-neighbours are reflexive) we would expect a proportion of $(\frac{2}{3})^1$, i.e. 0·667 (or 66·67%) of all the places in the distribution to be reflexive pairs if the distribution were random. If the actual proportion were higher, the distribution could be said to be uniform, and if it were lower the distribution would be tending towards grouping. The further the actual proportion is away from the expected proportion, the greater is the tendency towards either grouping or uniformity.

It was this method which we then applied to each of the six data sets in our study. For each of the six functions, we counted the actual number of first order reflexive pairs, expressed this number as a proportion of

Fig. 4.35 DISTRIBUTION OF FUNCTIONS: nearest-neighbour analysis of reflexive pairs

FUNCTION	OBSERVED PROPORTION	DESCRIPTION
food stores	·823	uniform
clothing stores	·667	grouped
household stores	·444	grouped
variety stores	·798	uniform
financial offices	·296	grouped
public offices	·298	grouped

Fig. 4.36 LOCATION OF FUNCTIONS IN THE CENTRAL AREA

FUNCTION	DISTANCE FROM PRVP (in metres)
food stores	165
clothing stores	77
household stores	44
variety stores	275
financial offices	120
public offices	210

the total number of points, and compared it with the expected proportion (0·667). The results are shown in fig. 4.35. As can be seen, only the food shops and variety stores show a distribution which is not grouped.

The distance from the PRVP of each establishment of each of the six function groups was then measured and tabulated, and the mean distance from the PRVP of each of the six functions was calculated (fig. 4.36). These figures appeared to show that each function was to be found at a different mean distance from the centre of the C.B.D. In order to verify our conclusions statistically, we decided to apply the standard test for significance to the data, that of 'Student's t' (Section 2C 1d), and in fact the mean distances from the PRVP of each of the six functions were found to be significant at not less than the 95% probability level.

As with all our projects, it is not this conclusion in itself which is interesting so much as the explanation we offer for it.

Watch-points The point to which the distance from the PRVP is measured must be the same in every case. It will probably be easiest to measure to the centre point of each premises' frontage. It is important that the *shortest* direct route of getting from the PRVP to the premises being measured is chosen.

FURTHER READING

Burghardt, A. F., 'The location of river towns in the central lowland of the

152

United States', *Annals of the Association of American Geographers*, (1959), 49, pp. 305–323.

Dacey, M. F., 'The spacing of river towns', *Annals of the Association of American Geographers*, (1960), 50, pp. 59–61.

Murphy, R. E., Vance, J. E. and Epstein, B. J., 'Internal structure of the central business district', *Economic Geography*, (1955), 31, pp. 21–46.

Murphy, R. E., *The American City* (McGraw-Hill, 1966).

4C 2c Land and property values

Within an urban area, the price of land varies. In general, land in the city centre is more expensive than land at the city boundary, so that land values tend to decline with distance away from the city centre. Similarly, it has been found that in most cities land values are higher along the major roads out of the cities and at the intersections of the routes than they are in the areas away from them (Berry, 1963) (fig. 3.12).

Many factors are of importance in causing the land values to vary in such ways within the urban area. There will obviously be certain pockets of land where the values are high because of some physically attractive feature of the landscape (the area may command extensive views, for example), or because they have been developed at a low density of housing. Conversely, areas of high density housing or areas in poor physical sites, with poor environments, will be less desirable and therefore less expensive. It is important to note how there is a circle of 'cumulative causation' in this process: low density housing is, basically, more expensive than high density housing because it requires more land to house one individual: once such an area has been developed, there will be many people trying to buy such properties (because they are thought to be, in estate agent's jargon, 'superior'!): many buyers seeking few properties (few for the reason already given) means that the price goes up ... and up ... and up! Hence, low density areas of housing increasingly become high land value areas.

But, apart from these considerations, it is thought that the most important factor affecting land value prices is 'accessibility'. The fundamental reason why most shops are located in the centre of the city is that everyone in the city can most easily get to the centre: it is the most accessible point of the system from which the largest possible market can be obtained. Hence, the central sites will be expensive to buy. Similarly, those areas where major roads run in to the city centre have a greater degree of accessibility than the areas behind them, and they, too, can therefore command a high price. But once again, the 'cumulative causation' principle begins to operate, because several potential buyers and users of the land will be bidding for a limited amount of accessible land. Inevitably, therefore, the *most* accessible land will go to the highest bidder.

From this, arises the distribution of urban land uses which is characteristic of all towns. The most accessible locations (i.e. the centre and the major arteries) will be occupied mainly by commercial uses because they can afford the site. Occasionally, private flats are found in these same locations and, for the same reasons, these are usually high cost and, therefore, high class.

The land market operates in a similar way with respect to different kinds of commercial use within the CBD. The most accessible land at the heart of the CBD will be the most expensive, and away from this 'peak' value points, costs gradually decline. Only those shops or services which can make high bids will be found on the most central sites: and, since the land at any point will always go to the highest bidder, we would expect to find a locational sorting of functions within the central area on the basis of the costs they can bear. This is the real reason why different types of function are found at characteristically different distances away from the city centre (as we saw in the preceding section, 4C 2b) with the function which can best afford the high property prices at the centre of the CBD, and the rest bidding for the intermediate sites. As Garner (1967) has pointed out: 'accessibility means different things for different activities'; thus, while clothing shops may find a central site the most 'accessible' and be able to afford it, ironmongers may regard a location near to car-parks (away from the central sites) as more profitable and not be willing to pay for any more central site.

Naturally, the detailed mechanism of the urban land value market is far more complicated than we have outlined, and many studies have been made both by economists and geographers to understand the processes involved. The works of Alonso (1960), Berry (1963), and Yeates (1965) are among the better known of these.

Local Study

Aim: To describe the relationship between land values and their location in the CBD.

In this project we shall show how land and property values vary with location in the CBD, and attempt to establish whether certain activities are associated with characteristically valued properties, as theory would seem to indicate. A useful measure of the value of a property is its rateable value. Every property-holder in Britain is required to give details of the physical size of his property, and these details are then used to assess the rates (taxes) which must be paid by the property-holder to the county or city rating office. The site of the building is also taken into account in assessing the rateable value — the most 'accessible' sites in an urban area being taxed most heavily. The rateable value of a property is, therefore, a land and building value combined. The properties with high rateable values will, therefore, be either the largest in size, built on a large amount of land, or else at a central 'accessible' location.

Traditionally, studies of land values have 'standardised' the rateable values so as to express the value of each property in terms of its frontage. Usually the value of the property per foot of frontage has been calculated (Murphy *et al.*, 1955), and this quantity has been referred to as the 'foot frontage value'. Rather than change the name of this much-referred to measure, because of metrication, we have decided, for the purpose of this study, to retain the term 'foot frontage value', and to make it refer

to a unit of 0·3 metres (almost the direct equivalent of one foot).

Data sources: Rating books at local council offices; field survey.

Method:

1 Plot the rateable value of every property in the city centre on a plan map (OS 1:2 500 scale) (this can normally be done at the rating office).

2 Calculate the front-footage value of each property. This can be calculated by substituting in the formula

$$\frac{RV \times 3}{L \times 10}$$

where RV = rateable value, and L = the length of the premises' frontage (in metres).

3 Plot the front-footage values on a map showing the location of each *kind* of business use.

4 Make a Chi-squared test to see whether rateable value (front footage) affects the distribution of the functions in the central area of the city.

5 Calculate the mean rateable value (front footage) of the premises used for each kind of function, and then test for any significant differences in their mean value, by Student's *t* test.

6 Make a series of transects through the central area (along the main streets) to show how the front footage values vary geographically. This is shown graphically by plotting the location of premises on the *x* axis of a graph (in scale), and their front footage values on the *y* axis (fig. 4.38).

7 On the map showing front-footage values, divide the streets into 30 metre (about 100 foot) 'lots', and for each of these lots calculate the mean front footage of the premises it contains (see fig. 4.39).

8 Define the CBD edge by drawing in an appropriate 'percentage value' line and analyse the variation of land values with distance from the PRVP.

Example

Area studied: Exeter CBD.

At the Exeter City Council Rating Office

Fig. 4.37 CALCULATION OF CHI-SQUARED:
clothing shops in Exeter

rateable values (£ per front-foot)

	<50	51–100	101–150	151–200	>201
Observed frequency	4	5	6	13	2
Expected frequency	6	6	6	6	6
$O - E$	−2	−1	0	7	−4
$(O - E)^2$	4	1	0	49	16
$\dfrac{(O - E)^2}{E}$	·66	·16	0	8·16	2·66

$$\chi^2 = \sum \frac{(O - E)^2}{E} = 11·64 \quad \text{degrees of freedom } (5 - 1) = 4$$

we plotted the rateable value of every property in the city centre on a 1:2 500 map. The front footage of each of the premises was measured and the value per front foot calculated; in turn, this value was plotted on the map which we had prepared for the preceding project (4C 2b) and which shows the location of seven different functions (fig. 4.34). In order to find out whether these different functions were associated with premises of a particular rateable value, as theory would assume, we used two statistical tests. First, we used a Chi-squared test to establish whether rateable value was a significant factor in explaining the distribution of each of the functions; then we compared the mean rateable values of each of the functions by means of student's t test.

It will be recalled from Sections 2B 3 and 2C 3 that the χ^2 test involves a comparison of actual frequency distribution with a theoretical one which is based on a null hypothesis. The actual distribution of each of the functions was plotted as in fig. 4.37 (notice that it was necessary to group the rateable value data into a number of classes: in the example shown here we made 5 classes: values under £50 per foot, £51–100, £101–150, £151–200, greater than £201). In this example, the null hypothesis was that 'rateable value did *not* affect the distribution of functions'. Hence, the cell frequencies for the expected null hypothesis distribution was 6 (30 clothing shops ÷ 5). The value of χ_2

was then calculated by the method explained in Section 2B 3. As can be seen in fig. 4.37, χ^2 in the case of clothing shops was 11·64 and with 4 degrees of freedom: this value in the statistical tables (Lindley and Miller, 1966, Table 5) occurs between 5% and 2·5%, which means that our null hypothesis would be correct in only 5–2·5% of all cases — in other words, there is a 95%–97·5% probability that the **inverse** of the null hypothesis was correct (i.e. clothing shops did locate with respect to rateable value). Similar calculations for the other six functions indicated that the location of business activity *was* related to property values, the null hypothesis in no case having a level of probability greater than 5%.

The mean rateable value of the properties occupied by each of the business activities was then calculated, and it was found that each of the activities appeared to be located in properties of a different value. For instance, the household shops were located in premises whose mean front footage value was £78, whereas the clothing shops were located in premises whose mean front footage was £168. The next obvious question was were these differences statistically significant? The application of a student's t test to the data (Section 2C 1d) showed that in all six cases the differences were statistically significant, and in no case, with less than a 95% level of probability. The theoretical assertions which we made earlier that

155

distance (metres) from east end of High St

rateable value
(£ per front foot)

Fig. 4.38 RATEABLE VALUES, transect along Exeter High Street

different activities would be associated with premises of different value were, therefore, proved.

It now remained to describe the way in which property values varied throughout the CBD. Even from casual inspection of the map showing front-footage values, it was clear that premises near to the 'centre' were more highly rated than those progressively further away, and that several minor peaks of high valued properties occurred throughout the area. This pattern was more clearly shown by making a series of transects along the main streets of the CBD, and by plotting the distribution of premises on the x axis of a graph against their rateable values on the y axis (fig. 4.38).

Clearly such transects can only show how property values vary along one side of a street. In order to locate the point at which rateable values are highest within the CBD it is, of course, necessary to consider the variation of values along both sides of the streets at the same time. This, however, is not so easy to do as it may at first sight appear, since the actual values on one side of a street may occur at a different location from the peak value on the other side. Hence, some way of generalising or averaging the values on both sides of a street has to be devised. We chose to divide the streets into 30 metre (about 100 foot) 'lots' and to calculate the mean front footage of the premises it contained. This mean value was then plotted on the map as the mid-point of the 'lot' to which it referred. For example, lot 'A' in fig. 4.39 consists of seven premises whose front footage values (in £) are respectively 30, 34, 38, 30, 33, 37, 34. The mean value of this set, £34, is then indicated as the central point of the 'lot'. Having plotted such values for the whole of the CBD, the peak rateable value point could be easily identified. These could then be used to construct graphs showing the distance-decay function which characterises the land value pattern.

Earlier (Section 4C 2c) we mentioned that property values had been used by several writers to define the limits of the CBD. The method is a simple one, and all that is needed is that the actual front-footage values for the 30 metre 'lots' be expressed as percent-

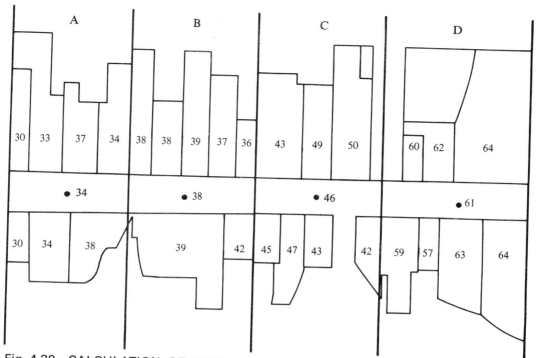

Fig. 4.39 CALCULATION OF FRONT-FOOTAGE VALUES FOR 30m LOTS

ages of the PRVP value, and then some critical percentage level is used to define the CBD edge. Murphy, Vance and Epstein (1955) suggested that the blocks having a front footage of less than 5% of the PRVP should be counted as non-CBD.

Watch-points Be particularly careful to choose meaningful transect lines when analysing the overall pattern of land values; transects which cover as wide a range of values as possible should be selected.

FURTHER READING

Alonso, W., 'A theory of the urban land market', *Papers and Proceedings of the Regional Science Association*, (1960), 6, pp. 149–157.
Berry, B. J. L. *et al.*, 'Commercial structure and commercial blight', *University of Chicago Department of Geography, Research Paper*, (1963), 83.
Garner, B. J., 'Models of urban geography and settlement location', ch. 9 in Chorley, R. J. and Haggett, P. (eds), *Models in Geography* (Methuen, 1967).
Murphy, R. E., Vance, J. E. and Epstein, B. J., 'Internal structure of the central business district', *Economic Geography*, (1955), 31, pp. 21–46.
Yeates, M., 'Some factors affecting the spatial distribution of Chicago land values', *Economic Geography*, (1965), 41, pp. 57–70.

157

4D MOVEMENT

Activity implies movement: since human geography is concerned with the location of human and economic activity, it must equally be concerned with human and economic movements. It is, however, only comparatively recently that studies of movement and interaction of people and commodities between one place and another have assumed any significant rôle in locational studies.

In general, it appears that movement is very strongly affected by distance and that many locational decisions are taken, and have been taken, so as to minimise the amount of necessary movement. It is also clear that in making such decisions, distance, movement and opportunities are perceived in different ways by different people. Early studies of 'push and pull' factors in explaining movements (Beaujeu-Garnier, 1956) have led, therefore, to refined statistical and theoretical testing not only of those same factors but also of the effects of movement-minimisation and perception.

Similarly, more detailed analysis has been made of the various forms of movement: the definition of trade areas, 'spheres of influence' or 'hinterlands' has become a major part of geographical studies of movement, whilst a renewed interest is being taken in the networks over which the movements take place. Statistical techniques, particularly, are being used to identify and describe the major structural characteristics of such interaction fields and networks.

4D 1 Movement-minimisation

Distance is fundamental to movement, since all movement involves a cost which in turn is related to distance. Thus, the direct costs of transport for any commodity are normally related in the first instance to the distance involved; in general, the greater the distance, the greater will be the cost of transport, though this relationship may be modified slightly in certain circumstances (Sharp, 1965; Alexander, 1953). There are also certain 'indirect' costs of distance which may not, in fact, be expressed in monetary terms, but which nevertheless affect movement: for example, travel *time*, *safety*, or *reliability* may be just as significant in affecting movement as the actual *linear* distance costs.

The overall effect of such 'distance-costs' is to cause a 'falling-off' of movement with increased distance. In a sense, therefore, distance can be thought of as a kind of 'friction' acting against movement, the net effects of which are to increase movement costs with distance and, therefore, to reduce movement over long distances. From this, it follows that 'locational decisions are taken, in general, so as to minimise the frictional effects of distance' (Garner, 1967, p. 304), and so the location of human and economic activity will reflect the need to minimise movement whenever possible.

Alfred Weber (1909) demonstrated theoretically that the most efficient location for any industry would be at the point at which movement costs of all kinds were at a minimum. This point would vary according to whether the transport costs of assembling the raw materials were greater than the costs of distributing the products; where distribution costs were higher than those of raw material assembly, the location would tend to be near the market ('market orientated'), and where the reverse was the case, the location would tend to be nearer to materials ('materials orientated').

Although the basic theory sounds attractive, it is doubtful whether industrial location, particularly at the present time, really operates in such a manner (Haggett, 1965; Hamilton, 1967; Isard, 1956; Greenhut, 1956). Weber recognised that under certain conditions industry would be attracted away from 'movement-minimisation' locations; thus, agglomerative and deglomerative tendencies or the existence of a large labour supply could cause a 'deviation' from the theoretical location.

Perhaps one of the most obvious effects of the movement-minimisation principle is in causing functions and populations to agglomerate. The producer, out to make maximum sales of any commodity, will need to be as accessible to as many people as possible; the customers, aware of increased movement costs with increased distance, also need to be as near as possible to the producer. Clearly in such a situation both producer and consumer will be able to minimise movements, and thereby reduce the frictional effects of distance by locating as close to each other as possible. Once people 'crowd in' to an area in order to minimise movement costs, certain other economies begin to take effect. In particular, it becomes cheaper to provide the basic services (such as sewerage and electricity) because the costs of operation can be spread over a greater number of people. Other producers of other commodities are in turn attracted to the area because of the possibility of reducing movement costs and creating a larger market. From then on, the process is self-perpetuating and the agglomeration of functions and population is assured. Hence, as we saw earlier (Section 4A 2), the density of population gradually declines with increased distance away from a production centre.

Patterns of land use are also affected by the need to minimise costs and distance. For agricultural land uses, Chisholm (1962) has shown that at all scales of operation, from the organisation of land use on an individual farmstead to the variation in land use on a regional scale, there is clear evidence of frictional effects of distance. Those commodities which require intensive care, involving a great deal of movement, will, *ceteris paribus*, be located near to the centre of organisation (farmstead or market town), whereas less intensive uses, requiring less movement, will be found at greater distances away from the organisation centre. Much the same relationship had been shown earlier by von Thünen (1826) who formulated his observations into a theory to explain why the pattern arose. The basic postulate of this theory was that each plot of land would be occupied by the activity which could pay most for it. The amount offered for each plot of land would vary according to its usefulness from the point of view of each activity, and one of the main determinants of this usefulness would be its accessibility. Thus, on a flat plain of uniform fertility with transport costs proportional to distance, the plots of land nearest to a village would be most useful for those activities which involved great amounts of labour (e.g. labour-intensive products). Hence, farmers who wished to cultivate vegetables, for instance, would make high bids for the plots nearest the village; the plots further away would involve greater movement costs and, therefore, less would be offered for them.

It can thus be seen that 'movement-minimisation' is basically responsible for the arrangement of land uses in a given region. Not only does this principle apply to agricultural land uses, as we have seen, but also to all other forms of land use. The arrangement of urban land uses is explained by the same basic argument. The sites which are thought to be the most 'accessible', from the point of view of any would-be entrepreneur, are those at which movement-costs would be minimised and for which he would be willing to pay more rent. Of course, for different activities the most 'accessible' (desirable) site varies, but usually it is the one at which movement costs are at a minimum. Hence, high bids will be made for the central sites by those functions for whom accessibility to the whole urban area is important, for it is only here that their total movement costs could be minimised. Other functions, for whom the accessibility requirements are different, will find other sites at which their movements are minimised. Since each site will be sold to the highest bidder, it follows that the location of urban land uses will be a reflection of the same principles of movement minimisation.

Using postulates and assumptions similar to those of von Thünen, Garrison (1959) and Isard (1956) have shown that the overall spatial effect would be to cause a concentric zoning of urban functions — a pattern which seems at least to underlie the location of different activities in many cities of the world, whether throughout the whole urban

G

159

area (Section 4A 2), or within the CBD (Section 4C 2b).

Movement-minimisation seems to be a fundamental factor, therefore, in the explanation of locational patterns.

Local Study

Aim: To show the effect of movement-minimisation and distance on crop location.
Data source: Land use map.
Method:

1   Place a transparent overlay on top of the land use map and, choosing a central town or village, construct around it a series of concentric zones each containing the same area. The radius of each successive circle can be calculated by substituting in the formula

$$R = \sqrt{(A/\pi)}$$

where A = the *total* area enclosed by that circle.

Thus, if the zones were each to be of 10 sq km area, the first circle's total area would be 10 sq km and would have a radius of $\sqrt{3 \cdot 18}$, while the second circle would enclose a *total* area of 20 sq km (its own zone (10 sq km) + the zone on its inner periphery (10 sq km)), and would have a radius of $\sqrt{6 \cdot 37}$.

2   Take a random sample of land use in each zone by constructing a reference grid over the study area and using random numbers to select the co-ordinates of the sample points (Section 1C 2).

3   Calculate the percentage of each zone occupied by each particular land use, and also the percentage of each land use in each zone.

4   Portray the information cartographically, using graphs, and attempt to explain the variations in land use and distance in terms of the 'movement inputs' (Haggett, 1965, pp. 162–164) each land use requires.

Example

Area studied: Abergavenny (area contained on Sheet 278, Land-use Survey of Gt Britain, 1:25 000).

A series of six concentric zones, each of area 8 km², were first constructed from the centre

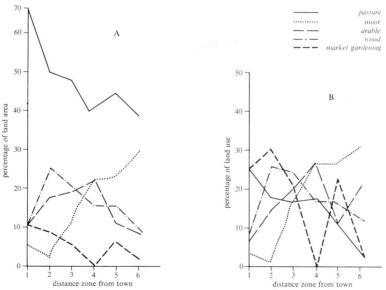

Fig. 4.40   RELATIONSHIP BETWEEN LAND USE AND DISTANCE, Abergavenny: A—percentage of land area in each zone occupied by a particular land use; B—percentage of total amount of land occupied by particular uses in each zone

160

of the town. Five different land-use types were selected for the study and, by means of random sample, the relative proportions of these land use types was estimated for each of the six zones. The data was analysed in two slightly different, but complementary, ways. First, we calculated the percentage amount of land in each zone which was devoted to each of the five different uses, and then we calculated the percentage amount of each land use type which occurred in each of the six zones. Both data sets were then plotted on a graph to show the variations of land use with distance from the market town (fig. 4.40).

It was clear that land use in this area varied according to distance in a manner not altogether unlike that described more theoretically by von Thünen. Thus, for example, 53% of the market gardening was located within the first two zones (i.e. within a radius of 2·27 km of the market town), whereas arable land becomes most important in the fourth zone (between 2·67 and 3·22 km) from the town centre. In terms of bid-rents we can hypothesise that market gardening must be bidding high in the first zone, whereas in the second and third zones woodland occupies a greater proportion of the land area than does arable and consequently its bid-rent curve must, at this point, generally lie above that of arable. In zones 5 and 6, moorland is clearly the highest bidder. The overall importance of pasture-land in the area is apparent from both graphs. It forms the greatest percentage of land area in every zone, but tends to be particularly concentrated near to the town where, we must conclude, it is able to make its highest bid.

The relative 'bids' are, of course, related to the amount of movement entailed in the particular form of land use in each successive zone. Since, for example, market gardening is concentrated near the town, its movement inputs, the total cost of transport (men, machines, materials and products) must lie above those of every other land use. Movement costs are so important that they have to be minimised by locating near the town.

Watch-points It is essential that the study

zones are equal in area. If they are not, an error may be introduced because the data will not be 'standardised' by area.

A useful sequel to this project would be to attempt a correlation between the proportions of land use and the variations in geology, soil type or morphology of the area.

FURTHER READING

Alexander, J. W. *et al.*, 'Freight rates: selected aspects of uniform and nodal regions', *Economic Geography*, (1958), 34, pp. 1–18.

Beaujeu-Garnièr, J. (translated 1965), *Population Geography* (Pergamon Press, 1965).

Chisholm, M. D. I., *Rural Settlement and Land Use* (H.U.L., 1962).

Garner, B. J., 'Models of urban geography and settlement location', ch. 9 in Chorley, R. J. and Haggett, P. (eds), *Models in Geography* (Methuen, 1967).

Greenhut, M., *Plant Location in Theory and Practice* (Cardma U.P., 1956).

Haggett, P., *Locational Analysis in Human Geography* (Arnold, 1965).

Hamilton, F. E. I., 'Models of Industrial Location', ch. 10 in Chorley, R. J. and Haggett, P. (eds), *Models in Geography* (Methuen, 1967).

Isard, W., *Location and Space Economy* (M.I.T. Press, 1956).

Sharp, C., *The Problem of Transport* (Pergamon Press, 1965).

Weber, A. (1909) (translated Friedrich, C. J.), *Theory of the Location of Industries* (Chicago U.P., 1956).

4D 2 Perception

Most of us have started off, optimistically, to walk from place *A* to place *B* only to find that it turned out to be much further than we had imagined. Had we known, we would probably either have gone by bus or not bothered at all (especially if the journey was not really necessary anyway). Similarly, the way in which we perceive *opportunities* at different locations may well affect our movements. If we think that place *B* does not have such a good selection of shops as place *A*, then our shopping expedition will undoubtedly be to place *A*. Our knowledge of the relative opportunities may not, however, be complete and so the journey we make may not be the ideal or 'best' one.

In focussing attention on the *perception* of the environment in this way, geographers have come a long way from the days when they explained behaviour in terms of the environment itself. Perhaps the first important behavioural concept to gain a hold in geography was that of 'environmental determinism'. Man's actions were, according to this view, largely determined by the environment in which he lived, and little place was afforded to the suggestion that man had 'free will'. The process of 'conversion' was hardly effected at Pauline speed! It was not really until the early 1950s that any alternative view of decision-making and the idea of a rational or 'economic' man gained wider support. In fact, like many other 'conversions', the effect has been extreme, and man's decision-making has often been over-stated in economic and rational terms. Generally, economic man's behaviour is thought to be concerned with the goal of 'optimisation', which may be achieved either by maximising profits and/or by minimising costs. Such a view clearly underlies many of the explanatory models which we have so far reviewed. Yet we have seen, repeatedly, that the observed patterns do not wholly coincide with the patterns which theoretically, according to this view, should occur. There are, of course, many reasons for this, but one of the main ones is simply that many of the explanations of economic behaviour (which are in every way just as rigidly 'deterministic' in their assessment of cause and effect) are based on assumptions of perfect knowledge. It was this realisation that perfect knowledge did not exist in the real world that pointed the direction of further research. If a man had incomplete knowledge it would be impossible for him to behave rationally, yet we can suggest that he would be acting rationally on the basis of the information that he received. It is this change in emphasis from proposals of an all-embracing external

knowledge to the information that is available that enables us to have a better insight into patterns of behaviour. In addition to this lack of knowledge, and partly a function of it, is the whole problem of uncertainty. In these circumstances, we are now in a position to appreciate that non-maximising behaviour can be rational and that sub-optimal decisions can be logical.

How does this situation of a lack of perfect knowledge arise? Partly it results from the sheer mass of information that is available which one man cannot hope to assimilate. Consequently there must be some process of sorting the information either consciously or unconsciously. Some things have more meaning than others because of a person's past experience or because they are more relevant to a given situation. The lack of knowledge also results from our lack of appreciation of the environment; we appreciate it not as it actually is, but as we think it is. This whole process of sorting, filtering and appreciating information is known as 'perception'.

A body of general theory relating to perception is being developed (Huff, 1960) at the same time as many empirical studies are relating general principles to the real world (Wolpert, 1964; Newby, 1971). Huff (1960) has shown that decisions are influenced by the endogenous factors of the individual decision maker, which include his sex, education, occupation, income and mental synthesising abilities. He indicates that the process of optimisation is much more complex and requires a greater mental synthesising ability than the processes associated with merely attaining a satisfactory level of benefit. Wolpert (1964) applied this concept to the productivity of farm labour in a part of Sweden and found that actual productivity was less than optimum productivity. He concluded that, in addition to imperfect knowledge and uncertainty as to the best product-mix, a major cause of this deviation was a desire on the part of farmers not to achieve optimum productivity but merely to be content with a level of production which would give rise to a satisfactory income.

162

In addition to general studies of the perceptive process in decision making, there have been more detailed studies into the nature of the information upon which decisions are based. Gould (1966) investigated the mental maps which people possess of the USA, Europe and West Africa and found that apart from a greater preference for and knowledge of the local area, the mental image that a particular cultural group had was remarkably similar. Gould and White (1968) have repeated the work in Britain, investigating the preferences that British schoolchildren have for living in different parts of the British Isles. Hägerstrand (1957) has attempted to fit a mathematical model to our perception of distance, suggesting that, in general terms, it is perceived logarithmically. If this is true, then it has important consequences for our ideas on population movement. On a smaller scale, a classic study by Lynch (1960) on the relationship between the process of finding one's way about a town and the mental images one has of that town, has given rise to a great deal of work along the same lines and the study of preferences has also been introduced into surveys of the perceived environment.

The last major approach to studying perception in a geographical context is through the attitudes of various cultural groups towards the environment, as expressed in their writings and their actions. Yi Fu Tuan (1968) contrasts the naturalism and animism of Oriental cultures with the desire to overcome and organise the environment inherent in Western civilisation. In much the same way, Lowenthal (1962, 1964, 1968) has looked at Americans' attitudes to America and investigated their aesthetic criteria. In Britain, Lowenthal and Prince (1964, 1965) have carried out similar surveys.

There can be little doubt that studies of perception and its effects on locational patterns will make an increasing contribution to geographical studies since, as we have seen, our perception of the environment in part influences our decision-making processes.

Local Study

Aim: To show how perceived distances differ from reality within an urban area.
Data sources: Field survey (questionnaire); large-scale map of the area (OS 1:2 500).
Method:
1 Choose a series of well-known features within the study area and use these as the 'control points' for the interview.

Fig. 4.41 PERCEIVED DISTANCES TO CONTROL POINTS (in metres)

RESPONDENTS	Control points — WESTERLY direction from interview point					
	1	2	3	4	5	6
males	217	265	448	829	1 098	1 274
females	194	303	406	579	927	1 104
both sexes	206	284	427	704	1 012	1 189

RESPONDENTS	Control points — EASTERLY direction from interview point					
	1	2	3	4	5	6
males	101	186	252	381	654	1 100
females	73	133	218	427	865	1 205
both sexes	87	159	235	404	760	1 102

2 Conduct a sample of interviews, asking the distance from the interview point to each of the established control points.

3 For each control point, calculate the mean and standard deviation of the interviewee's judgments of the perceived distance.

4 Relate the actual distances to the perceived distances.

Example

Area studied: The central area of Exeter.

Twelve control points were established and a stratified random sample of pedestrians at the centre of the city (as defined in Section 4C 2c) was taken. Residents who had lived in the city for at least one year were asked how far they thought it was from the interview point to each of the 12 control points.

The mean perceived distances to each control point were calculated, not only for the total sample, but also by sexes (fig. 4.41). Although at first sight there appeared to be some difference between the perception of males and females, no statistical significance could be established (tested by student's *t* test). Using only the figures for the total sample, we next constructed a map to show the difference between actual and perceived distances (fig. 4.42). It became clear that in one direction perceived distances were greater than the actual distances, whilst for the most part in the other direction, the reverse was the case. This relationship was also revealed by expressing the mean perceived distances as a percentage of the actual distance to each control point (fig. 4.43).

In general, it was found that people tended to underestimate distances to the eastern end of Exeter's High Street and to overestimate in the other direction. The reasons for this are obviously many and varied, but the configuration of the site may, perhaps, be

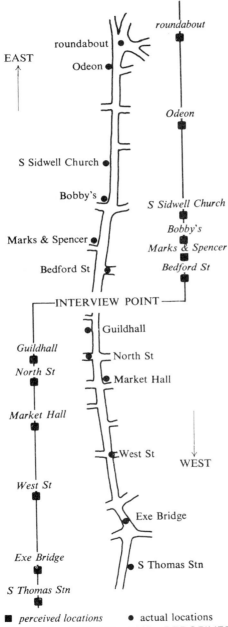

■ *perceived locations* ● *actual locations*

Fig. 4.42 ACTUAL AND PERCEIVED DISTANCES, Exeter central area

Fig. 4.43 DIFFERENCE BETWEEN ACTUAL AND PERCEIVED DISTANCES: derived from data in Figs. 4.41 and 4.44

DIRECTION	% difference to control points					
	1	2	3	4	5	6
West	+64	+13	+12	+19	+10	+18
East	−18	−23	−24	−32	− 8	+ 6

164

one major consideration. In the easterly direction, the High Street widens into a straight carriageway through a modern shopping centre, whereas in the opposite direction, the street is much more enclosed and, in addition, goes down a steep hill. Whether or not these differences in configuration do affect peoples' perception is, naturally, difficult to ascertain, but there was certainly evidence to suggest that overestimation was correlated with lack of familiarity with the control points (78% of all respondents claimed that they were not so sure about the distances to the points westward of the interview point).

It was also interesting to note that there was a general tendency for people to give progressively more inaccurate estimates for points at greater distances and for them to underestimate nearer distances and to overestimate greater distances. This was revealed by expressing the distance between one control point and its neighbour as a ratio and comparing this ratio with a similar ratio computed for the perceived distances. Thus,

for example, the distance between the interview point and control point 1 was 125 m, while to control point 2 it was 250 m. By dividing 125 into 250, a ratio of 2·00 was obtained, which compared with a ratio of 1·38 between the perceived distances of the same two control points (fig. 4.44). The actual ratio between control points 1 and 2 exceeds the perceived ratio in both directions; between points 2 and 3 they are about the same, whilst from points 3 to 6 the majority of perceived ratios exceed the actual ratios, indicating that error in judgment tends to increase with distance.

Watch-points The people we interviewed were asked to quote the distances in feet or yards, but because of metrication it has been necessary to convert all the distances quoted above into metres. It may well be that people still think mentally in terms of British Imperial units and, if it is found that this is the case, it would be better to make the conversions *after* the interviews.

Fig. 4.44 ACTUAL AND PERCEIVED DISTANCES : ratios between control points

DISTANCES (in metres)	Control points — WESTERLY direction from interview point					
	1	2	3	4	5	6
Actual	125	250	380	590	920	1 000
Ratio between control points		2·00	1·52	1·55	1·55	1·08	
Perceived	206	284	427	704	1 012	1 189
Ratio between control point		1·38	1·50	1·64	1·43	1·17	

DISTANCES (in metres)	Control points — EASTERLY direction from interview point					
	1	2	3	4	5	6
Actual	105	205	305	590	820	1 040
Ratio between control points		1·95	1·48	1·93	1·38	1·26	
Perceived	87	159	235	404	760	1 102
Ratio between control points		1·83	1·47	1·72	1·88	1·45	

Gould, P., *On Mental Maps*, (Michigan U.P. 1966).

Gould, P. and White, R., 'The mental maps of British school-leavers', *Regional Studies*, (1968), 2, pp. 161–182.

Hägerstrand, T., 'Migration and area', *Lund Studies in Geography*, Series B, (1957), 13, pp. 27–158.

Huff, D. L., 'A topographic model of consumer space preferences', *Papers and Proceedings of the Regional Science Association*, (1960), 6, pp. 159–173.

Lowenthal, D., 'The American scene', *Geographical Review*, (1968), 58, pp. 61–88.

Lowenthal, D. and Prince, H. C., 'The English Landscape', *Geographical Review*, (1964), 54, pp. 309–346.

Lowenthal, D. and Prince, H. C., 'English Landscape Tastes', *Geographical Review*, (1965), 55, pp. 186–222.

Lynch, K., *The Image of the City*, (M.I.T. Press, 1960).

Newby, P. T., 'Some attitudes to the assisted areas of the South-West as business environments' in Ravenhill, W. L. D. and Gregory, K. J. (eds.), *Exeter Essays in Geography*, (Exeter U.P., 1971).

Tuan, Y. F., 'Discrepancies between environmental attitudes and behaviour', *Canadian Geographer*, (1968), 12, pp. 176–191.

Wolpert, J., 'The decision making process in spatial context'. *Annals of the Association of American Geographers*, (1964), 54, pp. 537–558.

4D 3 Interaction Fields

Interaction between producer and consumer involves the movement of both people and commodities. Whereas the producer of a commodity is generally located at a given point in geographical space, his customers are distributed at varying distances around him, and so, before a transaction can take place, movement has to occur. From what we have said earlier, we would expect both the consumer and the producer to keep this movement to a minimum whenever possible although, of course, there would be certain exceptions to this general principle because 'optimisation' of opportunity does not always characterise decision-making. Other things being equal, customers tend to go to the *nearest* supplier of any commodity (though their definition of 'nearest' may vary). Hence, the producer's trading area, or 'interaction field', is to a large extent limited by the frictional effects of distance.

On the other hand, the producer of any commodity has to meet his 'threshold' requirements (Section 4C 1b) before production can occur. He has to ensure, therefore, that he can capture enough sales to make production viable, within the areal limits set by the increasing costs of distance. The location of competitors and also the distribution of potential consumers is bound to be a vital consideration.

Christaller (1933) and Lösch (1940) have shown how these considerations lead to the creation of 'ideal' economic landscapes. Assuming that transport costs were proportional to distance and that the population of a uniformly flat plain was equally distributed, they showed that the size of a business' interaction field (trading area) would be proportional to the threshold size requirements of that business: businesses with high threshold requirements would need larger trading areas than those with low threshold requirements. In turn, of course, this means that high threshold businesses, with large interaction fields, will be located at greater distances from each other (see Section 4B 1b).

Most of the initial assumptions of this theory do not, of course, occur in the real world. The distribution of population in any region is not uniformly distributed, as we have seen earlier in Section 4A 2, and different regions do not have identical population densities; both of these facts will cause the theoretical pattern to be modified. Isard (1956) has shown, for instance, how interaction fields could be modified theoretically by the 'agglomeration' of population near to the production points: in his model the trade areas for a given function become smaller in densely populated regions than in less densely populated regions because the necessary threshold population would be found within a smaller area. Berry and Barnum (1962) have shown, in a comparative analysis of market areas in the rangelands, wheatlands, corn belt and Chicago that, in general, the lower the population density of a region, the larger will be the trade areas of any given function. This is simply because in less densely populated areas the total population needed to meet the threshold requirements of any function will only be met by attracting customers from a larger area. The frictional effects of distance, therefore, are less marked in areas of low population density than they are in more populous areas.

One further assumption, that customers will go to the *nearest* supplier, also needs modification. Whilst this may be generally valid, it has been shown that this is not always the case and that there are often quite marked variations in consumer behaviour. Huff (1960) has suggested, for example, that a consumer's preferences for visiting one shopping centre or another vary with his or her own 'value system' and psychological drive, the way the alternatives are perceived and a whole range of 'movement imagery' considerations. Since these characteristics vary so much from individual to individual, it is not surprising to find that 'proximity' of facilities does not alone determine consumers' interaction fields, and that people from different cultural and social backgrounds have different patterns of spatial behaviour. Thus, for example, Murdie (1965) has shown how cultural differences may affect interaction fields by considering the differences in shopping behaviour between 'modern' and 'old' Canadians, the 'moderns' preferring to make their purchases at different shopping centres from those used by the 'older' generation.

Baumol and Ide (1956) have suggested that the *willingness* of consumers to travel various distances is related not only to the cost of travel but also to the difficulty of shopping at various places, a knowledge of the alternatives open and the probability of actually being able to get a particular item when the journey has been made.

Despite all these modifications to the premises, the basic principles of Christaller's and Lösch's theories cannot be denied. High order functions *do* have larger interaction fields than low order functions (fig. 4.46) and hence the interaction fields of settlements also vary according to the size of settlement, as Berry (1967) has shown.

The actual limits of an interaction field between producer and consumer are, therefore, determined by many factors but the frictional effects of distance still remain fundamental. Likewise, distance has frictional effects upon the volume or intensity of movement within the interaction field. Since movement over distance is costly, long-distance movement will take place less frequently than movement over short distances. This simple fact has been verified many times over, whether for commodity movements or for human movements. Near to the centre of a field, movement will be at its greatest intensity, but gradually as distance increases away from the centre, the amount of movement will begin to fall off or lapse. The general decline of movement with increased distance is known as the movement **lapse rate.**

Two other factors also affect this general tendency. Characteristically in the real world (as well as in the ideal landscapes of Christaller and Lösch), the edge of an interaction field could more accurately be described as a zone of competition between two centres. Thus, in settlements near the edge of the trade area of one town, not all the population will be trading with that particular centre. This has been demonstrated by Bracey (1953) in a study of spheres of influence of centres in Somerset. A questionnaire was sent to every settlement in Somerset, from which it was possible to determine which towns were used for each of fifteen different services. For each settlement a 'point score' was made; where that settlement used just one town for a particular service, it was allocated one point. If two towns were used for that service, it was allocated half a point, if three, then a third of a point, and so on. The maximum score a settlement could gain was, therefore, fifteen, and that would be where only one town (the same one) was used for all services. Such a place obviously falls in the 'core' of the town's interaction field. At the other end of the scale, a settlement with a low score (2 or 3 points) is clearly 'on the fringe' of the town's general interaction field. In between these extremes is a zone where the scores (7 or 8 points) indicate an 'intermediate' position in the urban interaction field. The scores of all the settlements within a town's maximum interaction field were then plotted on a map, from which it was possible to identify three areas: an 'intensive' area — country settlements with high scores; an 'extensive' area — country settlements with medium scores and a 'fringe' area — country settlements with low scores. Patently, therefore, the intensity of interaction declines due to increasing competition at a distance.

The other factor which affects the movement lapse rate is that of population distribution. We have already seen (Section 4A 2) that, generally, population density declines with increased distance from the centre of a settlement. It follows, therefore, that there will, in any case, be fewer people living at the periphery of any town's interaction field. Any tendency for less movement to occur within the population will, therefore, be magnified by the distribution of population.

The absolute geographical limits of any interaction field, whilst important, are not, therefore, all that significant. For instance, the maximum catchment area of the ABC cinema in Exeter is quite large (some patrons come from as far away as Barnstaple), but the vast majority of patrons come from an area within about 16 km. The recognition of different zones of interaction intensity within the absolute interaction field is much more useful.

Several methods have been employed to delimit the maximum extent of interaction fields. The fields of individual functions are relatively easy to define, for they involve no more than plotting on a map the distribution of the customers for the function. Thus, the catchment area of a school is defined by plotting the distribution of the pupils' homes, and the sales area of a local news-

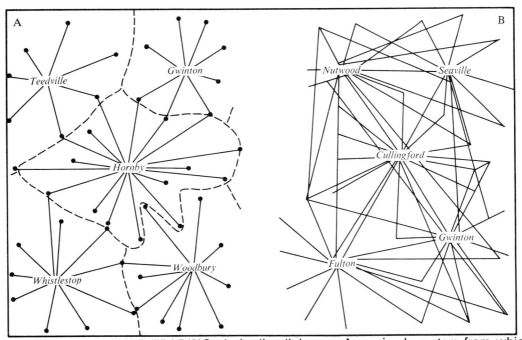

Fig. 4.45 FURNITURE TRADING, desire line linkages: A—a simple system from which the hinterland boundaries of each town can be estimated (indicated by the broken line); B—a more complex situation requiring more sophisticated analytical methods

paper is, likewise, defined by plotting the distribution of its readers. Once the distribution has been plotted, a boundary line can be drawn in to show the maximum extent of the field. Naturally, most of the information about customers has to come from direct field survey, since statistics are rarely published on this topic. There are two ways of approaching the collection of this information; either by conducting surveys at the location of the service in question, or else by conducting them in the surrounding area.

In the first situation this involves asking either the producer or the consumer of the function being analysed for any relevant information. For example, if we were making a survey of the trade area of a furniture store in a particular town, we could ask the store managers for details of their delivery area and/or we could ask the customers coming out of the shops for their home addresses. The alternative to this would be to ask people living in the area surrounding the town where they normally went to purchase furniture, and to plot their answers in the form of desire lines (Section

3B 2b). Thus, a line would be drawn on a map linking the town being studied with the places in its surrounding area from which shoppers come to purchase furniture. Where shoppers from a settlement used other places than the town being studied for furniture suppliers, lines would be drawn to show the link with its competitors. The maximum furniture trade area of a town could then be distinguished fairly clearly by visual inspection of the resulting map (fig. 4.45A). However, if the structure of movement were more complex (as in fig. 4.45B), more sophisticated analytical methods would have to be used to isolate the interaction fields.

Every function in the town has its own interaction field (Toyne, 1971), so that the more 'general' interaction fields, such as the 'hinterland' of a port or the 'sphere of influence' of a city, represent 'composite' fields made up of the individual fields of all the functions they contain. Thus, the spheres of influence of all the services in the city (e.g. hospitals, schools, cinemas), and the trading areas of all the commercial activities have to be considered together at the same time

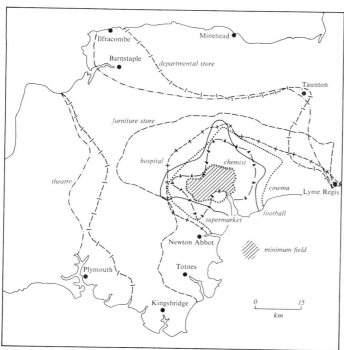

Fig. 4.46 TRADING AND SERVICE AREAS, City of Exeter

(Smailes, 1947). Naturally, it would be impossible to construct hinterlands for all the functions and so, normally, a representative sample has to be taken. Such a sample would probably include selected retail and wholesale establishments and various educational, social and occupational activities. Each of the sample fields is then superimposed on a map: a pattern of interdigitating and meandering lines emerges (fig. 4.46) and the 'maximum' field is easily identified.

The identification of intermediate boundaries within these 'maximum' fields has generally involved the calculation of some form of 'average' field. A useful concept is that of the 'mean' interaction field, which defines the area within which 50% of the total movements in the maximum field occur; similar 'percentage fields' could equally be constructed for different values (e.g. 30%, 20%). We have already shown how Bracey (1953) was able to distinguish intensive, extensive and fringe areas in urban fields using a 'point score' method of analysis.

Where the maximum field was defined on the basis of superimposition, it is clear that a 'core area' within which the influence of the central town in dominant could be defined (fig. 4.46). But between the maximum and minimum so defined there lies a zone within which interaction with the town varies considerably. It has been suggested that a 'median' boundary line could be defined within the zone (Green, 1955), but it is not exactly clear whether this newly defined line really represents any meaningful division (Haggett, 1965, p. 246).

Instead of superimposing several boundaries in this way, the maximum urban field can be defined by analysis of flow lines (Section 3B 4) on the basis of overall transport flows between the centre and its surrounding area. Green (1950) and Carruthers (1957), for example, were able to define the hinterlands of the towns of England and Wales based on the frequency of bus services on market days. Godlund (1956) also used this method to delimit urban hinterlands in Sweden. The difficulty here, however, is simply that bus flows show only bus movements, and it is by no means certain

that other movements within the urban region are of a similar nature. Detailed transport surveys of all movements within a region would clearly give a more accurate picture of the real interaction within a region. Where many movements are involved, however, it becomes difficult, as we have already mentioned, to distinguish meaningful interaction fields without the use of precise statistical methods. Thus, for example, using graph-theoretic methods to analyse regional structure based on telephone message flows, Nystuen and Dacey (1961) were able to identify urban interaction fields in Washington State, and Goddard (1970) has been able to identify interaction fields based on taxi flows within the city of London by means of factor analysis.

Local Study

Aim: To study the interaction fields and movement lapse rates for different functions.
Data source: Field survey.
Method:

1   Make a survey to establish the home address and the frequency of visit of customers to various stores.
2   Plot the interaction field of each function which you have decided to study (choose a representative range of the town's functions).
3   Plot the home location of all customers and then construct a series of concentric circles based on the town.
4   Construct a histogram to show how many customers come from each of the successive zones.
5   Repeat step 4 for each of the individual functions in turn, to show how the movement lapse rates vary from function to function.

Example

Area studied: Interaction fields based on Exeter.

In order to delimit the overall interaction field of the City of Exeter, we made surveys of several services which we thought to be typical of the total range of services offered by the city. Customers at supermarkets, furniture stores, chemists and department stores were sampled and asked where they lived. Similarly, interviews were conducted with people coming out of Exeter's Northcott Theatre, one of Exeter's cinemas and from an Exeter City Saturday football match, to find out where they lived. Finally, the local Hospital Board was able to define for us the normal area served by Exeter Hospitals. The information so obtained was plotted on a map of the area and, as can be seen in fig. 4.46, the areas served by each of these facilities varied quite considerably. A small 'core' area serving settlements within about 15 km of Exeter was apparent, but the contrast between this and the maximum field which included an area within about 50 km was admirably shown. It was also interesting to see that the 'theoretical' pattern of high threshold services being associated with large interaction fields was confirmed (c.f. supermarkets with department stores). But much more interesting than this was the map we drew to show the home location of all the people we inter-

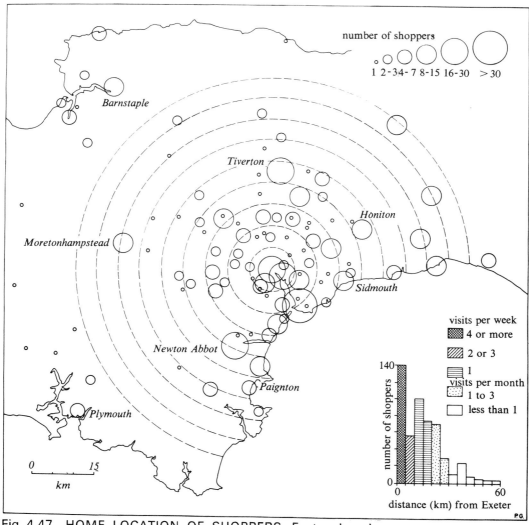

Fig. 4.47 HOME LOCATION OF SHOPPERS, Exeter shopping centre

viewed in our various surveys (fig. 4.47). Clearly, fewer people came from great distances away than they did from areas relatively close to the city: the frictional effects of distance, which we have mentioned earlier, were clearly causing movement to decline with distance. To show this in more detail, we constructed a series of concentric zones from the city centre: the smallest was of 5 km radius, and successive circles were each 5 km radius greater than the previous one. Next, we added up the total number of Exeter customers within each of these 5 km zones and plotted the figures as a histogram (fig. 4.47). Patently, although there was a progressively decreasing interaction with distance, as we expected, there were some important exceptions: notice, particularly, that the 5–10 km zone falls well below the level we might have expected, and that the 35–40 km zone falls above the 'expected' level. The reasons for this are, of course, to do with the regional distribution of population.

Naturally, the frequency of visits made to Exeter varies with distance: to demonstrate this we established for each of the 5 km zones what was the *majority* behavioural pattern, and plotted this information on the same histogram. As can be seen in fig. 4.47, the majority of people in the zone up to 5 km away from Exeter go to the city for various purposes daily, and progressively the frequency of visit declines with increased distance from the city centre.

Watch-points Be careful to establish meaningul zones: too many or too few can lead to distorted results.

The shopping survey should be based on a representative sample (see Section 1C).

FURTHER READING

Baumol, W. J. and Ide, E. A., 'Variety in retailing', *Management Science*, (1965), 3, 93–101.
Berry, B. J. L., *Geography of Market Centres and Retail Distribution*, (Prentice-Hall, 1967).

Bracey, H. E., 'Towns as rural service centres', *Transactions of the Institute of British Geographers*, (1953), 19, pp. 95–105.
Carruthers, W. I., 'A classification of service centres in England and Wales', *Geographical Journal*, (1957), 122, pp. 371–385.
Goddard, J. B., 'Functional regions within a city centre: a study by factor analysis of taxi flows in central London', *Transactions of the Institute of British Geographers*, (1970), 49, pp. 161–180.
Godlund, S., 'Bus services in Sweden'. *Lund Studies in Geography*, Series B, (1956), 17.
Green, F. H. W., 'Urban hinterlands in England and Wales', *Geographical Journal*, (1950), 116, pp. 65–88.
Green, H. L., 'Hinterland boundaries of New York city and Boston in southern New England', *Economic Geography*, (1955), 31, pp. 282–300.
Haggett, P., 'Locational Analysis in Human Geography', (Edward Arnold, 1965).
Isard, W., *Location and Space Economy*, (M.I.T. Press, 1956).
Murdie, R. A., 'Cultural differences in consumer travel', *Economic Geography*, (1965), 41, pp. 211–233.
Nystuen, J. D. and Dacey, M. F., 'A graph theory interpretation of nodal regions', *Papers and Proceedings of the Regional Science Association*, (1961), 7, pp. 29–42.
Smailes, A. E., 'The analysis and determination of urban fields', *Geography*, (1947), 32, pp. 151–161.
Toyne, P., 'Customer trips to retail business in Exeter' in Ravenhill, W. L. D. and Gregory, K. J. (eds.): *Exeter Essays in Geography*, (Exeter U.P., 1971).

4D 4 Networks

The location and form of the communications network basically reflects and affects the location and movement of goods, services and people within and between given regions. The precise relationship between networks, movements and location is naturally very complicated, though all too often it has been assumed that the location of settlements post-dated the communications network (the familiar logic contained in many a student's essay being that place X is where it is 'because it was well served by communications'). Although, in certain cases, this may well be the case, it is apparent that in many other cases the communications only came into being because there was sufficient demand for them. In other words, networks post-dated settlements. Yet again, it is also true that once networks have been established between a series of points, the points which are more likely to grow are those which are best served by, or are the most 'connected' of the whole network. The existence of the network is, in this sense, cumulative in its total effect and may lead to a progressive structuring of locations on a hierarchical basis. It follows, therefore, that networks may be regarded as a geographical feature underlying the whole of human and economic activity: without them, there can be neither movement, change, development nor function, all of which are the fundamental prerequisites of activity of any kind.

The description of networks is perhaps

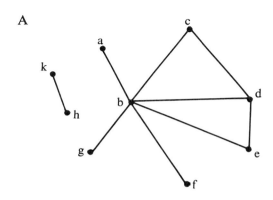

A

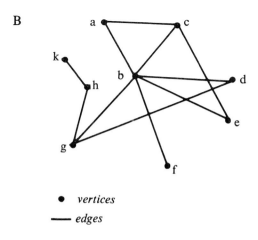

B

● vertices

— edges

Fig. 4.48 TOPOLOGICAL NET-WORK STRUCTURES: A—planar graph (note that the graph formed by the edges linking vertices *h* and *k* is a separate subgraph); B—non-planar graph

173

one of the most difficult parts of geographical study. Faced with a meandering and inter-digitating set of lines linking one place with another the traditional vocabulary becomes somewhat strained and the best that can be achieved is a detailed account of the route taken by each and every part of the total structure. The size of the network and the relative importance of each place on the network can similarly only be couched in rather vague and subjective terms. The problem, in fact, is rather like that of trying to describe the distribution of settlements in a given region. We saw earlier (Section 4B 1a) that one way round that particular difficulty had been found by measuring the settlements' distribution accurately and then calculating a mathematical index of distribution (the nearest-neighbour statistic, R_n), which served as a new and more flexible vocabulary. In a similar way, several attempts have been made to describe networks by the use of various index numbers derived from 'graph theory' which forms part of the study of topology in mathematics (Garrison, 1960: Kansky, 1963).

In order to apply such mathematical techniques, the network is considered to be a graph-like structure, made up of its points (referred to as **vertices** (V)), actual links (referred to as **edges** (E)) and also, possibly, some **sub-graphs** (P) (fig. 4.48A). Two different kinds of network, known as **planar** and **non-planar graphs,** can be identified according to the nature of their structure: planar graphs being those in which the edges have no intersections except at the vertices (fig. 4.48B).

Two of the main characteristics which can then be measured are the **extent** and the **connectivity** of the networks. The **extent** of the graph can be effectively measured by the Pi (π) index which compares the total mileage of the network (c) with the network's **diameter** (δ):

$$\pi = \frac{c}{\delta}$$

where δ = the maximum number of edges in the shortest path between each pair of vertices.

The greater the value of π, the greater is the extent of the network. Kansky (1963) has shown that, in general, network structures in developed countries have a greater extent (higher π index) than networks in relatively underdeveloped countries.

The connectivity of the graph can be measured by several different indices, of which the most useful is probably the α index developed by Garrison and Marble (1961) which consists of the ratio between the observed number of fundamental circuits and the maximum number that may theoretically exist in the network. The observed number of circuits is given by the formula:

$$\mu = E - V + P$$

where μ is called the **cyclomatic number** (or first **betti number**)

The maximum theoretical number of circuits is given by the formula:

$$2V - 5 \quad \text{for \textbf{planar graphs}}$$

and by $\frac{V(V-1)}{2} - (V-1)$ for **non-planar graphs.**

The values of α will occur in the range 0 to 1, with 0 indicating a branching form of network and 1 indicating a completely connected network. Once again, Kansky was able to show that there was a correlation between level of development and the degree of connectivity of a nation's transport network.

More refined techniques which give more efficient descriptions of network structure have been obtained by treating the network as a **connectivity matrix** (Pitts, 1965) and by the use of principal components or factor analysis (Goddard, 1968).

The **density** of a network can also be measured quite simply. In physical geography, particularly, various measures of drainage density have been devised: in human geography, the simplest, yet probably most effective, measure of network density is to divide the total length of the network (L) by the area which it covers (A). Ginsburg (1961) used this method and found that network density was correlated with the level of economic development in many countries of the world.

The explanation of network characteristics has traditionally been couched in rather environmental terms by geographers. Whilst there can be little doubt that routes *are* affected by physical considerations of relief, drainage and other topographical features, the significance of economic considerations has been rather under-stressed. Bunge (1962) has suggested that all networks can be thought of as derivations of two basic types: those which link a number of points by the shortest possible total mileage (the least-cost to build), and those in which all the points are completely interconnected by direct routes (the least-cost to the user). Cost-minimisation, in this sense, is seen to underlie the network design, and there is certainly evidence to suggest that elements of these two extreme network forms can be found respectively in rural areas where population density is low and urban areas where population density is high (Ullman, 1949). Similarly Lösch (1954) has suggested that cost differentials between network construction over topographical forms are just as significant a factor affecting route location as the actual forms themselves. The natural tendency would be for a route to follow the shortest possible path between two points, but where it became relatively more costly to follow that route (for example, where it would be necessary to build embankments or cuttings) the route may deviate because by doing so costs could be lessened *despite* the increase in distance involved. In many ways, of course, this represents only a slight change in emphasis from the purely deterministic viewpoint, but it is, nevertheless, a significant one.

Since the concept of accessibility, as measured by straight-line distance, underlies so many of the explanations of location, it is becoming important that the relationship between 'direct' straight-line routes and the actual 'detours' be clearly understood. This may well help us to reformulate some of our model theories in more realistic terms. In this context, it seems likely that the analysis of 'perceived' alternative routes may also be useful.

Local Study

Aim: To measure the change in connectivity of movement networks.

Data sources: Documentary sources; (timetables, directories, historical sources).

Method:

1   For the present day, plot the linkages that are feasible between all the settlements in the study area by bus and train. Use the 'desire-line' method (Section 3B 2b) to portray the information collected from local timetables.

2   Construct a similar desire-line map showing the linkages that were feasible by carriers' routes at a date in the last century (Carriers were the precursors of the present public transport — they carried goods on regular services by horse and cart between various settlements. Details of these operations will be found in most trade directories (e.g. Kelly's) which are normally available from most areas from about 1850 onwards (see Sections 1A 5 and 1A 6)).

3   Calculate the α measure of connectivity by counting the number of edges, vertices and subgraphs on the two maps and substituting in the formula:

$$\alpha = \frac{E - V + P}{V(V-1)} - (V-1)$$

4   Suggest why there have been changes in the connectivity of the networks over the study period.

Example

Area studied: Part of the West Riding of Yorkshire.

Two periods were selected for study, the present day and 1861, and for each of these periods 'desire-line' maps were constructed to show the movements of goods and peoples between all the settlements in the study area. We chose the year 1861 because a Kelly's Directory was available for that year, from which we were able to plot the links made by the carriers of the day. For comparability we plotted the bus and train services network for 1970. The two maps (parts of which are shown in fig. 4.49) reveal quite clearly that at the present time the network of move-

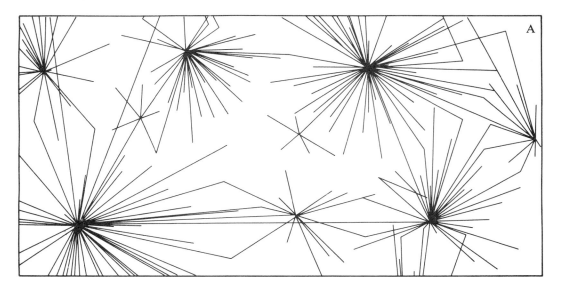

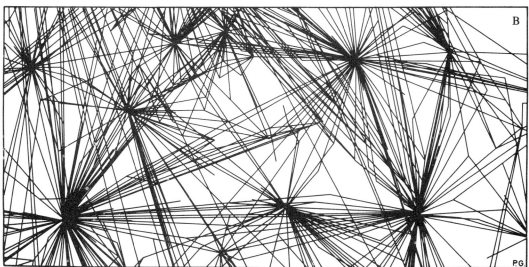

Fig. 4.49 MOVEMENT OF GOODS AND PEOPLE, West Riding of Yorkshire: A—carriers' services in 1861; B—bus and train services in 1970

ments is much more completely connected than it was in 1861. The difficulty, however, of comparing the two maps objectively was immediately apparent, and so we decided to calculate the α measure of connectivity for them both. It was found that in 1861 the value of α was 0·36, and that by 1970 it had increased to 0·82. Knowing that the range of α values can be between 0 and 1, we have

an immediate mathematical expression of the degree of connectivity of the two networks.

Watch-points A relatively large area should be chosen for this study so that a regional picture of network change may be obtained. It should be noted that the formula used for the calculation of α is for a **non-planar** graph.

FURTHER READING

Bunge, W., *Theoretical Geography*, (Gleerups, 1962).

Garrison, W. L., 'Connectivity of the interstate highway system', *Papers and Proceedings of the Regional Science Association*, (1960), 6, pp. 121–137.

Ginsburg, N., *Atlas of Economic Development*, (Chicago U.P., 1961).

Goddard, J. B., 'Multivariate analysis of office location patterns in the city centre', *Regional Studies*, (1968), 2, pp. 69–85.

Haggett, P. and Chorley, R. J., *Network Analysis in Geography*, (Edward Arnold, 1969).

Kansky, K. J., 'Structure of transport networks', *University of Chicago Department of Geography Research Papers*, (1963), 84.

Lösch, A., (translated Woglom, W. H.), *The Economics of Location*, (Yale U.P., 1956).

Pitts, F. R., 'A graph-theoretic approach to historical geography', *Professional Geographer*, (1965), 17, pp. 15–20.

Ullman, E. L., 'The railroad pattern of the United States', *Geographical Review*, (1949), 39, pp. 242–256.

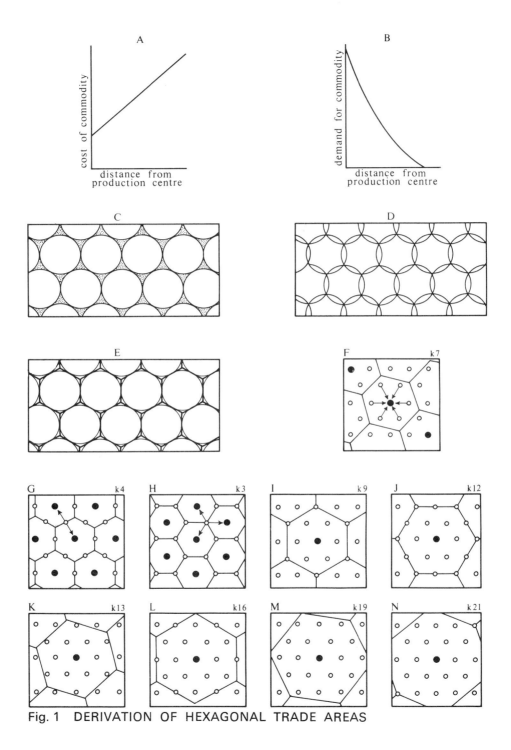

Fig. 1   DERIVATION OF HEXAGONAL TRADE AREAS

178

Appendix:
Elementary Central Place Theory

Various attempts have been made to explain theoretically the hierarchical structure and the regularities of spacing which appear to be characteristic of settlement functions in different regions (Section 4C). The basic postulate of such theories (known generally as central place theories) is that the location of economic activity is largely determined by conditions of supply and demand. Other factors (such as relief, population and transport) are, of course, important, but in order to test the effects of supply and demand *alone*, certain simplifying assumptions have to be made about those other factors in rather the same way that the assumption of *ceteris paribus* is often made in economic theory. Thus the simplifying assumption of central place theory is that of a region characterised by a flat featureless plain of uniform fertility in which the population has uniform tastes and preferences and is regularly distributed. Transport is assumed to be available in all directions at a cost which increases in direct proportion to the distance involved. Such an area, or land surface, is known technically as an **isotropic surface.**

In such a region, the cost of supplying any settlement with a particular commodity will be dependent upon the distance of that settlement from the place at which the commodity is produced, (fig. 1A). Since the demand for most commodities tends to decrease as the cost of the product goes up, it follows that the demand for any product in this theoretical region will decrease with increased distance away from the place at which it is produced, until the point is reached where transport costs make the product so expensive, that there is no longer any demand for it, (fig. 1B). In turn, because population is distributed regularly and transport costs are proportional to distance,

the sales area for any commodity will be circular in shape and the place at which the commodity is produced will be centrally situated to the trading area. The production place is therefore called the 'central place', and all the settlements which are supplied by that centre are called 'dependent places'. The actual size of the trading area for each commodity will be wholly determined by the price of the product at the central place, and the extent to which it can bear the cost of transport.

The whole region under consideration can then be divided into a series of such circular sales areas representing different commodities, though certain difficulties do arise: if the circles were fitted so that they just touched each other, there would be some areas left where the commodity could not be obtained (the shaded areas in fig. 1C); on the other hand, if the whole area had to be covered, there would be several overlapping zones (fig. 1D). For these reasons neither of these situations represents an efficient way of 'packing' the area. It has been suggested that a more efficient shape for packing any given area is the hexagon (even bees seem to appreciate this simple fact, by constructing hexagonal honeycombs!). Since hexagons are in a sense little more than 'collapsed' circles (fig. 1E), it is logical and feasible to replace the postulate of circular sales area with one of hexagonal sales areas (the same causative factors of supply and demand would still hold).

Just as there could be different sizes of circular trade areas, so there could be different sizes of hexagonal trade areas, each containing a different total amount of demand. The most obvious of these would be the situation where a central place supplied all of the demand from each of its nearest neighbouring dependent places, (fig.

179

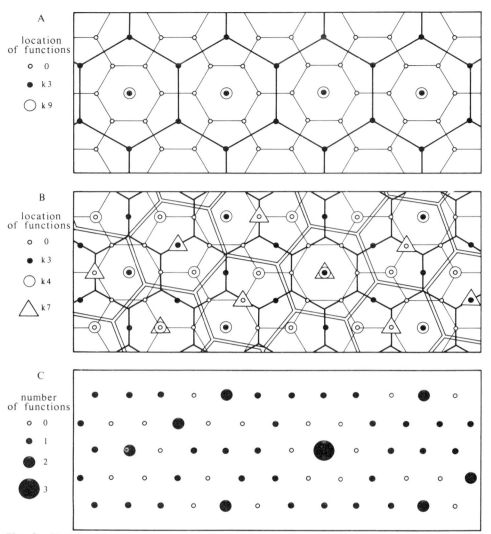

Fig. 2   THEORETICAL LOCATION OF SETTLEMENT FUNCTIONS: A—a fixed-*k* network (Christaller's Marketing Principle, a *k*3 system); B—a 'relaxed-*k*' network (Löschian system using *k*3, *k*4 and *k*7 trade areas); C—distribution of number of functions in each settlement (Löschian system as in Fig. 2B with hexagons removed)

1F). Since there are six dependent places immediately surrounding the central place and given the assumption that there would be a maximum demand of one unit from any one settlement (whether central place or dependent place) each trading area would then contain a total demand of 7 units (1 unit from each of the 6 dependent places plus the 1 unit of demand from the central place itself); it is this demand figure which is called the '*k*-value' of the central place, so that in this particular situation $k = 7$. However, not all of the total demand of the nearest settlements may necessarily be met by just one central place: it is possible, for example, that the demand for a particular commodity in each of the dependent places may be shared between two central places (fig. 1G), and in this case $k = 4$ ($\frac{1}{2}$ a unit from each of the 6 dependent settlements plus 1 unit from the central place itself); alternatively, each dependent place may share its total demand between three central places (all situated at the same distance from the settlement) (fig. 1H), so that $k = 3$ ($\frac{1}{3}$ of the demand from each of the 6 dependent settlements plus the 1 unit from the central place itself).

Many other k-value systems (or 'networks') can be constructed (fig. 1I to 1N), but it will be noted that they are all derivatives of the $k3$, $k4$ and $k7$ networks. (E.g.: the $k13$ and $k19$ networks are similar to the $k7$ network in that the total demand of all the dependent places is attributed to one central place.)

Examination of these different trade areas reveals that commodities which need a large amount of demand for their support (i.e. have high 'thresholds') will be provided in fewer central places than commodities with lower threshold requirements. In turn, it follows that central places offering goods with high thresholds will be spaced farther apart from each other than those which offer lower order goods. A hierarchy of settlements must therefore result with different combinations of commodities, being provided in different places. The precise form of this hierarchy and spacing of settlement functions will obviously be dependent not only on how many commodities are considered, but also upon the k-networks used to represent them.

Christaller (1933) based his theory on the assumption that the k-values in any region would be fixed according to one of three different 'principles'. In areas where the supply of goods from the central places had to be as near as possible to the dependent settlements, the **marketing principle** (the $k3$ system and its derivatives) would be operative. Under such a system the greatest possible number of central places would be created. However, where the cost of constructing transport networks was more important, central places would be located

on the **traffic principle** (a $k4$ system and its derivatives) because in such a system as many important places as possible would lie on one traffic route between larger towns. In areas where administrative control over the dependent places was necessary, central places would be established according to the **administrative principle** (a $k7$ network) since under such a system there would be no competition from alternative central places.

The main disadvantage of this 'fixed-k' theory is that it tends to exaggerate differences in demand between commodities; thus, in a system based on the marketing principle, the smallest threshold size which could be used would be $k = 3$, the next size would be $k = 9$ and the third size would be $k = 21$. In such circumstances, it is hardly surprising that a very marked hierarchy of functions is produced, with all the settlements of a given tier having exactly the same combination of functions, and all higher-order places containing all the functions of the smaller central places. The distribution of places of the same hierarchical order is also very regular, as can be seen in fig. 2A which shows the location of two functions, one requiring a $k3$ trading area, the other a $k9$ system.

A rather more realistic system was suggested by Losch (1940) who relaxed Christaller's 'fixed-k' assumptions and used *all* the possible alternative sizes of trade area in combination. Hence, the $k3$ network was used for the commodity with the lowest threshold requirements, the $k4$ network for the next largest, then the $k9$, $k12$, $k13$ and so on. Fig. 2B shows the location of three functions, one requiring a $k3$ network, and the others requiring respectively a $k4$ and $k7$ network.

With these 'relaxed-k' assumptions, a hierarchy of functions is still produced, but the combinations of function found in different places is more variable than in the 'fixed-k' system: high order places do not necessarily include all the same functions as places of lower order, and the distribution of settlements of the same hierarchical order is less regular (fig. 2C).

Empirical evidence, such as that reviewed

in Section 4C, tends to support the Löschian hypothesis rather more than that of Christaller. In detail, of course, no region will ever follow the precise form of the theoretically generated system because none of the original 'simplifying assumptions' of the theory are found in reality. There is, however, a sufficiently broad similarity between theory and reality to suggest that the factors of supply and demand are significant in determining the location of economic activity within settlements.

EXERCISE

On separate sheets of tracing paper (or plastic sheeting) draw, to the same scale, networks of central and dependent places according to various k-value systems. (e.g. $k3$, $k4$, $k7$).

(a) reconstruct Christaller's marketing principle theory by superimposing a series of networks which are derivatives of the $k3$ system.

(b) reconstruct Lösch's theory, by superimposing networks of various sizes.

Assume that each of the networks represents a different commodity (e.g. in the Löschian system the $k3$ network might be taken to represent grocery trading areas, the $k4$ network to represent butchery trading areas and so on).

For both systems:
(i) examine the combinations of function generated at each central place.
(ii) establish a hierarchy of central places.
(iii) examine the spacing of central places of the same hierarchical order.

What are the main differences between the two systems?

Index